The publisher and the University of California Press Foundation
gratefully acknowledge the generous support of the
S. Mark Taper Foundation Imprint in Jewish Studies.

On My Right Michael,
On My Left Gabriel

On My Right Michael, On My Left Gabriel

Angels in Ancient Jewish Culture

Mika Ahuvia

UNIVERSITY OF CALIFORNIA PRESS

University of California Press
Oakland, California

© 2021 by Mika Ahuvia

Library of Congress Cataloging-in-Publication Data

Names: Ahuvia, Mika, 1983– author.
Title: On my right Michael, on my left Gabriel : angels in ancient Jewish
    culture / Mika Ahuvia.
Description: Oakland, California : University of California Press, [2021]
    | Includes bibliographical references and index.
Identifiers: LCCN 2020051323 (print) | LCCN 2020051324 (ebook)
    | ISBN 9780520380110 (cloth) | ISBN 9780520380127 (epub)
Subjects: LCSH: Angels—Judaism.
Classification: LCC BM645.A6 A52 2021 (print) | LCC BM645.A6 (ebook)
    | DDC 296.3/15—dc23
LC record available at https://lccn.loc.gov/2020051323

Manufactured in the United States of America

29 28 27 26 25 24 23 22 21
10 9 8 7 6 5 4 3 2 1

For Aaron

CONTENTS

ACKNOWLEDGMENTS

This book has reached your hands thanks to the support of many teachers, colleagues, and friends, whom I am gratified to acknowledge here.

My teachers at Princeton University guided my research in its early stages, and
their insights stayed with me until the end: my gratitude goes to Martha Himmelfarb, Peter Schäfer, John Gager, Harriet Flower, Peter Brown, Naphtali Meshel,
and AnneMarie Luijendijk.

At Tel Aviv University, Gidi Bohak introduced me to the field of ancient Jewish
magic. At the National Library in Jerusalem, Ophir Münz-Manor mentored me in
the study of liturgical poetry in his spare time.

I was privileged to take a position at the University of Washington, where my
research has been supported by the Stroum Center for Jewish Studies, a Royalty
Research Fund fellowship, and a Gorasht Faculty Endowment. I want to thank
Reşat Kasaba, Noam Pianko, Joel Walker, and Sarah Zaides Rosen for ensuring
I had time to focus on this book. And I am especially grateful to my colleagues
Michael Williams, Christian Novetzke, Scott Noegel, Stephanie Selover, and
Hamza Zafer for their collegiality and feedback through the years. Beyond UW,
I am thankful to Nova Robinson, Rena Lauer, Greg Gardner, Loren Spielman,
and Eva Mroczek for fostering such a supportive intellectual atmosphere in the
Pacific Northwest.

Looking back, I appreciate Moulie Vidas's advice to center the ritual-magical
evidence and to open every chapter with a primary source. I learned so much
from the works of Michael D. Swartz, and I was thrilled to learn he was one of
this book's final readers and supporters. Laura Lieber encouraged me from afar,
visited Seattle during a city-stopping snowstorm, and offered valuable feedback

on my entire manuscript. Avigail Manekin-Bamberger kindly read and reread my chapters on ritual sources, helping me engage fruitfully with advances in the field of Jewish magic. Gillian Steinberg read every draft of this manuscript from start to finish and was my cheerleader every step of the way.

I will forever be grateful to the following two scholars for elevating my research: when I felt stalled, Ra'anan Boustan's support gave me new momentum, offering constructive feedback on every chapter of this book, challenging me to flesh out every argument, and to place my contributions in the field of late antique religion more broadly. Long before I thought of a book project on angels in Jewish sources, I heard Ellen Muehlberger lecture on angels in Christian sources. She generously shared her research with me through the years, and, in the end, she gave me the confidence to articulate my argument without any hedging, qualifiers, or disclaimers.

In the pandemic spring of 2020, I taught an online seminar on angels to a brilliant group of students. Their dedication, humor, and insight made finishing this book a pleasure (special thanks to Corinna Nichols and Grace Dy). My deep gratitude goes to Jennifer Hunter for being the best TA and RA during the worst of times and for enabling me to finish revisions of this book.

I am grateful to Eric Schmidt for shepherding this book through to publication and everyone at the University of California Press for making the publication of this book such a positive experience.

My book has a beautiful cover thanks to Sean Burrus, who kindly shared his photographs with me and patiently helped me acquire copyright permissions from the National Museum of Rome.

Only the word-limit prevents me from naming all the friends and family members in NYC, Israel, Japan, NC, MO, and MN, who have encouraged me along the way—thank you.

Having written a book on angels in the religious imagination, I feel qualified to say that many of us have entertained angels unawares: they are the strangers we serendipitously encounter or the companions on our journey who, with a word, a deed, or their very presence, set us on track. Sarit Kattan Gribetz and Helen Dixon have shown up in just this way in my life countless times. Like the ancients before me, I have no words to describe my gratitude for their interventions.

Introduction

Angelic Greetings or *Shalom Aleichem*

Peace be upon you, ministering angels, angels of the Most High,
Of the King, the King of kings, the Holy One, blessed be He.

Come in peace, angels of peace, angels of the Most High
Of the King, the King of kings, the Holy One, blessed be He.

Bless me in peace, angels of peace, angels of the Most High,
Of the King, the King of kings, the Holy One, blessed be He.

Depart in peace, angels of peace, angels of the Most High,
Of the Kings of Kings, the Holy One, blessed be He.[1]

—TRADITIONAL HEBREW SONG

Although many Jewish households begin the Sabbath by singing "Shalom Aleichem" (lit. "Peace be upon you") and welcoming the angels to their home, few people dwell on the literal meaning of this song's words. This popular seventeenth-century Hebrew song greets the angels of God beginning with "the ministering angels" and, alternating with calling them "the angels of peace," welcomes them to the home in peace, asks for their blessing, and wishes them a peaceful departure.[2] The song's most common melody was composed in Brooklyn in 1918, but

---

1. My translation of "Shalom Aleichem," following Israel Davidson's notes: "of the King of Kings" could also be translated "from the King of Kings," emphasizing that the angels are sent from God. Davidson attributes this piyyut to the Kabbalists (*Thesaurus of Mediaeval Hebrew Poetry* 3:1268, p. 465). Brettler observes that the verbs *come, bless,* and *go* relate to the order of these verbs in Deut 28:6 (*My People's Prayer Book*), 68.

2. Already in the eighteenth century, Jacob Emden (d. 1776 and known as *Ya'avetz*) was trying to correct the language of this piyyut, suggesting the *mem* in *mi-melech* be deleted (Davidson, *Thesaurus of Mediaeval Hebrew Poetry* 3:1268, p. 465).

1

it is sung by Jews around the world.[3] Despite the ubiquity of this song in Jewish domestic life, Christian conceptualizations of angels have become so powerful and pervasive that people often do not realize that angels have a firm biblical and Jewish pedigree. Twentieth-century scholarly accounts of Judaism's pure, monotheistic origins, taught in seminaries as well as the academy, have obscured the role of angels in the Bible, classical Jewish texts, and Jewish ritual practice.[4] This book aims to reveal the significance of angels in the foundation of classical Judaism.

The book makes three interrelated arguments. First, it argues that conceptualizations of angels were an integral part of late ancient Judaism and Jewish society. Descriptions of angelic beings can be found in every layer of biblical text, and, in the Hellenistic period, Jewish myths enlarged the role of angelic beings so that, by late antiquity, the praise of the seraphim was as sacred as the biblically commanded Shema prayer, the angels Michael and Gabriel were as familiar as the patriarchs and matriarchs, and guardian angels were as surely present as shadows on a sunny day. Contrary to common understanding, angels were not coupled with demons in the late antique Jewish imagination; they were imagined on their own terms and as independent beings. Angels served as intermediaries, role models, and guardians, with descriptions and invocations of them appearing in a range of contexts, including in ritual-magical, exegetical, liturgical, and mystical sources.

This book's second argument—as well as its methodological contention—is that considering additional sources provides a fuller account of the role that angels played in ancient Jewish culture. An array of sources from antiquity attests that people took for granted that the invisible realm was crowded with mediating beings: angels could be found at home, on the streets, in the synagogues as well as in the multilayered heavens. Scholarship of ancient Judaism has focused primarily on rabbinic texts, and scholars of rabbinics have, for the most part, explored other dimensions of rabbinic textual production, deploying literary, legal, ritual, exegetical, and comparative methods. Recent scholarship has shown, however, that rabbinic texts do engage meaningfully with theological questions.[5] This book argues that one neglected theological topic is angels in rabbinic literature. Moreover, and just as importantly, rabbinic texts only capture one dimension of late antique Judaism. Considering rabbinic and biblical sources alongside material evidence and seemingly less authoritative sources such as magical spells and synagogue poetry produces a more accurate picture of ancient Jewish thought about angels,

---

3. Frühauf, *Experiencing Jewish Music in America*, 22.
4. See Kaufmann's influential *The Religion of Israel*, discussed in the conclusion.
5. See Weiss, *Pious Irreverence*.

in part by capturing the output of more than just a small group of elite men, as has often been the case in previous scholarship. Indeed, angels appear frequently in incantation bowls, mystical sources, and liturgical poetry that existed alongside, in conversation with, and in tension with rabbinic sources.

Thirdly, examining references to angels in these diverse sources, in conversation with one another, demonstrates that rabbinic ideas about angels developed over time and in dialogue with other genres and materials. As time passed and angels became more prominent in other corpora, rabbinic writers began to accept that angels feature in other Jews' piety. Passages in the Babylonian Talmud suggest accommodation over time. This study of traditions about angels thus also reveals that the different registers of Jewish culture were, in fact, in contact in antiquity and that they evolved together: ideas about angels were exchanged and flowed between rabbis, ritual practitioners, synagogue poets, and mystics.

The fact that the function of angels was also debated by Christians and other adjacent communities in the late antique Mediterranean and Near East does not make angels any less significant for the study of Judaism. Abraham the patriarch is considered a foundational figure to Jews, Christians, Muslims, and others, and yet no one would question his significance for Jewish self-understanding. Likewise, angels were central to the religious communities of late antiquity, Jews among others. As I shall show, some conceptions of angels can be distinguished as specifically Jewish while others reflect the common beliefs of the inhabitants of the late antique Mediterranean. In the conclusion, I more broadly situate my findings about angels in Judaism in the religious landscape of late antiquity.

To return to the opening example: many of those Jews who sing "Shalom Aleichem" each Friday are unaware that it is believed to have been inspired by a tradition in the Talmud:

> Rabbi Yose the son of Yehuda said: two ministering angels accompany a man on the eve of the Sabbath from the synagogue to his home, one good and one evil. And when he arrives at his house, if a lamp is lit and a table is prepared and his bed covered, the good angel says, "may it be like this on another Sabbath too" and the evil angel answers "amen" against his will. And if it is not, the evil angel says, "May it be like this on another Sabbath too" and the good angel answers "amen" against his will.[6]

In a few sentences, this passage manages to address many of the problems and questions associated with angels in antiquity: How do angels relate to their charges? What do they do? How do angels respond to human behavior? Equally important

---

6. *b. Šabb.* 119b. Whether this rabbinic tradition inspired this sabbath song or not is ultimately unknowable. In any case, "Shalom Aleichem" correctly reflects enduring Jewish interest in relating to angels.

are the questions *not* asked by this rabbi: do angels exist? What do angels look like? Who oversees them? It was obvious to the ancients that angels were subordinate to God. The other two questions may seem natural to modern readers, perhaps, but were not to ancient people, who did not dwell on the appearance of angels and accepted the reality of divine beings crowding the invisible realm.

Though found only in the sixth century CE Talmud, this short story about angelic visitation is attributed to Rabbi Yose, one of the most quoted sages in rabbinic literature and a contemporary of Judah the Patriarch, the illustrious redactor of the Mishnah, the foundational document of the rabbinic movement (ca. third century CE). The story's attribution places it in chronological and geographical proximity to the beginning of normative Judaism. This tradition imagines that angels can be found wherever Jews congregate on the eve of the Sabbath (the holy climax of the Jewish week), and that angels follow people home from these gathering places. Once at the individuals' homes, the angels observe whether ritual and domestic preparations were made for the Sabbath and recite a benediction to God that affirms human behavior—for better or worse. In doing so, the angels, both good and evil, also acknowledge their limited authority under God.

As is the rabbis' way, they do not provide straightforward theology in their foundational documents, but formulate stories, legal pronouncements, and teachings instead. These traditions may be suggestive of the attitudes, at least, of the final redactors of the Talmud. The editors of the Talmud seemed to have no problem attributing a story about the active presence of angels in Jews' life to the son of Judah the Patriarch. They transmitted a story that admitted the presence of "good" and "evil" angels, who nevertheless appear to operate within certain parameters under God's authority. I discuss this source at great length among other later rabbinic sources (see chapter 6), but for now we may note that this story answers some questions but leaves others unanswered: Why are angels at home with Jews? And what is an angel exactly?

DEFINING ANGELS

No single definition of angels holds true across all time periods or across all religions.[7] The term *angel* in English derives from the ancient Greek *aggelos*, which can refer to a divine or human messenger. All the inhabitants of the Greco-Roman Mediterranean believed that the gods employed messengers that mediated between

---

7. In Reiterer, et al., *Angels: The Concept of Celestial Beings*, almost every contribution offers an instructive definition of angels, each representing a different corpus of text or religious community from the ancient Near East and Mediterranean world. I refer to many of these essays below. Schipper's "Angels or Demons?" offers the strongest critique of attempting a general definition of angels in comparative religions.

the divine and human realm (see *aggeloi* of the *Iliad* 2.26, 2.63, and 18.165).[8] As in Greek, so in Hebrew, the term *mal'akh* can refer to a divine or human messenger. *Mal'akh* is related to the Hebrew word for divine work, *melakha*, a crucial term in Genesis's description of the origin of the Sabbath: "On the seventh day God finished the *work* that He had been doing, and He ceased on the seventh day from all the *work* that He had done" (Gen 2:2). Work here is *melakha*, from the triliteral root for L-A-KH, "to send" or "to work."[9] *Mal'akhim*, or angels, are sent out to accomplish the work of God. The last prophetic book in the Hebrew canon is not named for a prophet but simply named Malachi: "my angel" or "my messenger." In Genesis the creation of the world and the Sabbath go hand in hand; so too do divine work and God's multitude of angels (Gen 2:1 states "Thus the heavens and the earth were finished, and all their *multitude*," with angelic beings implied). This is one clue as to the angels' function: look for them as agents in works of creation (broadly conceived), near the Sabbath (see the rabbinic tradition and song above), and as messengers from God. Less common terms in the Hebrew Bible for angelic beings include "sons of God," "holy ones," and "the heavenly host."[10] In the rabbinic corpus, angels are referred to as *mal'akhim* or, just as commonly, as the ministering angels (*mal'akhei ha-sharet*), with the latter term emphasizing the role of angels as servants of God.[11]

The stories of the Torah provided Jews with a great deal of material for conceptualizing angels, but the Psalms proved equally important. One influential verse averred that God "made his angels winds / his servants flaming fire," suggesting that angels were somehow insubstantial, fiery yet invisible (Ps 104:4).[12] That angels were made of fire was one of the only angelic characteristics upon which all later Jewish sources agreed.[13] Like the rest of the inhabitants of the ancient Near East,

8. See discussion in Speyer, "The Divine Messenger in Ancient Greece, Etruria and Rome," who notes that what Hellenistic poets and "their Roman successors say about the divine messenger often is just an imitation and variation of respective Homeric scenes and suggestions" (36). Iris and Hermes were the preeminent divine messengers.

9. For more on the ancient Near Eastern background of *mal'akh*, see Köckert, "Divine Messengers and Mysterious Men."

10. For *bnei elim* ("sons of gods"), see Ps 19:1. For *bnei ha-elohim* ("sons of the God"), see Gen 6:2–4 and Job 38:7 (discussed below). For "holy ones," see Deut 33:2. For the "host of the heavens," see Isa 13:2–5, Josh 5:13–15, and Dan 8:10–14, discussed in Quine, "The Host of Heaven and the Divine Army." Olyan devoted a monograph to the emergence of angelic brigades in ancient Judaism in *A Thousand Thousands Served Him.*

11. For "ministering angels," see *t. Soṭah* 4:1, *Mek. RI Bo* 9 (Horowitz and Rabin, 33), *y. Sanh.* 10:2, and *b. Sanh.* 96b.

12. See Kaduri, "Windy and Fiery Angels," 134–49.

13. These sources will be discussed in each corpus in turn: *Gen. Rab.* 78:1, *b. Ḥag.* 14a, Yannai's *qedushta* to Exod 3:1, Hekhalot Rabbati §213, Morgan, trans., *Sepher Ha-Razim*, 21; §31 of *Sefer ha-Razim*, ed. Schäfer and Rebiger.

Jews believed that the stars, moon, and sun were distant fiery divine beings, and scattered references in the Bible ensured they were understood as God's angels, fixed in the heavens but also able to exercise influence on earth.[14] And yet, this phrasing proved capacious enough for multiple interpretations of the changeable nature of the angels.

Alongside the view of angels as messengers of fire and wind, coexisted the imagining of angels as fantastic hybrid beings (so-called "Mischwesen") like the cherubim and seraphim.[15] Among the cultures surrounding ancient Israel, the cherubim and seraphim had distinguished iconography; no Israelite would confuse the fierce winged-lion cherub in the temple with the snake-like seraph. These animalistic features of cherubim and seraphim connoted power and the ability to ward off evil in ancient Mesopotamia and Egypt.[16] Though references to these creatures is found throughout the Hebrew Bible, it is the visions of Isaiah and Ezekiel, especially the verses that became part of the liturgy, that left a lasting impression in Jewish conceptualization of these divine beings who surrounded God's throne.[17] In time, the differences between these divine beings seem to have become blurred and forgotten in the minds of Jewish interpreters, who understood all of these different hybrid creatures as angelic beings worthy of imitation in liturgical practice and prayer.

By late antiquity, the rabbis commented that cherubim referred to beings with youthful faces, much like the cupids popular in Greco-Roman art.[18] Where the prophet Isaiah saw only the six-winged seraphim reciting "Holy, Holy, Holy" in the ancient Jerusalem temple, the late antique liturgical poet Yannai would imagine the cherubim, ophanim, holy creatures as well as "angels" in general reciting this praise of God, equating the various categories of these divine beings. Similarly, in incantation texts ritual practitioners did not dwell on the appearance of invisible beings but tended to be explicit about their invocation of God's subordinates, calling them *mal'akhim* before listing their names and describing what they hoped the angels would do for their clients.

14. For biblical references to angels as stars, see Job 38:7 and 38:31–33; Isa 40:26 and 45:11–12; Ps 147: 4.

15. On these figures in their Near Eastern context, see Hartenstein, "Cherubim and Seraphim." Cherubim, ophanim, and hayyot, appear together in Ezek. 10. For cherubim, see also Gen 3:24; Exod 25:18–22; Psalm 99:1. For seraphim, see also Isa 6:2; Num 21:8.

16. Hartenstein, "Cherubim and Seraphim," 157.

17. For a recent overview of the Mesopotamian parallels to winged biblical figures, see Noegel, "On the Wings of the Winds."

18. See *b. Ḥag.* 13b, discussed in chap. 6. For an analysis of cherubim from the angle of the rabbinic visuality, see Neis, "Heterovisuality, Face-Bread, and Cherubs" in *The Sense of Sight in Rabbinic Culture.*

Psalms and other biblical stories attest to the ancient Israelite belief that angels served ordinary persons, pious households, and the people of Israel on behalf of God. Psalm 91:11 assured hearers that God "will command his angels concerning you / to guard you in all your ways. On their hands they will bear you up / so that you will not dash your foot against a stone."[19] This verse suggested angelic intervention on behalf of the individual with God's approval. Biblical stories demonstrated that angels had appeared to the meritorious patriarchs and matriarchs, but also to disconsolate figures like Hagar, the mother of Ishmael, comforting her when she was expelled and abandoned with her son in the wilderness. The book of Tobit illustrated how an angel might intervene to protect a pious household with Raphael in disguise as a helpful relative. The Exodus story affirmed that God sent an angel to guard the nation of Israel in the wilderness (23:20), and the book of Daniel reaffirmed angelic protection of the nation with Michael fighting on behalf of Israel in the heavens against the angelic representatives of Persia and Greece (10:13–21). Late antique Jews believed that angels were available to ordinary men and women and they were aware that angels were a cross-cultural phenomenon.

The Hellenistic Jewish philosopher Philo explained that those beings whom the philosophers called *daemons* Moses called angels (*De Gigantibus* 1:6). This description highlights the neutral disposition of angels, who could be sent on beneficent or maleficent missions by God. As I shall show in the following chapters, both early and late rabbinic traditions agree with Philo on this point: there were angels of good (or peace) and angels of evil and destruction. Philo and the rabbis insisted on a divinely guided universe, where no invisible being could be out of step from God's plans. The existence of demons was also taken for granted by the peoples of the Near East, including the ancient Israelites, who were castigated for turning to demons in the Torah and in prophetic texts.[20] In my reading of the evidence, later Jews did not confuse angels of evil with demons; they had a different terminology and the rabbis even offered several etiologies for demons, which are not discussed in relationship to angels.[21] Demons were distinct and diverse beings, also at home

---

19. For reception history, see Breed, "The Example of Psalm 91."

20. van der Toorn provides a great overview of demons in the Bible in its Mesopotamian context through analysis of Isa 34:14, Deut 32:23, and Hb 3:5 in "The Theology of Demons in Mesopotamia and Israel." In Deut 32:17 and Lev 17:7, the people of Israel are castigated for sacrificing to *shedim* and to *se'irim* respectively.

21. According to *m. 'Abot* 5:6, demons (*mazzikin*) were created by God at twilight on the sixth day. A later tradition in *b. 'Erub.* 18b blames Adam, asserting he begat "spirits, demons, and liliths" (cf. Gen 5:3). Post-Talmudic midrash offers yet another origin story for demons: the mating of Adam and the first woman, later known as Lilith. See Harari, "The Sages and the Occult," 536. *Gen. Rab.* 1:3 is the earliest rabbinic text to collect interpretations about when the angels were created, debating whether angels were created on the third or fifth day, based on reading angels as winds or birds.

in the ancient Near East, and later linked to the Hellenistic Jewish myth of fallen angels on the one hand and in conversation with local traditions about demons in Persian Babylonia on the other hand.[22] Though people today may think of angels and demons as inseparable, angels had an independent existence in ancient Judaism. Indeed, though some of the sources analyzed in this book involve demons, most do not.

In the Jewish texts of the Hellenistic period, we find reference to angels by the names of Michael, Gabriel, and Raphael.[23] In the book of Daniel 10:20–21, Michael and Gabriel are called "princes" (*sar*), a title that will be used for top-ranking angels in the Hebrew mystical texts as well. In Greek texts, chief angels become known as archangels ("ruling angel").[24] In later Jewish interpretation, Michael, Gabriel, and Raphael were identified with the three anonymous men who visited Abraham at Mamre and foretold that he and Sarah would have a son (Gen 18).[25] This proved to be one of the most influential and popular stories about angels in antiquity, shared among Jews, Christians, polytheists, and later Muslims.[26] The location became a pilgrimage site in late antiquity."[27] Michael, Gabriel, and Raphael became part of the shared culture of the Mediterranean world: they can be found in the rabbinic, liturgical, ritual, and mystical texts of late antique Jews but also in the Christian and Hellenistic-Egyptian polytheistic texts more broadly.[28] This trio of angels can be found in incantation texts of late antiquity alongside other angelic names that are unpronounceable, recognizable only by their location in lists of angelic names or their "-el" suffix. From extant sources, we can see that Gabriel and Michael proved to be the most commonly invoked angels among Jews.

Late antique Jews did not feel the need to define the category of angels, nor did they write an angelology or attempt to place divine beings in a hierarchy. And yet a modern reader may need a general definition of angels before proceeding any further into the findings of this book. From an etic perspective, for the Jews of

22. See Bohak, "Conceptualizing Demons in Late Antique Judaism"; and Martin, "When Did Angels Become Demons?" Also see Gafni, "Babylonian Rabbinic culture," esp. 244–46. For demons in incantation bowls, see Hunter, "Who Are the Demons?"

23. Michael and Gabriel have small but important roles in Dan 10 (ca. 164 BCE) while Raphael is at the center of the book of Tobit, which likely dates to the third or second century BCE. Tobit is the only text to revolve around the angel Raphael, whose name contains the root verb for "to heal" in Hebrew.

24. As Berner observes in "The Four (or Seven) Archangels," the term archangel is found not in translations of the Hebrew Bible, but in Greek translation of 1 En 20:8 and 4 Ezra 4:36 as well as 1 Thess 4:16, and Jude 9 (396).

25. See Yannai's interpretation of Gen 18 in chap. 5. In Christian interpretation, one of these visitors to Abraham was understood as the pre-incarnate Jesus (Cline, *Ancient Angels*, 107–8).

26. Jones begins his book *Angels* with this story and its cultural significance.

27. Cline, "Mamre," in *Ancient Angels*, 107–18.

28. Sanzo and Boustan, "The Shared Magical Culture of Late Antiquity."

late antiquity, angels were subordinate yet powerful divine beings, usually invisible to the human eye, who were ever present both in the heavenly and earthly realms and who could intervene for good or ill in human life in accordance with human behavior and God's will. Angels were an integral part of the religious landscape in antiquity, one deeply grounded in the biblical heritage, and yet, as I shall show, the significance of angels in people's lives varied greatly based on personal and familial preference, local custom, communal practice, religious ideology, and regional factors. My corpus-by-corpus approach will demonstrate this variation, even as I highlight what is particularly Jewish about angels, and the ways Jews argued and exchanged ideas about angels in late antiquity. Only much later Jewish and Christian medieval angelologies would seek to overcome these deeply local and diverse perspectives on the invisible realms.[29]

This work makes no ontological claims as to the existence of angels but chronicles how ancient Jews believed in angels and made them into real presences in their everyday lives. These beliefs were anchored in biblical texts, in popular myths, and in dialogue with the other inhabitants of the ancient Near East. Angels were a particularly attractive mediating force because they could be used to circumvent established hierarchies even as they drew on the deep wells of inherited traditions. This book uncovers how angels made their way into the foundational practices and worldviews of ancient Jews and makes sense of why angels continue to play such a significant role within and without institutional Jewish settings.

METHODOLOGY AND SCHOLARSHIP

This book's interest in ancient Jewish "beliefs" about angels poses a tricky methodological challenge: How can modern historians know the intentions of ancient subjects? This study does not claim to uncover the thoughts of ancient Jews. Rather, each extant story, ritual incantation, liturgical piyyut, or mystical tradition about angels is treated as an example of one tradition once expounded in a rabbinic study house, one ritual object produced in a practitioner's workshop or performed in the home, one prayer recited in the synagogue, or one passage recited for mystical purposes. By placing each source in its historical and cultural context, insofar as is possible given our limited data from antiquity, I reconstruct the assumptions about angels that underpin rabbinic narratives, incantations, liturgical poems, and mystical texts about angels. Beliefs about and practices involving angels, just like any other Jewish beliefs or practices, were imparted and taught to

---

29. Jewish angelologies can only be found after the tenth century CE. For Christian angelology, see Muehlberger, *Angels in Late Ancient Christianity*, 207, in conversation with Frankfurter, "An Architecture for Chaos," in *Evil Incarnate*, 13–30.

ancient Jews in particular settings, and we can use these extant examples to think about how they were taught.[30]

In each chapter, I describe the particular methods and problems pertinent to each genre of evidence under examination, but I begin here with a few general remarks about my approach overall. The sources cannot be treated as transcripts, of course, or fully representative of a conversation in the homes or streets of ancient Jewish towns. Rabbinic attributions to named figures cannot be taken at face value or dated with any certainty. And yet traditions associated with leading figures may reveal what disciples of the rabbis wished to associate with their predecessors and may be indicative of later rabbinic attitudes toward angels. As I shall show, rabbinic traditions critical and supportive of engagement with angels are associated with some of the most famous historical rabbis.

In the 1960s and '70s, scholars of classical Judaism took note of the number of traditions about angels in rabbinic texts, and they paid special attention to the theological implications of traditions about angels in rabbinic literature.[31] However, lack of diachronically and synchronically precise studies elided tensions among various rabbinic corpora, which I hope to draw out over the course of three chapters on rabbinic texts. This book differs from previous surveys in that it tackles the biblical and rabbinic evidence in conversation with neglected sources, thus placing the "normative" sources and authorities in proper perspective. The emphasis on rabbinic religiosity in modernity has obscured the extent to which angels played an important role in the life of ancient Jews. By bringing other sources on angels into view, this book provides a very different description of Judaism than has been offered before, decentering the rabbis and showing their approach to the divine as one possibility among other equally Jewish options. I intentionally begin this book with ritual evidence from the sixth century CE, showing that angels feature prominently in Jewish ritual sources and not just in opposition to demons. After detailing the Babylonian and Palestinian ritual evidence, I turn back to the earliest rabbinic sources from the third century CE and then trace them diachronically forward. The rabbinic evidence may still occupy three chapters of this book, but in this arrangement, the rabbis are properly framed by other Jewish voices from ritual, liturgical, and mystical sources, who all had as much, if not more, to say about angels. This book shows the rabbis in conversation with ritual practitioners and synagogue leaders and argues that they accepted the influence of other Jews in shaping their own prayer and practices involving angels.

In recent decades, specialists in more neglected areas of Jewish studies such as magic, mysticism, and liturgy have demonstrated the contributions of their

---

30. My approach was in part inspired by Robert Orsi's theory that religion is fruitfully studied as a "network of relationships" (*History and Presence*, 9).

31. Urbach, *Hazal* (trans. *The Sages*); Schäfer, *Rivalität zwischen Engeln und Menschen*.

research to the reconstruction of late antique Jewish society.[32] They have also noted the role that angels fill in these texts, but their findings remained limited to publications in their respective fields.[33] Only scholars writing about Jews through a lens of comparative religious studies have highlighted that the world of ancient Jews was filled with angels, but they do not elaborate on this assertion.[34] The studies that have been devoted to angels on a corpus-by-corpus basis in recent decades, for example, in the Bible, in the literature of the Second Temple period, in rabbinic literature, and in patristic literature, now enable a more comprehensive study of angels in late antique Jewish sources.[35] This book will show these different genres of material may be fruitfully engaged for the reconstruction of daily Jewish life and the role of the angels therein.

My approach to Jewish magic differs from others in that I treat incantation bowls and amulets as the ritual practice of a wide swath of the Jewish population rather than the domain of male specialists alone. In part, this is because I argue that the performative aspect of incantations was key to their efficacy. As I have contended elsewhere, incantations are best viewed as collaboration between practitioners and clients seeking to overcome a problem in the invisible realm. Incantation bowls or amulets are the artifacts of these relationships and these ritual performances. As such, they offer a window onto the diverse relationships that Jews had with entities in the invisible realm.[36] I also treat Jewish magical objects as evidence of men's and women's concerns. Literacy in the ancient world may have been limited to a small segment of the population and slanted male, but a spectrum of literacy rather than a binary of literacy/illiteracy prevailed. Thinking about a spectrum of engagement with text provides a more accurate model of ancient people's engagement with reading and writing practices.[37] Women's engagement with textual production should not be ruled out a priori; indeed, at

32. Naveh and Shaked, *Amulets and Magic Bowls* as well as *Magic Spells and Formulae*; Bohak, *Ancient Jewish Magic*; Lieber, *Yannai on Genesis*; Swartz, *Mechanics of Providence*.

33. Schiffman and Swartz, *Hebrew and Aramaic Incantation Texts from the Cairo Genizah*; Schäfer, "Engel und Menschen in der Hekhalot-Literatur."

34. Schwartz writes that "The rabbis' world was, in contrast to ours, pervaded with gods" in *Imperialism and Jewish Society*, 185. See also Hopkins, *A World Full of Gods*. Peter Brown discusses the role of invisible beings in *Body and Society*, esp. 161–66 and in *The Making of Late Antiquity*.

35. Rofé, *The Belief in Angels in the Bible and in Early Israel*; Mach, *Entwicklungsstadien des Jüdischen Engelglaubens in vorrabbinischer Zeit*; Stuckenbruck, *Myth of Rebellious Angels*; Schäfer, *Rivalität zwischen Engeln und Menschen*; Muehlberger, *Angels in Late Ancient Christianity*.

36. Ahuvia, "Spatial and Social Dynamics of Jewish Babylonian Incantations."

37. This topic in the context of late antiquity has been explored recently at the SBL 2019 and 2020 conferences in the Social History of Formative Judaism and Christianity unit. On women's literacy as evidenced by the Cairo Genizah, see Kraemer, "Women Speak for Themselves," as well as Melammed and Melammed, "Epistolary Exchanges with Women."

least a few extant incantations proclaim a female identity and were written in the first-person feminine.[38]

Although all the known synagogue poets were male, men and women were in attendance in the synagogue. Reading the liturgical and ritual-magical texts closely, one senses that synagogue poets and ritual practitioners interacted with women regularly. Overall, the topic of angels in late antique Judaism does allow access to more ordinary men's and women's concerns than other subjects might. Investigating Jewish attitudes to angels reveals Jewish men and women as dynamic participants in late antique trends, both in Palestine and Babylonia.

My decision to examine evidence from Jewish communities as far apart as Roman Palestine and Sasanian Iran is based on the fact that religious ideas and rituals were not limited by geographical boundaries in late antiquity. Like Paul's epistles, which offer evidence of widely scattered religious communities communicating with each other, Jewish sources also provide a window onto a time when religious ideas were shared over a vast geographical area, despite the boundaries of the Roman and Sasanian Empires. Most famously, rabbinic traditions traveled with learned disciples from Palestine to Babylonia and back again.[39] Likewise, magical spells from Palestine influenced Babylonian incantation formulas and vice versa.[40] Jewish Palestinian synagogal poetry was exceedingly popular in Babylonia despite Babylonian rabbinic disapproval of it.[41] While a few traditions in the Hekhalot literature point to a Babylonian context, its complex literary development suggests development "at different places and different times," potentially in Palestine and in Babylonia.[42] Fully appreciating the complexity of Jewish sources on angels may require considering the possibility that ideas traveled from afar and were adapted by different sectors of society.

CHAPTER OUTLINE

In seven chapters, I traverse conceptualizations of angels among ancient Jews and provide a revised portrait of late antique Judaism. Each chapter begins with an example of the genre of evidence under investigation and ends with a section describing the legacy of this material: how this ancient evidence impacted other sectors of Jewish society or Jewish practice more broadly. The first two chapters

38. For a recent survey of evidence and the argument that women composed incantation bowls, see Kedar, "Who Wrote the Incantation Bowls."

39. Schwartz, "The Political Geography of Rabbinic Texts," 91.

40. Naveh and Shaked, *Magic Spells and Formulae*, 21.

41. Langer, *To Worship God Properly*.

42. Schäfer, *Origins of Jewish Mysticism*, 307 and 347; Schäfer, "Tradition and Redaction in Hekhalot Literature," in *Hekhalot-Studien*, 15.

center on ritual-magical evidence from Babylonia and the Levant before turning to the earliest rabbinic evidence (third century CE). Because the Babylonian
incantation texts are much longer than the Levantine amulets, they offer much
more social information and, for this reason, they are discussed first (although
they are arguably the latest ritual objects chronologically, dating from the sixth
and seventh centuries CE). Even though this order does not follow a simple
chronological progression through the sources, I have chosen this arrangement
because the ritual-magical evidence is too often relegated to the periphery rather
than treated as essential to the understanding of formative Judaism. Moreover,
the vivid descriptions of religious experience in incantation bowls and amulets
show what is at stake in rabbinic omission of angels in their foundational texts
and what ideas the Babylonian rabbis were reacting to in later centuries. To be
clear, I do not intend this arrangement to reflect an evolutionist outlook on the
development of religion from magic to orthodoxy to mysticism.[43] On the contrary, I hope this arrangement conveys how richly polyvocal and multicentered
Jewish society was in late antiquity.

In chapter 1, "At Home with the Angels," I begin with the ritual-magical
objects and texts that uncover an aspect of ancient life that is implicit but usually hidden from view in classical Jewish sources: one where relationships with
beings in the invisible realm mattered within the framework of Jewish monotheism. Buried under the floors of homes in ancient Mesopotamia, simple ceramic
bowls contained personalized incantations written in Aramaic and Hebrew.
These incantation bowls reveal how Jewish men and women appealed to God,
angels, biblical protagonists, rabbinic heroes, and others for aid. Incantation
texts show the choices available to Jews and the many ways people could relate
to angels in the invisible realm. The ritual evidence offers vivid testimony for
how Jews imagined angels relating to them, healing their illnesses, restoring love
in their marriages, increasing their business, or protecting their home from the
harm of antagonists and demonic forces. I close this chapter with reflection on
the relationship of incantations and prayers, reading the formula that invokes
the angels on all sides in many incantation bowls and much later in the Jewish
liturgy as well.

In chapter 2, "Out and About with the Angels," I focus on Jewish texts from
the Levant like amulets buried in ancient synagogues and the treatise *Sefer ha-
Razim* ("Book of the Mysteries"). Necklace-amulets reveal how Jews visualized
the angels among them in the Greco-Roman milieu of Palestine and how they
participated in the religious-magical practices of the Late Antique Mediterranean

43. For an overview of this historiography, see Harari, "Magic and the Study of Religion," in *Jewish
Magic before the Rise of Kabbalah*.

world. Alongside these amulets, I also examine *Sefer ha-Razim,* a multilayered composition from Palestine, parts of which date to the same time period as the late antique amulets and rabbinic midrashim. The framework of *Sefer ha-Razim* describes how a learned ritual practitioner from Palestine understood the role of angels in relation to biblical traditions and God. Taken together, the ritual sources provide a fascinating window into Jewish beliefs in angels in the fourth and fifth centuries CE in Roman Palestine, and help place rabbinic, liturgical, and mystical texts in proper perspective. The evidence examined in this chapter contributes to my argument that relationships with the angels mattered to ancient Jews everywhere, not just to one diaspora community in Mesopotamia but to Jews in the ancient world more broadly. This chapter closes with a reflection on the relationship between angels in ritual-magic, Jewish attitudes toward gender, and the implications for ancient Jewish society.

In chapter 3, "No Angels," I delve into the earliest rabbinic material, foregrounding the evidence in the Mishnah, Tosefta, and midrashei halakhah for Jewish engagement with angels as well as rabbinic ambivalence toward angels. This chapter focuses on how the rabbis of Roman Palestine downplayed interest in angels, even as their exegesis of Torah had to acknowledge (at times) that angels were integral to Israel's origin story. A few stray traditions betray that angels were integral to some sages' worldview, but, overall, angelic presence is repressed in earlier rabbinic sources. The earlier generations of Palestinian rabbis stand out for inveighing against angels and against Jewish preoccupation with angels. Recognizing this tendency reveals what the rabbis were worried about: loss of faith in a God committed to his people and still active on earth. Rabbinic attitudes to angels remained multifarious through the post-Talmudic midrashim, but they did perceptibly shift toward acceptance of engagement with angels over time. At the end of this survey of early rabbinic sources, I emphasize the relationship of ritual practices to rabbinic midrash, highlighting a possible origin for the invocation of angels on all sides in early rabbinic sources.

In chapters 4 and 5, I show how two competing frameworks were available to Jews in late antiquity, one associated with rabbinic settings and the other with worship settings: the former asserted that Jews should focus on relationship with God exclusively and imitation of God alone while the latter emphasized Jewish fellowship and imitation of the angels. In chapter 4, "In the Image of God, Not Angels," I trace the preoccupation with imitation of angels from the Second Temple period sources onward and the concomitant rabbinic reaction to it. One stream of the rabbinic movement distinguished itself by offering fellow Jews a way of relating to God that would arm them with confidence on the one hand and preclude other intermediaries, namely angels, on the other. Rabbinic disciples were encouraged to focus on God's love for them and the imitation of God alone. In effect, the rabbis who downplayed angels were drawing boundaries, distinguishing themselves from fellow Jews as well as other late antique religious communities. Ultimately, this rabbinic endeavor did not prove convincing to most Jews, who continued to seek fellowship with the angels, but it is worth examining to appreciate the intellectual investment of the rabbis in conceptualizing their relationship with God and the invisible realm.

In chapter 5, "In the Image of the Angels," we will see how angels took center stage in ever more vivid terms in the communal institutions of worship in late antiquity. I focus on the space of the synagogue and the liturgical poetry of Yannai, who openly encouraged Jews to imitate the angels during their worship of God and to think of themselves in angelic terms. While conceptualizing angelic fellowship and imitation was common to Jews and Christians at this time, I show how Yannai gave a particularly Jewish lens to this imaginative framework. Yannai's work has the advantage of showing us how one individual Jew in late antique Palestine synthesized ideas about angels from the Bible, the popular imagination, rabbinic midrash, and even ritual practice. This liturgical evidence also opens a window into a time when Jewish men, women, priests, rabbis, and ritual practitioners mingled in the communal space of the synagogue, reciting God's praise in synchronicity with the angels.

In chapter 6, "Israel among the Angels," I examine the late Babylonian rabbinic perspective on the angels, showing how later rabbis came to embrace the angels in storytelling, prayer, and practice. Whereas earlier rabbis downplayed angels in foundational narratives, later rabbis inserted them into retellings of stories about their own legendary heroes. Where earlier sources criticized praying to Michael and Gabriel, later rabbinic sources taught Jews how to pray to their accompanying angels. Only later Babylonian rabbinic traditions are detailed enough to allow for a discussion of Jewish beliefs on the nature of good and evil angels, angelic freewill, and angelic emotions. By analyzing rabbinic traditions alongside ritual and liturgical evidence, we can see how the rabbis responded to Jewish attraction to angels. Seeing that the popularity of angels could not be overcome, the rabbis decided to harness it instead. This chapter closes with a rumination on the rabbis and their intermediaries of choice, angels among them.

Reciting prayer in the synagogue with the angels in mind sufficed for some Jews, but not for Jewish mystics, who took preoccupation with the angels to unprecedented levels. In chapter 7, "Jewish Mystics and the Angelic Realms," I investigate the earliest manifestation of Jewish mysticism found in the esoteric Hekhalot literature ("Books of Heavenly Palaces"). These texts illuminate the worldview of circles of Jewish mystics, who strove to pray in unceasing synchronicity with the angels, to achieve mastery of Torah through the angels, to imagine ascent to the heavens, and even to command the angels to do their bidding on earth. Some mystics positioned themselves as the ultimate heroes, angelic figures above both angels and other humans. Focusing on the earliest treatise, Hekhalot Rabbati, I examine its component texts, elucidating a variety of Jewish mystical views about angels, all revealing engagement with other segments of Jewish society, even as their radical stance clearly sets them apart. Though Hekhalot mysticism would give way to the mysticism of the Kabbalah, this "way not taken" in early medieval Jewish society demonstrates how some Jews took belief in angels to radical extremes and in the process, expanded the Jewish religious imagination.

In the Conclusion, "Angels in Judaism and the Religions of Late Antiquity," I summarize the results of my survey of ancient Jewish society. Acknowledging ancient views about angels may necessitate expanding our definition of Jewishness and Judaism as well as reevaluating the importance of relationship with others, invisible and visible, within the study of religion. I place my findings in the larger context of the religions of late antiquity, showing how developments in Jewish thought remain distinctive though in dialogue with conceptions of angels in other religious movements. Thereafter, I trace how conceptualization of angels changed from antiquity through the medieval period to the present. In doing so, I account for the afterlife of angels in religious history, their popularity and eventual decline in significance among modern Jewish thinkers and Jews more broadly. This book establishes how writing angels into the history of Jewish religion offers both a more accurate view of the past and important insights into Jewish practice today.

. . .

A NOTE ON TERMINOLOGY AND CITATION

I define scholarly terms in every chapter, but some terminology is specific to the study of rabbinic literature (the focus of chapters 3, 4, and 6), and, for the uninitiated reader, I share it here.[44] I sometimes refer to the rabbis as sages, Tannaim, Amoraim, or Stammaim. The term *Tannaim* refers to early generations of rabbis cited in texts like the Mishnah and the Tosefta (both texts were compiled in the first quarter of the third century CE), while *Amoraim* refers to those rabbis cited in later Talmudic texts (no later than 500 CE); the term *Tannaitic* denotes rabbinic sources from before the mid-third century CE and *Amoraic* denotes sources from the subsequent period. A Baraita is a tradition attributed to an early sage yet

---

44. Rosen-Zvi, "Language, Terminology, and Citation Policy," in *Demonic Desires* inspired this section.

preserved outside the Mishnah. The Stammaim are the anonymous post-Amoraic editors and redactors of the Babylonian Talmud. The term *midrash* refers to works of rabbinic exegesis (e.g., *Genesis Rabbah*). The term *sugya* refers to a full unit of discussion within the Talmud.[45]

---

45. For reference, I list common abbreviations, critical editions, and translations here: For the Mishnah (*m.*), Kaufmann MS A 50 is online; see Danby, trans. (Oxford, 1939). For the Tosefta (*t.*), see Lieberman, ed. (New York, 1955–88) and Zuckermandel, ed. (Jerusalem, 1970); Neusner and Sarason, trans. (New York, 1977). For the Mekhilta of Rabbi Ishmael (*Mek. RI*), see Horwitz and Rabin, eds. (Jerusalem, 1970) and Lauterbach, trans. (Philadelphia, 2004). For the Mekhilta of Rabbi Shimon (*Mek. RS*), see Epstein and Melamed, ed. (Jerusalem, 1956) and Nelson, trans. (Philadelphia, 2006). For *Sifre Numbers*, see Horowitz, ed. (1966; reprint Jerusalem, 1992). For *Sifre Deuteronomy*, see Finkelstein, ed. (Berlin, 1939; reprint NY, 1969) and Jaffee, trans. (2016). For *Genesis Rabbah* (*Gen. Rab.*), see Theodor and Albeck, eds. (1936; reprint Jerusalem, 1965). For the Jerusalem or Palestinian Talmud (*y.*), see Schäfer and Becker, eds., *Synopse zum Talmud Yerushalmi* (1991). For the Babylonian Talmud (*b.*), see the Lieberman Institute's Talmud text databank. Abbreviations for tractate titles follow *The SBL Handbook of Style* guidelines.

At Home with the Angels

Babylonian Ritual Sources

Healing from Heaven, and sealing and protection for the dwelling, for the threshold, for the residence, for the house, and for the threshold of this Parrukdad the son of Zebinta and for Qamoi the daughter of Zaraq, and everything which they have, that they may be guarded—this Parrukdad the son of Zebinta and this Qamoi the daughter of Zaraq, they, their sons, their daughters, their oxen, their donkeys, their slaves, their handmaidens, and all large or small cattle which is in this dwelling and threshold—which is in it and which is going to be in it—[from now] and forever.

And there will cease from this dwelling and threshold of this Parrukdad the son of Zebinta and of Qamoi the daughter of Zaraq, Aramean sorceries, Jewish sorceries, Arabian sorceries, Persian sorceries, Indian sorceries, Greek sorceries, sorceries of the Romans, sorceries which are practiced in seventy languages, either by woman or by man.

All of them are brought to an end and annulled by the command of the jealous and avenging God, the One who sent Azza, Azzael, and Metatron, the Great Prince of His throne. They will come and guard the dwelling and threshold of Parrukdad the son of Zebinta and of Qamoi the daughter of Zaraq.

And may the gates of sustenance open for [them; omitting repetition of names] from the four corners of the earth, from above and below.

In the name of Kavshiel, who conquers everything bad from the threshold of this Parrukdad the son of Zebinta and of this Qamoi the daughter of Zaraq. YHWH is his name. Amen Amen Selah.[1]

— BABYLONIAN INCANTATION BOWL

1. Translation based on Gordon's (no. 6519, D) in "Aramaic Magical Bowls in the Istanbul and Baghdad Museums," 319, 328–30, with his correction later published in "Aramaic and Mandaic Magical Bowls," 106. "Arabean" in Aramaic is *Tayya'an*: a generalized term for a pre-Islamic Arabian tribe

To understand the significance of angels in ancient Judaism, it is best to begin with the words of personalized incantation texts such as this one, which evoke the interconnected world of the ancient Near East with its many peoples and languages. Incantation bowls offer a window into ancient Babylonian Jews' anxieties and the ways they assuaged their fears, by calling on God and the angels. This particular Aramaic incantation from ancient Mesopotamia tells us that a husband and wife sought protection for their children and their extensive household against sorceries (Aramaic *ḥarshin*) or the perceived nefarious intentions of others in their milieu. The composer of this incantation gave this family assurance of God's involvement in their lives. More than that, he offered a framework for conceptualizing the world wherein God's angels actively intervened to protect households. While this particular couple feared sorceries and the curses of others, they did not regard themselves as practicing aggressive magic when they commissioned this incantation bowl but were instead participating in a ritual of protection, one that brought God's angels into their home and daily life.

In this chapter, I analyze the incantation bowls, like the one quoted above, from late antique Jewish communities in Babylonia, demonstrating how this genre of evidence can give texture to conceptualizations of angels in the ancient Jewish imagination. I begin by explaining and defining what incantation bowls are, explaining who used them, and reviewing the history of scholarship on this topic and its relationship to Jewish and religious studies. Next, I present my survey and quantitative analysis of the incantation bowls, which lay out the proportions of texts appealing to God, angels, and others for assistance. I examine each of these permutations in turn, analyzing those calling on angels, those calling on angels alongside other heroes, and finally those incantations that focus upon other intermediaries instead of angels. Finally, I share the legacy of these incantations, showing how ancient texts invoking the angels still form a part of the Jewish liturgy. These texts reveal that angels were imagined to function in a variety of ways: healing sickness, restoring love in a marriage, increasing business, or protecting a home from the harm of human and demonic forces. More than rabbinic traditions, ritual objects like incantation bowls and amulets allow us to view the relationships that men and women imagined they had with angels apart from communal and institutional spaces, in the domestic space of their homes. Moreover, only incantation bowls and amulets shed light on the positive relationship women formed with angels, allowing for a more accurate description of Jewish beliefs about angels. Through incantation bowls and amulets, we can see how angels pervaded the lives of ancient Jewish men and women.

(cf. *b. Bat.* 36a; Jastrow, *Dictionary*, 531). Bohak also discusses this incantation in "Babylonian Jewish Magic in Late Antiquity," 104.

WHAT IS AN INCANTATION BOWL?
IS IT MAGIC? IS IT JEWISH?

Most Jewish incantation bowls are made of plain ceramic and are about the size of a cereal bowl.[2] Text fills the walls of the bowls, usually spiraling from the concave center to each bowl's margins. Sometimes, text continues on the outside of the bowl as well. They were composed mostly in Jewish Aramaic but also in other dialects like Syriac, Mandaic, Manichaean and, more rarely, in Middle-Persian as well.[3] The first few dozen incantation bowls that came to light over a century ago were from Nippur, one of the longest continually inhabited cities in the Near East, about one hundred miles southwest of Baghdad, once on a canal connected to the Euphrates river. Nippur was the leading center of the region known as Mesene, discussed in a variety of ancient sources.[4] Jews dwelled in this region since the Babylonian exile in the sixth century BCE.

Educated speculation estimates the population of Jews in Babylonia to have been about one million, "possibly exceeding the number of Jews in Roman Byzantine Palestine."[5] As in Palestine, some towns in Babylonia had Jewish majorities while others had more mixed populations.[6] Jews living in the Persian-Zoroastrian Empire benefited from intensive imperial investment in the cultivation of agricultural land as well as a generally more neutral religious policy, leaving them to live among Persians, Buddhists, Christians, Manichaeans, Arabs, and others in relative (though not perfect) prosperity and peace.[7] Jews dwelled in northern Mesopotamia where the city of Nisibis was a central node and in lands east of the Tigris River like Media and Elam, but we know the most about the rabbinic Jews who lived near the confluence of the Tigris and Euphrates rivers, in the area where canals crisscrossed the fertile plains. The rabbis of the Babylonian Talmud refer to this region, which they inhabited, as the "area of pure lineage," contrasting themselves with Jews of suspect lineage, who lived elsewhere to the north,

2. For example, in the British Museum's collection, the bowls range from 13.5 cm to 20 cm in diameter with most averaging 16 cm in diameter and 5 cm in depth. A few outliers are much larger, like the Aramaic bowl measuring 33 cm in diameter and 13.6 cm in depth (BM 102581) or the Mandaic bowl measuring 40 cm in diameter and 18.4 cm in depth (BM 91777). For a great overview of these bowls, see Morony, "Magic and Society in Late Sasanian Iraq" and idem, "Religion and the Aramaic Incantation Bowls."

3. Harari, *Jewish Magic*, 234–51.

4. For a survey of sources on Mesene, see Paz, "'Meishan Is Dead.'" For Roman sources, see discussion in Young, *Rome's Eastern Trade*, 129–32; for Jewish sources, see Oppenheimer, *Between Rome and Babylon*, 422–24.

5. Gafni, "The Political, Social, and Economic History of Babylonian Jewry," 805.

6. See Oppenheimer, *Babylonia Judaica in the Talmudic Period* for a survey of all the Jewish sites known from the Talmud.

7. Gafni, "The Political, Social, and Economic History of Babylonian Jewry," 794–801.

east, and especially the south, in the region of Mesene where Nippur was located.[8] Yakir Paz presents a compelling case that the Babylonian rabbis portrayed the Jews of Mesene negatively for a number of reasons, but mainly because Mesenean Jews "did not shift their allegiance to the Babylonian Sages but rather continued to conform to the halakhic hegemony of the Land of Israel."[9] Unfortunately, such polemic about the region of Nippur does not reveal much salient evidence about the composers of the incantation bowls.

According to the earliest excavation reports, the incantation bowls were found in one of the latest layers of habitation at Nippur, a residential area of plain houses, the remains of which were close to the surface of the mounds.[10] While Nippur's incantation bowls were not excavated under ideal conditions, they still have a firm provenance, which makes them better suited to an analysis of Jews in one community. In recent decades, hundreds of bowls have appeared on the antiquities market and in private collections without any indication of their find-spots and, making matters more complex, some of them appear to be forgeries.[11] The objects that were excavated earlier in the century have the advantage of authenticity and a secure provenance. For this reason, this study focuses on the earlier incantation bowls that came to light from Nippur and its environs.

In the field of ancient Jewish magic, the text is called an "incantation" because the language tends to be somewhat formulaic, composed of building blocks in diverse arrangements, sometimes including stock biblical verses.[12] Some bowls have images in their center, but the images' meanings are difficult to decipher and correspond loosely to the accompanying text.[13] Incantations usually begin with a request for divine assistance and close with the phrase "Amen, Amen, Selah." This phrase is found in late antique synagogue inscriptions like the Ein Gedi mosaic.[14] It is found in Palestinian amulets as well, suggesting it had wide

---

8. *b. Qidd.* 72a. For analysis of the full *sugya* (71b–72a), see Herman, "Babylonia of Pure Lineage."

9. Paz, "'Meishan Is Dead,'" 78. Paz adds that "the portrayal of the Mesenean Jews as slaves clearly serves also as a foil for the self-definition of the rabbis as free-men and noble" (93).

10. See Hilprecht et al., *Explorations in Bible Lands*, 447–48; Layard, *Discoveries in the Ruins of Nineveh and Babylon*, 509–26; Peeters, *Nippur*, 182–7; Fisher, *Excavations at Nippur*.

11. Rollston, "The Crisis of Modern Epigraphic Forgeries and the Antiquities Market." Indeed, most of the two-thousand bowls that have come to light since the mid-twentieth century excavations are without provenance.

12. Angel, "The Use of the Hebrew Bible in Early Jewish Magic," 785–98. Harari prefers the term "adjuration text" to incantation text and offers eight features that identify such texts (*Jewish Magic before the Rise of Kabbalah*, 172–73).

13. See Hunter, "Who Are the Demons?" More recently, Vilozny discusses "Stylistic Aspects of the Figures Appearing on the Incantation Bowls" in a short section of Shaked, Ford, and Bhayro, *Aramaic Bowl Spells*; see also book-length treatment in Vilozny, *Lilith's Hair and Ashmedai's Horns* (Hebrew).

14. Levine, *The Ancient Synagogue*, 386.

liturgical use in antiquity.[15] In their repetitive way, incantations share some characteristics with liturgical poetry and, indeed, the synagogue liturgy may have influenced incantations and incantations may have influenced the Jewish liturgy.[16]

The recipients of the incantation bowls' protection are always identified with their matronymic, in contrast with the public identification with one's patronymic (e.g., in legal and rabbinic texts).[17] The prophet Jeremiah's description of Rachel weeping for her children, the people of Israel in the context of the Babylonian destruction, and God's merciful response to her (Jer 31:15) may have provided the precedent for evoking the maternal line in the context of ritual requests for intercession, one that the rabbis would elaborate on in late antiquity, and that continues in prayers for healing in Jewish communal settings to this day.[18] In a rare quotation of a woman's voice in the Babylonian Talmud, the Rabbi Abaye relates that his mother (or a woman named Em) stated that "all incantations are in the name of the mother."[19] The most important difference between liturgical and ritual language is that incantations refer to individuals and their personal anxieties while the more formal synagogue liturgy addresses communal concerns more broadly.

The preservation of the incantation bowls has generally led scholars to hypothesize that these objects were ritually buried beneath the dirt floors of their homes.[20]

15. The benediction "Amen" would have been familiar to any readers or hearers of the Torah and the same is true of "Selah," found in Psalms, where it signals the end of a piece, though it is otherwise mysterious in meaning. "Amen" is said by the people of Israel as an affirmation already in Deut 27:15–26. See also Pss 41 and 72; "amen, amen" in sequence without conjunction appears only in the *sotah* ritual in Num 5:22 (known for its "magical" overtones) and Neh 8:6, just after Ezra opens the Torah and blesses God before the congregation of Israel. *Selah* is found often in Psalms, but is untranslatable (Pss 3, 4, 9, 20, 24, etc.).

16. See Schäfer, "Jewish Liturgy and Magic." I will also discuss evidence of this relationship at the end of successive chapters.

17. Lesses, "Exe(o)rcising Power," 363.

18. Scholars have given other explanations for matronymic naming practices in ritual sources and ancient Judaism more broadly, namely "the uncertainty of paternity" (on this, see Cohen, *The Beginnings of Jewishness*, 290). I thank Laura Lieber for suggesting this alternative explanation in private communication. On the intercessory power of Rachel and mothers' in ancient Judaism, see Gribetz, "*Zekhut Imahot.*"

19. See *b.* Šabb. 66b; Lesses, "Exe(o)rcising Power," 363; Ilan suggests that Em may be a proper name in *Silencing the Queen*, 27. Also discussed in Swartz, *Mechanics of Providence*, 30–31.

20. See Gibson, *Excavations at Nippur: Eleventh Season*, 121, 151. Gibson mentions that the Aramaic bowls were found on the site's surface and perhaps associated with rooms. Bohak notes that bowls were found "within the premises of a dwelling, or under the thresholds, or in a cemetery, or in large groups of bowls in one location (perhaps the atelier which produced them)," *Ancient Jewish Magic*, 184. More recently, Frankfurter has suggested that perhaps they were visible and above ground in "Scorpion/Demon," 9–18.

Ceramic bowls may seem like an unintuitive choice as a medium for an incanta-tion, but they offer the advantage of being cheap and widely available.[21] Scholars have tried to make sense of the shape's relevance to ritual ends, but no theory has gained widespread traction.[22] It is helpful to keep in mind that writing upon pot-tery and ceramic fragments was actually quite common throughout the ancient Near East; ceramic pieces were used for lists, for drawing lots, and even for legal contracts like divorce.[23]

During the fifth to seventh centuries CE, Jews, Christians, and other adjacent communities commissioned incantation bowls.[24] These ritual objects were in use in Mesopotamia only, not elsewhere in the Levant or in the Mediterranean world.[25] Based on the incantation bowls excavated in the ancient town of Nippur alone, Michael Morony observed that "73 percent were in Jewish Aramaic, 21 per-cent were Mandaic, and 5 percent were in Syriac."[26] Jewish Aramaic script is much more widely represented than the Mandaic and Syriac scripts. Why Jewish Ara-maic is overrepresented in this ritual medium has intrigued scholars for decades. For context, consider that Jews made up between one-eighth and one-tenth of the population of Sasanian Persia, probably constituting one of the largest minorities alongside Mandeans and Syriac-speaking Christians.[27] Though limited in circula-tion to this region of the Middle East, the incantation bowls still offer a great deal of useful information about the lives of late antique Jews.

Just over a century has passed since the landmark publication of incanta-tion bowls from the Mesopotamian town of Nippur.[28] For most of the twentieth

21. Bohak is surely right in stating that the bowls "were not produced by the magicians for the purpose of this specific ritual, but were bought in the marketplace in very large quantities, and then used as a surface on which to inscribe magical spells" (*Ancient Jewish Magic*, 185). See also Shaked et al., *Aramaic Bowl Spells*, 2.

22. See Isbell, "The Story of Aramaic Magical Incantation Bowls," 7–10 for a review of the pro-posed theories and their shortcomings. More recently, see Frankfurter, "Scorpion/Demon."

23. See discussion of writing on ostraca in Bülow-Jacobsen, "Writing Material in the Ancient World." Bülow-Jacobsen notes that ostraca overtake papyri as the most popular writing medium in Coptic in late antiquity. Notably, the rabbis mention that divorce documents are valid if written on any medium (*m. Giṭ.* 2:3). See also Bagnall, "Writing on Ostraka."

24. Shaked, Ford, and Bhayro state that bowls were certainly produced during the sixth and sev-enth centuries, but hypothesize that "the practice began somewhat earlier, in the fifth or possibly even the fourth century CE" (see *Aramaic Bowl Spells* 1, esp. note 2).

25. In "Incantation Bowls: A Mesopotamian Phenomenon?" Hunter analyzes an anomalous bowl associated with a private collection of Egyptian artifacts and highlights its Mesopotamian features; she rightly locates the cultural resonances of these ritual objects within a "Neo-Assyrian and Babylonian matrix" that "did not encourage the dissemination of incantation bowls in communities outside Meso-potamia, whether in Palestine, Syria, or Egypt" (227).

26. Morony, "Magic and Society in Late Sasanian Iraq," 95.

27. Neusner, *A History of the Jews in Babylonia*, 2:241–50.

28. Montgomery, *Aramaic Incantation Texts from Nippur*.

century, study of the incantations was the realm of philologists, who painstakingly deciphered the contents of myriad incantations and laid the groundwork for the research that continues to flourish today.[29] Where incantation bowls might have been dismissed as superstitious nonsense unworthy of study, Joseph Naveh and Shaul Shaked's surveys brought together Babylonian incantation bowls alongside Palestinian amulets and ritual texts from the Cairo Genizah, forming the field of ancient Jewish magic.[30] Casting these artifacts as evidence of syncretistic popular religion, Naveh and Shaked brought attention to these artifacts to a new generation of Jewish Studies scholars, who pulled the study of magic into religious studies and rabbinic studies.[31] Publication of collected translations of incantation bowls texts continues apace today alongside newer studies that seek to integrate the study of magic or ritual objects into the study of rabbinic texts, Jewish culture, history, and ancient Mediterranean religion more broadly.[32]

Although the term *magic* is enjoying a surge of positive associations in popular culture, it still carries connotations that distract from the meaning of ritual texts from Palestine and Babylonia.[33] Notably, the incantation texts themselves do not claim to be engaged in magic; they claim to fight curses, sorcery, and witchcraft.[34] Coercion of divine forces has long been seen as the key to differentiating magical from religious ritual.[35] However, in most of the Babylonian incantation texts, which form the bulk of the survey in this chapter, such a coercive attitude toward God and his angels is absent. Most incantation bowls are defensive in nature, not

29. Two recent publications provide excellent overviews of the historiography of this field. See Harari, "Jewish Incantation Bowls," pp. 133–40 in *Jewish Magic before the Rise of Kabbalah*, and Bohak, "Babylonian Jewish Magic in Late Antiquity."

30. See Naveh and Shaked, *Amulets and Magic Bowls* and *Magic Spells and Formulae*. For an overview of Shaked's oeuvre, see Harari, "Shaul Shaked on Jewish Magic." See also Schiffman and Swartz, *Hebrew and Aramaic Incantation Texts from the Cairo Genizah*.

31. Lesses, *Ritual Practices to Gain Power*. See also the many contributions of Swartz, collected in *The Mechanics of Providence*, and Bohak, *Ancient Jewish Magic*.

32. Most recently, see Shaked, Bhayro, and Ford, *Aramaic Bowl Spells* and other volumes in Brill's series like Paz-Saar, *Jewish Love Magic*. See also Manekin-Bamberger, "Jewish Legal Formulae in the Aramaic Incantation Bowls;" Sanzo and Boustan, "Christian Magicians, Jewish Magical Idioms, and the Shared Magical Culture of Late Antiquity."

33. See Ahuvia, "Popular Religion and Magic" and Harari, *Jewish Magic before the Rise of Kabbalah*.

34. Meyer and Smith, *Ancient Christian Magic*, 2. For examples of Jewish Aramaic incantations that fight magic, see Hunter, "Two Incantation Bowls from Babylon." For incantations aimed at curses, see Manekin-Bamberger, "The Vow-Curse in Ancient Jewish Texts." See also 034A published by Segal and Hunter, *Catalogue of the Aramaic and Mandaic Incantation Bowls in the British Museum*. Henceforth, Segal and Hunter's book is referred to as *CAMIB*.

35. From Frazer down to present anthropological research, "the terms most frequently associated with magic are 'impersonal,' 'mechanical,' 'automatic,' 'compulsive,' 'coercive,' 'efficient,' 'learned techniques,' and 'acquired skills' (see Hammond, "Magic,"1352).

aggressive.[36] To be clear, many incantations do endeavor to compel demons to depart. While demons are commanded to cease tormenting their victims, angels and God are more commonly petitioned for assistance.

Deployment of the term *magic* is gendered and tends to marginalize people associated with it, particularly women and their ritual practice. In ancient texts men arrogated authority to themselves and tended to accuse women of engaging in magic or witchcraft, even if they were engaged in identical behaviors.[37] Incantation bowls bring into view a wider range of people, social configurations, and perceptions than rabbinic sources do. The incantation bowls from the town of Nippur, for instance, were commissioned by men and women, individuals, couples, and families to fulfill personal, familial, and/or household needs. The evidence from Nippur indicates that about 60 percent of the beneficiaries of incantations were male while 40 percent were female.[38] At least in Nippur, slightly more men than women commissioned incantation bowls in Nippur, undermining the generalization that women were more prone to "magical" practice. Overall, incantation bowls show how individuals concretized abstract ideas about the angels and the divine realm in their daily lives.

The incantation texts also shed light on rabbinic culture. On the one hand, the rabbis of the Talmud never explicitly refer to incantation bowls. On the other hand, the incantation bowls quote Mishnaic texts and name rabbinic figures, and many show awareness of authoritative rabbinic texts, technical terms, and practices.[39] Some incantation bowls (examined below) suggest that a couple of rabbis became well known as folk heroes with expertise in anti-demonic ritual practices. A recent article by Shaked collected references to rabbis in incantation bowls (amounting to ten examples) and proposes "that the rabbis, among them possibly some who were prominent scholars, were just as much involved in the process of using incantation bowls, as other members of the Jewish community."[40] In some of the bowls Shaked analyzed, the rabbis were mentioned incidentally,

---

36. Levene has collected the curse texts that have come to light over the decades in *Jewish Aramaic Curse Texts from Late-Antique Mesopotamia*. Out of the roughly one thousand incantations known at the time of his publication, Levene identified only thirty curse texts.

37. Discussed in Ilan, *Silencing the Queen*, 240. Commenting on Exod 22:18, "You shall not allow a witch to live" (*maḵašēpāh lo ṯeḥayeh*), the rabbis in the Palestinian Talmud state that "scripture teaches you about the way of the world in which the majority of women are witches" (*y. Sanh.* 7:13, 40b); cf. *y. Qidd.* 4.11: "even the best woman is an expert at magic." Traditions in the Babylonian Talmud agree: "most women engage in witchcraft" (*Sanh.* 67a).

38. Morony, "Magic and Society in Late Sasanian Iraq," 101.

39. Manekin-Bamberger, "Jewish Legal Formulae." See also discussion of Schøyen 1929/6 in Shaked, et al., *Aramaic Bowl Spells*, 22–23; this bowl and another fragmentary one by the same practitioner is discussed in Shaked, "Form and Purpose in Aramaic Spells."

40. Shaked, "Rabbis in Incantation Bowls," 116.

as neighbors to clients.[41] Even though the rabbis of the Babylonian Talmud make no direct reference to *writing* incantation bowls, they do discuss ritual practices against demons and for healing. Gideon Bohak has examined the subject of rabbinic interest in magic and magical expertise in rabbinic texts, showing how the rabbis sanctioned some ritual practices while legislating against others.[42] Ritual practitioners were not disconnected from rabbinic communities and, moreover, the rabbis and their texts became recognized sources of authority for some producers of incantation bowls. The incantation texts help us to understand the milieu of the rabbis: who their neighbors were, how these rabbis were popularly perceived, and how the rabbis themselves were influenced by other non-rabbinic Jews. Even though these bowls are chronologically later than most classical rabbinic literature from Palestine, beginning with the ritual texts will help us make sense of the variety of the rabbis' reactions to angels.

My analysis of angels in Babylonian incantations and Palestinian amulets joins in the efforts to illuminate neglected aspects of Jewish religiosity by focusing on the invocation of angels in the bowls in the context of Jewish daily life. Thus far in scholarship, a focus on the production rather than reception of the incantation bowl has prevailed in the field of ancient Jewish magic.[43] In my view, incantation bowls can be analyzed in one of three ways: (1) as fixed formulae intractable for social analysis; (2) as specialized texts reflecting the views of ritual practitioners; and (3) as reflecting a collaboration between the practitioners who made them and the clients who used them in their homes. The significance of my observations regarding the role of angels in these incantations will depend on one's approach to texts and their reception in antiquity.

My reading of well over one hundred ritual texts led me to approach ritual texts like Babylonian incantation bowls and Palestinian amulets as the end of a long collaborative ritual process.[44] Much of the content of the bowls can be understood as relevant for Jewish beliefs if a more inclusive perspective on religion, Jewish identity, and Jewish practice is adopted. Incantation bowls written in Jewish Aramaic script show a clear tendency to appeal to Jewish divinities. It is true that incantations written in Syriac scripts sometimes parallel Jewish incantations and may have been written by Jewish practitioners for Christian clients, but that does not negate the value of Jewish incantations for the study of

---

41. See MS 1928/49, where the border of Rav Aḥa's and Rav Huna's house is mentioned in Shaked, "Form and Purpose in Aramaic Spells," 20–21.

42. See Bohak, *Ancient Jewish Magic*, especially chapter 6: "Magic and Magicians in Rabbinic Literature." And more recently, Bohak, "Babylonian Jewish Magic in Late Antiquity."

43. Since I have discussed my methodology in detail in "The Spatial and Social Dynamics of Jewish Babylonian Incantations," I only summarize my approach here.

44. See the table of incantation bowls in the appendix.

Judaism.[45] There was enough common ground between ancient Jews and Christians that a Jewish incantation appealing to God and his angels could suit some Christians as well. Syriac incantations are just as diverse as Jewish ones in terms of the figures they invoke for aid: some invoke Jesus or the Trinity, but most of the published incantations do not.[46] Research on angels in Syriac bowls remains a desideratum. Meanwhile, Jewish Aramaic bowls remain an untapped source for understanding the network of divine-human relationships of which ancient Jews understood themselves to be a part.

Thinking about the ritual construction of an incantation bowl, I hypothesize that there was first a moment when a client decided that a ritual object written by a specialist was necessary to confront a problem; secondly, an occasion when a client encountered a specialist and explained the predicament; thirdly, a process of producing the incantation bowl; fourthly, a performance or recitation of the incantation in the home, and finally, the deposition of the incantation bowls at a fitting location within the home. While there must have been variation in practice, this may serve as a general outline of the entire process. In this collaborative process, the ritual practitioner, the clients, God, the angels, and others would each play a role. Each incantation bowl encourages conceptualizing a different constellation of relationships among the clients, their household or community, and the invisible realm of the angels. Focusing on angels within these various permutations is key to understanding their function in the religious imagination.

HOW DO ANGELS FUNCTION IN INCANTATIONS?

Previous scholars have suggested that incantation bowls rallied angels to fight against demons.[47] My study, however, has yielded the following observations (see the table in the appendix): Angels and demons are arrayed against each other in only about one-third of incantations.[48] When angels are invoked in incantations,

45. See Juusola, "Who Wrote the Syriac Incantation Bowls?"; Moriggi, *A Corpus of Syriac Incantation Bowls.*

46. See Moriggi, *A Corpus of Syriac Incantation Bowls,* Bowl 2, p. 28 and Bowl 6, p. 48, also discussed in this book's conclusion.

47. Levene, "Curse or Blessing."

48. I began with investigating the few dozen bowls published with provenance, and then turned to later publications of bowls without a provenance; this study revealed that the presence or absence of provenance did not substantially affect the distribution of beings invoked in the incantation bowls. See the appendix for the references and acronyms of bowls cited in the table. My results here are slightly different from those presented in my doctoral thesis: for one, I eliminated some accidental counting of identical formulas in different publications. More importantly, I now think that I underestimated the role of the practitioner in the performance of incantations. If we keep in mind that a practitioner always mediated these incantations, separating out some textual formulas that emphasize the first-person singular of the practitioner seems unnecessary.

they are called on to help with a variety of issues: in addition to guarding people from demons, angels provide protection from other people's curses, they enable commercial success, they bring health, and they restore good marital relations. The most popular incantation formula, known as Refrain A, appeals to angels alone to counteract the curses of one's in-laws.[49] More often, angels play a supportive role of protection alongside other intermediaries: 40 percent of incantation bowls invoke angels alongside or under God's authority. Another 13 percent call on angels, God, and a folk hero like Rabbi Joshua b. Perahia or Rabbi Hanina ben Dosa to achieve their aims. Relatively few (5 percent) rely on the practitioner's powers alone without calling on God's approval, the angels' aid, or a predecessor's example. Only about one-fifth of the incantation bowls are directed toward God alone. Paying attention to why angels are invoked by some incantations and not by others holds the key to understanding their function in the religious landscape.

Calling on Angels

I begin with examples of the largest category, the 40 percent of incantation bowls that explicitly call on the angels under God's authority. Returning to the bowl with which this chapter opened, we can home in on a representative Jewish household in late antique Iraq whose members invoked angels for well-being. This incantation bowl, unfortunately without provenance, brings into relief the makeup of a particular household in an ancient community in Iraq.[50] Possessing slaves and servants, this couple was likely wealthy, and they worried about the jealous and nefarious intentions of others toward them. They particularly worried about aggressive magic from others in their vicinity, which apparently had quite a diverse population: the ritual practitioner lists Arameans (possibly Christians), Jews, a pre-Islamic Arabian tribe, Persians, Indians, Greeks, and Romans as potential sources of aggressive magic. He may list them in descending order of magnitude, but we lack enough data about the population of late antique Iraq to be sure. What is certain is that, to make themselves feel protected and safe, they solicited a Jewish ritual practitioner to write them an incantation bowl that would invoke God and the angels for assistance. The incantation opens with a formula typical of Jewish Aramaic incantations: it requests rescue, healing, or salvation from the heavens.[51]

---

49. It is difficult to quantify this incantation alongside others as only one bowl with Refrain A has a firm provenance, and we do not know the geographic scope of this formula. For this reason, I count only distinct formulae in my table, counting even popular ones like Refrain A, only once.

50. Gordon, "Aramaic Magical Bowls in the Istanbul and Baghdad Museums," 319, 328–30 (D, no. 6519).

51. Though this opening formula resembles the liturgical Aramaic phrase *besiyata dishmaya*, "with the help of heaven," this phrase only became widespread among Orthodox Jews in the beginning of the twentieth century.

The fact that this family chose a Jewish ritual specialist who appealed to the Jewish God and his angels suggests their Jewish affiliation. The practitioner did not call on the famous angels Michael or Gabriel for their protection but rather Aza, Azzael, Metatron, and Kavshiel. In this list, only Metatron eventually developed a widespread reputation; the rest of the names seem to have been invented, like Kavshiel, the angel "who conquers" evil, whose name includes the Hebrew verb for "conquer." Likewise, *Az* means "strong," "firm," and "vehement" in Hebrew, and Azzael's name seems to have been constructed from this adjective.[52] Much debate centers on the meaning of the name Metatron: it may derive from Greek *metath-ronos*, designating one serving beside or behind the divine throne, or it may relate to the Latin *metator*, the term for a Roman officer who acts as forerunner.[53] Metatron became an increasingly well-known figure in the early medieval Jewish world, acquiring the characteristics of the archangel Michael, other famous angels, and eventually the antediluvian patriarch Enoch.[54] Scattered references to Metatron appear in the Babylonian Talmud, in the Aramaic translations of the Hebrew Bible known as the Targumim, and in early mystical texts.[55] This pattern of combining both well-known angelic names with invented ones is typical of late antique Jewish ritual and mystical texts. After invoking these angelic names, the ritual practitioner pronounced the powerful and taboo Hebrew name of God, another common practice of the incantations.[56] To close, the incantation signed off with the liturgical formula "Amen, Amen, Selah."

This incantation constructs a worldview in which the Jewish God is supreme, and only God can bring an end to others' "sorceries" by his command, a task that is executed through his angels, who themselves descend to earth to guard this household. This ritual practitioner encouraged this family to imagine that angels were available to help people like them on earth. Notably, the ritual practitioner did not *order* the angels to do his bidding. He only described a reality in which God and the angels protected their household and were the source of sustenance for people on earth. Here, the angels were imagined as responsible for ensuring safety from all harm as well as providing daily nourishment.[57] This incantation

52. See Jastrow, *Dictionary*, who also notes that the name appears in Targum Y. Gen 6:4.

53. For discussions of etymology, see Alexander, "From Son of Adam to Second God"; Orlov, *The Enoch-Metatron Tradition*; Miller, "Folk-Etymology, and Its Influence on Metatron Traditions."

54. Schäfer, *The Jewish Jesus*; Orlov, *Yahoel and Metatron*; and most recently, see Paz, "Metatron is not Enoch."

55. See *b. Sanh.* 38b, *b. Ḥag.* 15a, *b. 'Abod. Zar.* 3b, *Bem. R.* 12:12, summarized in Ahuvia, "Metatron."

56. As Bohak explains, "The great sanctity surrounding the Tetragrammaton" was "a unique feature of Jewish religion," which was deployed often in Jewish magical practices (see *Ancient Jewish Magic*, 119).

57. The rabbis begrudgingly admit that an angel may bring about redemption (per Gen 48:16), but assert that God controls sustenance, a far more difficult action! See *Gen. Rab.* 97:3, discussed in chapter 6.

therefore reveals a hierarchy wherein people turned to a ritual expert who appealed to the angels, who were subordinate to God. Once the ritual practitioner had left, the family could continually reinvoke the angelic presence, imagining the angels around them. Others might have employed their own ritual experts and still directed sorceries in their direction, but this family relied on the angels to maintain their safety.

According to incantation texts, angels could be called on to protect from a danger far closer to home, indeed within the home. In Refrain A, the most-copied ancient incantation formula known to date, angels were invoked to counteract the curses of one's in-laws against the client(s).[58] To understand why familial in-laws were a source of anxiety, it is helpful to understand that in antiquity, households were multigenerational agglomerations where people lived in very close proximity to each other, with little privacy and sometimes in tense configurations. On this atmosphere, Peter Brown observed that "claustrophobia and the tensions of living in a face-to-face society, not loneliness or rootlessness, are the leitmotifs of the specifically late Antique form of being unhappy."[59] Worries about the criticisms and curses of parental or sibling in-laws preoccupied many individuals who turned to ritual practitioners. Their response was not commissioning a curse tablet but instead procuring a defensive incantation.[60] The ritual practitioners who employed Refrain A invoked only the angels and the angelic names against the curses of relatives.

A typical incantation of this category begins with the refrain "Overturned, overturned, overturned is the earth and heaven, overturned are the stars and the planets, overturned is the talk of all the people, overturned is the curse of the mother and of the daughter, of the daughter-in-law and of the mother-in-law, overturned is the curse of men and women who stand in the open field and in the village and on the mountain and the temple(s) and the synagogues(s)."[61] Three incantations include the phrase "in the temple and the synagogue,"[62] grounding these formulae in the mixed Jewish and polytheistic regional landscape of the

58. Refrain A has been found in over a dozen bowls since its discovery in 1851. For a thorough recapitulation of all the parallels and variations of this formula, see Hunter, "Manipulating Incantation Texts: Excursions in Refrain A"; also briefly discussed in Secunda, *The Iranian Talmud*, 34 and 164. The earliest discovered incantation bowls (the so-called Rawlinson group) that contained Refrain A turned out to contain an interesting variant (see especially BM 91727): it blamed female in-laws for conjuring up demons that were sent against the client, revealing a belief that people could send demons against each other.

59. Brown, *The Making of Late Antiquity*, 4.

60. Levene numbered thirty such aggressive texts out of the one thousand incantation bowl texts known in 2013 when he published *Jewish Aramaic Curse Texts from Late-Antique Mesopotamia*.

61. Here following Naveh and Shaked, *Amulets and Magic Bowls*, 134–35, Bowl 2.

62. See also BM 91713 and BM 91758 in Segal and Hunter, *CAMIB*.

ancient Near East. The incantation emphasizes overturning the natural order of the celestial bodies and overturning the power of female in-laws, ostensibly those related to the client. In this worldview, personal strife was raised to cosmic proportions and only the heavenly intercession of the angels could remedy it.

Next, the incantation formula calls on specific angels to remedy this situation. Section II states "In the name of Betiel and Yequtiel, and in the name of YY the Great, the angel who has eleven names." A list of foreign names known in scholarship as *nomina barbara*, follows. These vary in their spelling between the different attestations of this formula. The incantation then warned against transgressing against those names. I conjecture that Betiel was considered the appropriate angel for this situation because the name Betiel derives from *byt*, meaning home or wife; the angel of the home has obvious relevance in these tense household configurations. The precise derivation of Yequtiel is unknown: in one late antique Palestinian midrash, Moses is said to be called Yequtiel because he looked like an angel of God, suggesting angelic connotations to the name.[63] In the Babylonian Talmud, this name applied to Moses was interpreted as relating to the verb for hoping or trusting in God.[64] Perhaps the mystery of the name was part of Refrain A's power. Betiel, Yequtiel and "YY the Great Angel who has eleven names" appear in every variant of this incantation.[65] The names of the angels were thus key to the operation of this incantation. Another section, which appears in about three-quarters of the incantations sends against "the woman who cursed" the angels NKYR and YY. A number of translations have been suggested for NKYR, some pointing to ancient Akkadian etymology referring to "hostile one," "enemy" or "warrior" and others pointing to the angel of death from the Islamic period.[66] YY is a common abbreviation for God in scribal texts but here is evidently listed as the name of "the Great Angel." Notably, this formula relied only on angelic names, which the practitioners saw as deployable for family conflict. Some matters did not require God's attention. Whereas people today might find calling on angels for household drama strange, the incantation bowls show us that this approach was acceptable, encouraged, and deemed useful by Jewish practitioners in Mesopotamia.

Shifting to a different challenge, an incantation bowl from Borsippa only invoked angels to ask for commercial success. A man named Aban, son of Daday, commissioned the incantations and buried two duplicate bowls at the entrance to

63. The name is found in 1 Chr 4:18 and interpreted by *Pirqe R. El.* 48:7 to apply to Moses.

64. The name Yequtiel (Jekuthiel) is also applied to Moses in *b. Meg.* 13a but with a different folk-etymological explanation.

65. In medieval Hebrew manuscripts, *YY* usually refers to God, but this formula makes it clear that *YY* was understood as an angelic representative of God.

66. I thank Scott Noegel for the reference to Akkadian *nakāru* and *nakīru* (stranger, foe). See other possibilities summarized in Hunter, "Manipulating Incantation Texts: Excursions in Refrain A," 269n58–60.

his shop, which was also probably his home. The first line seems to indicate where the incantation bowl ought to be deposited (the edge or threshold of the home). Although this is the only incantation that seeks commercial success found to date, its existence suggests that people could imagine that the angels could help them with their businesses:[67]

> For the edge.
> Hark! A voice heard in the heavens and howling in the earth. A voice in all (things). Call him that they may open the gates of the heavens and [the gates of] the earth and the winds of the heavens. For the [ed]ge. Sustaining the house and the shop of Aban son of Daday to provide (for him) and to help him and to give him plenty. Cause every evil eye to desist from his house and from his shop. And in the name of Qanayel Anangiel Barqiel Gabriel Hasdiel Hizel and Hananiel (and) 'Atriel, in the name of these seven angels [. . .], they will drive out and will open the gates of all the children of Adam and Eve to the gates of Aban son of Daday. Amen Amen Selah Hallelujah.[68]

Like the first incantation we encountered in this chapter, the beginning and end of this incantation imagine the gates of the heavens, where the angels stand guard.[69] Ancient Jews imagined heavenly storehouses (e.g., of rain, wind, destruction, or blessing) with gates that the angels of God patrolled.[70] The oral dimension of the text is prominent, describing a call heard in the heavens and on earth, a call for the angel guarding the gates between the heaven and the earth to open them for the client. One can imagine the practitioner reading it aloud, the client hearing it and internalizing it, and the incantation bowl serving as a permanent manifestation of this performance in his shop and home. In this incantation, angels are portrayed as gatekeepers, essential to successful commerce in the earthly realm. The formula invoked a particular high angel, asking him to have other angels open the gates of the heavens for his client.

The middle of this incantation centers on the danger of the evil eye. Fear of the evil eye (a jealous look or ill-intentioned gaze) as a source of misfortune was widely shared by peoples in the Mediterranean and ancient Near Eastern world.[71]

---

67. Segal and Hunter, CAMIB 021A (BM 127396). Another incantation with a similar purpose was published by Levene and Bhayro, "'Bring to the Gates . . . Upon a Good Smell and Upon Good Fragrances': An Aramaic Incantation Bowl for Success in Business."

68. The scribe erroneously listed eight angels, not seven, probably because Anangiel is a misunderstanding of the Greek for angel, αγγελος.

69. Cf. the example with which this chapter began: "And may the gates of sustenance open for [them] from the four corners of the earth, from above and below" (Gordon D, no. 6519).

70. Such "storehouses" ('wtsr) are mentioned in the Hebrew Bible (cf. Deut 28:12, Ps 135:7). On this topic, see Houtman, Der Himmel im Alten Testament.

71. Kalmin, "The Evil Eye in Rabbinic Literature of Late Antiquity."

The client likely hoped that the angels would keep the evil eye from harming his business. Again, the angels' role was not combative but protective and beneficent. As in Refrain A, the incantation warding off the curses of in-laws, there is no reference to God's sacred name but only reliance on the angels for help. The client and/or specialist thought that appealing to God for business matters was inappropriate, but that the angels were available and present for such problems. In any case, for this client, appealing to the angels alone sufficed to give him confidence in his livelihood. Thanks to the angels, all people ("all the children of Adam and Eve") would come to his shop through the "gates of Aban son of Daday."

Returning to familial concerns, another incantation bowl from Nippur was preoccupied with love, marriage, and childbearing.[72] Contrary to some people's expectations of so-called erotic magic, this incantation is not coercive. This incantation stands out for the intimacy of the household scene it brings to life: neatly divided in two, the first part in the interior of the bowl describes three angels compassionately embracing, clothing, and protecting a woman named Bachmanduch bat Shema. When it was recited out loud, this description allowed Bachmanduch to imagine herself cared for by angels. The second part of the incantation, written on the exterior of the bowl, explains why this intervention was necessary: this woman was lovelorn in her marriage and was desperately hoping for a child. Asserting that all mouths (i.e., potential sources of criticism and curses) are closed before her, the practitioner wrote that "the angel Rahmiel and the angel Habbiel and the angel Hananiel—these angels have mercy and love and [. . .] embrace Bachmanduch bat Shema" (3–5). The angelic names themselves play on verbs whose meaning is love, honor, and favor. According to the incantation, these three angels clothed her "with grace from on high" and "they sit with her" in the name of God (6–7). The exterior lines of the bowls describe her suffering and inability to bear a child. Next, her husband Ephra is addressed in the second person singular to return to her quickly. The end of the incantation closes piously with "Amen, Amen, Selah, salvation and peace from heaven for ever and ever and ever." This incantation attests to the way one Jewish woman was comforted by imagining angels surrounding her. Considering the scarcity of representations of women's experiences from antiquity, this incantation provides important evidence for how women imagined the divine realm and were comforted by angelic presence.

Notably, this incantation is not unique: another incantation bowl, without provenance, similarly enlists angels to support Mahdukh daughter of Ispendarmed with glory, mercy, splendor, and the general favor of others.[73] It begins by appealing to 'Aniel to answer her, Michael to teach her, Hadariel to clothe her

---

72. Here I examine Montgomery, *Aramaic Incantation Texts* (hereafter *AIT*) no. 13; *AIT*, no. 28 is also focused on restoration of love in a marriage but is fragmentary.

73. See MS 1927/2 in Shaked, "Form and Purpose," 8–10, and pp. 25–26 for transcription.

with glory, Karmiel to clothe her with mercy, and Ziviel to add splendor to her.[74] Calling on the "holy angels," the incantation asks that she be granted grace in the eyes of all: "May she speak and be heard, may she come to trial and win it, may she ask and take (that which she has asked for), may she say (something) and be listened to."[75] The incantation also appeals to the angel Zarpiel to give grace to Hilion, daughter of Ispendarmed, perhaps the sister of Mahdukh. The women hearing these words believed the angels were on their side, available to help them in ordinary day-to-day conflicts.

These incantations are striking because we do not encounter this level of personalization and of divine and human intimacy in the communally oriented Jewish liturgy. While the rabbis portrayed themselves as having intimate, personal interactions with God, Elijah the prophet, or angels, the rabbis did not portray ordinary women in this way. Where the rabbis did admit that the Jewish matriarchs spoke with angels, they did so only condescendingly to emphasize that God never spoke with women.[76] In these incantations, the relationship of women and angels is described in vivid, positive, and personal terms. The incantation bowls are important in demonstrating how ancient women related to the invisible realm as informed by the Bible and by Jewish traditions. The wife from Nippur was confronting a difficult period in her marriage, and she relied on the angels and a ritual practitioner to help her through it. As more incantation bowls are translated and published, more such fascinating examples will come to light.

Whereas the previous incantation bowls each tackled one specific issue, the majority of incantation bowls take aim at a wider range of issues, covering all of their bases, as it were. In the following incantation bowl from Nippur, God and the angels were enlisted in the fight against a litany of sources of trouble:

> A Song of praise to the King of the World, YHWH of Hosts
> The Rock of the Worlds, I-am-who-I-am, Yah, the King who speaks [and] creates
>   dry land, the Savior who is called DWRPS, PWDWP' of spirits.
> Bound and Sealed is the threshold of Ulla the son of Rehud, from Satan, from the
>   demon, from the curse and the invocation, from the vow, and from the knocking.
> In the name of [skipping 26 variations on the name YHWH].
> In the name of Yhws, Yhws, Yhws, and 'Hws, and 'Grybt. Qumiel, Qutiel, Yhw,
>   Sbhw.[77]

---

74. Shaked, "Form and Purpose," paraphrasing Shaked's translation; and see p. 25, line 1. Some of these names are puns and may have been invented ad hoc, but interestingly, the angel 'Aniel or 'Anael (God responds) evidently had a reputation for answering women's prayers in late antiquity and in the medieval period.

75. Shaked, "Form and Purpose," MS 1927/2, line 3, p. 8.

76. See *Gen. Rab.* 20:6, 45:10 and 48:20. The rabbis single out Sarah as the exception that proves the rule.

77. Isbell, "Two New Aramaic Incantation Bowls," 20–23 (Oriental Institute Text N-IV).

The practitioner who wrote this incantation introduced it as a song of praise to God (Hebrew, *shir*), reminding us of the performative aspect of these texts: the practitioner likely sang or recited the incantation as part of its introduction to the home of Ulla.[78] This incantation targeted Satan, demons, curses, vows, and the frightening knocking sounds of the night. We can learn from this that ancient Jews in Nippur were anxious about the demonic realm alongside curses and vows from the human realm, as well as those inexplicable noises of the night that could originate from either the demonic or human realms. The practitioner appealed to God and the angels to protect the home of Ulla from them all. The epithets for God in the first two lines of this incantation can be found in the book of Psalms and the Jewish liturgy. From the practitioner and client's perspective, this incantation was a pious appeal to God. The practitioner pronounced twenty-six permutations of the tetragrammaton, likely because YHWH is equivalent to the number 26 by way of gematria (Hebrew numerology).[79] Even as this formula traveled far and wide and the variations for God's name changed, the number of divine names remained the same.[80] The incantation closed with a list of angelic names. There is no physical description of how these angels were present for the client, but we must deduce that for this practitioner and client, reciting the divine names of God and the angels was understood as sufficient to make the angels present and subdue demonic, human, and indeterminable sources of affliction.

Other incantations describe the angels in a more active role against the demons. An incantation bowl for a couple from Nippur states "Rescue from Heaven for Gurio bar Tati and for Ahath bath Doda his wife, that there vanish from them in their dwelling all demons and *devas* and that they be saved by the mercy of Heaven."[81] Evidently, this couple believed demons and devas were infesting their home. With the rise of Persian mazda-worship and Zoroastrianism, devas, divinities indigenous to the Hindu tradition, were demoted to the status of demons.[82] To counteract these demons, the ritual practitioner addressed God and his angelic representatives. He listed angelic names that are used to address God: "Yophiel is your name, Yehiel they call you . . . Metatron Yah"). Then he

78. The phrase "A song of praise to the King" can also be found in two other incantation bowl texts translated by Jeruzalmi and republished in Isbell, *Corpus*, nos. 67 and 69.

79. I thank Scott Noegel for drawing my attention to this numerical significance and the following related references: Labuschagne, "Significant Compositional Techniques in the Psalms"; Youngblood, "Divine Names in the Book of Psalms"; and Knohl, "Sacred Architecture."

80. See the amulet at opening of chapter 2; Isbell, "Two New Aramaic Incantation Bowls," 23, line 6.

81. Montgomery, *AIT*, no. 25:1 (with Epstein's corrections in "Commentary on Babylonian-Aramaic Words").

82. On this, see Yamauchi, "Aramaic Magic Bowls," who observes that in some incantation bowls we see the degradation of deities to demonic forces. *Deva* may also be transliterated as *dewa* or *daeva*.

singled out lesser known angels ("Tigin, Trigis, Balbis, Sabgas, Sadrapas") and asserted that these latter angels "bring salvation to all the children of men. *They will come and ascend* with the salvation of this house and property and dwelling of his, of his [family] . . . from this day even for the sphere of eternity."[83] This practitioner was explicit in stating the angels came and went, presumably between the heavens and the home of the client, and that the angels took the time to rid the home of demons. There is no description of a fight or confrontation narrated here. The ritual practitioner needed only to request the angels' presence to make the demonic specter disappear.

Overall, in this section, we see that angels were called into the home for a variety of personal needs—they provided protection from others' curses (including familial curses), they provided daily support for people's livelihoods, they could restore love in a marriage, and they could defend homes against demons as well as other sources of trouble. They were seen as present in homes, amenable to helping Jews who requested their assistance through incantations. They were also seen as in charge of gates in the heavenly realm, which they could open to bring success to people in the earthly realm. The ritual experts called the angels by name, sometimes stressing their subordination to God and sometimes invoking the angels alone. In incantation bowls, clients and ritual practitioners envisioned angels as mediators between God and themselves, available to help them with familial and personal needs.

ANGELS ALONGSIDE OTHER HEROES

To understand the place of angels in the ancient Jewish imagination, it is necessary to examine the other figures who were invoked alongside them in about 15 percent of the incantations. These include the biblical figures Adam, Noah, Abraham, Isaac, Jacob, Moses, David, and Solomon.[84] By late antiquity, these men had become heroes in the religious imagination with myths that enlarged their reputation and stories that overlooked their transgressions. Intriguingly, two rabbinic sages, Rabbi Joshua ben Perahia and Rabbi Hanina ben Dosa, are also found invoked alongside angels in the incantation bowls in historiola (short stories) that practitioners deployed to frame their approach to the invisible realm.[85] What the

83. Montgomery, *AIT*, no. 25:5.

84. All abbreviations are explained in the appendix: For Adam, see Montgomery, *AIT*, no. 10; VA 3854 in Levene, "Heal O'Israel"; or M123 in Levene, *A Corpus of Magic Bowls*. For Noah, see *AIT*, no. 10 as well. For the biblical patriarchs, see *AIT*, no. 8, discussed below. For Moses, see MS 1927/2 and M123. For David, see M117 and *AIT*, no. 14. For Solomon, see Gordon B; Gordon 1932.620; Faraj-Moriggi 62265; MS 1927/9; and Isbell, *Corpus*, 66.

85. I discuss examples invoking both figures below, but see the section devoted to Rabbi Hanina ben Dosa in Shaked, Bhayro, and Ford, *Aramaic Bowl Spells*, 53–94 for more.

permutations demonstrate is that angels were additive in the Jewish imagination, seen as supportive figures who could work in tandem with heroes from the ancient past like the biblical patriarchs or more recent folk-hero rabbis.

Incantation bowls invoked Rabbi Joshua ben Perahia and his so-called "writ of divorce" to expel demons from homes and break demonic attachment to individuals. Classic rabbinic literature gives no hint that this rabbi was known for exorcisms of demons. In tractate 'Abot (the treatise containing quotations of the "fathers" of the rabbinic movement), Rabbi Joshua ben Perahia is attributed the saying: "Provide yourself with a teacher and find a fellow-disciple; and when you judge a man, incline the balance in his favor" (m. 'Abot 1:6). This emphasis on learning and judging typifies the interests of the rabbis and does not set this first century CE rabbi apart. What does set Rabbi Joshua ben Perahia apart is a strange Babylonian Talmudic story where he is assigned blame for Jesus's apostasy.[86] According to the story, Rabbi Joshua was too strict with Jesus, and a misunderstood gesture cemented Jesus's alienation from the rabbis and turned him toward idolatry. This story has nothing to do with demons, but it may be relevant that Jesus himself, according to the earliest gospel, gained renown through his exorcisms of fellow Jews in the synagogue.[87] Perhaps the story indicates some guilt by proximity. Despite Rabbi Joshua ben Perahia having no direct associations with demons or exorcisms in rabbinic literature, he seems to have gained such a reputation for expelling demons in Babylonia both among Jews and Christians. The evidence of the incantations reveals a popular perception of the rabbis that the rabbis themselves never claimed.[88]

In incantations, Rabbi Joshua is attributed a powerful writ of divorce that could expel demons from homes. Scholars have struggled to explain how the idea of the divorcing demons fit into ancient people's worldview.[89] Did they really believe they were married to demons and had to divorce them to exorcise them?[90] The Book of the Watchers is the only ancient Jewish narrative that explicitly sets out an etiology for demonic attachment: the archangels killed the giants' physical bodies, leaving behind dispossessed angry spirits that thirst, hunger, and seek other bodies.[91] To

86. See b. Soṭah 47a and Schäfer's discussion of this story in Jesus in the Talmud, 34–40.

87. See the Gospel of Mark, where descriptions of Jesus's exorcisms are most detailed. For a detailed investigation, see Geller, Joshua b. Perahia and Jesus of Nazareth.

88. See Sanzo and Boustan, "Christian Magicians, Jewish Magical Idioms."

89. For shared language between rabbinic texts and incantations, see Manekin-Bamberger, "Jewish Legal Formulae in the Aramaic Incantation Bowls." Levene reviewed the literature on this topic in Corpus of Magic Bowls, 18–21. Montgomery and Yamauchi detected Hos 2:3–5 and Ezek 16:35 behind this ritual (Yamuachi, "Aramaic Magic Bowls," 520). See also Shaked, "The Poetics of Spells Language."

90. So Thomas Ellis, an early archaeologist believed. See his "Jewish Relics," in Discoveries in the Ruins of Nineveh and Babylon.

91. Stuckenbruck, The Myth of Rebellious Angels, 82.

judge from the threats against demons found in incantation texts, it seems that some Jews in late antique Babylonia worried about demonic attachment to themselves (whether they were male or female), to their children (who were especially vulnerable to being killed), or to the very structure of their homes. Ritual practitioners envisioned a landscape in which demons could not be killed: at best one could expel them, contain them, seal one's house against them.[92] With the language of divorce, ritual practitioners focused on expelling demons from households, borrowing elements of the most well-known Jewish legal ritual in antiquity. Divorce proceedings in Jewish law required a written text, oral assent, delivery by witnesses, and acknowledgment on the part of the wife. These elements are also found in the ancient incantations, with angels as witnesses to the legal proceeding.

Rabbi Joshua b. Perahia was not always cited when a divorce from a demon was necessary, but his writ of divorce comes up often in these contexts. Incantation bowl no. 9 from Nippur, which sought to exorcise a haunted home, is a representative example of an incantation that calls on this rabbi.[93]

> This lot I cast and take and this ritual I practice, and it was as in [the way of] Rabbi Joshua bar Perahia. I write for them divorces, for all the liliths who appear to them, in this [house of] Babanos bar Kayomta and of Saradust bath Sirin his wife, in dream by night and in slumber by day; namely a writ of separation and divorce; in virtue of letter from letter, and letters from letters, and of words from words, and of gaps from gaps; whereby the heavens and earth are brought low and the mountains are uprooted, and by them the heights are down cast.[94]

Although there is an illegible word in the first sentence, it is clear that the practitioner was drawing on the reputation and ritual practice of Rabbi Joshua against demonesses using his divorce ritual. These "liliths" are tormenting the residents, particularly in their sleep, in nightmares that afflict them by day and night. The practitioner used the power of the divorce writ, the power of the words and letters themselves, to effect a powerful change that cast out the liliths.

Lylyn and *Liliths* were understood as demons, both masculine and feminine respectively, in the ancient Near East.[95] The Jewish Lilith appears to be related to the ancient Mesopotamian demonesses Lilitu or Lamashtu, who felt jealous of married women and mothers and tried to usurp their position, often with fatal consequences for marriages and infants.[96] She already appears as a notorious fig-

---

92. See Ahuvia, "The Spatial and Social Dynamics of Jewish Babylonian Incantations," 241–45.

93. Montgomery, *AIT*, no. 9. Cf. Levene, *Corpus of Magic Bowls*, M50 (p. 32).

94. Montgomery's translation of *AIT*, no. 9, lines 1–6 of 10 with my corrections.

95. See Sokoloff, *Dictionary*, 626; Shaked et al., *Aramaic Bowl Spells*, 305.

96. Scurlock, "Popular Religion and Magic: Ancient Near East;" also discussed in Hutter, "Demons and Benevolent Spirits in the Ancient Near East," 29.

ure in the Babylonian Talmud, but her narrative is only found in later medieval popular folktales.[97] Both the singular Lilith and the plural *Liliths* and *Lylyn* coexisted in the imaginative world of Jewish incantations. This category of demons is found in incantations alongside other demons like shades (*shedim*), devas, and a litany of others. Just as there was no Jewish angelology in this period, there was also no Jewish demonology, so there is much variation in the way demons were referenced in the incantations. In ancient sources, angels and demons were gendered both masculine and feminine. Extant sources, however, overrepresent masculine angels and feminine demons. This evidence should not be taken to mean that all people were inclined to imagine angels and demons in such gendered ways, but rather that surviving sources—authored primarily by men—tended in this direction.[98]

The exterior of the same bowl from Nippur named famous angels as witnesses to the divorce: "In thy name have I wrought, YHWH, God, Sabaoth, Gabriel, and Michael and Raphael."[99] *Sabaoth* is a transliteration of the Hebrew "hosts" or "armies" as in "the Lord the God of Hosts" (cf. Jer 15:16, Is 10:23, 1K 19:10). Here *Sabaoth* seems to be referenced as a name for God. The most famous three angels are named alongside three of God's names. For this client and practitioner, the precedent of Joshua b. Perahia and his powerful divorce writ was essential, but the authority of God and the witnessing role of the angels was necessary to execute this divorce writ against demons in the invisible realm.

Incantation bowl no. 8 from Nippur also appealed to Rabbi Joshua b. Perahia, God, and the angels to counter demons and called in additional backup against Lilith and her male and female offspring.[100] Because the incantation is rather long, I paraphrase its contents. Following the customary opening formula requesting help from the Lord of salvation, it specified that "this bowl is for the sealing of the house" of the client (lines 1–2). The practitioner described a scenario of the demons being expelled from the home just as divorced wives were expelled in the name of God the scatterer (2–3).[101] He announced that Rabbi Joshua b. Perahia had sent the divorce writ against them (5–6) from the heavens. The practitioner

97. See *b. 'Erub.* 100b, *b. Nid.* 24b, *b. Šabb.* 151b, and *b. Bat.* 73a. See "Lilith" in van der Toorn, Becking, and van Der Horst, *Dictionary of Deities and Demons in the Bible*. The legend of Lilith being the first wife of Adam is found in later medieval midrashim like *The Aleph Bet of ben Sira*, for which see Yassif, *The Tales of Ben Sira in the Middle Ages*, as well as Stern and Mirsky, *Rabbinic Fantasies*. See also Kosior, "A Tale of Two Sisters."

98. See discussion of winged women in chapter 5 and Agrat the angel of destruction in chapter 6. I summarize the evidence for Jewish imaginings of feminine angelic beings in "Gender and the Angels in Ancient Judaism."

99. See Montgomery, *AIT*, no. 9.

100. Montgomery, *AIT*, no. 8 (with Epstein's corrections).

101. Cf. Num 10:33.

adjured the demons with their full names and even the name of their parents, Pal-has and Pelahdad, paralleling the clients, who were called in incantations by their mother's names (6–7). The practitioner repeated twice more that Rabbi Joshua's divorce writ had come down from heaven and from across the sea to expel the demons (7–10). Next, the specialist threatened the demons with signet rings—another distinctive mark of status and authority in antiquity—one of God and one of Rabbi Joshua b. Perahia himself (10–11). Then the practitioner again adjured the demons to leave by the authority of the "the Strong One of Abraham, by the Rock of Isaac, by the Shaddai of Jacob" (12). This is a variation on the manner in which God is named in biblical and liturgical traditions as the God of Abraham, Isaac, and Jacob; we see it here invoked in a domestic ritual context. The formula then reiterated that the document had come down from heaven "through holy angels" (13). The following section has some indecipherable lacunas but referred to the Chariots, the holy creatures known from the vision of Ezekiel, and the legions of God's angels, finally naming "'Azriel the great angel," "Kabkabkiel the great angel," and 'Akariel the great angel" (13–15). The incantation closed with a final warning to the demons to depart forever according to the "letter of divorce" and the customary "amen, amen, selah," filling up all the space possible in the bowl with writing (15–17). Although the language of this incantation may seem foreign to readers today, it is important to keep in mind how Jewish all of these elements are: the beings of the invisible realm were as familiar as Abraham, Isaac, and Jacob to ancient Jews.

In the fight against demons, this practitioner apparently wanted to use all the methods and formulas at his disposal to seal the house against demons, expel them, and ward them off forever. He highlighted the physicality of the bowl itself, the divorce-writ of Rabbi Joshua b. Perahia, the role of the angels, and the signet rings of God and Rabbi Joshua b. Perahia, even invoking the God of Abraham, Isaac, and Jacob before also invoking the names of other angels. Incantation texts 8 and 9 from Nippur, where the angels and this folk-hero-rabbi are foregrounded, teach us that the angels coexisted on a spectrum of intermediary figures between the human clients and God.

Looking to the unprovenanced bowls that invoke Rabbi Hanina ben Dosa, we see these patterns recapitulated, this time for the sake of healing the migraine headaches of two women.[102] The practitioner began by invoking God's authority ("By your name I act, great holy one"), requesting healing from heaven, calling on God's angels, including Raphael and Michael and others (4, 11), naming the demoness (5–7) and adjuring her to depart by deploying the historiola of Hanina ben Dosa (8–9), and finally closing with a warning that if the demoness failed to

---

102. These women may have been related to each other and all of the examples of this formula may have been written by the same practitioner (*Aramaic Bowl Spells*, 53–94).

listen, angels would be sent against her just as they had been sent against "mighty fortified cities" (10–11). Like Joshua b. Perahia, the first century sage Hanina ben Dosa appears in sources from the Mishnah through the Talmud, where he is remembered as a charismatic miracle-worker.[103] Whereas Rabbi Joshua b. Perahia had a powerful writ of divorce the practitioners liked to invoke, Hanina b. Dosa featured in a historiola that centered on his meeting an evil spirit and quoting a verse of psalm 104 to assert his power over it; this verse reminded the demon of God's ultimate authority over creatures of the night.[104] It thus lent itself to anti-demonic use ("You make darkness and it is night, wherein all the animals of the forest creep" [Ps 104:20]).[105] The practitioner makes this explicit, warning the evil spirit against becoming "a companion of the night" of the client (10). In this incantation, the historiola is insufficient by itself: the angel Raphael, whose name connotes healing, is invoked both at the beginning and at the end of the incantation alongside other angels whose power is necessary to maintain God's divinely ordered world.

Angels and folk-hero sages were helpful in the fight against demons. Neither alone was sufficient, and one did not necessarily exclude or compete with the other. For these practitioners and clients, invisible intermediaries closed the gap between humans and God. Jews needed only to ask for help, and angels, alongside biblical and more recent Jewish heroes, were available to them.

NO ANGELS NECESSARY?

Beyond studying these angel-centered texts, we can learn about the function of angels in ancient Judaism by examining incantations that *avoid* calling on the power and presence of the angels. This may seem counterintuitive, but I have observed that where angelic beings are not imagined, other Jewish figures come to the foreground, like prophets, priests, rabbis, or ritual practitioners, who themselves take on angelic characteristics. According to my analysis, incantations without angels form about one-third of the extant incantation formulas. The remaining two-thirds of incantations with angelic presence demonstrate that such intermediaries (within a monotheistic framework) were central to Judaism and Jewish daily life in late antiquity. Acknowledging this evidence undermines reductive descriptions of difference between Judaism and Christianity and produces more accurate history and theology.

---

103. Bokser, "Wonder-Working and the Rabbinic Tradition: The Case of Hanina ben Dosa."
104. In chapter 6, I discuss a Babylonian rabbinic story about R. Hanina ben Dosa encountering Agrat daughter of Mahlat and her retinue of 180,000 angels of destruction. As with R. Joshua b. Perahia, the rabbis and ritual practitioners transmitted independent traditions about the same figure.
105. See MS 1927/8 (=JBA 1) and its parallels in Shaked, et al., *Aramaic Bowl Spells*, 56–98.

"A unique magic bowl from Nippur" was excavated by the Oriental Institute in the 1960s and was composed entirely of strung-together quotations from Ezekiel and Jeremiah, repeating verses in Hebrew and then in the Aramaic translation, specifically quoting Targum Pseudo-Jonathan.[106] This practitioner turned to prophets associated with the Babylonian exile to confront challenges over one thousand years later in the same region. To this day, it is still the only incantation bowl known to contain these scriptural quotations and to quote the Masoretic and Targumic texts so carefully.[107] The spiraling text begins in medias res with a quotation from Ezekiel, wherein God is warning the Israelites of the avenging sword he is about to unleash on them through the might of the Babylonian Empire:

> Attack to the right!
> Engage to the left!
> —wherever your edge is directed.
> I too will strike hand to hand,
> I will satisfy my fury;
> I the Lord have spoken.[108]

If this practitioner were confronting invisible or mortal enemies in his local environs in Babylonia, one can imagine these words empowered him or the clients to feel confident. The incantation continued with a quotation from Jeremiah 2:2–3 immediately afterward, followed by the Aramaic translation of the same verse. In between, the practitioner inserted three words identifying Jeremiah as the prophet being quoted.

> "Go and proclaim in the hearing of Jerusalem: Thus says the Lord:
> I remember the devotion of your youth, your love as a bride,
> how you followed me in the wilderness, in a land not sown."
> Jeremiah the prophet prophesied. "Israel was holy to the Lord, disaster came upon
>   them, says the Lord."

These verses emphasize God's continued loyalty to Israel despite disasters that have come upon them, words that could be comforting to Jews, even in faraway Babylonia. Cryptically, the text of the incantation bowl then ends with the words "The word of the Lord came to me," repeated in Hebrew and Aramaic, quoting either Jeremiah 2:1 or Ezekiel 21:23. I imagine the performance of the practitioner picked up at this point, where the text of the incantation bowl ends. The practitioner positioned himself as a prophet, perhaps delivering a specific message for

---

106. Kaufman, "A Unique Magic Bowl from Nippur," 170–74.
107. Confirmed by Shaked, et al., *Aramaic Bowl Spells*, 20.
108. Ezek 21:21; in Christian Bibles, this verse is numbered as Ezek 21:16.

the clients receiving this bowl. Much like the Hebrew prophets and the angels, he became a messenger between God and the clients.

In the next example, the ritual practitioner conjured priestly and rabbinic authority. This short incantation text was written for the protection of a married couple and their household from demons as well as other sorcerers, their curses, and other misfortunes.[109] This incantation contains an extended quotation of the Mishnah, which elaborates on the biblical command to present burnt offerings (Num 28:11 and 15) at the temple.[110] Treating the entire passage as if it were a powerful name, the ritual practitioner used this passage to evince his command over the invisible realm:

> The Sin-offerings of the congregation and of individuals (these are the Sin-offerings of the congregation: the he-goats offered at the new moons and at the set feasts) were slaughtered on the north side and their blood was received in a vessel of ministry on the north side, and their blood required to be sprinkled with four acts of sprinkling on the four horns [of the Altar]. After what manner? The priest went up the Ramp and went around the Circuit and came to the south-eastern horn, then to the north-eastern, to the north-western, and to the south-western horn. The residue of the blood was poured over the southern base; and the offerings were consumed within the Curtains by males of the priestly stock, and cooked for food after any fashion, during that day and night until midnight.[111]

This description of the procession around the altar and the emphasis on the cardinal directions appealed to the ritual practitioner who composed and performed this incantation. The incantation bowl that opened this chapter also appealed to the four directions, but this description is more temple-centric. The movement described in the passage would also be especially fitting for the deposition of bowls in the home. While reciting the priestly cultic act as formulated by the rabbis, the ritual practitioners may have sought to embody the authority of both priests and rabbis. The couple hearing it would presumably have been comforted by this performance and the appeal to traditional sources of authority. Notably, there is no mention of angels, no explicit mention of God, and no first-person

109. See discussion of Schøyen 1929/6 in Shaked, et al., *Aramaic Bowl Spells*, 22–23 (lacks provenance); this bowl and another fragmentary one by the same practitioner is discussed in Shaked, "Form and Purpose in Aramaic Spells."

110. See *m. Zebaḥ.* 5:3. It is possible the ritual practitioner knew this text from the liturgy. By the ninth century CE, Num 28:1–8, *m. Zebaḥ.* 5:3, and the introduction to the *Sifra* were part of an anthology of texts on temple sacrifices included in the morning prayers of Seder Rav Natronai Ga'on. See Tabory, "The Prayer Book (Siddur) as an Anthology of Judaism." On the other hand, we cannot rule out the possibility that the performance of *m. Zebaḥ.* 5:3 was popularized by ritual practitioners and then incorporated into the morning liturgy.

111. Danby, trans., *Mishnah*, 474.

singular subject emphasizing the practitioner's own immediate presence. The ritual performance itself would have highlighted the practitioner's authority. In this incantation, the ritual practitioner evoked priestly and rabbinic authority instead of invoking angels, acting as an intermediary between this household and malevolent forces.

The final two incantations that I wish to examine highlight the climax of practitioner confidence. The original Nippur collection featured two bowls wherein two male practitioners named Pabak and Abuna, cast protective spells for their shared households, each naming himself and declaring the action he was taking on the other's behalf.[112] For the sake of brevity, I summarize the three actions described in Abuna's incantation for Pabak: this incantation claimed (1) to cover and "hold in the sacred angels," (2) bind evil spirits with a powerful binding used to fix the stars and zodiac signs in place, and (3) to have surrounded the household with a "great wall of bronze."[113] Abuna's incantation envisioned a new reality wherein perhaps the incantation bowl itself was seen to fix the angels' presence in the home, protecting its residents. Secondly, he made the home impenetrable to demons by claiming access to a powerful binding spell. In doing so, he projected the view that the stars were celestial beings that could be bound in place. Finally, Abuna claimed to have surrounded the home with a wall of bronze, a material thought to repel the demonic.[114] The belief that practitioners could command angels is found in some incantation bowls and reflects the heightened sense of self-confidence of the practitioner.[115] Abuna emphasized his authority in the closing of the incantation: "I, what I desire I grasp, and what I ask, I take. You are in the place of Abuna b. G. and in the place of Pabak b. K." In this incantation, the practitioner asserted his own power, even over angels, to feel secure. If Abuna seemed overconfident, Pabak went even further, likening himself to an angel:

> Again, I come, I, Pabak bar Kufithai, in the power of my own self, polished armor of iron on my body, my head of iron, my figure of pure fire. I am clad with the garment of Hermes, *Dabya*, and the Word, and my power is in him who created heaven and earth. I have come and I have smitten the evil Fiends and the malignant Adversaries. I have said to them: if at all you sin against Abuna bar Geribta and against Ibba bar Zawithai, I will lay a spell against you, the spell of the Sea and the spell of the monster

112. Montgomery, *AIT*, nos. 2 and 4.

113. Montgomery, *AIT*, no. 4, translated by Montgomery with my corrections based on Epstein's commentary.

114. Cf. Num 21:9 on Moses and the bronze snake. See also Häberl, "Production and Reception," 133 on the Mandaic ritual practice of circumscribing a home in a circle of flour to keep out demons.

115. See also Gordon 6 (= Isbell, *Corpus*, text forty-three, pp. 102–3), which directly adjures angels to remove all sorceries and a litany of demons, even as it calls the angels "holy, chosen, pure, holy, glorious, and religious" (103). My thanks to Avigail Manekin-Bamberger for bringing this text to my attention.

Leviathan. If at all you sin against Abuna b. G., and against his wife and his sons, like a bow I will bend you and like bowstring I will stretch you.[116]

This formula declared that the practitioner Pabak had a body of pure fire. One of the only angelic characteristics that all ancient Jewish sources agreed upon was that angels were made of fire.[117] This agreement likely stems from Daniel's description of the angel who spoke to him as having "a body like beryl [or topaz, in any case of yellow color] and a face with the appearance of lightening and eyes like torches of fire and arms and legs like gleaming bronze" (Dan 10:6). By claiming that he himself was made of pure fire, this ritual practitioner was describing the most famous angelic appearance.

Moreover, he claimed to possess the garments of Hermes, a divine messenger figure so well known that he transcended his Greek cultural background in the ancient Mediterranean.[118] Adhering to conceptions of angels in biblical and Jewish conceptions, Pabak affirmed that his strength was from God, "him who created heaven and earth." Like the angels, Pabak claimed to possess divine knowledge: spells powerful enough to subdue the sea and the biblical monster Leviathan. In this angelic guise, Pabak could threaten the demons. His self-representation provides a sense of how practitioners believed they could interact with the invisible realm. If they were as powerful as angels, they did not need to call on them. These last two practitioners already saw themselves as so accomplished they could deal with their foes without politely invoking the angels. Calling on angels, then, may be seen as a measure of the confidence of the practitioner in his place in a network of relationships that stretched between himself and God.

Pabak's angelic identification can be further understood in the context of ritual practice from elsewhere in the Mediterranean world. Practitioners in non-Jewish incantation texts often declared themselves to be divinities, such as in the Greek magical papyri that survived from the Egyptian desert. We find there such statements as "I am Anubis . . . I am Osiris";[119] "I am Sabertoush, the great god who is in heaven";[120] "I am Horus";[121] "I am Hermes."[122] A Coptic spell states, "I am Mary,

116. Montgomery, *AIT*, no. 2 was also republished by Isbell, *Corpus*, as no. 2. This incantation has a duplicate published in Montgomery, *AIT*, no. 27, where a man uses this formula to protect himself and his wife. See also Gordon, "Aramaic Incantation Bowls," 273–74 (text 11).

117. Cf. *Gen. Rab.* 78:1, *b. Hag.* 14a, Yannai's *qedushta* to Exod 3:1, Hekhalot Rabbati §213, Morgan, trans., *Sepher Ha-Razim,* 21; §31 of *Sefer ha-Razim,* ed. Schäfer and Rebiger.

118. On this topic, see Sanzo and Boustan, "Christian Magicians, Jewish Magical Idioms." See discussion of his Greek and Hellenistic origins in Speyer, "The Divine Messenger," 37–39.

119. Betz, *Greek Magical Papyri in Translation*, PGM I. 247–62.

120. Betz, *Greek Magical Papyri in Translation*, PGM IV. 52–85.

121. Betz, *Greek Magical Papyri in Translation*, PGM IV. 1075.

122. Betz, *Greek Magical Papyri in Translation*, PGM IV. 2999.

I am Mariham, I am the mother of the life of the whole world."[123] These claims of identity prepared the way for the actions the practitioner wished to effect in the world. I posit that one of the distinguishing features of Jewish incantation texts is that Jewish practitioners only aspire to the status of angels. Even then, these practitioners made sure to affirm God's singular supremacy. Unlike the polytheistic practitioners, they never placed themselves on the same level of divinity as God. The incantations written in Jewish Aramaic script make sense within the realm of the biblical and Jewish imagination. They cannot be fully understood outside a Jewish context.

These examples illustrate the various ways Jews related to invisible beings and the divine realm and the essential roles of angels in diverse ritual formulas. People could appeal to practitioners who only invoked God or only the angels under God. They could turn to practitioners who appealed to God, the angels, and heroes like Rabbis Joshua b. Perahia or Hanina b. Dosa. They could appeal to practitioners who reminded them of other intermediaries with prophetic powers, priestly cultic associations, or rabbinic legal authority. They could appeal to practitioners confident in their adjuration powers or who conceived of themselves as being as powerful as the angels themselves.

BLURRING THE BOUNDARIES:
FROM RITUAL PRACTICES TO PRAYER

In this section, I discuss how the material found in incantation bowls impacted Jewish beliefs and practices beyond Babylonian ritual practices. Observant Orthodox Jews today, who recite the nighttime Shema, use a surprising number of biblical verses favored by the ritual practitioners as well.[124] One in particular proves relevant to this study: "In the name of the Lord the God of Israel, on my right is Michael, on my left is Gabriel, in front of me Uriel, and behind me Raphael, and upon my head is *Shekhinat-El*." This so-called "invocation of angels on all sides" is found in Amram Gaon's ninth-century CE Seder, but it only became part of the daily fixed liturgy in the thirteenth century, when it became part of the bedtime Shema. Scholars who study Jewish magic noticed in recent years that this formulaic prayer is already found in ten incantation bowls and two amulets (all, unfortunately, without provenance), texts from the Cairo Genizah, and in ritual texts in other languages.[125] The invocation of angels on all sides is not found in

---

123. See translation in Meyer, "The Prayer of Mary in the Magical Book of Mary and the Angels," 59.

124. Angel, "The Use of the Hebrew Bible in Early Jewish Magic."

125. Levene, Marx, and Bhayro, "Angelic Protection in Jewish Magic and Babylonian Lore," 186–87. This formula is found not only in Hebrew and Aramaic, but also in Syriac, Manichaean, Coptic, and Arabic texts (see 186n5 for references).

the Hebrew Bible or other ancient Jewish texts, and it may be that it originated in popular ritual practice.[126] A typical example of this invocation can be found in the following incantation bowl:

> Gabriel is on the right of Dudita, daughter of Duday, and her sons and her daughters, And Michael is on her left, and before her is Susiel, and behind her is Menuha, and above her is *Shekinath El*. "The LORD of hosts is his name" [Isa 51:15]. Remove from her, from Dudita, daughter of Duday, and from her sons and from her daughters, every evil affliction demon and every evil satan and every evil living creature and every evil word and every evil utterance and all the spirits of copulation in the world. "I Am that I am" [Exod 3:14]. Amen, Amen, Selah, Hallelujah and established and sound. This seal is forever. Amen and Amen and sound.[127]

In this incantation, the angel Gabriel is positioned on the right, Michael on the left, Menuha ("repose" in Hebrew") is behind, and Susiel (*sus* is "horse" in Hebrew) is in front of Dudita. Above her is *Shekhinat El*. The publishers of this incantation read *Shekhinat El* as an angel too, but I believe a reference to God is more likely, especially as "the Lord of hosts" is invoked immediately after *Shekhinat El*. Overall, the angels under God's presence are envisioned as protecting Dudita and her children from an exhaustive list of threats, particularly demonic ones.

The use of *Shekhinah* in this formula and the later Jewish liturgy is worth lingering on. The targumists, the rabbis, and the ritual practitioners all used the term *Shekhinah* for God. The term *Shekhinah* is first found in the Mishnah and no earlier. Generally, it was used by the rabbis and later targumists to emphasize that God was not a distant figure in the heavens above, but one that dwelled among the people of Israel still, despite their exiled state.[128] *Shekhinah* is gendered feminine and came to be understood as the immanent aspect of God. We can see how the *Shekhinah* is used in the ritual objects to conjure intimacy as well. The expression "under the wings of the *Shekhinah*" occurs in three instances in Palestinian rabbinic writings, bringing to mind the winged angels.[129] It is fitting therefore that this aspect of God, *Shekhinat El*, is conjoined with the motif of angels surrounding an individual, which is found in amulets, incantation bowls, and finally in the standard Jewish liturgy. Even lacking provenance, these objects demonstrate that this

---

126. I describe a possible rabbinic origin for this formula at end of chapter 3.

127. SD12, trans. Levene, Marx, and Bhayro, "Angelic Protection in Jewish Magic and Babylonian Lore," 189.

128. The most thorough and recent study of *Shekhinah* can be found in Danan's unpublished dissertation, "The Divine Voice in Scripture: *Ruah Ha-Kodesh* in Rabbinic Literature." Danan notes that a century after its publication, Abelson's *The Immanence of God in Rabbinical Literature* remains the most influential and popular volume on this topic.

129. See *y. Soṭah* 1:10; *y. 'Abod. Zar.* 1:4; *Sifrei Deut Haazinu* 306.

prayer technique circulated among ritual practitioners and their clients before it became part of the standard liturgy.

As Jews increasingly insisted on a divine aspect of God in exile with them (sometimes termed the *Shekhinah*), the conception of God directly above them and angels all around them may have become part of the Jewish imagination. Alternatively, we can see the angels on all sides as a development of the intimate images of angels embracing and protecting individuals as described in the incantation bowls from Nippur. What is certain, however, is the proliferation of evidence demonstrating that Jews imagined angels actively engaged in their daily life.

CONCLUSION: ANGELS IN BABYLONIAN INCANTATION BOWLS

Babylonian incantation bowls give us but glimpses of ancient interactions among people and the ways they conceptualized the invisible realm around them. Attempting to understand the Jewish individuals behind the bowls brings to mind Clifford Geertz's description of ethnography: "Doing ethnography is like trying to read (in the sense of 'construct a reading of') a manuscript—foreign, faded, full of ellipses, incoherencies, suspicious emendations, and tendentious commentaries, but written not in conventionalized graphs of sound but in transient examples of shaped behavior."[130] When we attempt to study individuals through actual faded texts on bowls, the problems are only compounded. There is much we cannot recover. Still, the incantations offer salient lessons.

If ancient Jews chose to take their concerns (whether with human or demonic opponents) to ritual practitioners, they were offered a variety of ways to interact with the invisible forces around them. Each bowl represents a negotiation between clients and a specialist over how to imagine the network of relationships to which they belonged: angels, folk-heroes, God, prophets, priests, and rabbis were all possibilities. According to my survey, the most common request was for the assistance of the angels and God, forming 40 percent of unique incantation bowl formulas. Moreover, even when angels are not explicitly present, other intermediaries took their place, themselves sometimes assuming angelic tropes.

From the Babylonian incantation bowls, we learn that angels were imagined as present in people's homes but also as opening gates of success for them in the heavens or delivering heavenly divorce documents to demons. While the common angelic names Michael, Gabriel, and Raphael are found in the incantations, we find many more unfamiliar and even unpronounceable names. The evidence of the bowls highlights the diversity of ways Jews situated themselves in the networks

---

130. Geertz, *The Interpretation of Cultures*, 10.

of relationships between themselves and God, showing Jews to be just as focused on mediating divinities as their non-Jewish neighbors (albeit within a monotheistic framework). Without the evidence of the incantation bowls, we would not have a full account of the variety of ways angels were imagined as active in the lives of ancient Jews.

2

Out and About with the Angels

Palestinian Ritual Sources

A song of praise to King of the Worlds
Yah, Yah, Yah, the Hastener of the Worlds, I-am-
That-I-am, the King who speaks with distinct mystery
to every bad and evil-doing spirit—you should not
cause pain to Rabbi Eleazar the son of Esther,
the servant of the God of Heaven, Strong and Mighty [One]
Send Wprt, Trgyn, Astd and Bqth,
Slslyrh, Qllqm, Yqyps, Suriel,
Raphael, Abiel, Anael, Nahariel
Nagdiel, Aphaphel, and Ananel Ms
Ps Yqrndrys Yahu Krmsys
The great God Thth Ghgh Thth
Mrmr Psps Yнwн Holy in every
place where this amulet will be seen,
you [evil spirits] will not detain Eleazar
the son of Esther. And if you detain him,
"immediately you will be cast into a burning
fiery furnace" [Dan. 3:6]. Blessed are you our Lord,
the Healer of all the earth, send healing
[and] cure to Eleazar. Bwbryt, Tbryt,
Bstarwt, the angels that are app[ointed]
over fever and shivering, cure Ele[azar]
by a holy command.

— PALESTINIAN AMULET

Dating to the fifth–sixth century CE, this Hebrew and Aramaic incantation text
is from an amulet discovered in the excavations of a village in the Golan Heights

of modern Israel.[1] Now known as Horvat Kanaf, this Byzantine-era Jewish village was located to the northeast of the Sea of Galilee, just south of Qasrin. In this ancient village long ago, Eleazar was suffering from illness and he turned to a ritual practitioner to write him an amulet that he could wear around his neck. This incantation began as a song of praise to God, warned evil spirits to desist from afflicting Rabbi Eleazar, son of Esther, and enlisted numerous angels to protect and cure him. The practitioner and Eleazar believed that the amulet would ward off demons and, simultaneously, called in the ministering angels to heal Eleazar.

In this chapter, I present the evidence for Jewish interaction with angels in the Late Antique Levant (the areas now known as Israel, Palestine, Jordan, and southern Turkey) by surveying the functions of angels in amulets from the Levant and in the treatise *Sefer ha-Razim* ("Book of the Mysteries"), which was likely composed in Palestine.[2] The amulets, worn by ordinary Jews, and *Sefer ha-Razim*, shared among ritual practitioners, together reveal how both practitioners and clients related to the invisible realms of spirits, angels, and God. The ritual objects and texts offer us not a view from the fringe but views of a broad swath of the Jewish population, which provide insight into the attitudes toward angels in rabbinic, liturgical, and mystical sources in turn. Overall, the evidence demonstrates angels' centrality to Jewish religiosity in the dynamic period of development of late antiquity.

WHAT IS *SEFER HA-RAZIM*? WHAT IS AN AMULET?

Sefer ha-Razim is a late antique manual written in lucid Hebrew by a learned ritual practitioner for practitioner consumption. As it was transmitted from generation to generation, additions were made to this treatise, giving us a sense of how generations of Jews received and used this text. The opening of the treatise proclaimed that it was transmitted by an angel named Raziel (*raz*, "mystery") to Noah and his descendants and it promised its users wide-ranging powers and knowledge of the angelic realm. The treatise demonstrates that the memory of the antediluvian age with angels transmitting secret knowledge to biblical heroes was alive and

1. Reproduced from Naveh and Shaked, *Amulets and Magic Bowls*, 51, amulet no. 3: this is their translation with minor corrections for readability (e.g., I capitalize the first letter of every divine name). I also follow their alternative interpretation of lines 6–7, which brings this amulet into closer alignment with a line from another incantation bowl (Isbell, *Corpus*, 67:3), discussed below. "Hastener" is Hebrew *yahish*—that is, the one who hastens, as in "the God of Israel will hasten and will bring the Messiah in our day to comfort us" (*Pirqe R. El.* 29:24); in *Amulets and Magic Bowls*, Naveh and Shaked suggest reading *Yahish* as a proper name, which maintains the alliteration of this incantation.

2. For English, see Michael Morgan's translation of *Sepher Ha-Razim*. For the various manuscript editions, see the synoptic edition by Schäfer and Rebiger, *Sefer Ha-Razim*, discussed in greater detail below.

well, long after the *Book of the Watchers* had fallen out of favor with rabbinic and Christian authorities. Much of *Sefer Ha-Razim* contains lists of angelic names, many as unfamiliar as the ones from Babylonia. Close analysis of this treatise, alongside the extant ritual and mystical texts of antiquity, offers insight into the dynamic relationships Jewish ritual practitioners imagined with angels in the eastern Roman Mediterranean.

Ancient amulets (Hebrew, *qame'a*) were small objects that people could wear on their bodies to ward off malevolent spirits (demons, etc.) or to call in divine protection from God and the angels. As Yuval Harari observes, the "word *qame'a* derives from the root *qm'*, which means 'to tie'" and relates to the fact it was often "tied to or hung on its user's body."[3] Ritual practitioners made amulets for clients by drawing symbols or by writing a short incantation on a narrow strip of material, rolling up the text tightly, and enclosing it in an ornamental case, which was then attached to a string and could be worn around the neck by the client. Alternatively, some amulets may not have been created as accessories but as objects to be buried or hidden in a location that would aid its efficacy (e.g., in a room in a house, a synagogue, a cemetery, a crossroads, etc.).[4] The wearing of necklace amulets stretches back to the ancient Mediterranean world and was a cross-cultural phenomenon.[5] For the purposes of this book, I focus on the function of angels in Jewish Aramaic amulets from the late antique Levant.

In the period after the destruction of the second temple, surviving evidence suggests that Jews increasingly commissioned amulets inscribed with incantations for personal use.[6] The Mishnah itself attests that Jews were wearing such amulets. While discussing laws related to clothing and jewelry that may be worn on the Sabbath, the Mishnah prescribes that a man may *not* wear an amulet that was *not* prepared by a specialist—in other words, he *may* wear one that was prepared by a specialist of whom the rabbis approved.[7] Other early rabbinic authorities inquired as to what distinguished a specialist's "effective" amulet.[8] The response was that an effective amulet was one that had healed a person three times, whether it was made of text or of roots. This ancient opinion reminds us that we only have one

---

3. Harari, *Jewish Magic*, 216.

4. Harari, *Jewish Magic*, 219.

5. A quick search of the British Museum catalog brings up dozens of examples of cloth and metal amulets from Northern Africa to Europe to south Asia dating to recent decades and centuries. See the introduction and several articles in Gordon and Simón, *Magical Practice in the Latin West*.

6. Aside from two intriguing silver amulets found in a late seventh-century BCE tomb near Jerusalem, there is a surprising dearth of evidence for the use of amulets in the Second Temple period. On this see Bohak, *Ancient Jewish Magic*, 30 and 114. See also Swartz, "Jewish Magic in Late Antiquity."

7. *m. Šabb.* 6:2.

8. NB: in Hebrew, *expert*, *effective*, and *specialist* are all the same word: *mumcheh*. See *t. Šabb* 4:9; Lieberman, ed. *Tosefta Ki-Fshuta*, 65.

slice of the surviving material culture of the ancient world: we only have texts preserved on metal, not the ephemera that people may have carried with them for protection or healing.

Sefer ha-Razim itself seems to have come into the hands of a rabbinic Jew at some point, who inserted the sages into its chain of transmission, bringing to mind the opening lines of Mishnah *'Abot*.[9] With the surviving evidence, it is much easier to point out the amulets that directly flouted rabbinic prescriptions than ones of which they would have approved (see example below). Still, the fact that the rabbis acknowledged the use of amulets and that one ancient disciple of the sages may have transmitted *Sefer ha-Razim* requires us to expand our definition of normative Jewish identity and practice. Jews, both rabbinic and non-rabbinic, wore amulets.

The language of the amulet quoted above suggests that it was a visible accessory, and that the person who wore it expected encounters with malicious spirits and benevolent angels as he went about his day ("in every place where this amulet will be *seen*, you should not detain Eleazar the son of Esther"). The client and practitioner believed that God, angels, and demons knew the content of this text, even as it was hidden in an amuletic case: it addressed itself to God with praise, to the demons in the second-person plural (warning them of punishment), and finally to the angels with the hope that they would cure Eleazar with God's approval. In this sense, the amulets from Roman Palestine take us out of the domestic sphere and show us how Jews positioned themselves in a landscape crowded with invisible beings. The amulets offer a glimpse of what it was like for ancient Jews to be out and about with the angels in the villages, towns, and cities of Roman Palestine. Eleazar did not walk alone: he wore a reminder that demons and angels were present and active in his life as well.

HOW DO AMULETS COMPARE TO MAGIC BOWLS?

Readers may notice that this amulet recalls an incantation bowl from Nippur, which began with the same song of praise to God.[10] This parallel reminds us that the Jews of remote towns like Nippur in Mesopotamia and the Jews of a Galilean village were not utterly disconnected and imagined their relationship with invisible beings in similar ways. It would seem that ritual practitioners, like the rabbis,

9. Morgan, *Sepher Ha-Razim*, 19n9. See Schäfer and Rebiger, *Sefer Ha-Razim*, §13. On "the chain of tradition motif," see Swartz, *Scholastic Magic*, esp. 172–205.

10. See chapter 1, pp. 51–52 and Isbell, "Two New Aramaic Incantation Bowls," 15–23, esp. 23; cf. Naveh and Shaked, *Amulets and Magic Bowls*, 50–54. The opening formula "A song of praise to the King" can also be found in two other incantation bowl texts translated by Isak Jeruzalmi and published in Isbell, *Corpus*, nos. 67 and 69.

traveled between Palestine and Babylonia, sharing formulas and practices that appear in the texts and ritual objects they composed.

Like the incantation bowls, surviving amuletic texts project a world that is full of invisible beings: angels are present in a majority of the amulets but not all of them. Amuletic incantations quote biblical and Jewish motifs. As in Babylonia, so in Byzantine Palestine: Jewish men and women went to ritual practitioners with a specific problem (often an illness, according to surviving amulets), and the practitioner offered the clients an amulet, personalized with their name, divine angelic names, and other strategies intended to secure a positive outcome. Late antique Palestinian ritual experts who composed amulets acted in the name of the angels and God much like their Babylonian counterparts and invoked similar strategies against the demonic. As with the incantation bowls, we must speculate that the success of the practitioners and their amulets was contingent on reassuring the client that their problem had been competently addressed. Each amulet can be seen as the product of negotiation, not only reflecting the practitioner's perspective, but also the client's. In this way, the personalized content of Jewish amulets offers a glimpse of Jewish daily concerns and how angels featured in the networks of relationships Jews imagined themselves in. The deployment of incantation bowls in Babylonia seems to have been popular among Jewish ritual practitioners and their adjacent religious communities, but not widespread otherwise. In contrast, wearing necklace amulets was a common practice in antiquity and would *not* have distinguished Jews from other inhabitants of the Levant in any way.[11]

A few more differences between incantation bowls and amulets can observed: whereas the religious affiliation of the incantation bowls still provokes debate, the Jewish character of the Hebrew and Aramaic amulets recovered in Palestine is widely accepted.[12] Archaeological excavations have brought to light these amulets from all over ancient Roman Palestine, personalized with names, often including biblical quotations, and invoking the name of God and angelic names to protect the client. Non-Jewish amulets are generally found in tombs buried with their owners, but most Aramaic and Hebrew amulets have been found in synagogues or monumental buildings.[13] Hanan Eshel and Rivka Elitzur Leiman hypothesize that because ancient Jews treated the written name of God with a deep sense of sacrality, they endeavored to discard amulets in fitting locations: when the client died or no longer needed the amulet, the amulet was deposited in synagogues, either behind the apse or in storage areas specifically designated for discarded liturgical materials (*genizahs*).[14] Overall, much more is known about the daily life of the

---

11. Most recently, see Edmonds, *Drawing Down the Moon*, esp. 119–41.
12. Eshel and Leiman, "Jewish Amulets."
13. Eshel and Leiman, "Jewish Amulets," 199.
14. Eshel and Leiman, "Jewish Amulets," 198.

Jews of Roman Palestine than the Jews of Babylonia.[15] The abundance of Roman and Byzantine texts helps us contextualize surviving Jewish texts from this region in a way that is not yet possible for Jewish Babylonia.

Whereas thousands of incantation bowls have been excavated and a few hundred published, only a few dozen amuletic texts have been discovered and deciphered from Roman Palestine and its environs. Moreover, amuletic texts are generally shorter than the texts on ceramic bowls and often more challenging to decipher. For both of these reasons (small sample size and terse texts), making generalizations about their differences is necessarily tentative. That said, Avigail Manekin-Bamberger recently highlighted two noteworthy differences between the corpora: "Jewish magic from Palestine does not contain rabbinic material" and "Palestinian amulets lack legal terminology."[16] I would add that in Palestinian amulets, angels were assigned to particular spheres of influence (e.g., linked with features of the landscape or appointed over parts of the body), associations that are not foregrounded in incantation bowls. Additionally, in amulets published thus far, an emphasis on the High Priest Aaron and priestly imagery distinguishes Palestinian amulets from Babylonian incantations (discussed below). Overall, the similarities between bowls and amulets prove more important than their differences: like the incantation bowls, there is much variation among the amulets and their approach to God and the angels; and, like the Babylonian amulets, the Palestinian amulets were made for both men and women, who imagined that angels could be ongoing guardians for all.

CALLING ON GOD AND THE ANGELS IN AMULETS

This chapter began with an amulet from a village in the Golan written for a rabbi Eleazar the son of Esther. This amulet has a partial parallel in a Babylonian incantation bowl from Nippur. Like most rabbis who show up in the inscriptional evidence from Roman Palestine, this Eleazar cannot be identified with any member of the rabbinic movement, and it is likely the title was used honorifically in this incantation.[17] Perhaps he was a great man, but this Eleazar was not one of the rabbis named Eleazar known from the Talmud. When this Eleazar was struggling with illness, he turned to a Jewish ritual practitioner for help. The practitioner, in turn, appealed to God and the angels for assistance.

15. See Hezser, *The Oxford Handbook of Jewish Daily Life in Roman Palestine*; Ahuvia, "Jewish Towns and Neighborhoods."

16. Manekin-Bamberger, "Who Were the Jewish 'Magicians' Behind the Aramaic Incantation Bowls?" 251–52. Her essay was published as this book was in the final stages of production, and I regret that I cannot devote more attention to her thought-provoking insights.

17. For a summary of the discussion of the term *rabbi* in rabbinic texts and epigraphical evidence, see Lapin, "Epigraphical Rabbis: A Reconsideration."

This incantation, more than the one from Nippur, begins and ends in a hurry, with an emphasis on the speedy recovery of the client from demonic infection that is causing physical suffering: God was addressed as *Yahish*, literally the Hastener and later, quoting the book of Daniel, the incantation threatened evil spirits with being *immediately* cast into fire. The epithets for God, "Yahish of the Worlds, I-am-that-I-am, the King," are noteworthy and will be discussed more below. The middle of the incantation consisted of a list of angelic names, some familiar like Suriel and Raphael, some less familiar, and a few variations on God's name or written in cipher.[18] The demonic threat and the named angels in this amulet themselves are very different than the ones in the bowl from Nippur.[19] Based on my approach to the evidence, I posit that this reflects the particular and local preferences of the ritual practitioners and/or the clients. Practitioners and clients invoked the local and particular manifestation of the divine that they knew and related to—otherwise, the amulets would not have had impact on the clients. *Sefer ha-Razim* contains long lists of angelic names, some easily pronounceable and recognizable from an etymological standpoint, and still many that appear as foreign as names we come across in Babylonian incantations. To the ritual practitioners who employed these names, these were names of powerful beings who could be near to them and enlisted for assistance. For this practitioner and client, only this particular combination of divine names could overpower the demons in Eleazar's body.

In a manner characteristic of Palestinian amulets, this incantation targeted against evil spirits (*ruha bishah*) that were believed to cause ailments in the body. Whereas Babylonian incantations worried about the general health of their clients and tended to list many possible demonic enemies, Palestinian incantations tended to be more explicitly focused on physical health matters and the demonic source of the ailment. Whereas the parallel incantation from Nippur that began with the "song of praise" was worried about addressing all manner of misfortune (Satan, demons, curses, invocations, vows and knocking), this amulet targeted only fever and shivering caused by the evil spirits.[20] In tandem, it appealed to the

18. For example, *Msps* which is an *atbash* of *Yhwh* (Naveh and Shaked, *Amulets and Magic Bowls*, 52).

19. According to the bowl, the client is threatened by Satan, demons, curse, invocations, vows, and knocking; in the amulet Eleazar is protected from "every bad and evil-doing spirit." Most of the angelic names in the bowl from Nippur are variations on the tetragrammaton, excepting Quti'el and Qumi'el (Isbell, "Two New Aramaic Incantations," 23).

20. Similarly, the other amulet found in Horvat Kanaf also declares that its purpose is to heal feverish illness caused by demons in the body. Naveh and Shaked, *Amulets and Magic Bowls*, 45 (no. 2). This amulet was written for Ya'itha (lit. beauty or grace) daughter of Marian. Whereas evil spirits (*ruha bishah*) troubled Eleazar with illness, female demons (*shydtah*) afflicted Ya'itha with fever and shivering.

angels that are appointed to resolve the matter. This amulet from Horvat Kanaf specifically appealed to the angels appointed over fever (Bwbryt, Tbryt, Bstarwt), who could heal Eleazar by a holy command. The ritual practitioner requested that God send the appointed angels to protect the client in the future and to heal the client from the damage that had been inflicted already.

Similar operating principles can be seen in an amulet found in Ḥorvat Kannah (also spelled Qana, or Cana, perhaps the village mentioned in John 2:1–12) in the lower Galilee, where the ritual practitioner targeted fevers afflicting Simon the son of Katia and appealed to the angel(s) in charge of healing illness. Here we see the angel Abraxas take center stage, as he does in a number of Hebrew and Aramaic amulets.

> A good[21] amulet to expel the great
> fever and the tertian [fever] and the chronic fever
> and the semi-tertian [fever] and any spirit and any
> misfortune and any [evil] eye and any [evil] gaze
> from the body of Simon, son of
> Katia, and from all his limbs,
> to heal him and to guard him.
> In the name of all these holy names
> and letters which are written in this amulet,
> I adjure and write in the name of Abraxas
> who is appointed over you [i.e., the fever], that he may uproot
> you, fever and sickness, from the body
> of Simon, the son of Katia.
> In the name of the engraved letters of the name.
> [lines 16–33 contains magic names and then a repetition of the opening formula]
> I make an oath and adjure in the name of
> Yashar Temanuel who sits on
> the river whence all evil
> spirits emerge; and in the name of Yequmiel,
> who sits on the roads;
> Nahariel, who sits over the [light,]
> Tomïel, who sits [on . . .]
> and in the na[me of . . .].[22]

What distinguishes this amulet from Babylonian bowls is an underlying belief in angelic appointment to places and the particular roles filled by angels in the process of healing. For the writer of this amulet, there are angels appointed over fevers (Abraxas) as well as over rivers (Yashar Temanuel) and roads (Yequmiel);

---

21. Naveh and Shaked translate *tov* as "proper."
22. Naveh and Shaked, *Magic Spells and Formulae*, 60–66, amulet no. 19.

the latter two are liminal spaces from whence illness or evil have the potential to come. Abraxas was appointed over healing the client, but other angels were responsible for control over the places whence fever-causing spirits emerge. For this practitioner, it was not enough to heal the fever that was present; the client's environment had to be made safe. Knowledge of the divine names empowered this practitioner to interact with the angels of the invisible realm and to enlist their assistance.

One fragmentary and difficult-to-read amulet written for Theodosius son of Theodora (a surprisingly common Jewish name in antiquity) enumerated the angels and their spheres of influence: "the name that rules in the heaven," "He who rides the clouds," "He who rules over *She'ol*" (the depths), "He who rules over the sun," possibly Malal "who rules over the moon," and finally ". . . his servant . . . who rules over the ocean."[23] This emphasis on angels and their particular realms of authority may have to do with the Greco-Roman cultural milieu of Palestine. Roman religion places a strong emphasis on place and spirits associated with particular places.[24] Jewish practitioners and rabbis internalized such knowledge and references to the angels of the sea and other places can be found in their respective texts.[25]

Abraxas shows up in the above-mentioned amulet from Ḥorvat Kannah in lower Galilee, Horvat Kanaf in the Golan, and in an amulet from Nirim in the Negev, all rural Jewish settlements.[26] Abraxas was a very popular divine figure in ancient ritual practices of Jews, Christians, and others in antiquity. Abraxas in Greek is spelled with seven letters whose numerical values adds up to 365, a number of significance to Jews as well as to others in the Greco-Roman Mediterranean.[27] These lucky numerical associations would ostensibly have endowed Abraxas with a reputation that appealed to practitioners and clients alike. As with Hermes in the Babylonian incantation bowl, Abraxas's appearance in an amulet should not be surprising, nor should it be seen to detract from the amulet's Jewish

---

23. Naveh and Shaked, *Magic Spells and Formulae*, 73–75, no. 22 (unknown provenance).

24. Beard, North, and Price, *Religions of Rome*; on angels and sacred sites in Roman Empire, see Cline, *Ancient Angels*, chap. 5.

25. See *b. B. bat.* 74b where God orders the prince of the sea to swallow waters to make room for land. I was reminded of two more sources by Gideon Bohak, who kindly shared with me a draft of an article on prayers to angels in ancient Judaism: See the story of R. Yehoshua commanding the prince of the sea to swallow a heretic (*y. Sanh.* 7:13, 25d) and the story of R. Elazar b. Dordya seeking the intercession of (the angels of) mountains, hills, heavens, earth, sun, moon, stars, etc. (*b. 'Abod. Zar.* 17a). It may also be relevant that Jews, Christians, and polytheists were gathering to commemorate the angels' visit to Abraham at the well of Mamre, not far from Hebron (Gen 18). See Cline, *Ancient Angels*, esp. chapter 5; Cline also observes that a legend recorded in John 5:2 may attest to an association of healing angels with the Bethesda pool in Jerusalem (*Ancient Angels*, 125–28).

26. Naveh and Shaked, *Amulets and Magic Bowls*, 45–49 (no. 2) and 94–97 (no. 12).

27. Bohak, *Ancient Jewish Magic*, 247–50.

character. A motif does not have to be uniquely Jewish to part of the Jewish imagination. An amulet found in a synagogue in Nirim in the northwest Negev, written for the son of a woman named Shlomzo (short for Shlom-Zion, "peace of Zion"), also appeals to Abraxas alongside Hebrew names of God for assistance and protection from evil spirits.[28] Jews could adopt figures from the Greco-Roman divine realm as divinities subordinate to their own Jewish God.[29] These Jews looked to Abraxas as well as the better-known Michael and other angels whose names end in 'el, including 'Ezriel, whose name means "aid of God" or "God is my aid."

A third example from a gold amulet from Syria illustrates the association of angels with rivers and abstract spaces in the Byzantine Levant.[30] It was written for a woman named Arsinoë, a name found among Jewesses in late antiquity.[31] In this amulet, the ritual practitioner enlists four angels associated with skies, seas, rivers, and the abyss to "rescue and save" Arsinoë from "strange, difficult, and frightening" destroying demons.[32] It begins with the words "I am writing [this] so that Arsinoë will be healed. In the name of Yešrumiel and Yešymel and Nahariel, who is [appointed] over the rivers of God, and Tehomiel whom God set up."[33] The first two angelic names are difficult to decipher, but Roy Kotansky, who published the amulet, suggested Yešrumiel may be connected with the heights or skies (Hebrew, *rom*) while Yešumel may relate to depths of the sea (Hebrew, *ym*).[34] Nahariel contains the Hebrew word for river (*nahar*) and Tahomiel contains the Hebrew word for abyss (*tehom*). I mentioned rivers above as a source of illness, but the abyss was also a source of particular anxiety to the people of the Roman Near East.[35] Imagining an angel appointed over the abyss may have helped mitigate that fear. This incantation shows a practitioner enlisting powerful but unfamiliar angels to rescue and heal Arsinoë from demonic illness.

The same ritual practitioner composed another silver amulet for Arsinoë, this one enlisting *only* angels for healing.[36] This time the practitioner chose to invoke more well-known angels and, after giving the first four angels special attention, he added a much longer list of lesser known angels. The practitioner described each of the first four angels with epithets, quoting biblical verses for Michael and

28. Naveh and Shaked, *Amulets and Magic Bowls*, 94–97, no. 12.

29. See discussion in Horbury, "Jewish and Christian Monotheism in the Herodian Age" on how some streams of Jews, particularly in the late Second Temple period, viewed the gods of other peoples as subordinate to YHWH.

30. Kotansky, "Two Inscribed Jewish Aramaic Amulets from Syria."

31. See Ilan, *Lexicon* III: 405 for Arsinoe the daughter of Yohanan in Egypt as well as Cyrenica.

32. Kotansky, "Two Inscribed Jewish Aramaic Amulets from Syria," 270.

33. Kotansky, "Two Inscribed Jewish Aramaic Amulets from Syria," 270.

34. Kotansky, "Two Inscribed Jewish Aramaic Amulets from Syria," 272.

35. Ahuvia, "Darkness upon the Abyss."

36. Kotansky, "Two Inscribed Jewish Aramaic Amulets from Syria," Amulet B, 274.

Gabriel and, apparently, drawing on common knowledge for the second pair of angels, Raphael and 'Anael:[37]

> I call upon you Holy Angels that you heal Arsinoë from every illness:
> "Prince of the hosts of *Yhwh*" [Josh. 5:14–15], Michael;
> "And the man, Gabriel" [Dan. 9:21];
> And Raphael, master of healing;
> And 'Anael, who answers [the prayers of] the daughters of Eve.

Michael, Gabriel, and Raphael were, of course, the most famous trio of angels in antiquity, but Raphael was termed a master of healing only in other ritual texts.[38] 'Anael appears in the amulet from Horvat Kanaf quoted at the beginning of this chapter and in an incantation bowl described in the previous chapter.[39] 'Anael contains the verb for answering or responding in Aramaic (*'-n-h*), but why this practitioner describes this angel as partial to the prayers of women is not self-evident today.[40] Comparison with other incantations and treatises in which 'Anael appears suggests that this angel had a reputation in antiquity for answering women's prayers and was even conceptualized as a feminine being.[41] The practitioner's choice of names, combined with the epithets, suggests that the angels' identity and function mattered to clients and was not arbitrary. Perhaps Arsinoë needed further reassurance that her prayer, as a woman in particular, would be heard.

The amulet continues with a list of twenty-seven more angelic names, most of which also have recognizable etymologies like Sadqiel (justice of God), Uriel (light of God), Nahariel (river of God, again), and so on. It closes with the statement "I pray of you, heal Arsinoë from every evil spirit" and quotes three words from Psalm 138:2, obliquely alluding to God's "loving-kindness and faithfulness." The closing verse from the Psalms is the only oblique allusion to God in this incantation. In this incantation, the practitioner calls upon "Holy Angels" to heal Arsinoë, particularly invoking familiar established angels, an angel emphatically associated with answering women, and a long list of angels with recognizable names that would comfort her and protect her from evil spirits.

---

37. Kotansky, "Two Inscribed Jewish Aramaic Amulets from Syria," 275.

38. See sources listed in Kotansky, "Two Inscribed Jewish Aramaic Amulets from Syria," 277.

39. 'Aniel was the first angel invoked in an incantation bowl for Mahdukh, daughter of Ispend-armed, for the sake of garnering her grace in the eyes of all (Shaked, "Form and Purpose," 8–10, also discussed in chapter 1).

40. Saar observes that 'Anael is "sometimes identified with the planet Venus or mentioned in spells of love magic," but this amulet was not a love spell (*Jewish Love Magic*, 230); as she observes, most erotic magic was commissioned by men (see 157ff.).

41. See sources listed in Kotansky, "Two Inscribed Jewish Aramaic Amulets from Syria," 277, especially *The Wisdom of the Chaldeans*, which makes apparent that some Jewish ritual practitioners pictured 'Anael as a feminine being. I discuss this evidence in "Gender and the Angels in Ancient Judaism."

More than the Babylonian incantation bowls, the Palestinian amulets emphasized the power of the revealed name of God. Many Babylonian incantation texts begin with the formula "In your name" and include the tetragrammaton.[42] But the Palestinian amulets emphasized the epithet "I-am-that-I-am" more frequently, quoting Exodus 3:14, where God revealed himself to Moses with the "I-am-that-I-am" name.[43] At least seven of the thirty-two amulets published by Naveh and Shaked invoke God with this biblical verse. This seems to have been a particularly cryptic saying that lent itself to incantational use among Jews in the Greco-Roman Mediterranean. The scene of the theophany where God reveals his name to Moses and his loyalty to the Israelites was likely a very evocative passage for these Jews. Amulets thus shed light on another way biblical stories about God and his divine name were known and ritualized among late ancient Jews.

A golden amulet written for a woman named Klara (unfortunately without provenance, but likely from the Roman East) shows us a Jewish ritual practitioner carefully curating divine names, both of God and the angels, to confront an invasive spirit. I-am-that-I-Am takes pride of place:

> Adjured are you, spirit, in the name of I-am-who-I-am and in the name of His Holy Angels, that you may move away and be expelled and keep far from Klara daughter of Kyrana, and that you may have no longer from now on power over her. May you [the spirit] be bound and kept away from her, in the name of Afarka'el, Ahi'el, Raphael, Mafri'el, Ofafi'el, Kefuya'el, 'Ami'el, Turi'el, and in the name of Michael, Besam'el, Nedav'el. May she [Klara be] sealed from you and also from all evil. In the name of the Word [mymr] of the Holy one of the World. [six lines of "magic characters, incomprehensible Hebrew and Greek letters" follow].[44]

This ritual practitioner directly adjured the spirit to depart from Klara in the name of the revealed name of God. God's "holy angels" were enlisted to bind the spirit and keep it away from Klara. The first named angel, Afarka'el, has a name that may derive from Greek επαρχος or the military title of prefect, the practitioner named the lieutenant or prefect of God first among the angels. Raphael and Michael were then mentioned among other angelic names less familiar to us today, but ones that would have been familiar to this practitioner and client.

---

42. The tetragrammaton had a long history among Jews as "the apotropaic mark par excellence" (Bohak, *Ancient Jewish Magic*, 117). Bohak points to the example of the high priest in the Jewish temple, who wore the tetragrammaton on a golden plate as part of his headdress (Let. Aris. 98; Wis 18.24; Philo, *Mos.* 2.114; Josephus, *J.W.* 5.235 and *A.J.* 3.178, 8.93, 11.331). For the tetragrammaton in amulets, see Naveh and Shaked, *Amulets and Magic Bowls*, no. 17, lines 2–7, and *Magic Spells and Formulae*, no. 27.

43. Naveh and Shaked, *Amulets and Magic Bowls*, nos. 2, 4, 6, 11, 12, and *Magic Spells and Formulae*, nos. 18 and 28.

44. Naveh and Shaked, *Magic Spells and Formulae*, 57–60, no. 18, lines 1–6 of 12. Provenance unknown, but likely Levantine.

Interestingly, just before delving into nonverbal symbolic characters, this practitioner also invoked "the name of the word of the Holy one" (*shma d-mymr kadish alma*). This is striking because *mymr* is used as a circumlocution for God in Aramaic translations of the Hebrew Bible, known as the Targumim. In late antique synagogues, Jews would have heard the Torah both in Hebrew and in the Aramaic Targumim. In the Targumim, God is most frequently referred to by the phrase "the Memra of the Lord," where spelling out the tetragrammaton is avoided with various multiplications of the letter *yod* instead.[45] Although much debated, the general consensus among Jewish Studies scholars is that *Memra* is a non-anthropomorphic circumlocution for God.[46] Like the Targumists, this ritual practitioner did not use the tetragrammaton but played with many other combinations of Hebrew and Greek letters. Even as this practitioner sought to be circumspect in the way he addressed God, he saw fit to employ the names of angels and ritual symbols to encircle and protect his client.

GOD, ANGELS, AND OTHER HEROES
IN LEVANTINE AMULETS

As with the Babylonian bowls, there is much variation among Palestinian amulets in their approach to the invisible realm, with most invoking God and the angels, some invoking the angels alongside other heroes, one invoking angels alone, and a few avoiding angels altogether. Only a few of the published amulets with provenance do not mention angels, and these focus on God alone instead.[47] I shall describe one of these amulets, whose technique has a long afterlife, before surveying some other interesting permutations from the late antique Levant.

The following amulet for Esther was one of nineteen Aramaic and Hebrew bronze amulets discovered in the apse of a synagogue in Nirim in the northwest Negev.[48] Of the three amulets published from Nirim, two amulets appealed to angels, while the following one did not.[49] This range demonstrates that, even within one rural Jewish community, a variety of approaches to the divine realm

45. McNamara, *The Aramaic Bible: Targum Neofiti 1*, 37 and 52.

46. See Ahuvia, "Memra."

47. See also Kotansky, "A Jewish Liturgical Fever-Amulet," for a Greek amulet discovered in western Galilee that combined quotations from the Septuagint with Hebrew liturgical language and focused on the Creator God of Genesis. Two amulets discovered in Sepphoris lack any signs of personalization and appeal to God's justice with variations on the tetragrammaton; for these, see also McCollough and Glazier-McDonald, "Magic and Medicine in Byzantine Galilee."

48. Naveh and Shaked, *Amulets and Magic Bowls*, 98–101, no. 13.

49. See Naveh and Shaked, *Amulets and Magic Bowls*, 90–95, no. 11, which invokes a number of angels like Barqiel, Uriel, Milhamiel, and so on. I discussed no. 12, which invokes Abraxas above.

prevailed. Instead of angels, this amulet relied on a biblical verse that emphasized God's protection of the people of Israel:

> A good[50] amulet for Esther daughter of Tate,[51]
> to save her from evil tormentors, from evil eye, from spirit, from demon from
>   shadow-spirit, from all evil tormentors, from evil eye, from imp[ure] spirit.
> . . . "If you will give heed hearkening to the voice of the L[ord] your God,
> and do what is right in His sight, and give ear to His commandments and keep
>   all His statutes, None the diseases which I put upon the Egyptians; [will I place
>   upon you] [for I, the LORD, am your healer]"

This amulet for Esther seeks to protect her from demonic illness by harnessing the promises made to Israelites long ago. The verse quoted from Exodus 15: 26 conveys the idea that piety and observance guarantee freedom from plague. Here it is applied in written form to protect Esther from demons. Interestingly, the famous rabbi Akiva is said to have considered the incantational use of this exact verse by a ritual practitioner for healing a wound tantamount to the worst of heresies.[52] It may be that its use here as a form of protection, rather than verbal ritual use, would not have been seen as problematic by the rabbis.[53] In any case, this biblical verse had a long history of use in ritual objects and rabbinic prohibition could not discourage it.[54] This biblical verse continued to be part of the incantational tradition of healing and eventually became one of the embellishments of the nighttime Shema, a prayer said nightly by observant Jews to this day. A spectrum of possibilities was open to ancient Jews in their approach to their illnesses: some ancient Jews relied on ritualized verses of the Torah (like God's promises to the Israelites), while others relied on angels when they sought protection or healing.

---

50. Hebrew "*tov*," Naveh and Shaked prefer "proper." The more literal translation makes better sense.

51. Ilan transliterates *T'tys* as "Tate" (a woman's name in keeping with the ritual use of matronymic), noting Greek Τατης is found in a fourth-century epitaph in Beth She'arim (*Lexicon of Jewish Names in Late Antiquity* 2:260).

52. See *m. Sanh.* 10:1. The amulet from Nirim is from a much later date than the Mishnah, but evidently the verse was already being used by ritual practitioners for healing wounds in the second century CE. This Mishnaic text is also discussed in Schäfer, "Magic and Religion in Ancient Judaism," 34–35.

53. See *b. Šebu.* 15b where the Stammaim of the Babylonian Talmud discussed the use of biblical verses, distinguishing between apotropaic use (permitted) and use for healing rituals (prohibited).

54. See the discussion in Bohak, *Ancient Jewish Magic*, 379. As the COVID-19 pandemic emerged in the winter of 2020, the Israeli ultra-orthodox party *Shas* distributed an amulet quoting this same verse from Exodus.

In addition to angelic names, two amulets from the Levant invoke the priestly and royal heroes of Israelite traditions.[55] To date, explicit references to Aaron and the high priesthood have not been found in Babylonian incantations. As more bowls and amulets come to light, it will be interesting to see if this turns out to be a particularly Palestinian emphasis. A silver amulet for healing a woman named Ina daughter of Ze'irti was recovered in the early twentieth century in a cemetery close to Tiberias. Ina was suffering from fever and illness. In her amulet, the ritual practitioner placed special emphasis on the divine name on Aaron the High Priest's holy garments, specifically his miter, which (according to Exod 28:36) had a gold plate with the words "holy to the Lord" upon it. For the sake of brevity, I quote only the most distinctive section of the amulet here (lines 2b–7 and 17–22 of 36):

> In the name that is *yzwt yh yh*
> [*y*]*h*, which was written on the plate [*tsitsa*] which was
> [roll]ed on the miter [*klilah*] of Aaron the High Priest
> who was serving with it, and he descended in order to fu[lfill]
> [. . .] his name, who carries those on high
> [and] those below, [and all] tremble before him. This is it.

> [skipping divine names of God and angels, including 70 repetition of *yh*]

> Eradicate from the body of Ina daughter of Ze'irti a[ll]
> hectic fever and illness and sickness in the name of *Yhwh*
> who is enthroned among the cherubim, Amen Amen Selah. Blessed be He.
> "The Lord of Hosts is with us, the god of Jacob our refuge
> Selah" [Ps 46:7 and 12]
> Holy Holy Holy Holy[56]

This opening section is somewhat difficult to decipher, but the figure of Aaron and his holy garb is key. The practitioner evokes this priestly and biblical precedent for wearing God's name even as he inscribed it on an amulet for an ill woman. In the case of an amulet, only beings from the invisible realm could see the tetragrammaton: if they were angels, they would be drawn in to assist Ina, and if they were demons, presumably they would flee from her; this is in contrast to the high priest's holy garb, which broadcasted the tetragrammaton.[57] Combining the images of high priests and angels is not altogether surprising, as ancient Jews believed that God was in a physically accessible throne room (in the tabernacle

---

55. Naveh and Shaked, *Magic Spells and Formulae*, nos. 17 and 27.

56. Naveh and Shaked, *Magic Spells and Formulae*, 50–57, no. 17, reproduced with my emendations.

57. According to a poignant tradition preserved in the *b. Šabb.* 63b, R. Eleazar b. Yose even saw this priestly gold plate in Rome after the destruction and looting of the Jerusalem temple. For discussion of the fate of the temple implements in rabbinic literature, see Boustan, "The Spoils of the Jerusalem Temple at Rome and Constantinople."

or temple), surrounded by angels, and priests were the only ones who had access to this divine meeting space.[58] It is possible that with the repetition of "Holy," the practitioner had in mind Isaiah's vision of seraphim in the temple, who recited "Holy, Holy, Holy."

Aaron's golden plate makes another appearance in an amulet found in Irbid in modern Jordan (just east of the southern tip of the Sea of Galilee), alongside other biblical heroes and objects associated with each respectively. This amulet was written for a woman named Marian, daughter of Sarah, who was seeking protection for herself and her unborn baby.[59]

> And by the rod of Moses and by the front-plate [*tsitsa*] of Aaron
> the High Priest and by the signet-ring of Solomon and [. . .]
> [. . .[60]] of David and by the horns of the altar and by the nam[e]
> [of] the living and existent God: that you should be expelled, [you,]
> [s]pirit and the evil assailant and every demon
> des[troyer] from the body of Marian daughter of [Sarah]
> and her fetus that is in her belly from th[is day]
> to eternity, Amen, Amen, Selah.[61]

The ritual practitioner invokes these heroes and their symbols of power to expel and exorcise demons from the body of Marian. The order of figures invoked is not chronological: the incantation begins with Moses and Aaron, then invokes Solomon before David. The patriarch Abraham and the name of God are featured in the more fragmentary middle portion of the amulet and finally, names of angels, are mentioned at the end of the amulet. It seems that this practitioner believed that inscribing these figures and their respective objects of power (rod of Moses, front-plate of Aaron, signet ring of Solomon) into a necklace amulet (that Marian would wear) would protect Marian from demonic assailants. Boustan and Beshay have observed that Solomon's signet ring was one of the most well-known sacred insignia in late antique ritual sources, "moving with ease across religious, linguistic, and political boundaries" and associated with anti-demonic powers in magical objects from Roman Egypt, Roman Syria, and Sasanian Iraq.[62] The other

---

58. Himmelfarb, *A Kingdom of Priests*, describes the creative tension this created in ancient Jewish society.

59. First published as Amulet A by Montgomery, "Some Early Amulets from Palestine"; reevaluated and retranslated by Naveh and Shaked, *Magic Spells and Formulae*, 91–95, amulet 27.

60. King David's associated object was probably musical in nature because of his association with the book of Psalms. See incantation bowl no. 3 from Montgomery, *Aramaic Incantation Texts*, p. 183, which invokes *mizmor* (the song) of David. The shield of David, used to refer to the hexagram associated with Jewish identity today, is a much later medieval development (Scholem, "Magen David").

61. Naveh and Shaked, *Magic Spells and Formulae*, 93–94, amulet no. 27, lines 1–8 of 32.

62. Boustan and Beshay, "Sealing the Demons," 100.

references, especially to imagery of the temple, locate this object more firmly in the Jewish imagination. Through amulets, we can see how biblical heroes, famous insignia, and sacred spaces remained active resonances in the lives of the Jews of late antiquity.

A final example of angels in necklace amulets comes from an amulet found in central Turkey. Inscribed on a silver sheet and placed in a bronze container, the amulet describes its request ascending to the angels in the heavenly throne room. This is the only amulet known to me that describes the location of the angels relative to God in the heavens. The practitioner specified that angels stand in the throne room of God. The way the practitioner imagined addressing the demonic antagonists recalls the language of incantation bowls more than the Palestinian amulets examined so far.

> Put mercy from heaven
> on Sloneh. In the name of Michael, Raphael,
> Azzael, Azriel, Ariel, [. . .] the great
> [. . .] you, the holy angels who stand
> in front of the throne of the Great God. May there be extinguished
> the evil spirit and the shadow-spirit, and the demon,
> whether male or female from Sloneh
> son of Demetrion. In the name of . . .
> [skipping two lines of esoteric angelic names]
> under *Yhwh*. In your name, sacred God,
> may there be extinguished the evil spirit and the demon
> and the shadow-spirit and the tormentor and the destroyer. In your name
> God of Israel, may the words rise up to heaven
> at the side of the throne of the great, powerful, awful,
> sacred, magnified and praised, and exalted God. Those
> three: one who is hungry, but does not eat, one who
> is thirsty, but does not drink, and one who is drowsy,
> but does not sleep. I said to the hungry one: Why are you
> hungry, but you do not eat? [I said] to the thirsty one: Why are you thirsty
> but you do not drink? [I said] to the drowsy one: Why are you drowsy, but you do
> not sleep? The three answered and said: d'n.[63]

Though located on the body of the client in the earthly realm, this amulet positioned the client in the midst of a cosmic battle between angels and demons, all under the beneficent control of God. This practitioner began by enlisting the angels of the throne room of God to help Sloneh. More mysterious angelic names took up the middle-part of the incantation before the practitioner appealed to

63. Naveh and Shaked, *Amulets and Magic Bowls*, 68–77, no. 7 (following their addendum on p. 76). Findspot: Agabeyli, Turkey.

God's authority directly. The practitioner hoped his words would rise up to the side of the heavenly throne, presumably to the angels standing there, who would execute God's will.

In the second section of the amulet, the practitioner himself addressed the demons, using reverse psychology to disempower them, and recalling the language of some incantation bowls from Babylonia.[64] With the mysterious answer *d'n*, the demons seem to express assent. What was the role of the angels in this incantation? Although the practitioner does begin with requesting heavenly mercy for his client, this incantation is otherwise mum on angels protecting Sloneh. Instead, the focus is on the incantation-prayer itself reaching the angels in the throne room and God. It seems more likely that the angels (under God) undergirded the authority of the practitioner himself, as he confronted the demons. Sloneh likely took comfort from having a practitioner take up his cause, appeal to angels and God, and directly address demons on his behalf.

RITUAL PRACTITIONERS AND ANGELS
IN *SEFER HA-RAZIM*

Unlike the Palestinian and Babylonian amulets, which represent a product of negotiation between ordinary Jews, practitioners, and perceived divine powers, *Sefer ha-Razim* is a composition by a learned specialist for specialist consumption (or by a specialist for other would-be specialists).[65] Mordechai Margalioth first produced an edition of this composition based on eclectic manuscripts in 1966.[66] He argued that the treatise dated to the third or fourth century CE based on internal references to the Roman calendar, its sophisticated Hebrew, the similarities of its contents to Greco-Coptic ritual practices, its use of Greek technical terms and loan words, and the cultural motifs in the work.[67] More recently, Peter Schäfer and Bill Rebiger reevaluated the evidence, noting the heterogeneous character of the text, that its Greek loan words could easily date to the Byzantine or early medieval period, and that no other sources refer to it before the ninth century CE.

---

64. Cf. no. 9731 in the Iraq Museum and no. 91776 in the British Museum, both published by Gordon in "Aramaic Incantation Bowls," 349 and 342–44. Also discussed in Ahuvia, "Spatial and Social Dynamics," 243–44.

65. See a survey of other such surviving manuals in Harari, "Instructional Literature: Magic Recipes and Treatises" in *Jewish Magic*, 255–89.

66. Margalioth, *Sefer ha-Razim*. Morgan published an English translation of this eclectic text in *Sepher Ha-Razim*. Schäfer and Rebiger observed that *Sefer ha-Razim* survives in two main versions, one reflecting its Greco-Roman milieu and another, which is a later abridgement. As previously mentioned, their two-volume edition of *Sefer ha-Razim* is synoptic. For the reader's convenience, I cite Morgan's translation alongside Schäfer and Rebiger's synoptic edition and the relevant manuscripts.

67. Margalioth, *Sefer ha-Razim*.

Acknowledging that the text has a long tradition-history, they place its final redaction in the late Byzantine or Geonic period (seventh to eighth century CE) either in Egypt or Palestine.[68] Bohak, meanwhile, writes that this text "is so deeply influenced by the Greco-Egyptian magical tradition, and so full of Greek loanwords, as to assure of its Palestinian origins and of its date sometime in the Early Byzantine period, prior to the Muslim conquest."[69] I follow Schäfer and Rebiger's later dating of the spells, but think it is safe to say that the opening framework of the treatise belongs to the cultural milieu of late antiquity.

As many scholars have noted, two strata of texts are discernible within this treatise: a cosmological narrative framework and a collection of ritual practices. The narrative framework of the manual does not match the spells contained within it. My research suggests that the framework matches attitudes toward the invisible realm seen in other late antique texts, while the spells in the manual parallel later sixth-century texts. Of importance to this work is the fact that angels are approached differently in the narrative framework and in the spells themselves. While the framework bears some resemblance to the language and worldview of the ritual specialists that we have encountered, the spells reflect a different worldview that positions the ritual expert as powerful, independent, and free to adjure the angels. I will examine the conception of angels in the framework and in the spells in turn.

Although we must be careful not to read one body of evidence through the lens of another, *Sefer ha-Razim* has the potential to shed light on the moment before the composition of the amulet and the performance of the incantation. The incantation bowl or amulet is the created product, just one aspect of the ritual practice. By its very nature, an amulet will not necessarily tell us about the libation or offering made with it or the timing required to execute it properly. Read carefully, *Sefer ha-Razim* may supply pertinent details to the understanding of the full context of the incantations. The opening lines of the book, written in lucid Hebrew are worth quoting at length and analyzing closely, one section at a time:

> This is a book from the books of the mysteries, which was given to Noah son of Lamech, the son of Methuselah, the son of Enoch, the son of Jared, the son of Mahalalel, the son of Kenan, the son of Enosh, the son of Seth, the son of Adam, by Raziel the angel in the year when he came into the ark before his entrance.[70]

---

68. Schäfer and Rebiger, *Sefer ha-Razim*, 2:9.

69. Bohak, "Babylonian Jewish Magic in Late Antiquity," 89. Bohak also discusses the linguistic context of this and other magic sources in "Jewish Amulets, Magic Bowls, and Manuals in Aramaic and Hebrew."

70. Morgan, *Sepher Ha-Razim*, 17 with minor corrections. Schäfer and Rebiger, *Sefer ha-Razim*, §2 (M248 and G1). Schäfer and Rebiger prefer M738 which states, "This is the book of the mysteries, which was revealed to Nuriel according to Raziel in the 300th year of Noah" (Schäfer and Rebiger, *Sefer ha-Razim*, 2:126).

The first angel encountered in *Sefer ha-Razim* is Raziel, a revelatory angel with a long afterlife in medieval mystical writings.[71] According to the opening lines of the treatise, Raziel conveyed this book, just one of many books of mysteries, to Noah in the year before the latter entered the ark. The choice of Noah, the last antediluvian patriarch, as the original recipient of the book, might have to do with his renewed popularity in late antiquity.[72] Though the *Book of the Watchers* featured Enoch as the hero and role model, other Jewish traditions, including *Sefer ha-Razim*, centered on Noah. Though the era of angelic and human commingling ended in the total destruction of the flood, this treatise promised that angelic and human communication could continue productively because Noah recorded everything that he learned from Raziel for future generations.

> And he [Noah] inscribed it upon a sapphire stone very distinctly. And he learned from it how to do wondrous deeds and mysteries and categories of understanding and thoughts of humility and concepts of counsel, how to master investigation of the strata of the heavens, and to roam in all that is in the seven abodes, to observe all the astrological signs, to examine the course and to explain the observations of the moon and to know the paths of the Great Bear, Orion, and the Pleiades [Job 9:9], to declare the names of the overseers of each and every firmament and the realms of their authority, and by what means they [can be made to] cause success in each thing [asked of them].[73]

In this section the text transitions from what Noah did and learned to what anyone can do if they achieve the proper level of purity. The treatise promises that the practitioner can roam the heavenly abodes like the angels themselves. Achieving the power and knowledge of the angels is a prominent theme in the opening of the treatise, which we have seen described by practitioners in the Babylonian amulets as well. We will return to this theme shortly. The treatise explains that myriads of angels are distributed over the multilayered heavens under the authority of various overseers, ready for service in the earthly realm. What *Sefer ha-Razim* explicates, that we might not have known from the Babylonian and Palestinian amulets, is that the angels cannot go forth from the heavens without the approval of their overseers. This idea is explained in more detail in the framing description of the first firmament, where we find seven overseers in charge of encampments of angels. The angels "do not go out without permission to perform any

71. See *Tg. Qoh* 10:20; *Zohar* I:117b–18a, discussed in Schwartz, *Gabriel's Palace: Jewish Mystical Tales*, 292–93 and Schwartz, "The Book of Raziel."

72. Stone, Amihay, and Hillel, eds., *Noah and His Book(s)*. See also Lieber, "Portraits of Righteousness: Noah in Early Christian and Jewish Hymnography;" Koltun-Fromm, "Aphrahat and the Rabbis on Noah's Righteousness in Light of the Jewish and Christian Polemic."

73. Morgan, *Sepher Ha-Razim*, 17–18; cf. Schäfer and Rebiger, *Sefer ha-Razim*, §3 (M248, lines 19–28).

action, not until one of the seven overseers, who sits upon the throne and who rules them, gives them approval, for only according to their will and authority do they proceed."[74] The angels, then, do not quite have free will, but are subordinate to higher angelic authorities. This elucidates one previously examined incantation bowl from Borsippa, which stated, "Call him that they may open the gates of the heavens."[75] Presumably, by this the ritual practitioner meant to call the appropriate overseer angel (in the singular) to tell the subordinate angels (in the plural) to open the gates of success for the client.

This section of the treatise also describes the biddable nature of the angels: "And each and every one of them goes about his work, set to hurry to all such (errands) to which he might be sent, whether for good or evil, for feast or famine, for war or peace. And they are all called by names from the day they are created." The mention of the names of the angels right after describing their nature is likely not coincidental—knowing the names of the angels is essential to requesting their help. It also echoes a motif that God knows the names of each angel, no matter how countless the host of heaven may seem.[76]

Sefer ha-Razim reveals another aspect of the amulets: timing is of the essence. The opening section of the treatise continues by emphasizing that Noah learned "the proper times" for calling on the angels. From the book of mysteries, Noah learned

> the names of their ministering attendants and the proper times [at which they will hear prayer, so as] to perform every wish of anyone [who comes] near them in purity.
>
> [Noah learned] from it rituals of death and rituals of life, to understand evil and good, to search out [the right] season and moments [for magical rites], to know the time to give birth and the time to die, the time to strike and the time to heal, to interpret dreams and visions, to arouse combat, and to quiet wars, and to rule over spirits and over demons, to send them so they will go out like slaves.[77]

In this way, the treatise promises to teach practitioners the right times and seasons for invoking angels for aid in ritual practices. According to the book, both the calendric period and timing within the day is important. For the first camp of angels, ruling over matters of healing, we learn that "these are the angels that are biddable in every matter in the first and second year to the 15-year cycle according

---

74. My translation of §31, lines 24–29 (M248) in Schäfer and Rebiger, *Sefer ha-Razim*.

75. Segal and Hunter, *CAMIB* 021A, discussed on p. 46.

76. Cf. the sixth-century poet Yannai: "The rest of the stars can neither be counted nor reckoned, / yet all of them are called by name / by the One who dwells upon the Cherubim" (trans. Lieber, *Yannai on Genesis*, 310).

77. Morgan, trans., *Sepher Ha-Razim*, 18 with minor corrections, hewing more closely to Schäfer and Rebiger, *Sefer ha-Razim*, §3 (lines 28–30) and §10 (lines 32–38) following M248.

to the reckoning of the Greek kings."[78] Apparently, some years were considered better for angelic healing than others.

Furthermore, and of particular interest for this project, here the opening of the treatise promises to teach how to rule over spirits and demons, to send them out like slaves. As with the Babylonian incantation bowls and the Palestinian amulets, only demons are ruled over, not angels. The framework of the treatise promises to teach the user the times at which the angels hear prayer and "perform every wish of anyone [who comes] near them in purity," but it does not teach the user how to command the angels. Only the spirits and demons can be commanded like slaves.[79] The spells within the treatise, as we shall see, differ dramatically.

The final lines of the introduction reiterate that the treatise will teach the practitioner how to become like the angels:

> To watch the four winds of the earth, to be learned in the speech of thunderclaps, to tell the significance of lightning flashes, to foretell what will happen in each and every month, and to know the affairs of each and every year, whether for plenty or for hunger, whether for harvest or for drought, whether for peace or for war, to be as one of the awesome ones and to comprehend the songs of heaven.[80]

From the end of this introduction, which culminates in a promise to become angelic, we can deduce what abilities were thought of as the preserve of the angels. To be an angel was to have (1) knowledge of the movements of the celestial bodies, (2) free movement through the seven heavenly realms, (3) proficiency in the hierarchies of the angels and their overseers, (4) the ability to properly interpret dreams (5) power over lowly spirits and demons (*ruhot* and *pegaim*), (6) comprehension of natural phenomena (storms, lightning, etc.), (7) knowledge of the future and (8) knowledge of the heavenly liturgy. Because no Jewish angelology was produced in this period, no text states this explicitly. Indirectly, however, we may learn from this treatise how ancient Jews conceptualized angels and desired to become like them.

Although they are found in Jewish communities thousands of miles away, the assertions of specialists in the incantation bowls of Babylonia seem to reflect the fact that some practitioners believed they had achieved this level of expertise: for example, Abuna, who could claim to possess the fiery body of an angel and the spells to subdue the sea and monster Leviathan and the ability to command

---

78. Morgan, trans., *Sepher Ha-Razim*, 23; Schäfer and Rebiger, *Sefer ha-Razim*, §37 (G4 and M738)

79. Notably, the treatise does not use the term for demons found in rabbinic literature (*mezikin*), calling demons *ruhot* and *pegaim* instead. This difference in vocabulary might indicates that the ritual practitioner operated in separate circles from the rabbis, even as they shared a belief that they could command authority over demons.

80. Morgan, trans., *Sepher Ha-Razim*, 18, lines 15–18; Schäfer and Rebiger, *Sefer ha-Razim*, §10 (M248).

demons to depart. What this book promised, some believed, acted out, and put in writing on other objects as well.

Although *Sefer ha-Razim* mentions antediluvian patriarchs like Enoch and Noah as well as figures like Moses and Solomon in the opening framework, they do not recur in the spells or other sections of the book. *Sefer ha-Razim* has excluded them and instead foregrounded the role of the angels and, of course, God. Even more central is the specialist himself, who uses the angels to imagine another way of being in the world. In contrast with the opening framework of the treatise, some spells contained within the treatise *do* command the angels (as well as demons and spirits). Some spells only act in the name of the angels or make requests of angels as we saw in the amulets.[81] But many adjure the angels directly, and command their intervention, particularly for coercive erotic spells.[82] The first coercive erotic spell in *Sefer ha-Razim* relayed to male practitioners how they could acquire the favor of a high-status woman:

> If you wish to bring a great wealthy and distinguished and beautiful woman to you so that she loves you, take some perspiration from your face [and place it] in a new glass vessel [or flask] and write on tin foil [i.e., a *lamella*] the names of the angels and the name of the overseer, and cast it [the tin lamella] into the glass [flask] and say thus over the perspiration of your face: I adjure you overseer and I adjure you angels of favor and grace and angels of knowledge, that you will turn [to me] the heart of N daughter of N to love me and let her do nothing without me, and let not thoughts of me leave her mind, and let her heart be [joined] with my heart in love.[83]

To compel a wealthy woman into a binding relationship, the practitioner used coercive language with the angels. There are three steps to this ritual: physically placing perspiration in a glass vessel, inserting a tin sheet inscribed with angelic names into the vessel, and verbally commanding the angels to turn the heart of woman toward the practitioner. Relating to the angels as beings that the practitioner could command represents a major shift in attitude toward God's servants among ancient Jews, one that the evidence intimates remained esoteric. When people think of ancient magic, this is the kind of coercive spell that often comes to mind. It is noteworthy that no lamellae matching this description (in a glass vessel or only inscribed with names, without any other description of purpose) has been found.

That said, an incantation for igniting desire was found in the remains of Horvat Rimmon, just north of Beer Sheba in the Israeli desert, showing that Jews did

---

81. Schäfer and Rebiger, *Sefer ha-Razim I*, §111 and §160.

82. Schäfer and Rebiger, *Sefer ha-Razim I*, §67, §75, §93, and §96.

83. Schäfer and Rebiger, *Sefer ha-Razim I*, §§74–75 (M738); cf. Morgan, trans., *Sepher Ha-Razim*, 35.

enact ritual practices described in manuals.[84] Inscribed on ceramic, this fragmentary object was found in the upper remains of a fill associated with a synagogue and dates to fifth to sixth century CE and was reconstructed through comparison with Hebrew and Aramaic spells found in the Cairo Genizah.[85] The incantation begins with the circled names of six unfamiliar angels and then states:

> You holy and mighty angels
> [I adjure] you, just as this shard
> burns, so shall burn the heart of R[achel daughter of]
> [Mar]ian after me, I [. . .][86]

In this incantation the practitioner seems to command the angels to kindle a relationship.[87]

Notably, this incantation was inscribed on an unbaked piece of clay with incisions so that it could be ritually burned and broken. This matches no ritual instruction in *Sefer ha-Razim*. This ritual only finds explication in several of the Cairo Genizah erotic spells that command the practitioner to write "on an unbaked potsherd" that should be "thrown into the fire" for making the heart of one person burn for another, and which then appeals to angelic names and to particular angels (e.g., Abrasax) for intervention on the client's behalf.[88] What this ceramic object makes clear is that Jewish practitioners were engaged in coercive erotic spells in late antiquity, in proximity to synagogues, and that the angels were active in Jewish conceptualizations of the invisible realm. *Sefer ha-Razim* was likely just one treatise among many that circulated in late antiquity. In addition to the ritual technology of bowls in Babylonia, and amulets in Greco-Roman Mediterranean, ceramic objects were also used and many more may be discovered in time.[89]

84. As Saar notes in *Jewish Love Magic*, "the words written on behalf of an enamoured man around the fifth century CE resound in recipe manuals up until the twentieth century, accompanying the same ancient practice that left behind the burnt shard of Ḥorvat Rimmon," 120.

85. Naveh and Shaked, *Amulets and Magic Bowls*, 85–89 (no. 10), and cf. their *Magic Spells and Formulae*, 217–19 (Geniza no. 22). Discussed thoroughly in Saar, *Jewish Love Magic*, 29–30, 118–20, and passim. Saar tentatively suggests the client's name is Rachel, daughter of Marian, and situates this amulet in the context of the principles of Jewish love magic through time.

86. I reproduce Saar's version here from *Jewish Love Magic*, 118; she reconstructs the name Rachel.

87. I equivocate because Naveh and Shaked reconstruct the missing verb addressing the angels as "I adjure" from the parallels, but none of the Cairo Genizah fragments they cite for comparison actually contains this combination of "adjuring" with angels as objects of speech. In the spells they cite as parallels, the practitioner claims to act "in the name of the angels," but only malicious spirits are adjured. Still, it is not impossible that Jewish practitioners called on the angels for coercive erotic spells.

88. Naveh and Shaked, *Amulets and Magic Bowls*, 231.

89. Hamilton, "A New Hebrew-Aramaic Incantation Text from Galilee," describes an intriguing ceramic object found near Nazareth that invoked God and the angels Michael and Raphael against two brothers (Nehemiah and Jonathan, both sons of Elisheba), identified as evil sorcerers.

Returning to *Sefer ha-Razim*, we find other spells that adjure the angels for both weighty and trivial reasons. The angels of death and wrath could be adjured for violent ends.[90] The angels of the chariot races could be adjured so that the client's team would win the race.[91] One spell adjures the angels simply to create the illusion of fire within a house in order to impress people with his power: "I adjure you the angels wrapped in fire by him who is all fire and whose seat is fire and his servants are flaming fire and camps of fire serve before him. By his name I adjure you that you show me this great miracle and fill this house with your fire so that I and all that are with me will see this great miracle without fear."[92] Unlike other incantations that we encountered for health or protection, this spell is for personal power and gain. What this difference may reveal to us is that there was a variation in religious worldviews even among Jewish ritual practitioners. Some viewed the angels as intermediaries to be respected as divine messengers between Jews and God, whose assistance could be requested for remedying personal woes. Others viewed them in a more utilitarian way, as invisible beings to be commanded for any desired end.

The massive quantity of medieval documents preserved in a synagogue in old Fustat (known as the Cairo Genizah) attests to the continued circulation of some incantations found in ritual objects from Palestine and in *Sefer ha-Razim*. Scholars of Jewish magic agree that there is continuity between Jewish ritual-magical practices of late antiquity and the medieval period.[93] That said, already a century ago, reading the Talmudic and Kabbalistic evidence alone, Ludwig Blau observed that in "the Talmud, angels were the instruments of God; in the Middle Ages, the instruments of man, who, by calling their names, or by other means, rendered them visible."[94] My reading of the rabbinic and ritual evidence aligns with his observations: Jewish attitudes toward angels shifted between the late antique rabbinic sources and the medieval ritual evidence of the Cairo Genizah. Studying the late antique and medieval evidence, scholars like Michael D. Swartz and Erica Hunter also observed that most late antique ritual sources are more neutral or passive in their invocation of angels, while later medieval sources more actively adjure and command angels to do their bidding.[95] On the other hand, scholars of ancient magic like Gideon Bohak, Ortal-Paz Saar, and Yuval Harari emphasize the continuity in magical practices from the late antique period into the medieval period and beyond, marshalling an array of ritual sources from Palestine and

---

90. Schäfer and Rebiger, *Sefer ha-Razim*, §§48–49.

91. Schäfer and Rebiger, *Sefer ha-Razim*, §194.

92. My translation is based on composite reading of manuscripts, especially §M248 and §TA42 in Schäfer and Rebiger, *Sefer ha-Razim*; some manuscripts have the "flying angels" rather than "the angels wrapped in fire."

93. See Bohak, "Magic" and other scholarship cited below.

94. Blau, "Angelology." His reflections on Jewish angelology are discussed in the conclusion.

95. Hunter, "Incantation Bowls," 222–23; Swartz, *Mechanics of Providence*, 37.

the Cairo Genizah, which demonstrate that later ritual practitioners continued to transmit late antique formulae, some of which command or adjure angels.[96] Settling this question is beyond the scope of this book, but certainly the practices and formulae of ritual practitioners did not fade away after late antiquity. The attitudes toward angels may have shifted, but it is unquestionable that angels remained essential to the imagined efficacy of these Jewish ritual incantations.

BLURRING THE BOUNDARIES: ANGELS, GENDER, AND SOCIETY

I began this chapter by reflecting on the shared magical traditions between Babylonia and Palestine in late antiquity, emphasizing that both rely on angels in similar ways, albeit with diverse permutations of invoked beings. In this section, I briefly reflect on the legacy of these Palestinian traditions among Jews into the medieval period, focusing specifically on attitudes toward gender and angels found in *Sefer ha-Razim*. Attitudes toward women and angels in this ritual treatise were ambivalent. On the one hand, angels were enlisted on behalf of women. On the other hand, *Sefer ha-Razim*'s language makes it obvious that it was directed at male practitioners and that proximity to women was perceived as antithetical to the purity required for interaction with the divine realm. The treatise contained many warnings to stay away from women, especially the impurity of women, in order to ensure success in interacting with angels.[97] At the same time, many incantations claimed to protect women and relied on the intimate presence of the angels.

For example, to protect a woman giving birth from demonic attack, the book prescribed making her (before she was even pregnant) a metal amulet inscribed with angelic names to be worn around her neck.[98] At the time of childbirth, it recommended placing four silver lamellae inscribed with angelic names in the four sides of the house to keep out evil spirits. In effect, the practitioner and the angels had to be present at the messiest and most precarious moment in human life. This set up a tension between the expectations for ritual purity necessary to invoke the angels and the work that angels were expected to do for women. In ritual texts, this was a tension that remained unresolved and hints at the gendered tensions within late antique Jewish society itself. It is worth naming the androcentric and patriarchal assumptions that dominate most surviving texts from the ancient

96. See Bohak, "The Magical Rotuli from the Cairo Genizah," 321–41, and other essays in the same volume; Saar, *Ancient Jewish Love Magic*, 28; Harari, *Jewish Magic*, 207–16.

97. Morgan, trans., *Sepher ha-Razim*, 43, 56, 57, 59, 75. I developed my thinking on this topic in dialogue with Swartz's "'Like the Ministering Angels,'" where he discusses these "concepts of purity" in relation to ritual practices.

98. Schäfer and Rebiger, *Sefer Ha-Razim* §160.

world. In texts written by male practitioners, there was an emphasis on rhetorically asserting distance from women, some of whom might have been engaged in the same practices. This male rhetoric was apparently successful, as women are the ones that bear the brunt of rabbinic criticism for ritual practices.

So, for example, according to a Babylonian Talmudic tradition, if a person was traveling by a Jewish town and smelled incense, they would *not* recite the benediction for smelling spices, because Jewish *women* were likely burning it for magical ends: "Even if the majority [of the town] is Israelite, you do not say a blessing [on smelling spices] because the daughters of Israel burn incense for magic."[99] Meanwhile, the very first ritual-instruction of *Sefer ha-Razim* called for burning incense in the evening while reciting seventy times the names of seventy-two angels.[100] Evidently, ritual practitioners who wished to engage in healing practices followed these instructions, but it is only Jewish women who were referenced with opprobrium by the rabbis. Modern readers, then, must be careful not to collaborate with the rabbis and the practitioners in such stereotyping of Jewish women. Jewish men and women engaged in ritual practices that called on angels, and angels were imagined to approach women whether they were ritually pure or not. Other ritual texts show that some angels even had the reputation of responding to "the daughters of Eve," a topic that deserves more attention.

If in ritual texts tension about ritual practices, women, and angels remained unresolved, in the mystical texts that will be examined at the end of this book, that tension was erased: the mystics' language of the divine realm utterly excluded feminine imagery, and the goals of their encounters with the divine were radically and rigidly exclusive of the feminine in a way that is unparalleled in the ritual texts.[101] And that too, speaks of a society in which men could self-segregate to the extent that they could facilitate more exclusive and rigid gender norms. Ritual sources provide a fuller account of Jewish beliefs in late antiquity, and their ability to imagine angels among men and women reveals important information about attitudes toward gender roles and sexuality in Jewish society.

CONCLUSION: ANGELS IN RITUAL
SOURCES FROM THE LEVANT

Much remains to be discovered that will illuminate attitudes toward angels among Jewish practitioners and the Jews of Syro-Palestine. What is clear is that the Jews

99. See *b. Ber.* 53a; *b. ʿEruv.* 64b. Discussed in Green, *The Aroma of Righteousness*, 139. Also discussed in Ahuvia and Gribetz, "Daughters of Israel," 20.

100. Morgan, trans., *Sepher ha-Razim*, 24; Schäfer and Rebiger, *Sefer Ha-Razim* §38.

101. See Lesses, "Women and Gender in Hekhalot Literature," as well as Swartz, "'Like the Ministering Angels,'" 231–56.

of Mesopotamia cannot be dismissed as outliers at the periphery of the Jewish world. The extant evidence shows that Jews of Byzantine Palestine and Persian Babylonia shared a worldview of beneficial angels and malevolent demons under the aegis of God. In Roman Palestine, amulets were a popular ritual technology to which people could turn in times of need. Jews wore amulets that positioned angels all around them, protecting them from evil spirits, illness, and the evil eye of others. A few amulets relied on God alone and biblical verses that reinforced his active engagement in the world and with Jews in particular. The overwhelming majority of amulets were apotropaic and called on the angels to deliver messages, to heal illness, to remove demons, and to guard over an individual. In some amulets and in the redacted layers of *Sefer ha-Razim*, we see a shift in attitude among some Jews toward angels, an attitude not of awe and respect, but of equality with the angels, and even superiority over the angels that would continue among Jews in late antiquity and into the medieval period and beyond. The ritual evidence from the Levant provides a fuller account of Jewish life, practices, and beliefs in late antiquity. What it shows is that angels were popular sources of comfort and protection for Jewish men and women; so popular, in fact, that the rabbis eventually had to accept and harness belief in them.

3

No Angels?

Early Rabbinic Sources

Behold, I am sending an angel before you to guard you along the way and to bring you to the place that I have prepared. Pay heed to him and listen to his voice; do not defy him, for he will not forgive your transgressions, since My Name is in him.

—EXODUS 23:20–21

"And the Lord brought us forth out of Egypt," not by means of an angel, and not by means of a seraph, but the Holy One, blessed be He, himself in his glory, with a mighty hand.

—THE PASSOVER HAGGADAH

The rabbis inherited biblical texts that made it evident that the angels played key roles in Israel's origin stories. From the angel's announcement of Isaac's conception to the Exodus narrative and beyond, no hearer of the Torah could deny the role of the angels as heralds, guardians, or executors of divine punishment.[1] And yet, we can see that the rabbis endeavored to override some pivotal stories to reduce the role of angels and to enlarge the presence of God—and to some extent, they were successful, judging by the Haggadah passage above.[2] From the earliest to the latest generations, the rabbis were aware that popular Jewish ritual practices involved angels, but alone among other Jews, the early rabbis took issue with attention to the angels. In this topic, as with every other, the rabbis did not

---

1. On Paul's statement that seems to imply Sadducees do not believe in angels, see Daube's compelling explanation in "On Acts 23." For heraldic angels, see Gen 18. For guardian angels, see Exod 14:19 and Ps 91:11 as well as Dan 10. For destructive angels, see Gen 19:13 and angels of evil in rabbinic sources in chapter 6.

2. Goldschmidt, *Hagadah Shel Pesaḥ*, and see the section below, "Me and Not an Angel" for references in Tannaitic midrashim.

speak univocally, but it is notable that only among the earlier generations of the rabbis (the Tannaim and early Amoraim) do we find the attempt to make angels disappear from Jewish memory and Jewish practice.

In this chapter, I highlight the early rabbinic tendency to downplay the angels' role in Israel's national narratives, and I argue that these interpretive moves betray how powerful conceptions of angels were in ancient Jewish society. Rabbinic sources alone do not allow us to see what was at stake in rabbinic discourses about angels. Only examining rabbinic sources in conversation with biblical, ritual, and liturgical sources demonstrates that rabbinic ideas about angels developed over time and in conversation with non-rabbinic Jewish beliefs and practices.

After discussing the history of scholarship on angels in rabbinic literature, I focus on the earliest rabbinic sources: the Mishnah, Tosefta, the *Mekhiltot* of Rabbi Ishmael and Rabbi Shimon Bar Yohai, *Sifra*, and *Sifre* to Numbers and Deuteronomy, which were redacted by the mid-third century CE in Roman Palestine. Contrary to previous claims, angels do appear in the Mishnah, and rabbinic attempts to minimize the angels' role in foundational narratives (while producing some memorable refrains like "Me and not an angel") ultimately failed to curtail their popularity.

PREVIOUS SURVEYS OF ANGELS IN RABBINIC SOURCES

Three towering scholars of Jewish studies undertook the study of angels in rabbinic literature over the course of the twentieth century: Arthur Marmorstein's study is the earliest (1937), while Ephraim Urbach's (1969) and Peter Schäfer's (1975) studies are the most comprehensive and highlight many important themes and tendencies in the rabbinic corpus.[3] In *The Old Rabbinic Doctrine of God: Essays in Anthropomorphism*, Marmorstein suggested that the key to understanding rabbinic sources about angels lies in recognizing that two underlying and opposing interpretive forces operated in the foundational sources in rabbinic literature. Marmorstein asserted that literal and allegorizing approaches to the body of God operated side by side in the Tannaitic sources, both of which have implications for the rabbis' treatment of the angels. Rabbis of the allegorizing school (like Rabbi Ishmael and his students), assigned every anthropomorphic depiction of God to the angels. They took for granted the presence of angels in many biblical episodes, even as they emphasized the angels' subordination to God. In contrast, rabbis of

---

3. Marmorstein, *The Old Rabbinic Doctrine of God*; Urbach, *The Sages*; Schäfer, *Rivalität zwischen Engeln und Menschen*. A few recent studies deserve attention as well: Rebiger, "Engel und Dämonen," Bar-Ilan, "Prayers of Jews to Angels"; Steinberg, "Angelic Israel"; Septimus, "Talmudic Ritual Texts with Addressees Other Than God."

the literalizing school were not bothered by the anthropomorphic descriptions of God and were not inclined toward seeing angels in every theophany; they viewed the action of angels as undermining signs of God's devotion to Israel. Marmorstein's conflation of rabbinic hermeneutic and theology has been challenged, and much has changed since Marmorstein's day in religious studies.[4] Still, some of his insights about the rabbinic motivations for diverse depictions of the angels hold true. His work reminds us not to essentialize rabbinic sources and to keep in mind the internal interpretive motivations for diverse conceptions of angels. My reading of rabbinic sources affirms that every generation of rabbinic disciples had disagreements about the role of angels.

Urbach, in his chapter on the angels in *The Sages: Their Concepts and Beliefs*, noted that the rabbis were well aware that the Bible had no consistent angelology and they developed their own decisive ideas about angels, always careful to maintain God's omniscience and omnipotence. In his reading of the sources, Urbach sought to discern prevalent theological ideas about the angels, and he privileged the allegorical school of thought in rabbinic literature, which multiplied angels in the sources in order to maintain the transcendence of God. While his collection of the sources is most impressive, the shortcoming of this approach is that it reads early and late rabbinic literature as speaking in one voice and often reads later sources into earlier ones. His analysis focuses upon larger theological implications as well, not the historical development of Jewish belief in angels. Furthermore, Urbach takes rabbinic authority in late antiquity for granted, which I argue prevented him from understanding the function of some traditions about angels. My work places traditions about angels in proper historical context, in conversation with other Jewish authorities and popular non-rabbinic beliefs about angels.

Peter Schäfer's *Rivalität zwischen Engeln und Menschen: Untersuchungen zur Rabbinischen Engelvorstellung* (1975) surveyed and analyzed the diverse conceptions of angels in the Bible and non-canonical Second Temple period sources, and traced continuities and innovations in traditions about angels in rabbinic interpretive literature (midrashim). Schäfer shed light on the theme of human and angelic community in the sources from Qumran, the theme of human and angelic rivalry in the midrashic sources, and the (particularly Palestinian) tendency to uphold the status of Israel over that of the angels. Moreover, he stressed that the rabbis lacked a defined angelology and, instead, addressed beliefs about angels on an ad hoc basis. Some scholars sought to explain the rabbinic attitude to angels as a reaction to Gnosticism.[5] Schäfer, however, focused on the internal Jewish

---

4. Gottstein, "The Body as Image of God in Rabbinic Literature."

5. Altmann, "The Gnostic Background of the Rabbinic Adam Legends"; Schultz, "Angelic Opposition to the Ascension of Moses and the Revelation of the Law."

interest that led to such motifs, namely election theology.[6] The rabbis were intent on conveying God's faithful and loving relationship to Israel in spite of a political reality that might indicate the opposite (namely, that they were in exile and under occupation because they were rejected by God). He reads the insistence on Israel's superiority to the angels as part of an emphasis on their election and their covenant with God. I address this evidence in the next chapter, situating these sources in a wider cultural context, where imitation of angels was being popularized by sectarians, synagogue leaders, and ritual practitioners and the rabbis had to respond with their own framework for relating to the divine.

In his more recent book *The Jewish Jesus*, Schäfer again addressed the topic of angels, this time in the context of Jewish and Christian interaction in late antiquity. Here he writes that "there can be little doubt that Judaism was well on its way to developing or even institutionalizing an intermediate level of angelic powers between God and his creatures and that the rabbis consciously and quite effectively put a halt to this trend."[7] I am less sure that the rabbis succeeded in their efforts than Schäfer is. While no evidence exists to suggest a cult of angels existed among late antique Jews, certainly not from the rabbis, other corpora of evidence help us to see the broad appeal of angels and what the rabbis may have been reacting to. Not only did the rabbis find the idea of "an intermediate level of angelic powers" offensive, but they also found in the angels a threat to their own position of mediation. Along with the evidence from other corpora, this suggests that angels played a larger role in Jewish religious life than has been recognized.

NO ANGELS? DISCUSSIONS OF ANGELS IN THE MISHNAH AND TOSEFTA

"As is well known, there are no angels in the Mishnah"—thus one scholar summed up the absence of angels from the rabbis' founding document.[8] Indeed, the most common word for angels in Hebrew (*mal'akh*, pl. *mal'akhim*) cannot to be found in the Mishnah. This is striking, considering that the creation of demons (Hebrew, *ha-mazzikin*) is enumerated among other creations in this text.[9] It turns out that closer reading locates the angels just below the surface of the text and exactly where we might expect them: in discussions of Jewish popular practice, Jewish prayer, and the relationship between Israel and God. Much as with the opening

---

6. Schäfer, *Rivalität zwischen Engeln und Menschen*, 233.

7. Schäfer, *The Jewish Jesus*, 196.

8. Bar-Ilan, "Names of Angels," 39 (my translation) and echoed by Rebiger, "Angels in Rabbinic Literature."

9. In *m. 'Abot* 5:6 demons are mentioned among the ten things created at twilight of the sixth day of creation.

chapters of Genesis, reference to angelic beings can be found only by reading against the grain. This is no accident: it is likely that the framers of the Mishnah sought to downplay the role of angels in Jewish prayer, practice, and worldview.

The most well-known example of this phenomenon can be found in a rule prohibiting profane sacrifices. In Mishnah *Hullin* 2:8, we find the ruling "He who slaughters in the name of mountains, in the name of hills, in the name of the seas, in the name of rivers, or in the name of wildernesses, his slaughter is invalid."[10] Ostensibly, this prohibition is directed at Jews who offer sacrifices to the spirits of particular places, a common practice in the Greco-Roman Mediterranean. We may recall the amulet from Horvat Kannah that aimed to heal Simon son of Katia "in the name of Yashar Temanuel who sits on the river whence all evil spirits emerge" and other amulets that describe the appointment of angels over places. The amulet written for Simon did not indicate that sacrifices had been offered to the beings appointed over rivers or other places, but it shows that Jews, like other inhabitants of Roman Palestine, believed that divine beings inhabited rivers, caves, mountains, and other natural features.[11] In that amulet, Abraxas's name was invoked alongside lesser-known angels of rivers and crossroads to heal Simon. If some Jews were invoking the names of angelic beings in amulets, some may have been invoking them in more direct offerings as well.

Reviewing stories of angels from the Hebrew Bible may help us see why some Jews might have thought this practice was divinely sanctioned. Judges 6 relates the story of the hero Gideon, whom God selects to lead the Israelites against the Midianites and, concomitantly, to eradicate Israelite idolatry. When the angel of the Lord appears to Gideon to enlist him, Gideon asks for proof that the messenger is indeed an angel.[12] Gideon then makes him a sacrifice of meat and unleavened bread, and miraculously, the angel touches the offering with the tip of his staff and consumes the offering with fire. For some hearers of this tradition, the lesson may have been that the angels of God accept sacrifices—especially when there is no central temple in Jerusalem. The Mishnah's and Tosefta's rulings then, may have been an attempt to clarify biblical precedent that misled some Jews into thinking offerings to angels were appropriate.

---

10. *L-shem*, literally "in the name of" seems to connote "for the purpose of, for the sake of, with reference to" (Jastrow, *Dictionary*, 1590).

11. This order of places recalls the story of the rabbi who sought intercession from mountains, hills, and so on, likely referring to the angels of those places (*b. 'Abod Zar.* 17a). Among the thousands of lamp-votive offerings found in a late antique bath complex in Corinth, one lamp is inscribed with the Greek words: "the angels who dwell upon these waters." See Noy, Panayotov, and Bloedhorn, eds., *Inscriptiones Judaicae Orientis*, 1:340. This site and its relevance for angel veneration is discussed in Cline, *Ancient Angels*, 118–25.

12. See *m. Ber.* 9:5 which quotes Judg 6:12 as precedent for using God's name in a greeting, as the angel there says to Gideon "The Lord is/be with you, man of valor."

The presence of angels in the background of Mishnah *Hullin*'s ruling becomes more obvious when we look at the parallel for this ruling in Tosefta *Hullin* 2:18.[13] There, sacrifices to angels are directly acknowledged: "He who slaughters in the name of the sun, in the name of the moon, in the name of the stars, in the name of the planets, in the name of Michael the great commander of the host, and in the name of the small earthworm—lo, this is considered flesh derived from sacrifices to the dead."[14] The structure of the prohibition is the same, repetition of "in the name of" (*l'shem*), but instead of earthly bodies like rivers and the sea, the Tosefta lists the celestial bodies and most explicitly, the archangel Michael, here the great commander of the host (Hebrew, *sar tzvah hagadol*).[15] As we saw in the previous chapter, Michael is a frequent presence in incantation bowls and amulets. The Tosefta shows that sacrificing to the angelic beings, from greatest celestial divinity (the sun) through the archangel Michael to the smallest earthworm, is unacceptable. In Hebrew, the juxtaposition of these beings makes more sense: the alliteration of the series of terms linked by "in the name of" (*l'shem*), ending with the earthworm (*shilshol*) is pleasing and the contrast between "the great" Michael and the "small" earthworm is sharp and symmetrical.[16] In other words, both consideration of actual practice (invoking the Sun or Michael) and literary reasons (alliteration) contributed to the formation of this statement. Tosefta *Hullin* 2:18 thus preserves a tradition prohibiting sacrifice to a spectrum of divine beings, celestial bodies and angels among them, recalling the Deuteronomic prohibition on worshipping celestial bodies. Meanwhile, the Mishnah has excluded mention of angels, preserving an echo of a practice wherein Jews sacrificed to the spirits of more earthly places like hills and rivers and the wilderness. In general, the Tosefta seems to preserve more traditions that reflect Jewish preoccupation with celestial bodies and angels.[17]

---

13. *t. Hul.* 2:18, ed. Zuckermandel, 503. Both the Mishnah and Tosefta versions are discussed in Schäfer, *Jewish Jesus*, 191. There and in *Rivalität zwischen Engeln und Menschen*, 69, Schäfer suggests that a Baraita in the Babylonian Talmud that combines these two lists was the original version.

14. While Neusner translated this as flesh derived from sacrifices of corpses (*The Tosefta*, 73), I think "flesh derived from sacrifices *to* the dead" is a better translation. The term *zivchei metim* appears once in the biblical sources in Ps 106:28, "They joined themselves also to Baal-peor, / And ate sacrifices offered to the dead." And compare *m. 'Abot* 3:3 where eating from sacrifices to the dead and eating from the table of God are contrasted.

15. Michael's title comes from the unnamed angel in Josh 5:14, who introduces himself as *sar tzeva* YHWH (Bar-Ilan, "Names of Angels," 40).

16. Tzemah Yoreh and Naphtali Meshel helped me make sense of this deceptively simple text in private communication. Meshel pointed out a tradition in *Gen. Rab.* 8:1 (cited in Ben Yehuda's dictionary), which also contrasts the ministering angels and the *shilshol*.

17. For determining when Jews ought to recite the Shema in the evening, the framers of the Tosefta suggest looking to the emergence of the first stars (Ber. 1:1).

We can find more evidence of Jews praying to angels from a tradition preserved in the Palestinian Talmud. In mid-fourth century CE Palestine, a tradition attributed to Rabbi Yudan encouraged Jews to pray to God directly and not to call on Michael or Gabriel in their prayers. This tradition explained that whereas Jews might seek help through bureaucratic agents in their day-to-day lives, in prayer Jews ought to appeal directly to God, bypassing his angelic subordinates:

> Rabbi Yudan said on his own authority: If a man of flesh and blood has a patron, when he is in trouble, he does not suddenly enter his [patron's] presence, but comes and waits at the entrance and calls to a slave or a member of the household, who tells the patron: "there's a man waiting at the entrance to your courtyard," to ascertain whether or not to let him in. But the Holy One, blessed be He, is not like this: "If a person faces trouble, he should cry out neither to Michael nor to Gabriel, but should cry out to Me, and I will answer him immediately."[18]

In the text the rabbi does not just advise Jews to cry out directly to God, but has God assert in the first person that people ought to appeal to him directly. In doing so, this rabbinic tradition portrays God as less transcendent and more like the approachable angels. Perhaps the rabbis worried that invoking angels to convey one's prayers to God could easily transition to invoking angels alone. If Jews were not calling on Michael and Gabriel, there would be no need for the rabbis to criticize this practice.

Whether any room existed for prayers praising God *alongside* the angels is a topic of discussion in the Mishnah. In tractate *Berakhot*, the section of the Mishnah devoted to benedictions, we find discussion of the appropriate liturgical praise of God and, unsurprisingly, whether God should be praised in relationship to his angelic armies.[19] The topic is how one ought to recite the grace after meals in consideration of the number of men present (whether three, ten, one hundred, one thousand or finally ten thousand). In this Mishnah, every exponential increase in the number of men present causes the description of God to become more elaborate: it begins simply with "Let us bless the Lord, our God," but becomes "the Lord, our God, the God of Israel" and finally at the ten thousand mark, escalates to "Let us bless the Lord our God, the God of Israel, the God of Hosts, Who sits upon the cherubim, for the food that we have eaten." The hosts are, of course, the armies of angels. The epithet "Lord of Hosts" for God is quite common in the Bible, in the ritual incantations, and in the liturgy to this day. The prevalence of the phrase "Lord of Hosts" should not make us lose sight of its original angelic connotations.

---

18. See *y. Ber.* 9.1, 13a (Schäfer and Becker, *Synopse zum Talmud Yerushalmi*, 224–27). Schäfer discusses this passage in *Jewish Jesus*, 194, in the context of rabbinic polemic against the Roman system of patronage.

19. *m. Ber.* 7:3. Bar-Ilan acknowledges and dismisses this reference in a caveat, "Names of Angels," 39.

The next epithet for God listed in this prayer is "who sits upon the cherubim," which evokes the guardian figures first introduced at the edge of Eden in Gen 3:24 and described in the wilderness tabernacle of Exod 25:20, and finally in the construction of the first temple in 1 Kgs 6:32. In the idealized era of the tabernacle and the first Jerusalem temple, the presence of God was believed to dwell between the wings of the sculpted cherubim in the chamber known as the Holy of Holies. Reciting this epithet brought to mind an ideal period of worship of God and implicitly a hope for restoration in the future. Such a prayer is in line with the Mishnah's tendency to preserve the memory of the temple in Jewish practice (cf. *m. Ber.* 1:1). In this liturgical prayer recorded by the framers of Mishnah, praise of God with the angelic hosts and cherubim is accepted. A quotation attributed to Rabbi Yose the Galilean closes this section by affirming that God is praised according to the size of the assembly (citing Psalm 68). In an ideal world, past or future, when the masses of Israel eat together, God is praised with the angels and the angelic service of God is affirmed.

Rabbi Yose does not have the last word, however. In the same section, the famous Rabbi Akiva is attributed the question and answer, "What is found in the synagogues? It is one and the same whether there are few or many. [Recite] Blessed is God." This transition, from a discussion of grace after meals among tens of thousands to communal gatherings in the synagogue service, is most unusual. The former refers to an idealized Israel of the future; the latter to synagogues in Roman-occupied Judea. The rabbis rarely refer to synagogue practice to justify their rulings. And here a tradition attributed to Rabbi Akiva seems to use synagogue precedent to discourage the piling on of epithets of God. This statement might be construed as a reality check, but since we know little about synagogue practice in his day, we cannot be sure. We do know that a few centuries later in the synagogue, liturgical praise of the divine hosts, cherubim, and the angels is ever more elaborate (see chapter 5). What can be said with certainty is that traditions attributed to Rabbi Akiva will turn out to be very important in the delineation of the proper relationship between Israel, the angels, and God. Already in this Mishnah, we can see that traditions associated with Akiva downplay the role of angels in the Jewish imagination more broadly and in liturgical practice in particular.

Whereas the Mishnah is oblique in its references to angels, one tradition in *Pirqei 'Abot*, the Jewish equivalent to the Christian *Sayings of the Fathers*, is more direct about the existence of evil spirits or demons. Among the ten fateful things created at twilight at the end of the sixth day, the rabbis specify the creation of demons (Hebrew, *mazzikin*).[20] This pronouncement rejected the myth of fallen angels and its explanation for the presence of disembodied evil spirits in the world.

---

20. See *m. 'Abot* 5:6. *Gen. Rab.* 1:3 is the earliest rabbinic text to collect interpretations about when the angels were created.

The rabbis acknowledged the existence of demons, but only as part of God's creation. The Tannaitic rabbis would flatly contradict the plain meaning of Gen 6:1–4 and read the sons of god (*bnei elohim*) as sons of judges.[21] Still, the founding rabbis included demons in their description of the created world, acknowledging their presence in the invisible realms. Only in the later midrashim of *Genesis Rabbah* do we find the rabbis contemplating the origin of angels as directly (see chapter 6). The presence of angels in the worldview of the framers of the Mishnah requires more careful reading.

A reference to angelic intervention may be hiding in plain sight in a statement attributed to Eliezer ben Yaakov, who said that "he who performs one precept acquires for himself one intercessor, and he who commits one transgression acquires for himself one accuser."[22] In other words, good deeds led to the acquisition of heavenly intercessors—that is, angels that speak on a person's behalf—while transgressions led to the acquisition of accusers in the heavenly court. It is true that in rabbinic literature, a paraclete could refer to an angel, a human intercessor, or an abstract mediating action. That said, already in the Palestinian Talmud, an early generation of Amoraim discuss how one angelic defender can overcome one thousand angelic accusers.[23] Medieval rabbinic traditions made the angels' presence in Eliezer ben Yaakov's statement explicit by restating this adage using the term *mal'akh* rather than the vague intercessor or accuser.[24] I posit that this ambivalence about angels may have led to more subtle references to them among the earliest generations of rabbis. This tradition attributed to Rabbi Eliezer ben Yaakov is thus reflective of the lengths to which the editors of the Mishnah went to suppress or at least obscure the role of angels in Jewish tradition and practice.

ANGELS IN THE TOSEFTA

Although the Tosefta mentions angels more explicitly than the Mishnah, it only contains a handful of traditions that explicitly acknowledge the significance of angels in Jewish origins, practice, and belief (and most of these are concentrated in tracate *Soṭah*, see below). In addition to the ruling from tracate *Ḥullin*

---

21. *Sifre Num* 86 and *Gen. Rab.* 26:5–7. See Reed, *Fallen Angels and the History of Judaism and Christianity*, especially the chapter on "The Interpenetration of Jewish and Christian Traditions: The Exegesis of Genesis and the Marginalization of Enochic Literature."

22. See *m. 'Abot* 4:11. *Paraclete* (παράκλητος) is the loan word used for intercessor here.

23. See *y. Qidd.* 1:9 (Vilna 22b).

24. *Tanh. Mishpatim* §19 on Exod 23:20. If a man performed one precept, he is given one angel; if he performed two precepts, he is given two angels; if he did all the precepts, he is given many angels as it is said (quoting Ps 91:11) "For he will command his angels concerning you," etc. In the Targum to Job 33:23, *paraclete* was used to translate the Hebrew for an intercessory angel (*mal'akh melitz*).

prohibiting sacrifice in the name of the archangel Michael, the idea that piety resulted in angelic guardianship is discussed in two traditions in the Tosefta. The most important early tradition conceptualizing angels in ordinary Jewish life can be found in Tosefta 'Abodah Zarah 1:17, where it is the middle of three rabbinic proscriptions on traveling.[25] The previous halakhah proscribes traveling with caravans because of worries about gentile influence, robbers, an evil wind or spirit, and idolatry. The next two concern the company one keeps as well:

> Rabbi Eliezer, the son of Rabbi Yose the Galilee said "If you see a *Tzadik* [righteous man] set out on a journey and you wish to journey the same way, precede him within three days or follow him within three days so that you may journey with him. Why? Because the angels of peace accompany him as it is said 'for he will command his angels concerning you / to guard you in all your journeys'" (Ps 91:11).[26]

This recommendation does not teach Jews to invoke or appeal to angels for guardianship, but it teaches Jews to imagine that beneficent angels surround righteous individuals. Implicitly, good deeds bring about angelic presence. The tradition attributed to Rabbi Eliezer permits Jews to imagine travel, a hazardous activity in antiquity, with the framework of good company, both human and angelic, in mind. The advice is to travel within three days of the righteous man in order to benefit from his angelic retinue. This tradition is important, as it shows that imagining angelic companionship or guardianship was not alien to the early rabbis, even if they did not encourage it outright. Here angelic presence was a function of piety, not a benefit that had to be pursued through prayer or ritual invocations. Angels of peace accompanied righteous people—no amulets required.

Conversely, the next halakhah in the Tosefta warned about the adverse impact of traveling with an evil man: "If you see an evil man set out on a journey and you wish to journey the same way, precede him by three days or follow him after three days so that you do not journey with him. Why? Because angels of satan accompany him as it is said: "appoint an evil man over him" (Ps 109:6). The rabbis cite the psalm as a prooftext for the idea that God appoints "angels of satan" over "evil" men; it is not demons who are appointed to accompany individuals, but "angels of satan." This belief sounds very much like what is found in the Dead Sea Scrolls, where the "entire world is divided, with each faction including both humans and angels," in keeping with that sect's "belief in predestination."[27] These angels of satan affirm the negative impulses of their human charges. They are not angels of the capital S Satan/Devil, ruler of an underworld, known from the later medieval Christian imagination. As in the rest of the Dead Sea Scrolls, the

---

25. On the topic of travel more broadly, see Hezser, *Jewish Travel in Antiquity*.

26. Ed. Zuckermandel, 461; cf. Lieberman, *t. Šabb.* 17:2, p. 283.

27. Flusser, "The Dead Sea Sect and Its Worldview," in *Judaism of the Second Temple Period*, 1:2.

perception of satan here "generically denotes someone—anyone—who destroys by cutting short the life of human beings."[28] But where the sectarians of Qumran follow a doctrine of double predestination with a very narrow view of human choice, the rabbis emphasized free will, given to the first human and thereafter to every Jew.[29] This halakhah in the Tosefta, then, ought to be understood as emphasizing the choice that Jews have in associating with pious men and their angels or, conversely, with sinful individuals and their angels.

Early rabbinic traditions do not provide more commentary on the idea of accompanying angels, whether good or evil. I can only surmise that the creation story of Genesis 3 provided the prooftext for God's angelic retinue as knowledgeable of Good and Evil and this was combined with biblical prooftexts on angelic guardianship.[30] Only much later rabbinic traditions would elaborate on the idea of good and evil angels accompanying Jews (see chapter 6). It is important to note here that the conceptualization of angels as accompanying Jews was present at an early stage and is not a later or foreign development. We can see echoes of the idea of angelic guardianship in the closing of tractate *Berakhot*, where a section describing the inherent piety of the Jewish people and their many good deeds culminates in a quotation of Psalm 34:8, "The angel of the LORD camps around those who fear Him and rescues them" (*t. Ber.* 6:25). No sage is attributed this saying about the presence of angels, but the biblical prooftext expresses the idea that an angel guards the pious and faithful. By the time of the Tannaitic sages, the idea that multiple angels accompanied or guarded the faithful prevailed. And yet, there is little direct discussion of this idea in early rabbinic sources.[31]

As several scholars have noted, ideas about guardian angels, both good and evil, were shared among ancient Jews and early Christians.[32] The Alexandrian Jewish philosopher Philo wrote that people were assigned two guardians at birth, one good and one evil.[33] Similarly, the Christian thinker Origen, who lived and wrote in Caesarea at the end of his life (d. 253 CE), believed that people either

---

28. Stuckenbruck, "Demonic Beings and the Dead Sea Scrolls," in *The Myth of Rebellious Angels*, 94.

29. Flusser, "The Essene Worldview," in *Judaism of the Second Temple Period*, 1:27.

30. Gen 3:5 and 3:22 refer to the worry that Adam and Eve become like the *elohim*, "like one of us, knowing good and evil" and see Ps 91:11 for angelic guardianship. See chapter 6 for fuller discussion of angels of good and angels of evil.

31. Rosen-Zvi discusses how the Second Temple formulation of two ways or "two angels" may be related to the later rabbinic conceptions of the *yetzer*; see his chapter "*Yetzer* at Qumran: Proto-Rabbinic" in *Demonic Desires*, 44–64, esp. 55.

32. See Flusser's discussion of the "The Two Ways" as a Jewish text that was incorporated into the Didache, a Christian work from ca. 100 CE in "The Essene Worldview," in *Judaism of the Second Temple Period*, 25–31; cf. Flusser "There Are Two Ways," 235–52 [Hebrew]. In "Guardian Angels," Hannah argues that "It is clear that early Christians adopted, with very little variation, Jewish conceptions regarding guardian angels" (432).

33. See Philo, *Quaestiones et Solutiones in Exodus* 1:23; Hannah, "Guardian Angels," 425.

had a good angel or an evil angel assigned to them, depending on the merits of their behavior.[34] As he explains in his Commentary on the Gospel of Matthew, every person was assigned an angel at birth, but the goodness or wickedness of that angel depended on the proportion of the person's virtue or wickedness. The angel amplified or affirmed a person's innate virtue or lack thereof. Origen envisions that the angels and their human charges were works in progress, coupled like husband and wife, and one or the other could lead the way to right behavior and relationship to God. Rabbinic traditions on guardian angels do not dwell on angelic-human relations in such vivid detail but do assume that the pious attract good angels and the impious attract evil angels.

In light of Jewish and Christian beliefs in angelic relations with people, an idiomatic expression found only in the Tosefta deserves further attention. In a heated exchange attributed to Rabban Gamaliel and Rabbi Akiva, the former asked the latter how he dared to contradict the ruling of his senior colleague, but his exact words in Hebrew were: "How dare the angel of your heart transgress the words of your colleague?"[35] Scholars usually do not translate this sentence word for word, but a literal translation may gesture toward the belief in the angel associated with every individual, a belief that happened to transcend religious communal boundaries in Roman Judea and later Palestine.[36] If this is the case, Rabban Gamaliel is said to have asked Akiva not "how dare you?!" but, more euphemistically, "how could your angelic companion let you to be so disrespectful?" This phrasing mitigates the weight of a direct accusation of improper behavior. It may gesture toward how deeply embedded the belief in angelic doubles were in the ancient world, even among the sages. It is ironic that we find this expression applied to Rabbi Akiva, a figure who was associated with opposition to angels in other rabbinic texts, which will be discussed in the next chapter.

Tractate Soṭah of the Tosefta includes three more traditions that mention angels indirectly; in two of these, the angels are incidental to a lesson that the rabbis are imparting.[37] In the third, the ministering angels are observers of the Israelites singing God's praises after the miraculous parting of the sea.[38] In the last tradition, some of the ministering angels that observe the Song of the Sea are mentioned

---

34. See Origen's *Commentary on Matthew* 13.28, discussed in Muehlberger, *Angels in Late Ancient Christianity*, 98–99.

35. My translation of *t. Dmai* 5:24 (ed. Zuckermandel, 56: *hyach malach lybch* . . .); Lieberman, *Tosefta*, notes the absence of these words from the manuscripts before him (1:262–63).

36. Belief in angelic doubles can be found in Mandaeism, Manichaeism, and elsewhere. See discussion of angels in the religions of late antiquity in the conclusion.

37. The rabbis use the example of Abraham running toward the angels (Gen 18) as an example of proper practice with guests (*t. Soṭah* 4:1) and note that God humbles great nations and kings through his angelic subordinates (*t. Soṭah* 3:18).

38. See *t. Soṭah* 6:5 commenting on Exod 15:2.

in passing as the same ones that were antagonistic to humanity's creation. Only a later midrash found in *Genesis Rabbah* explains this description of the angels, according to which the angels protested the creation of humanity.[39] That midrash, in turn, seems to have been prompted by the ambiguous plural in the statement "Let *us* make man" or "humanity" (*adam*, Gen 1:26), which seems to imply that God consulted other beings. According to later midrash, while the angels debated the merits of humanity's creation among themselves, God went ahead and created humanity without their input. While this story is not elaborated upon here in the Tosefta or in other Tannaitic sources, evidently it was already a well-known interpretation of the creation story in Genesis 1. It served to affirm God's omnipotence and cosmic sovereignty, but, secondarily, it imparts the sense that the angels did not even want humankind created. In this framework, people ought to be skeptical of angelic support, since the angels were apparently not on humanity's side to begin with. In the context of the Tosefta, the brief reference to the antagonistic angels serves to highlight the merit of the Israelites' song, forcing those same angels to acknowledge the wonder of earthly (as opposed to heavenly) praise. This short-hand reference to those antagonistic angels in the Tosefta may be read as part of an overall strategy of discouraging interest in angels.[40] The exegesis of the passages about the Exodus narratives forced rabbinic interpreters to wrestle with angels and their role in the Jews' relationship to God, and it is to these sources that we now turn.

"ME AND NOT AN ANGEL": DOWNPLAYING ANGELS IN TANNAITIC MIDRASHIM

In Jewish memory, God led the Israelites through the wilderness, "by day in a pillar of a cloud" and "by night in a pillar of fire" (Exod 13:22). To uphold this memory, the rabbis had to downplay the biblical text. According to the book of Exodus, a nameless angel led the Israelites and protected them through their travels in wilderness (Exod 14:19, 32:34, and Num 20:16, 22:22–27).[41] The fullest description of this representative angel can be found after Israel receives the Ten Commandments and the Law at Mount Sinai, where the text has God proclaim (Exod 23:20–24 NRSV):

---

39. Schäfer has discussed this tradition under the heading of angelic and human rivalry in *Rivalität zwischen Engeln und Menschen* and in *The Jewish Jesus*, 166–69.

40. Rebiger cites a tradition from *y. Šabb.* 6:9 (mistakenly referenced as *t. Šabb.* 6:1), which discusses the righteous and the angels at the end of days ("Angels in Rabbinic Literature," 630).

41. For a study on the angels of Exodus from a biblical studies perspective, see Fischer, "Moses and the Exodus-Angel."

I am going to send an angel in front of you, to guard you on the way and to bring you to the place that I have prepared. Be attentive to him and listen to his voice; do not rebel against him, for he will not pardon your transgression; for my name is in him. But if you listen attentively to his voice and do all that I say, then I will be an enemy to your enemies and a foe to your foes.

When my angel goes in front of you, and brings you to the Amorites, the Hittites, the Perizzites, the Canaanites, the Hivites, and the Jebusites, and I blot them out, you shall not bow down to their gods . . .

In this section, it is not God himself but an angel that accompanies Israel on their journey to the promised land. Obedience to the angel brings God's beneficence, while rebellion against the angel brings God's wrath. The text states that *the name* of God is in the angel, which seems to mean that the angel possesses God's authority.[42] If some Jews looked to angels for mediation, they had biblical precedent for doing so. The rabbis address this issue in several traditions in their midrashim and their refutations have become a part of Jewish memory, particularly through the celebration of Passover.

The statement "not by means of an angel," with which I began this chapter, is found in several places in midrash as well as in all the recensions of the Passover Haggadah, which celebrates God's redemption of the Israelites from Egypt through narrative, benedictions, midrashic comments, and psalms. It seems to be targeting exactly these verses in Exodus cited above, which so emphatically suggest that angelic representatives led the Israelites on their journey. The rabbinic reframing asserts that God alone is responsible for all the saving interventions in Egypt—not the angels in all their various manifestations:[43] "'And the Lord brought us forth out of Egypt,' not by means of an angel, and not by means of a seraph, etc., but the Holy One, blessed be He, himself in his glory, with a mighty hand."[44]

42. The Babylonian rabbis addressed the ramifications of a plain reading of this passage in a tradition that has received much attention (*b. Sanh.* 38b): see Kister, "Metatron, God, and the Problem of the Two Powers; Schäfer, *The Jewish Jesus*, 104–7; Boyarin, "Metatron and the Divine Polymorphy of Ancient Judaism."

43. Cf. this fragment of *Mek. RS Sanya*: "Do I not possess [heavenly] messengers, do I not possess troops, do I not possess *seraphim*, do I not possess angels and [heavenly] beasts and *ophanim* and the wheels of the chariot that I could send to Egypt so that I might bring out My people? But you say, 'Make someone else Your agent!'" (Nelson, 5). This is one of the texts that makes clear that angels, seraphim, and divine messengers were understood as equivalent divine creatures in late antiquity.

44. See Goldschmidt, *Hagadah Shel Pesah*. Flusser argued that this phrase is based on a vorlage of Isaiah 63:9, which was "preserved in the Septuagint, and is also reflected in the War Scroll and the Passover Haggadah" (Flusser, *Judaism of the Second Temple Period*, 61–64). For this phrase in rabbinic sources, see *Mek. RI Ki Tissa* 1 (Horowitz and Rabin, 340; Lauterbach, 493): "'And the Lord spoke unto Moses.' Directly and not through the medium of an angel or a messenger." See also *Sifre Devarim Ha'azinu* 325:1 in Martin Jaffee's online translation.

Implicitly, this emphasis suggests that some Jews believed that God acted through mediators and that the rabbis sought to repress this idea. According to Goldschmidt, even Genizah fragments of the Passover Haggadah which are missing every other midrash still cite this statement.[45] The plain meaning of the expression emphasizes God's active and direct role in Israelite history over and against the angel described in Exodus.[46] This emphatic statement does not directly challenge the prooftext but asserts a framework for Jewish conceptualization of this important narrative that excludes angels from the imagination.

Contributors to the Mekhilta of Rabbi Shimon bar Yohai (fourth century CE) chose a different interpretive strategy to the texts in Exodus that referred to the angelic guardian of the Israelites.[47] Let us examine this source and see how it treats this important angel: "'I am sending an angel before you [to guard you on the way and to bring you to the place that I have made ready]' (Exodus 23:20): This [refers to] a prophet. And thus Scripture says, 'An angel of the Lord came up from Gilgal to Bochim'" (Judg. 2:1). Though the original context makes it self-evident that an angel was appointed by God for leading the Israelites, the sages chose to understand this divine messenger as a prophet instead. Replacing an angelic figure with a human prophet like Moses denies angels a central role in the Israelite origin story. The exegetes here cite a prooftext from the book of Judges, where a messenger reproves the Israelites in the style of the prophets (Judg 2:1–5). Since the next section of the text discusses the death of Joshua ben Nun (Judg 2:6–9), they could interpret the aforementioned messenger as the prophet Joshua himself. To extrapolate from Judges back to Exodus is typical of the rabbis but a stretch nonetheless. I argue that this reading is a reflection of a larger strategy of downplaying the role of angels in the biblical heritage.

A tradition in *Leviticus Rabbah* (dated to the fourth–fifth century CE), where the role of a different angel in the exodus is discussed, also replaces the angel with a prophet and provides a more totalizing explanation for this replacement. The prooftext being discussed is Num 20:16, where Moses sends messengers to recount the exodus event to the king of Edom. The sages quote Moses and then interpret his words. "'And he sent an angel and brought us forth out of Egypt.'

45. Goldin collected all the mentions of this expression in rabbinic literature, particularly elaborating on philological aspects of this expression in *Sifre Deut*, but he was not interested in its historical or theological implications. See Goldin, "Not by Means of an Angel and Not by Means of a Messenger."

46. Yuval placed this expression in the context of Jewish polemic against intermediate figures like Jesus; see *Two Nations in Your Womb*, 79–81.

47. *Mek. RS Kaspa* 81:1 (Nelson, 370). *Mek. RI*, whose subject is the laws of Exodus, stops just before this verse, evidently because it is no longer entirely legal in character. This section of the Mekhilta is dependent on *Midrash HaGadol*, whose antiquity is suspect. If this tradition is not ancient, only a Babylonian Talmudic source remains that refers to this verse (discussed below). For a study of this angel of the Lord at the biblical level, see Rofé, *The Belief in Angels in the Bible and in Early Israel*.

But was he an angel, was it not Moses? and why then was he called an angel? This teaches us that the prophets are called angels."[48] Reading the angel as Moses himself goes against the plain reading of the biblical text. Contrary to the plain meaning of the biblical words of Exod 23:20 and Num 20:16, the rabbis asserted that the appearances of angels in the Torah referred to human prophets only. Steinberg sees in this rewriting an "angelification of the prophets."[49] I contend, however, that the rabbis have less interest in promoting the ancient prophets to the status of angels than in reducing the roles of angels in the Israel's foundational stories. These midrashim suggest that some rabbis were uncomfortable with assigning the angels any significant role in the redemption from Egypt. This is an especially striking tendency, as it is the opposite of the tendency that we see in the Aramaic translations of the biblical writings and the liturgical poetry of the synagogue, which, as we shall see, inserts and multiplies angels in biblical traditions.

The expression appears elsewhere in early midrashim, affirming God's sole role as caretaker of Israel. In the following traditions, God's unique role as a provider of rain and justice is emphasized. Each of the following verses from Deuteronomy is followed by its rabbinic interpretation. In both cases, the sages make explicit that what God promised he would do for the Israelites in the book of Deuteronomy— whether providing rain or executing justice—would be handled by him personally and not by angelic messengers. Deut 11:13–14 states the following:

> If you will only heed his every commandment that I am commanding you today— loving the Lord your God, and serving him with all your heart and with all your soul—then he will give the rain for your land in its season, the early rain and the later rain, and you will gather in your grain, your wine, and your oil.

> "Then I will grant": I—not by means of an angel and not by means of a messenger. (*Sifre Deut* 42)

Elsewhere in this midrash, the rabbis quote Deuteronomy 32:35 ("Vengeance is mine, and recompense") noting that God "personally will exact retribution from them, not by means of an angel and not by means of a messenger" (*Sifre Deut* 325). While in the biblical book of Deuteronomy these statements are soon followed by reaffirmations of God's singularity (reflecting the Deuteronomist's exclusive monotheism), the need to exclude angels in particular likely arose in a context where some Jews were speculating that angels handled the details of God's affairs. These sages strive to make it clear that God is omnipotent and needs no angelic assistants. This rabbinic contention only makes sense in an environment in which other Jews are attracted to the mediating role of the angels. The rabbis' uniquely

---

48. *Leviticus Rabbah* I, 1 (ed. Margalioth, 2).
49. Steinberg, "Angelic Israel," 352.

ambivalent standpoint on angels can only be fully understood with this context in mind.

Although many scholars have juxtaposed the rabbinic prohibition on making images with the gorgeous mosaics of late synagogues, not enough attention has been paid to the role of angels in ancient Judaism in this debate. Reframing this "controversy" in the context of ancient Jewish belief in angels is productive. The Mekhilta of Rabbi Ishmael brings together the prohibitions against making images in Exod 20:4 and worshiping the heavenly host in Deut 4:19.[50] In this synthesis, the rabbis are explicit that making images of the heavenly angels is prohibited:

> But perhaps he may make an image of the sun, the moon, the stars, or the planets? Scripture says: "And lest thou lift up thine eyes unto heaven," etc. (ibid., v. 19). He shall not make an image of any of these. But perhaps he may make an image of the angels, the Cherubim or the Ophanim? Scripture says: "Of anything that is in heaven." As for "that is in heaven," one might think it refers only to sun, moon, stars, and planets? But it says: "Above," meaning, not the image of the angels, not the image of the Cherubim, and not the image of the Ophanim. He shall not make an image of any of these. But perhaps he may make an image of the deeps and the darkness? Scripture says: "All that is in the water under the earth."[51]

Adding to prohibitions against sacrificing to angelic beings, these rabbis ruled out making images of divine beings like cherubim and ophanim. As in the Mishnah and Tosefta, in the Mekhilta divinities of the heavens and the earth are explicitly pronounced off-limits. Since several late antique synagogue mosaics depict the zodiac encircling the personification of the sun (Helios), it is evident that some Jews did not heed these rabbinic prohibitions or understand the biblical law the same way that the rabbis did. There was a multiplicity of opinions among Jews about the proper role of angelic subordinates.

Scholars have tried at great length to solve "the problem" of the Helios mosaics in late antique Palestine.[52] But this problem needs to be placed in the context of the contested significance of angels among ancient Jews. For many Jews, the sun and stars were obviously angelic beings subordinate to God, beings who sometimes

50. Exodus 20:4 (JPS) states "You shall not make for yourself a sculptured image, or any likeness of what is in the heavens above, or on the earth below, or in the waters under the earth." And Deut 4:19, "And when you look up to the sky and behold the sun and the moon and the stars, the whole heavenly host, you must not be lured into bowing down to them or serving them. These the LORD your God allotted to other peoples everywhere under heaven."

51. *Mek. RI, Bahodesh* 6 (Horowitz and Rabin, 225; Lauterbach 322).

52. Smith, "Helios in Palestine"; Foerster, "The Zodiac in Ancient Synagogues and Its Place in Jewish Thought and Literature" [Hebrew]; Weiss, "The Sepphoris Synagogue Mosaic and the Role of Talmudic Literature in Its Iconographical Study"; Miller, "'Epigraphical' Rabbis, Helios, and Psalm 19"; Magness, "Heaven on Earth."

helped the people of Israel. In the song of Deborah, Jews were reminded of the days when "stars fought from heaven, From their courses they fought against Sisera" (Judg 5:20).[53] The author of Sefer ha-Razim included a hymn to "Holy Helios," which is sometimes cited as evidence of the treatise's non-Jewish character, but notably, this hymn was framed by prayers that acknowledged God's sovereignty over the sun (the sun is called Or-pny-el, "light of the face of God" in closing).[54] The synagogue poetry of Yannai, discussed in the next chapter, praised the celestial bodies as creations of God: "The rest of the stars can neither be counted nor reckoned, / Yet all of them are called by name by the Dweller upon the Cherubim."[55] When we think about the images in the synagogue in dialogue with the liturgy recited there, we can understand how Jews perceived the angelic stars to be under God's rule.[56] Making images of the sun alongside other heroes like Abraham and Moses, ancient Jews celebrated the many beings through which God had communicated with the people of Israel. The rabbis were opposed to particular attention to angels, but some Jews related to God through angels, whether through prayer, ritual objects, or figural depictions of celestial angels in the synagogue.

ACKNOWLEDGMENT OF ANGELS
IN EARLY RABBINIC TEXTS

As I noted at the beginning of the chapter, no Jewish reader of the Torah could deny the role of angels in Israelite foundation stories. Schäfer observed that the rabbis addressed angels on an ad hoc basis in their exegesis of biblical text, emphasizing that attention to angels was not systematic.[57] I argue that the pattern of erasure of angels and insertion of angels where it is not mandated by the biblical text at all point to something more intentional. These selections show at least some rabbis acknowledging the most popular motifs associated with angels among Jews in their own time. Alongside sources that read angels out of biblical narrative, halakhic midrashim also preserve traditions that insert angels into biblical scenarios. These additions may point to traditions about angels that could not be denied, but only tamed within a rabbinic framework.

The narrative of Exodus, for example, describes God going through Egypt and striking the firstborn. Multiple instances of first- and third-person singular in this chapter affirm that God acts alone (Exod 12:12, v. 13, and v. 29). At the same time, one biblical verse undercuts this depiction by describing God in the third

---

53. This prooftext is cited in Sifrei Num 84 as evidence of God's love for Israel.

54. See prayers framing Sefer ha-Razim §213; Morgan, trans. Sepher Ha-Razim, 70–72.

55. Lieber, Yannai on Genesis, 304–5.

56. See Münz-Manor, "In Situ: Liturgical Poetry and Sacred Space in Late Antiquity."

57. Schäfer, Rivalität zwischen Engeln und Menschen, 233.

person barring "the destroyer" (*ha-mašḥit*, an angel of destruction) from entering the home of the Israelites: "For when the Lord goes through to smite Egypt and he sees the blood on the lintels and upon the two doorposts, the Lord will pass over the door and will not let the destroyer enter and plague your home (Exod 12:23)." Rather than addressing this textual ambiguity directly and comprehensively, the rabbis ignored it completely in the Mekhilta of Rabbi Ishmael. They focused on the verses where God's singular action is described. The Midrash quotes "'And I will smite' (v. 12). I might understand this to mean, through an angel or through an agent. But it says: 'that the Lord smote all the firstborn' (v. 29)—not through an angel nor through an agent."[58] The rabbis thus precluded the possibility of any destroying agent participating in this awe-full moment in the narrative. Where God was in the role of savior figure, his unique status was affirmed.

Still, just a few verses later, the rabbis seem to allude to the angel of destruction when they described the danger of an Israelite leaving his home in violation of God's instructions: "'*And None of You Shall Go Out*' (v. 22). This tells that the angel, once permission to harm is given him, does not discriminate between the righteous and the wicked."[59] The biblical verse does not refer to the angel of death or destruction, but evidently, the sages could not ignore the presence of God's executing angel altogether. In a later chapter, when God hurls the Egyptians into the sea (Exod 14:27), the rabbis deflected this slaughter of Egyptians to the angels via wordplay: "He delivered them into the hands of youthful angels, so to speak; into the hands of cruel angels."[60] Allusions to the angels in both of these traditions are not necessitated by the biblical text itself, but by popular understandings of the angels' involvement in the Exodus narrative. The rabbis could ignore some traditions, but not all of them. This text is an example of the allegorizing approach of the rabbis, as they replaced God's overly anthropomorphic depiction with angels as actors instead. These examples stand uneasily with the earlier emphasis on God alone smiting the Egyptians, not the angels, within the same composition.

Chapter 14 of Exodus and its exegesis in the Mekhilta of Rabbi Ishmael is illustrative of this tension: angels are inserted where they are not mentioned in the biblical prooftext and excluded where they are in the original text. When the Israelites were encamped by the sea and the armies of Pharaoh came upon them,

---

58. *Mek RI, Bo* §7 (Horowitz and Rabin, 23; Lauterbach, 38).

59. *Mek RI, Bo* §11 (Horowitz and Rabin, 38; Lauterbach, 60).

60. *Mek RI, Besh.* §6 (Horowitz and Rabin, 111; Lauterbach, 163). The Hebrew word for "hurl," *ynʿr* has the root letters of male youths; Egypt (*mizrayim*) sounds like the verb "delivered" (*msrm*). Together, the verbs suggest God delivered Pharaoh's soldiers to youths, hence to youthful angels. The rabbis read male youths as angels, elsewhere associating cherubs with youthful features and further describing them as cruel, presumably because young men are known for their capacity for cruelty. See *b. Sukkah* 5b: "And what is [the form/face of] a cherub? Rabbi Abbahu said: Like that of a child [*ke-ravya*] as in Babylonia they called a baby a *ravya*" (cf. *b. Ḥag.* 13b).

the Israelites cried out in fear to God and Moses (Exod 14:11–12). One rabbinic tradition in the Mekhilta retold this dramatic moment thus: "Then the Israelites said to Moses: 'Moses, our Master, we have not the strength to endure.' At that moment Moses prayed and God caused them to see squadrons upon squadrons of ministering angels standing before them."[61] Moses's prayer temporarily made the invisible realm visible. This popular conception of angels remained with Jews through late antiquity: myriads of the angels were invisible and present to assist the Israelites.[62]

Just a few verses later, the Exodus narrative states, "The angel of God [mal'akh Elohim], who had been going ahead of the Israelite army, now moved and followed behind them; and the pillar of cloud shifted from in front of them and took up a place behind them" (Exod 14:19). The rabbis handled this difficult verse in two ways that completely erased the presence of the angel here: first, with a parable that likens this scenario "To a man who is walking on the road with his son walking in front of him,"[63] deflecting attention from an angelic figure back to God himself entirely. Second, Rabbi Simon is quoted as saying, "Elohim everywhere means the judge. This passage therefore tells you that Israel at that moment was being judged whether to be saved or be destroyed with the Egyptians."[64] The rabbis could only address these difficult verses by completely deflecting attention away from their plain meaning.

If a national guardian angel could not be acknowledged for the Israelites in the exodus narrative, he could be acknowledged and dismissed for the Egyptians. Based on the book of Daniel, Jews believed that each nation had a national angelic guardian. According to the book of Daniel, Gabriel tells the prophet that he is off to fight "the prince of Persia" and that no one is helping him against that nation except "your angelic prince Michael" (10:20–21). This became a widely known and accepted Jewish belief, assumed in the background of many traditions in rabbinic literature.[65] In the Mekhilta of Rabbi Shimon bar Yohai, the rabbis interpreted the so-called Song of Moses and the Israelites (Exod 15:1, "I will sing to the LORD, for He has triumphed gloriously; Horse and driver He has hurled into the sea") as a reference to God hurling *the angel of the Egyptians* into the sea. Hence, they said:

> When Israel saw that the guardian angel of Egypt had fallen, they began to give praise before Him.

---

61. *Mek. RI, Beshallah* §2 (Horowitz and Rabin, 94; Lauterbach, 141).

62. Similarly, see *Mek. RI, Bahodesh* §9 (Horowitz and Rabin, 236; Lauterbach, 340) where God sends angels to comfort the Israelites terrified by the theophany on Mount Sinai.

63. *Mek. RI, Beshallah* §4 (Horowitz and Rabin, 101; Lauterbach, 149).

64. *Mek. RI, Beshallah* §4, (Horowitz and Rabin, 101; Lauterbach, 150).

65. See also Deut 4:19, 32:8–9, Jub 15:31, and Sir 17:17. Flusser discusses the latter three sources in "Heavenly Beings," in *Judaism of the Second Temple Period*, 2:40.

Thus it is said, ". . . He has hurled (into the sea)" (Exod 15:1).

And thus you find that God does not exact punishment from kingdoms until their guardian angels first fall.

As it says in Scripture, "In that day, the Lord will punish the host of heaven in heaven, etc." and after this Scripture says, "and the kings of earth, etc." (Isa 24:21).[66]

Using prooftexts from Isaiah, the rabbis connected the hosts of heaven with the kings of the earth. They admitted the existence of a national guardian angel, but only for the fallen Egyptians. Despite the narratives of Exodus providing an obvious parallel guardian angel figure, the rabbis denied him such a role. They acknowledged the angels in uncalled-for scenarios and deprived the most important angel of any role in Israel's foundational narrative. In the process of differentiating themselves from fellow Jews and non-Jews, the early rabbis chose to uphold a worldview that excluded angels and emphasized relationship with God alone, a topic that will be explored more deeply in the next chapter.

BLURRING THE BOUNDARIES: FROM RITUAL PRACTICES TO RABBINIC INTERPRETATION

One final early rabbinic tradition about the Israelites in the wilderness brings the challenges of conceptualizing divine intimacy without angels into relief. Found both in the Mekhilta of Rabbi Ishmael and the Mekhilta of Shimon bar Yohai, this tradition elaborates on biblical texts that describe God accompanying the Israelites through the desert in a pillar of cloud by day (Exod 13:21, Exod 40:34, and Num 9:15). In the narratives of the Torah, the cloud was a physical manifestation of God's presence in the desert wanderings, on Mount Sinai (Exod 19:16), and in the Tabernacle (Exod 40:34). In the Torah this cloud could be a comforting and, at times, terrifying presence. The rabbis chose to focus on this image's more intimate aspects and in this interpretation in the Mekhilta of Rabbi Ishmael, this pillar of cloud was multiplied into seven clouds of God's glory that surrounded the Israelites: "there were seven clouds, four on the four sides of them [lit. "from the four winds of them"], one above them, one beneath them, and one that advanced before them on the road, raising the depressions and lowering the elevations."[67] In this retelling, the Israelites were surrounded and enveloped by divine presence. The rabbis justified this elaboration through a collation of a number of verses, but

---

66. *Mek. RS, Shirata* 28:2 (Nelson, 126).

67. *Mek. RI, Beshallah* 1, (Horowitz and Rabin, 81; Lauterbach, 124). This same tradition is found in the *Mek. RS, Beshallah* 22:5 (Nelson, 85). See also Tanh. *beShallah* 3:13, "Seven, four from the four winds, one from below, and one from above, and one preceding them, raising the depressions and lowering the elevations."

none explicitly mentions angels.[68] Instead, each interpretation emphasized God's sole intervention.

The Mekhilta's interpretation is striking because the biblical sources lend themselves to an angelic interpretation: Exod 14:19 equivocates between the angel of God preceding the Israelites and the pillar of cloud, implying they were one and the same. The descent of God onto Sinai in a "dense cloud" in Exod 19:16 is recalled in Deut 33:2 as his approach with "myriads of holy ones." The sages who composed *Sifra* betray this understanding when they hashed out whether the ministering angels overheard God's communication with Moses in the cloud in the tabernacle.[69] When the angels are *not* the main topic of debate, the rabbis are willing to admit their presence. Seven clouds would suggest seven angels, but the early rabbis evidently choose not to entertain this interpretation.[70]

A parallel tradition in the Tosefta counts the clouds of glory differently and adds the *Shekhinah* as well, stating:

> God gave his children seven clouds of glory in the wilderness: one on their right, one on their left, one before them, and one behind them and one above their heads and one for the *Shekhinah* that was among them, and the pillar of cloud that would proceed before them would kill snakes and scorpions and burn thorns, barbs, and prickly things and bring down the heights and raise the depressions and he made their way straight as a road that pulled them along.[71]

This language is more vivid than the Mekhilta's in conjuring the divine presence in four directions and in specifying what the manifestations of God on earth would do for his people. This text, of course, also recalls the popular ritual text about the angels on four sides with the *Shekhinah* above. This Toseftan passage raises the possibility that this was a rabbinic tradition adapted by ritual practitioners in Palestine, who exchanged the clouds of glory for individualized angels and who shared the formula with Babylonian ritual practitioners, whereafter it took on a life of its own, entering Syriac, Manichaean, Coptic, and Islamic ritual contexts. Named angels were evidently easier presences to relate to than the more abstract clouds of glory. As discussed at the end of chapter 1, the invocation of the angels on all sides became popular in ritual use and eventually entered the

68. In *Mek. RI*, they cite Num. 14:14, 9:19; Exod 40:36–38. In *Mek. RS*, they carefully count the number of mentions of clouds in Exod 13:21, Num 14:14, Num 9:19, Exod 40:36–38, adding up to seven.

69. *Sifra Nedavah* 2.9.

70. Cf. *Sifre Zuta* 10 (Horowitz, Jerusalem, 1966): "This teaches that seven clouds of glory were with them, one in front of them, and one behind them, and one to their right, and one to their left, and one upon their heads because of the sun, and one below their feet so they would not be walking barefoot, and the cloud of the *Shekhinah* was three days ahead of them bringing down mountains, raising ravines and making them a way and a path to go forth" (my translation).

71. My translation of *t. Soṭah* 4:2 (Lieberman, 645).

fixed Jewish liturgy. This visual motif represents an interface between rabbinic, ritual, and liturgical texts; it shows sages, ritual practitioners, and later liturgical poets in conversation with each other as well as the adjacent religious communities of the late antique world. Reconstructing the conversation among Jews about angelic presence helps us understand not only the development of Jewish beliefs and practices but also late antique religious beliefs on angels more broadly.

CONCLUSION: THE TANNAIM ON ANGELS

The early rabbinic sources, properly situated in the context of popular belief in angels, show the rabbis carefully negotiating with inherited traditions about angels. Jewish interest in angels is addressed in all of the earliest rabbinic compositions: the Mishnah, the Tosefta, and the Tannaitic midrashim. Rulings in the Mishnah and Tosefta prohibited worship of angels but acknowledged that God is properly praised with the angelic hosts. Strikingly, a few Toseftan traditions admit that pious Jews can count on angelic guardianship as well. People required frameworks to conceptualize the beings of the invisible realms. Legal instructions and stories had the power to teach Jews to imagine God as present with them—without any angelic interference—or to teach the Jews to conceptualize the angels with them on their journeys. Aside from the exceptional examples noted above, no early rabbinic tradition provided a framework for engaging with angels.

As I demonstrated in this chapter, the Tannaim discouraged imagining angels in retellings of the Exodus narratives. For the rabbis, the Exodus was the age of the most intimate relationship between God and Israel. The rabbis could not permit angels to interfere in that relationship. Taking a wider view of contemporary Jewish sources and attitudes toward angels helps to clarify what the rabbis were responding to and how they related to other Jews and developed their views of the invisible realm. From the standpoint of the rabbis, the role of angels in Jewish religiosity was still up for debate at this time. The rabbis would continue to wrestle with the problem of relating to God and the angels, especially when people sought to imitate the angels, a problem which is the subject of the next chapter.

4

In the Image of God, Not Angels

Rabbinic Sources

Rabbi Pappias also interpreted "Behold, the man is become as one of us" (Gen 3:22)—like one of the ministering angels. Rabbi Akiva said to him: "That is enough, Pappias."

—MEKHILTA OF RABBI ISHMAEL

He [Rabbi Akiva] would say "Beloved is man for he was created in the image [of God]; still greater was the love in that it was made known to him that he was created in the image [of God], as it is written, 'For in the image of God he made humankind'" (Gen 9:6).

—MISHNAH AVOT

As these two traditions from early rabbinic texts indicate, the relationship among people, angels, and God was a contested issue in the first centuries of the Common Era.[1] Among other aspiring leaders in Roman Palestine, the rabbis tried to offer fellow Jews ways to conceptualize an intimate relationship with God. This was particularly challenging in the face of the catastrophic failed revolts, with the province under Roman occupation, and with many Jews enslaved and displaced. After the destruction of the temple, Jews had to reconceptualize their relationship with God and the attendant angels. In this chapter, I argue that there is a long history of Jews imagining the angels surrounding them, especially in congregational settings, and that the early rabbis developed an alternative framework to overcome this view. The assertion about God's love and human likeness to God ought to be read as one rabbinic response to Jewish interest in relating to the angelic realm. The rabbis offered fellow Jews a way of relating to God that would arm them with confidence on the one hand and preclude other intermediaries, namely angels, on the other.

---

1. The first is *Mek. RI, Beshallah* §7 (Horowitz and Rabin, 112; Lauterbach, 1:164); parallel in *Gen. Rab.* 21:5 (MS Vat. 30) and 8:4. See also *Mek. RS, Beshallah* 26:4 (Nelson, 115). The second is *m. 'Abot* 3:14.

I begin by reviewing prophetic texts attesting to angelic presence in the Jerusalem temple and explain how these visions of angels came to play a role in conceptions of angelic fellowship and imitation in the Jewish imagination. I highlight how generations of ancient Jews from the Second Temple period through the first century CE adopted imitation of the angels as a practice, particularly in communal settings. In the next two sections, I trace the development of rabbinic traditions that upheld a relationship with God alone and imitation of God alone, rather than imitation of or fellowship with angels. I argue that these traditions are responses to angelic imitation among Jews. Through close reading of rabbinic traditions, I show how the rabbis reacted to other Jews and attempted to draw boundaries differentiating themselves from fellow Jews.

Only a diachronic examination of a wide array of sources provides an accurate account of the role of angels in the formative period of Judaism and fully contextualizes rabbinic statements about the imitation of God. Ultimately, the rabbinic contentions studied here did not prove convincing to most Jews, which will become clear in the next chapter, where I discuss imitation of angels in Jewish synagogal settings. Nevertheless, it is worth examining this "way not taken" to appreciate the intellectual investment of the rabbis in conceptualizing their relationship with God and the invisible realm. Only by carefully analyzing and contextualizing rabbinic texts can we see how the rabbis reacted to Jewish preoccupation with angels and changed their attitudes to angels over time.

ANCIENT JEWS AND THE ANGELS: FELLOWSHIP AND IMITATION

Lingering in angelic company was certainly a concern for pious Jews in the ancient Mediterranean, whether they were priests in the temple, sectarians in the Qumran community, attendees of Paul's congregations, or Jews in late antique synagogues. To understand the roots of this belief, we must return to Isaiah's vision of the seraphim. In a highly influential passage firmly attributed to the historical Isaiah, we find the idea that God and his winged retinue inhabited the temple: "In the year that King Uzziah died, I beheld my Lord seated on a high and lofty throne; and the skirts of His robe filled the temple. Seraphs stood in attendance on Him." (Isa 6:1–2). The belief that God and his retinue were present in the earthly temple correlated with the prestige of the Solomonic temple and the unassailable character of Jerusalem, which are resolutely upheld by Isaiah.[2] In this text, then, the

---

2. This belief stands in continuity with the belief that God was physically present on earth surrounded by the angelic hosts in the wilderness tabernacle (discussed in chapter 3 and see *Sifra Nedavah* 2.9). Concrete details in this passage from Isaiah make it evident he is describing the earthly temple, not a heavenly one (see the doorposts of v. 4 or the coal from the altar of v. 6).

priest and prophet Isaiah saw God in the temple and the invisible winged beings worshipping Him. Modern biblical scholars confidently state that seraphim and cherubim were in a typologically separate category from angels.[3] Centuries later, however, Jews understood all of these beings as angels as well.[4] Isaiah's vision provided the only eye-witness account of how otherworldly beings worshipped God. For this reason, their liturgical praise (known as the Qedushah or Sanctus) eventually became a central part of Jewish and Christian liturgy.[5]

The Jerusalem temple never fully recovered from the loss in reputation it suffered with the Babylonian destruction.[6] Ezekiel's vision of the departure of the heavenly throne from the temple proved particularly influential. No biblical text following Ezekiel dwells on the imagery of God in the earthly temple with his angelic retinue, but Zechariah's visions come close.[7] Zechariah's symbolic visions have often been seen as precursors to the apocalyptic genre because of their complex imagery and the omnipresence of angelic figures.[8] The third chapter's vision is particularly important as the scene opens with Joshua standing between the angel of the Lord and the accuser. Although not explicitly set in the temple, this vision is significant in according the High Priest the privilege of moving among the angels of the divine council and in bringing together the imagery of the heavenly court with the earthly temple (Zech 3:6–7):

> And the angel of the LORD charged Joshua: "Thus said the LORD of Hosts, 'If you walk in My ways and if you keep my service, then you will render judgment in my House and you will administer my courts; I will give you access to those who are standing here.'"

The High Priest is said to give judgment in the House of God, clearly the courts of the temple on Earth, even as he is granted access to the divine council. ("Those standing here" clearly refers to the angels in the Heavenly Court.[9]) In the absence of the monarchy, explain Carol Meyers and Eric Meyers, "the priesthood filled this gap in social organization and . . . the temple precinct rather than the palace became the seat of justice."[10] They also point out the innovative nature of "priestly

---

3. Hartenstein, "Cherubim and Seraphim in the Bible."

4. Newsom, "Angels: Old Testament."

5. For more on the different trajectories of these liturgical verses, see Gerhards, "Crossing Borders—the Kedushah and the Sanctus." Following a separate trajectory, the thrice-repeated "holy" would become part of the fixed Christian liturgy in the fifth century, mainly due to John Chrysostom's influence. The *Qedushah*'s role in the synagogue is discussed in the next chapter.

6. Himmelfarb, *A Kingdom of Priests*, 20.

7. Himmelfarb draws attention to the Enochic writings' debt to Ezekiel's throne vision, especially God's departure from the temple (*Ascent to Heaven*, 10–13).

8. Collins, "From Prophecy to Apocalypticism."

9. Meyers and Meyers, "Haggai, Zechariah," 197.

10. Meyers and Meyers, "Haggai, Zechariah,", 195.

access to the Divine Council," which they see as directly correlated with the priests' assumption of judgeship, a role that necessitated divine input.[11] Overall, the prophecies of Zechariah show evidence of a conception of priests who interact with the angels in the second temple in Jerusalem.

If angels were found wherever God was properly worshipped, it is no wonder that the sectarians at the Dead Sea Community insisted polemically that the angels of holiness were in their midst, not in the inferior Jerusalem temple. The sectarians at Qumran believed that the corrupt priests in Jerusalem, in charge since the Maccabean revolt, repelled the divine presence. The sectarians might have lacked the visible manifestations of power and authority, but they believed that the invisible angels' presence with them substantiated their claims. In the Community Rule found at Qumran, high purity standards were explained with reference to maintaining the presence of the angels in the community:

> No man afflicted by any form of human uncleanness shall enter the assembly of God; no man afflicted by [any of] these shall hold a position in the congregation.
>
> No one afflicted in his body, crippled in his feet or his hands, lame, or blind, or deaf, or dumb, or afflicted in his body with a physical defect visible to the eye, or an old and tottery man unable to keep still in the midst of the congregation—none of these shall en[ter] to take their place [in] the midst of the congregation of men of renown because the angels of holiness are [in] their [congregat]ion.[12]

The text here combines language from a number of biblical sources on priestly standards and on maintaining holiness because God is in the camp.[13] What is new is the insistence that angels of holiness are present in the congregation. The sectarians even composed a liturgical text, which presents itself as the liturgy of the angels, wherein angels were envisioned as priests in a heavenly temple, praising God.[14] Reciting this liturgy, the sectarians could conceive of themselves as angelic priests, with unique access to heavenly mysteries and angelic fellowship.[15]

---

11. Meyers and Meyers, "Haggai, Zechariah,", 197.

12. See 1QSa II.3–12, known as the Community Rule (*Serekh ha-Yaḥad*); Knibb, *Qumran Community*, 2:151. Another very similar statement appears in the *Damascus Document* (4QD^b, Fragment 17): "And no-one stupid or deranged should enter; and anyone feeble-minded and insane, those with sightless eyes, [and] the lame or one who stumbles, or a deaf person, or an under-age boy, none [of] these [shall enter] the congregation, for the ho[ly] angels [are in its midst]" (trans. from Martinez, *The Dead Sea Scrolls Translated*, 54; cf. CD XV.15–17 on p. 39).

13. See Lev 21:18, Exod 4:11, Deut 23:14. Knibb, *The Qumran Community*, 152.

14. Newsom, *Songs of the Sabbath Sacrifice*, and "'He Has Established for Himself Priests'" Alexander, *Mystical Texts*.

15. For further discussion, see Dimant, "Men as Angels;" Hayes, "'The Torah Was Not Given to Ministering Angels'"

Among the books found in the library of Qumran was the book of Jubilees. The author of this book was anxious about overcoming sectarian divisions within the people of Israel and used the angelic ideal as a call for unity.[16] The author asserted that by imitating the angels' observance of the Sabbath and circumcision, the observant men and women of Israel could resemble the angels and stand in fellowship with the angels. Sabbath and circumcision were two of the most distinctive markers of Jewish identity in antiquity. The author of Jubilees elevated these practices to the heavenly realm. Warning that whoever is not circumcised would be cut off from Israel, the author writes, "For this is what the nature of all the angels of the presence and all the angels of holiness was like from the day of their creation. In front of the angels of the presence and the angels of holiness he sanctified Israel to be with him and his holy angels" (*Jub.* 15:27).[17] The author asserts that the angels were created circumcised, implying that when parents circumcise their sons, they not only fulfill divine obligation but enable their sons' bodies to match the physical holiness of the angels. Already in the Second Temple period, some Jews proposed using angelic imitation as a call for unity and differentiation from other peoples.

In the first century CE, Paul warned the women of Corinth to veil their heads while praying in the congregation "because of the angels" (1 Cor 11:10). Like the desert sectarians, Paul assumed the angels were present in his congregation and that this was so self-evident that it required no further explanation. The presence of the angels required decorous behavior and dress, especially among women, who, according to the myth of the Watchers, had seduced the fallen angels.[18] Paul used belief in angelic presence to discourage disruptive behavior in his congregations. Paul's polemic shows that some first-century Jews believed that God and his angels were present in their congregations, even before the temple's destruction. Later Christians would also adopt this belief and it became more widespread in religious practice in late antiquity. In time, practicing a high level of holiness to commingle with the angels was seen as possible not only in sectarian settings but also in urban congregations.

Meanwhile, at the Jerusalem temple, the Jewish priests themselves continued to uphold the idea that God and the angels were in the temple with them. In the late first century CE, the Jewish historian Josephus (himself of priestly descent) recounted the sound of the angels and God's departure from the temple only on the eve of the Roman conquest: "For before sunset throughout all parts of the

16. Compellingly described in Himmelfarb, *Kingdom of Priests*, chapter 2; she places the composition of *Jubilees* between 133 and 100 BCE (p. 77).

17. Vanderkam, *The Book of Jubilees*, 92.

18. Definitively discussed in Stuckenbruck, "Why Should Women Cover Their Heads Because of the Angels (1 Corinthians 11:10)," in *The Myth of Rebellious Angels*.

country chariots were seen in the air and armed battalions hurtling through the clouds and encompassing the cities. Moreover, at the feast which is called Pentecost, the priests on entering the inner court of the temple by night, as their custom was in the discharge of their ministrations, reported that they were conscious, first of a commotion and a din, and after that of a voice as of a host, 'We are departing hence.'"[19] Underlying this statement is the view that when God departed from the temple, his multitudinous retinue departed with him. Josephus's account bears a striking resemblance to earlier descriptions of angelic warriors who do battle in the heavens on behalf of the nation of Israel.[20] His account also reflects an understanding of God together with his angels in the temple. Josephus also alludes to Ezekiel's throne vision, which states that the sound of the creatures moving was "a tumult like the din of an army" (Ezek 1:24) and Isaiah's description of God preparing to do away with Babylon, which sounds like "a tumult on the mountain—as of a mighty force" (Isa 13:4). For some Jews, God, the angels, and the priests were believed to be in close proximity in the First *and* Second Temple period.[21] After the second temple's destruction, some Jews had to reconceptualize their way of communicating with God, but some Jewish congregations had already been imagining the angels with them for decades.

THE RABBIS' RESPONSE: RELATIONSHIP
WITH AND IMITATION OF GOD ALONE

While some Jews looked to the angels for proper behavior, some early rabbis encouraged their disciples to look to God alone as their model. I posit that statements from the Mishnah through the Mekhilta and the Babylonian Talmud that use the framing device "beloved are (the people of) Israel" (*havivin yisra'el*) must be understood as part of a larger argument in antiquity about the relationship of Jews to God and the angels. While Peter Schäfer has investigated some of the same material under the heading of Israel's rivalry with the angels, I see a different issue at stake for the rabbis. In my reading, rivalry is not so much at stake as how Jews are to imagine and relate to the invisible realm.[22] Surviving ritual, rabbinic, liturgical, and early mystical Hekhalot texts reflect different frameworks for imagining relationship with the invisible realm. We have seen how ritual texts offered Jews several options for relating to this realm (God alone, the angels alone, God and the

19. Thackeray, trans., Josephus, *The Jewish War* 6.299 (LCL 210: 264–65).

20. Cf. Dan 10:13–21 and 2 Macc. 5:1–4 description of people seeing visions of angelic armies fighting over Jerusalem for forty days.

21. See Luke 1:11, where Zechariah encounters an angel on the right side of the altar of incense in the Temple.

22. See the summary of Schäfer's work in chapter 3 under "Previous Surveys of Angels in rabbinic sources."

angels, other biblical figures, etc.). The early rabbis offered Jews several options too. Many statements attributed to Rabbi Akiva and his followers strove for focus on God alone and imitation of God alone, while most Jews, I argue, chose to imagine the angels and to focus on imitation of the angels instead.

It is from this perspective that we must understand the statement in the Mishnah attributed to the famous sage Akiva, which established the principle of imitation of God, and which was influential for generations to come:

> Beloved is man for he was created in the image [of God]; still greater was the love in that it was made known to him that he was created in the image [of God], as it is written, "For in the image of God he made man" (Gen 9:6).
>
> Beloved are Israel for they were called children [of God]; still greater was the love in that it was made known to them that they were called children of God, as it is written, "You are the children of the Lord your God" (Deut 14:1).
>
> Beloved are Israel, for to them was given the precious instrument; still greater was the love, in that it was made known to them that to them was given the precious instrument by which the world was created, as it is written, "for I give you good teachings; do not forsake my Torah (Prov 4:2).[23]

Noteworthy in this passage is the refrain "beloved are Israel" (*ḥavivin Israel*). Each time this refrain is employed, the semblance, the relationship, and mutuality of the people of Israel and God are emphasized. The first statement is most broad, asserting the beloved status of the Israelites before God. God's love for them is made known in that they are made in God's image, and that the Torah tells them so. The next statements emphasize that Israel is the sole recipient of this love—they are beloved because they were called the children of God and because they alone were given the Torah.

Whether people were created in the image of God was not a settled question in antiquity, even among Jews. Some rabbis upheld creation in the image of God and yet seemed to admit it was a tenuous position. In a tradition recorded both in the Palestinian Talmud and *Genesis Rabbah*, so-called heretics questioned the use of the plural in Gen 1:26 to describe creation of man ("Let *us* make man in *our* image, after *our* likeness"), asking whether other divinities were involved in the creation of humanity.[24] Rabbi Simlai responded by pointing out that the next verse in Genesis returns to the singular "And God created the human in *his* image," not *their* image, suggesting creation in the image of God alone. Interestingly, this is one of a series of traditions wherein the rabbi's students tell their master that they do

---

23. *m. 'Abot* 3:14. All the biblical proof texts are in the marginalia of MS Kaufmann (fol. 171r, see 3:17); trans. Danby, *Mishnah*, 452, with updated translations of Bible.

24. *Gen. Rab.* 8:9 (Theodor and Albeck, 62); *y. Ber.* 9:1. These midrashim are discussed in Schäfer, *Jewish Jesus*, 27–37.

not find his answer convincing, albeit only once the outsiders have left the discussion. Rabbi Simlai's response was that the plural "in our image" in Genesis must be understood as referring to the image of God, Adam, and Eve altogether.[25] This would imply that humanity was made in the image of the first humans and God.

Meanwhile, in the context of discussions of human life and capital punishment, other Tannaim emphasized the creation of humans in the image of Adam alone, not God: "For a man strikes many coins from the same die, and all the coins are alike. But the King, the King of Kings, The Holy One [blessed be He] strikes every man from the die of the First Man, and yet no man is quite like his friend" (*m. Sanh.* 4:5). This passage presents an analogy between creation of humans in the image of Adam and the minting of coins. By analogy, the rabbis insert one step of remove between God and humans without appealing to the angels but also without addressing the topic of divine-human resemblance directly.

The formulation attributed to Rabbi Akiva on creation in the image of God held sway for generations of rabbis, but the surviving evidence suggests other rabbis' answers may have proved more attractive to Jews, such as that attributed to Rabbi Pappias, which emphasized that humanity was created in the image of the angels:

> Rabbi Pappias also interpreted: "Behold, the man is become as one of us" (Gen 3:22), like one of the ministering angels. Said Rabbi Akiva to him: "That is enough, Pappias." He then said to him: "And how do you interpret: 'Behold, the man is become as one of us'" Said Rabbi Akiva: "'As one of us' does not mean like one of the ministering angels. It only means that God put before him two ways, the way of life and the way of death, and he chose for himself the way of death."[26]

According to this midrash, Rabbi Pappias proposed that humanity was made in the image of the angels, partially because of the first-person plural pronoun in verse 22 (Hebrew, *mimenu*). Rabbi Akiva's response was that the meaning of the comparison between humans and God is not about angelic resemblance, but about divine knowledge, thus adhering to the plain meaning of the rest of verse 22 in Genesis ("as one of us, knowing good and bad, what if he should stretch out his hand and take also from the tree of life and eat, and live forever!"). Without awareness of how many Jews were preoccupied with resembling angels, Pappias's interpretation would seem forced at best. I maintain that comments like Pappias's and many others' need to be contextualized in light of Jewish preoccupation with relating to the angels.

---

25. *Gen. Rab.* 8:9 (Theodor and Albeck, 63).

26. *Mek. RI, Beshallah* §7 (Horowitz, 112; Lauterbach, 1:164); parallel in *Gen. Rab.* 21:5 (MS Vat. 30) and *Gen. Rab.* 8:4. See also *Mek. RS, Beshallah* 26:4 (Nelson, 115).

This is one of a series of challenges that Pappias posed to Akiva collected together in the Mekhilta of Rabbi Ishmael.[27] Arthur Marmorstein argued that Pappias belonged to the allegorical school of thought within the early rabbinic movement, which preferred the idea that humanity was made in the image of the angels; Marmorstein located Rabbi Akiva, on the other hand, in the literal school of thought, which was more comfortable with anthropomorphic depictions of God. In my reading, not only anthropomorphism was at stake for the rabbis but also the deeper implication of the relationship of humanity, the Jews in particular, to God. If Jews could relate to God directly, imagine God truly present for them, presumably as Akiva was able to, they would be unlikely to be drawn toward other intermediaries, angelic or human.

What was at stake was not just creation in the image of God or the angels, but the ability to imagine relationship to God directly, beyond an abstract notion of covenant. This emphasis on relationship can be seen in the way Akiva was quoted by later generations in stories of God's intimate care for Israel. One of Rabbi Akiva's students, Rabban Simeon ben Gamaliel, was said to have used Akiva's words when he explained how the Israelites received manna in the wilderness: "Come and see how *beloved the Israelites* [*havivin yisra'el*] are by him by whose word the world came into being. Because they are so much beloved by him, he made for them a change in the natural order of things. For their sake he made the upper region like the lower and the lower like the upper."[28] The "lower" and "upper" regions are how the rabbis refer to the heavenly and earthly realms. God engaged with the Israelites directly when he traveled with them in the wilderness and provided them with food much as a parent might feed a child. By being in the desert wilderness with them, God made the earthly realms like heaven and by descending from heaven to the earth, he made the heavens more like earth. Intimate relationship is stressed in this story.

Two of Rabbi Akiva's other students are also attributed sayings with the refrain "Beloved is Israel" although these are recorded only in the Babylonian Talmud in conjunction with Tannaitic midrashim. Rabbi Simeon ben Yohai is attributed the following rumination on the loving relationship of God and Israel in exile, recorded also in the Mekhilta of Rabbi Ishmael:

Come and see how beloved are Israel [*havivin yisra'el*] before the Holy One blessed be He—everywhere that they were exiled, the *Shekhinah* went with them. They were exiled to Egypt, the *Shekhinah* was with them as it is said: "Lo, I revealed myself to the house of your father when they were in Egypt" (1 Sam 2:27). They were exiled to Babylonia and the *Shekhinah* was with them as it is said: "For your sake I send to Babylon" (Isa 43:14). And even in the future when they are to be redeemed, the

27. *Mek. RI, Beshallah* §7 (Horowitz, 112–13; Lauterbach, 1:164–65).
28. *Mek. RI, Vayassa,* §2 (Horowitz, 160–61; Lauterbach, 1:234).

Shekhinah will be with them as it is said: "Then the Lord your God will return with your captivity" (Deut 30:3). It does not state He will bring [the exiles] back, but *He* [God] will return, which teaches that the Holy One, blessed be He, returns with them from the diaspora.[29]

Countering ancient religious beliefs that connect divinities to specific locales, this tradition emphasizes that even in exile, God is present with the Jewish people. The redactors combined Akiva's refrain with this evocative tradition from the Mekhilta of Rabbi Ishmael to emphasize God's close relationship with his people wherever they went. The proximity of the divine to human believers in the earthly plane mattered and had to be articulated by the rabbis.

This point is emphasized in the Talmud by the discussion that immediately follows about where exactly the divine presence is in late antique Babylonia. The anonymous redactors ask in which synagogues God's presence dwells, and a terse story is introduced, featuring the third-generation Babylonian rabbi Rav Sheshet in the "rebuilt synagogue in Nahardea," where the "*Shekhinah* came, but did not go out." This rabbinic story portrays God's ministering angels as jealous and pestering the rabbi as he attempted to linger in the presence of the *Shekhinah* in the synagogue. When Rav Sheshet called attention to his wretched state and appealed to God to intervene on his behalf, God duly stops the angels. Angels in this imagining only interfere with a rabbi's ability to linger in God's presence.

We might contrast the awful angels in this story with the rabbinic and ritual motif of the divine presence on four sides with the *Shekhinah* (see end of chapters 1 and 3). In the incantation bowls and amulets, the angels are explicitly on four sides while in the halakhic midrashim, those positions were held by clouds of glory, vague enough to refer either to God or the angels. Whereas the ritual evidence is intended to comfort and inspire with its imagery of the harmony of the angels together with the *Shekhinah* surrounding an individual, in this rabbinic story the ministering angels that accompany the *Shekhinah* are a nuisance at best. Considering the emphasis on praying with the angels that we will encounter in synagogue poetry, this image of angels interfering with prayer in the synagogue is particularly jarring (and strikes me as polemical considering the Babylonian attitude toward piyyut).[30] The quotation of Akiva's refrain, combined with this story, emphasizes that the relationship with God was at stake and so too was the exclusion of the angels. These rabbinic disciples were encouraged to imagine the *Shekhinah* alone when they desired a sense of divine presence, a divine presence that was available to them even in exile.

---

29. *b. Meg.* 29a; cf. *Mek. RI*, Pisha, Bo §14 (Horowitz, 51). See Fishbane, "Myths of Participation and Pathos," in *Biblical Myth and Rabbinic Mythmaking*, 134–35.

30. Langer, "The Language of Prayer: The Challenge of Piyyut," in *To Worship God Properly*, 110–36.

Similarly, the second-century CE Rabbi Yose is attributed the statement "Beloved are Israel [*havivin Israel*], for scripture did not require them to have an intermediary" only in the Babylonian Talmud.[31] In the context of the Talmudic argument, it is cited to support the description of the arrangement of furniture in the Holy of Holies, which the High Priest could enter directly, not circuitously, because "Beloved are Israel, etc." Like Akiva's saying in *'Abot*, this statement emphasizes God's direct relationship with Israel. It encourages unmediated interaction with God rather than roundabout worship techniques or attention to popular intermediaries like the angels. Notably, over 60 percent of incantation bowls from Babylonia appealed to other intermediaries alongside God, and only about one quarter of incantations appealed to God alone. Rabbinic circles in Babylonia likely knew about the Jews of Nippur and the region of Mesene, some of whom commissioned incantation bowls. When Babylonian sages recited Rabbi Yose's words in late ancient Babylonia, they were distancing themselves from Jews who were invoking angelic intermediaries. In the Babylonian context, Yose's words from the second century CE became a reaffirmation of their own stance on Israel's direct relationship with God. While the statement attributed to Rabbi Yose reminded them that they needed no other intermediary, Rabbi Simeon ben Yohai's statement emphasized the intimate presence of the *Shekhinah* with the Israelites wherever they go in exile. Both echo the words attributed to Akiva in the Mishnah about the Israelites' loving relationship with God.

An anonymous Baraita in the Talmud declares that "Beloved are Israel (*havivin Israel*) that the Holy One, blessed be He, surrounded (*sybbn*) them in mitzvot, tefillin upon their heads, tefillin upon their arms, and tzitzit on their clothes and a mezuzah for their gates."[32] The statement underscores some of the physical markers rabbinic Jews wore during prayer or placed in their homes.[33] This Baraita paraphrases Rabbi Meir's statement in the Tosefta that "there is not a single member of Israel who does not have seven mitzvot surrounding (*mekifot*) him: tefillin upon his head, tefillin upon his arm, mezuzah, four tzitzit surround him" (*t. Ber.* 6:25). Interestingly, in the Tosefta this passage ends with a quotation of Psalms 34:8 about the angel of the Lord encamping around (*sbyb*) those who are pious. This saying is recast in the Babylonian Talmud to fit into the Akivan framework (with the refrain *havivin Israel*) and with stress on God's love alone; no allusions to the angels exist in this reformulation. This reformulation supports my argument that the emphasis attributed to Akiva on imitation of God alone effectively excluded angels from the Jewish imagination of some rabbinic disciples. We might also note here that these rabbis preferred that Jews use these sanctioned accessories

---

31. *b. Yoma* 52a.
32. *b. Menḥ.* 43b.
33. Cohn, *Tangled Up in Text*.

(tefillin, tzitzits, mezuzahs) rather than wear amulets or place incantation bowls in their home for protection. These rabbis asserted that Jews already had ways of surrounding themselves with markers of relationship with God.

In a passage in the Babylonian Talmud, we see the rabbis downplaying the significance of the seraphic praise from Isaiah (the "Holy, Holy, Holy" known as the *Qedushah*, the subject of the next chapter), explicitly in confrontation with Jewish interest in praying like the angels.[34] The invisible hand of the final redactors juxtaposed an observation from a Babylonian sage on the angelic praise with the reaction of unnamed rabbis, who employed the refrain of *havivin Israel* to uphold the status of ordinary Jews and the Shema prayer over the *Qedushah* prayer:

> As Rav Hananel said that Rav said: Three classes of ministering angels sing praise every day: "One says Holy, another says Holy, and another says Holy is the Lord of Hosts."
>
> Others objected saying, "Israel is more beloved [*havivin Israel*] by god than the ministering angels. Whereas Israel recites prayers repeatedly, the ministering angels recite only once a day. Some say [they recite] only once a Sabbath; some say only once a month; some say only once a year, and some say once a week [of years, i.e., seven years] and some say only once a Jubilee, and some say just once forever.
>
> Moreover, Israel invokes God's name after only two words as it is said:
>
> "Hear O Israel, the LORD, etc." (Deut 6:4, the Shema). And the ministering angels do not invoke the name until after three words as it is written:
>
> "Holy, Holy, Holy, the LORD of Hosts. . . ." (Isa 6:3, the *Qedushah*). And the ministering angels do not recite prayers up above until Israel says them below.[35]

This text begins with an interpretation of Isaiah's vision of the seraphim in the temple, using the thrice-repeated "Holy" as a way to imagine what the ministering angels do in the heavens. The speculation about the liturgical praise in the heavenly realm is then undercut by a tradition from anonymous rabbis, who firmly redirect attention to the people of Israel and their prayers. There is no sign that Rav Hananel or Rav believed that the *Qedushah* was more important than the Shema, but the framers of the Talmud used this speculation as an excuse to insert this tradition comparing the merits of these two prayers. The anonymous tradition asserts there was proof that Israel was more beloved by God than the angels: The people of Israel pray more often than the angels do (three times a day as opposed to once), Israel's prayer, the Shema, declares God's name earlier in the liturgical verses than the angelic *Qedushah* (compare the position of the name of God in the verses), and the angels have to wait for the people of Israel to finish

---

34. In the *sugya* from *Ḥullin*, the rabbis discussed the prohibition on consuming the sciatic nerves based on the story of Jacob's injury from wrestling with the angel (Gen 32:25–33). Another tradition that strikingly ignores synagogue *Qedushah* practices can be found in *y. Ber.* 7:5.

35. *b. Ḥul.* 91b.

their prayers.[36] This description is fascinating because practices around the *Qedu-shah* were still evolving in late antiquity and the rabbis were clearly trying to make a claim for the importance of the Shema over the *Qedushah*.[37]

Preoccupation with praying with and like the angels predates the rabbinic movement and continued in various ways as the rabbinic movement developed. The rabbis would have liked the biblical Shema to suffice for ordinary Jews, but the evidence from the liturgy shows that Jews also demanded the inclusion of the *Qedushah* in their fixed liturgy. The principle attributed to Rabbi Akiva on imitation of God was enough for some rabbinic Jews and continued to develop in a number of legal traditions discussed below.

IN THE IMAGE OF GOD OR IN THE IMAGE OF THE ANGELS?

In his book, *In God's Image: Myth, Theology, and Law in Classical Judaism,* Yair Lorberbaum advances the thesis that in rabbinic writings, we find the foundational idea that man is not just created in the image of God, but that each human is an icon of God, actually containing a part of God within himself.[38] Lorberbaum argues that this foundational idea is reflected in halakhah and Haggadah and can be seen most vividly in the laws related to the death penalty. His research is relevant for this work, too, because it provides a framework for the rabbinic conceptions of self, the angels, and God. I argue that part of the reason that some rabbis resented attention to angels was because the imitation of God (*imitatio dei*) was foundational to their way of life and to their halakhah. Attraction to angels and the angelic life distracted from their approach and authority.

A tradition in *Sifrei* emphasizes the importance of *imitatio dei* when it interprets Joel 3:5 "And it will come about that whoever calls on the name of the LORD will be delivered." The sages ask whether a man can really call on the *name* of God. Their answer is that rather than reading "whoever calls on the name of God," one should read "whoever is called in the name of God" (reading the verb passively rather than actively):

> And how can a person call on the name of the Holy One, blessed be He? Rather, just as God is called compassionate and gracious, so you be compassionate and gracious

---

36. Cf. *Gen. Rab.* 65:21 (Theodor and Albeck, 739–40), which also states that the angels must keep silent while Israel recites the Shema.

37. See Fleischer, "The Qedushah of the Amidah," 311. As we shall see in the next chapter, the liturgical poet Yannai would equate Israel's *Qedushah* with the angelic *Qedushah*. In the Jewish communities of late antique Palestine, popular participation in the *Qedushah* would become an increasingly important phenomenon, albeit one that the rabbis barely comment on (303).

38. Lorberbaum, *In God's Image.*

and give freely to all. Just as the Holy One is called righteous as it said, "The Lord is righteous in all His ways and kind in all His deeds" (Ps 145:17) so you be righteous. The Holy one is called kind as it is said "Kind in all His deeds" so you be kind. Hence it was said "whoever *is called* in the name of the Lord will be delivered."[39]

In Hebrew, the phonetic similarity of "calling on the name" and "being called in the name" allows the sages to encourage fellow Jews to act in Godly ways. According to their teaching, being called in the name of God means imitating God, and this act brings about deliverance.

Another tradition from the Palestinian Talmud uses *imitatio dei* to teach the importance of judging with peers, in the framework of a rabbinic courthouse, rather than alone. Here the encouragement to be God-like is specifically directed at the sages, not all of Israel. "As it is taught, do not judge alone as no one may judge alone except one. Rabbi Judah b. Pazzi said even the Holy One, blessed be He, does not judge alone, as it is said 'And all the host of heaven standing by him on his right and on his left'—these inclining toward acquittal and those inclining toward conviction."[40] A sage ought not to judge alone because God does not judge alone. According to Rabbi Judah b. Pazzi, God judges with the host of heaven. By analogy, a sage ought to judge alongside other sages. Thus, the judge is God-like and fellow judges are like divinities as well, but only implicitly and for the sake of emphasizing the importance of godly behavior—that is, not being so presumptuous as to judge alone.[41]

It is well known that the sages imagine that God has a heavenly courthouse that both corresponds to and is subordinate to the rabbinic courthouse.[42] The Palestinian Talmud describes a scene in heaven in which the rabbis establish the date of the New Year. God orders the angels to set up the podium for the heavenly advocates and prosecutors to begin the judgment proceedings. After describing God's assembling of his heavenly court, the text is quick to mention that if the sages change their minds and decide that the New Year actually begins the next day, God duly orders his angels to deconstruct the platform, presumably to be assembled on the new date set by the sages.[43] According to this conception of the

39. *Sifre Deut* §49 (Finkelstein, 114).

40. *y. Sanh.* 1.1/5, 18a, Schäfer and Becker, *Synopse zum Talmud Yerushalmi* IV, 157.

41. The next tradition in the *sugya* asserts that God does not take any action until it is affirmed by the heavenly courthouse (see *y. Sanhedrin* 2a; also discussed by Schäfer in *Rivalität*, 41–42).

42. *y. Ber.* 9:5, 14c "The earthly court decreed three things and the heavenly court assented." The phrase heavenly courthouse also appears in *Sifre Num* 92 (Horowitz, 93); see also *b. Pesaḥ.* 53b, *b. B. Meṣi'a* 85a and 86a, discussed in in Goodblatt, *Rabbinic Instruction in Sasanian Babylonia*, 63–107; Gafni, "Yeshiva and Metivta," 23 and 29.

43. The sages read Ps 81:4, "this is a statute for Israel, a law of the God of Jacob" as if it stated, "this statute for Israel *is* a law *for* the God of Jacob." This tradition is also discussed by Schäfer in

heavenly sphere, the court-house of the rabbis and its decisions dictate reality, most importantly in establishing the new month and the new year, which depend on empirical observation of the moon.[44] Since the moon was part of God's heavenly host, the establishment of the calendar according to the rabbis' observation of the moon may also be seen as an expression of the rabbinic attitude of authority over the angels.[45] This is in keeping with rabbinic preoccupation with their own authority over heavenly sources of authority: with the rabbis, legal and calendrical decisions are achieved through legal exegesis and consensus, no longer by revelation or even divine intervention from God and His angels.[46]

When the rabbis do discuss the Jews' resemblance to angels, usually in response to biblical citations, they are more ambivalent than other contemporaneous Jewish thinkers. The reception history of Malachi 2:7 is illuminating in this regard: "For the lips of a priest preserve knowledge and they shall seek Torah from his mouth for he is an angel of the Lord of Hosts." The plain meaning of this line is that in the priest's capacity as guardian of biblical knowledge, he acts as a messenger of God to the people of Israel. The liturgical poet Yannai (the subject of the next chapter) applied this prooftext to priests and sages, equally positively, praising their respective merits. In contrast, this quotation appears in three contexts in rabbinic literature and, in each case, the rabbis undermined the positive valences of the statement, adding disclaimers to the analogy of an angel, whether it applied to the priests or to members of their movement. The key to the rabbinic interpretation of the verse is reading the conjunction *for* (as in "for he is an angel") as *if* (as in "if he is an angel"), a possible but non-contextual meaning. This turns an unqualified statement into a conditional one.

In *Sifrei Numbers*, the rabbis offer a vivid interpretation of Jacob's dream of the ladder of angels, reading it as an allegory for the Jerusalem temple and its priests, ascending and descending the ramp. Although it begins with "Beloved are the priests," recalling "Beloved are Israel," this statement is qualified: "Beloved are the priests. When he refers to them, he compares them to the ministering angels as it is said, 'For the lips of a priest preserve knowledge and they shall seek Torah from his mouth *if* he is an angel of the Lord of Hosts'—when the Torah is in his mouth, behold, he is like a ministering angel, but if it is not, behold, he is like an animal and a beast that does not recognize its creator."[47] While the rabbis allow

Rivalität, 234. See *y. Roš Haš.* 1.3/14, 57b, Schäfer and Becker, *Synopse zum Talmud Yerushalmi* II/5–12, pp. 188–89.

44. See *m. Roš Haš.* chaps. 1–3, which discuss the laws of witnessing the new moon and establishing the months and feast dates and especially 2:8–9, which describes the famous controversy between Rabban Gamaliel and R. Joshua about the date of the Day of Atonement.

45. I thank Naphtali Meshel for suggesting this to me.

46. The *locus classicus* for this idea is the story known as the "Oven of Aknai," *b. B. Meṣiʿa* 59b.

47. *Sifre Num, Korach*, §119, on Num 25:53 (Horowitz, 143).

that Jacob's dream of angels refers to the priests, the effect of the rest of the interpretation undermines this positive description. The rabbis manage to limit the truth-value of Malachi's statement: angelic status is contingent on pious behavior. No priest is inherently angelic from this perspective. This rabbinic tradition draws attention away from priestly and angelic ideals, prevalent among other Jews.

Elsewhere, the rabbis employ the verses from Malachi to disqualify the standing of rabbinic disciples.

> There was once a young scholar whose reputation was bad. Rav Judah asked: what it is to be done—excommunicate him? But scholars can still make use of him. Not to excommunicate him? But the name of heaven is profaned. He said to Rabbah b. bar Hana: Have you heard of such a case? He said to him, thus said Rabbi Yohanan: what can be learned from "For the lips of a priest preserve knowledge and they shall seek Torah from his mouth *if* he is an angel of the Lord of Hosts"? If a scholar resembles an angel of God, they ought to seek Torah from his mouth, but if he does not, they should not seek Torah from him. Rav Judah excommunicated him.[48]

Again, the rabbis use this prooftext from Malachi with a disclaimer. They do not use these verses to claim that they inherently resemble the angels in their role as custodians of the Torah, but to say that sometimes scholars do, and sometimes they do not, achieve angelic semblance. In the two instances this prooftext is employed with regard to rabbinic scholars, the scholars in question fail and are excommunicated.[49] These statements do not necessarily reflect a polemic against angels, but they do show, I contend, a disinterest in the relationship between the sages and the angels.

In the only instance I found where the rabbis liken themselves to angels, they also simultaneously distance themselves from angels: "Said Rabbi Zeira in the name of Rava bar Zimuna 'If the earlier [sages] were like angels, we are like mortals. If the earlier [sages] were like mortals, we are like donkeys, and not like the donkey of Rabbi Hanina ben Dosa and that of Rabbi Pinhas ben Yair, but like the common donkeys."[50] These Amoraim who traveled between Palestine and Babylonia emphasize their generational and qualitative difference from angels. In describing the glorious past and glorious future to come of Israel, the rabbis used angelic imagery, but I argue that this attitude is absent among the rabbis with regard to themselves precisely because it undermines their self-understanding.[51]

---

48. *b. Moʻed Qat.* 17a.

49. The second instance, employed in a discussion of Elisha ben Abuya's (a.k.a. Aḥer's) excommunication, can be found in *b. Ḥag.* 15a–b.

50. *b. Šabb.* 112b (only Vilna MS begins the quotation with "like sons of angels").

51. While Steinberg argued that the rabbis identified with angels or aspired to angelic status, no source shows the rabbis unequivocally likening themselves to angels. At best, scouring all the midrashim, he states that "the angelification of the Patriarchs, of Moses and the Prophets, of Israel

Emphasis on imitation of God correlated with imagining a direct relationship with God. Exclusion of imitation of angels also excluded the need to conceptualize angelic presence.

CONCLUSION: IMITATION OF GOD, NOT ANGELS

In this chapter, I mapped out an ancient debate among Jews, about how to understand themselves in relation to God and the angels. Statements attributed to Rabbi Akiva and other rabbis after him encouraged Jews to focus on God directly and to focus on God's loving relationship with Israel. In the traditions associated with Rabbi Akiva, God was not distant and inimitable but could be a presence for Jews. More than that, God could even be a role model for Jews without any other intermediary beings (mortal or divine) coming between them. The development of *imitatio dei*, the imitation of God, in the writings of the rabbis from the Mishnah through Babylonian Talmud shows this endeavor was successful among the sages. Because some rabbis upheld this principle as their highest value, they rejected imitation of angels.

This chapter does not offer a section on blurring the boundaries because I posit that in rejecting preoccupation with angels, these rabbinic traditions were drawing boundaries, particularly between rabbis and fellow Jews (not to mention non-Jews). Angels were a part of the biblical heritage and were a part of the Jewish worldview, even for some Tannaim. This could not be denied. Relating to God directly without intermediaries in the early centuries CE was more unusual. In the face of the catastrophe of the temple and the Judean state's destruction, it is not surprising that Jews reevaluated how to relate to the God of Israel. While much scholarship has been devoted to analyzing the intellectual efforts of the sages, including how they defined themselves apart from others through legal texts, less has been devoted to the emotional aspects of this process. This was an era in which relationship to God and the heavenly realms had to be reinvented. At that time, some sages endeavored to conceptualize a relationship with God that was direct and loving and did not require angelic mediators. In this, the rabbis stood apart from other Jews even as they hoped to draw them into their nascent movement. In the following chapter, we shall see that angelic mediation and imitation proved more popular among Jews and Christians in congregational settings. Yannai, the poet of the synagogue examined next, managed to find a middle ground, encouraging imitation of angels and upholding priests, sages, and prayer leaders like himself as intermediaries for the people of Israel.

---

at Sinai, and of the righteous in the time to come, *amounts* to an angelic anthropology of Jewish humanity that includes the rabbinic proponents themselves as well" ("Angelic Israel," 382, emphasis added).

5

In the Image of the Angels

Liturgical Responses

And each priest who ministers / ministers like the ministering angels
And the Levites composing song / are like the holy creatures breaking
*   into song*
And Israel sanctifying and answering amen / is like the seraphim who
*   open with "Holy"*

—LITURGICAL POEM BY YANNAI

About the same time as ritual practitioners were composing incantation bowls in Babylonia, a learned Jew named Yannai was composing liturgical poetry for synagogue worship in Byzantine Palestine. His surviving corpus confirms which approach to imagining the invisible realm prevailed among Jews in late antiquity.[1] If the traditions of the rabbis showed ambivalence toward the angels, Yannai's corpus of liturgical poetry shows the opposite: an unabashed celebration of God's angels as well as a desire to imagine their involvement in Jewish life. In this chapter, I delve into the space of the late antique synagogue, explain how the angelic praise became part of Jewish liturgy and Jewish life, and demonstrate how surviving liturgical texts illuminate the role of angels in ancient Jewish society.

Although Yannai is relatively unknown today, his view of the angels is more representative of late antique Jewish society than the rabbinic views examined so far.[2] After giving a historiographical overview of this field, I foreground two insights we can draw from Yannai's surviving works: First, through his compositions, recited in ancient synagogues, we learn how Yannai taught Jews to think of themselves in angelic terms and in fellowship with angels. Even as he engaged with

1. See Yannai's qedushta to Num 15:1 in Rabinovitz, *The Liturgical Poems of Yannai*, 2:56.
2. Lieber's book *Yannai on Genesis* has done the most to introduce English-speaking audiences to the genre of late antique Jewish liturgical poetry.

rabbinic midrashim, Yannai's liturgical poems (piyyutim) departed from rabbinic precedent and helped Jews imagine themselves in synchronicity with the angelic realm. As I show, Yannai offered Jews new ways of being angelic that aligned with biblical and Jewish norms. Second, Yannai's poetry allows us to see how one late antique Jew, who composed works with a Jewish audience in mind, synthesized diverse traditions about the heavenly angels and shared them with others. Yannai had a Jewish audience before him when he recited this poetry, and thus his surviving texts allow Jewish men and women of late antique Roman Palestine to come into view more than redacted rabbinic traditions do. When Yannai's poetry was recited, it was not in the context of a male-only rabbinic study house but in the context of the public synagogue. Including liturgical poetry therefore allows for a fuller account of the role of angels in ancient Jewish society.

BACKGROUND: WHAT WAS HAPPENING IN THE LATE ANTIQUE SYNAGOGUE?

Late antique synagogues in Byzantine Palestine were communal institutions attended by men and women, full of sights and sounds evoking scripture.[3] There the languages of Greek, Hebrew, and Aramaic intermingled (at the very least on the mosaic floors, if not in the recitation of Torah).[4] Unlike the prevailing custom today among Jews, which is to read the five books of the Torah over the course of the Sabbaths of one year, in antiquity, Jews who attended the synagogues of Palestine would hear the Torah read over a three- or three-and-a-half-year cycle, in short portions, which left time for hearing a line-by-line translation into Aramaic as well as for communal and individual prayer, and for the performance of a homily as well as liturgical poetry.[5] In these communal worship settings, conceptualization of angels took center stage.

One of the most significant developments in late antique worship was the increasing importance of the liturgical use of the verses from Isaiah 6:3, "Holy, Holy, Holy, is the Lord of hosts / the whole earth is full of his glory," known as the

3. On women's presence, see Brooten, "Female Leadership in the Ancient Synagogue;" cf. Levine, "Women in the Synagogue," in *The Ancient Synagogue,* 499–518. On synagogues as sites of scriptural and liturgical recitation, see Münz-Manor, "*In situ*"; Talgam, *Mosaics of Faith.* For the mosaics of Palestinian synagogues, see Fine, *Art and Judaism in the Greco-Roman World,* esp. 185ff.

4. The synagogue in Sepphoris has inscriptions in Greek, Hebrew, and Aramaic. See Hachlili, *Ancient Mosaic Pavements,* 236. See also Fraade, "Rabbinic Views on the Practice of Targum, and Multilingualism in the Jewish Galilee of the Third–Sixth Centuries."

5. Yahalom has suggested that it was the brevity of Torah portions in the triennial cycle that created the space and time that encouraged the prolific growth of interpretive literature and poetry in Late Antique Palestine (*Poetry and Society in Jewish Galilee of Late Antiquity,* 182).

Qedushah in Hebrew, the *Trisagion* in Greek, and the *Sanctus* in Latin.[6] Over the centuries, Isaiah's vision of seraphim praising God's holiness in the temple had become the paradigm for prayer for Jews and Christians. The ritual of reciting these words set the stage for conceptualizing humanity in the image of the angels. The ritual recitation itself likely preceded any theological justification for it. When they recited "Holy, Holy, Holy," people were not only thinking about God but blurring the lines between themselves and angelic figures.

The figure most closely associated with the popularization of the *Qedushah* in the late antique Levant was the prayer leader and poet (Hebrew, *payyetan*) Yannai, whose efforts should be compared with the efforts of the rabbis. Yannai took the first three benedictions of the fixed Hebrew liturgy and embellished them with themes related to each week's lectionary reading from the Torah. The culmination of each of his compositions was the *Qedushah* itself, recited not just by the seraphim but by the heroes of that week's Torah reading *and* the worshippers in the synagogue. The genre of liturgical poetry he developed is called the *qedushta* because, in it, the recitation of the *Qedushah* is the culmination and climax of prayer.[7] This genre of poetry (Hebrew, *piyyut*) has also been called "sung sermon," "liturgical story-telling," or "liturgical poetry" and each of these terms highlights a different aspect of its nature.[8] Poeticizing the *Qedushah* on a theme related to each week's lectionary reading, Yannai turned the angelic praise into a participatory event in the synagogue, often likening the people of Israel to angels.[9] Yannai gave his Jewish congregation frameworks for relating to angels, God, and themselves in new ways in the late fifth and early sixth centuries. Writing in Hebrew for Jewish congregations, Yannai nonetheless participated in broader regional trends wherein Greek and Syriac poets were revolutionizing the late antique religious landscape with the introduction of sacred song into their respective communities' worship spaces.[10]

6. For more on the different trajectories of these liturgical verses, see Gerhards, "Crossing Borders— the Kedushah and the Sanctus." Following a separate trajectory, the thrice-repeated "holy" would become part of the fixed Christian liturgy in the fifth century, mainly due to John Chrysostom's influence.

7. To be clear, the *Qedushah* refers to the verses of the angelic praise from Isaiah ("Holy, Holy, Holy"), which became a popular prayer. The *qedushah* (NB: in lower case) refers to the ninth poem of the composition of the *qedushta* (plural *qedushta'ot*), which refers to this genre of nine-part compositions for Sabbaths and holidays that culminate in the *Qedushah*. All of these are based on the Hebrew word for "holy," *qadosh*. For deeper analysis, see Lieber, "Anatomy of a Qedushta: How Form Shapes Meaning and Meaning Shapes Form," in *Yannai on Genesis*, 35–92.

8. See McGuckin, "Poetry and Hymnography," 649.

9. The Qallir (or Qaliri), perhaps a student of Yannai, composed *qedushta'ot* for holidays that proved enduringly popular. Yannai composed *qedushta'ot* for every Sabbath. While a comparison of Yannai and the Qallir's corpora of poetry remains a desideratum, it is beyond the scope of this study. On the Qallir and Yannai, see Elizur, *Sod Meshalshei Qodesh*.

10. See Brock, "Syriac and Greek Hymnography"; Münz-Manor, "Liturgical Poetry in the Late Antique Near East." It may be relevant that the Church of the Holy Sepulcher (then known as the

HISTORIOGRAPHIC NOTES

The history of the development of the fixed Jewish liturgy, the *Qedushah*, and liturgical genre of the *qedushta* is somewhat obscure.[11] What seems certain is that in the late antique Palestinian context, reciting the *Qedushah* became a holy ritual, recited communally only on the Sabbath or holidays (unlike today, when the *Qedushah* is recited on a daily basis in observant Jewish congregations).[12] Elizur proposed that the *qedushta* as a liturgical genre originated in fourth- or fifth-century Palestine; Yannai happens to be the earliest named poet associated with this genre.[13] As Laura Lieber suggests, it may have been popular desire to recite the angelic verses that eventually led to the regular recitation of the *Qedushah* as part of the liturgy.[14] The rabbis do not comment on this important development, much in the same way they do not comment on the rise of Christianity or other important events that were not germane to their sense of identity. Unfortunately, the prayer leaders only bequeathed us their liturgical books to make sense of their motives.

How Jews related to the angels in their worship in late antique synagogues and particularly through *qedushta'ot* has not been addressed in depth. Lieber devoted one essay to the topic angels and mysticism in her book on the poet Yannai.[15] She noted that Yannai generally agrees with statements about angels in rabbinic literature, although he tends to view Israel's and the angels' relationship as more harmonious than the rabbis do. My research on conceptualization of angels among Jews foregrounds how much Yannai departed from Tannaitic and Amoraic precedents, which downplayed angels in key moments in foundational biblical narratives.

Anastasis Church) was a major center of liturgical production in the Levant (McGuckin, "Poetry and Hymnography"). See also Krueger, *Writing and Holiness.*

11. On the history of the *Qedushah*, see the magisterial work by Elizur, *Sod Meshalshei Qodesh.*

12. Fleischer suggests that prayer leaders recited alone first and that later the congregation followed suit. See "Qedushah of the Amidah" (Hebrew). Due to the influence of Babylonian rabbis in the early medieval period, the public recitation of the *Qedushah* began to be performed on a daily basis as part of the fixed liturgy, and this remains the custom in synagogue worship to this day. See Langer, *To Worship God Properly,* 197.

13. Elizur, *Sod Meshalshei Qodesh,* 403–5.

14. Lieber, *Yannai on Genesis,* 233. The two approaches to this topic encapsulate the scholarly differences in the study of piyyut and liturgy: Fleischer takes an institutional perspective, focused on how the prayer leaders and the rabbis shaped the liturgy and what philological analysis of the Hebrew liturgy may reveal. Lieber leaves open the possibility that factors outside the rabbinic movement may have shaped the liturgy. The former considers the reasons for the development of public recitation of the *Qedushah* as ultimately mysterious and unknowable; the latter sees it as a natural outgrowth of popular fascination with angels, recognizable in surviving literary evidence from Qumran and elsewhere, including non-Jewish sources. On this topic, see Langer, "Revisiting Early Rabbinic Liturgy."

15. Lieber discussed Yannai's interest in the angels and Jewish preoccupation with angels in late antiquity in one section of her book entitled "Poetry, Angels, and the Heavenly Hekhalot," in *Yannai on Genesis,* 227–40.

Yannai is in agreement only with the latest strata of rabbinic traditions, which came to embrace angels, perhaps catching up to Jewish trends around them (see chapter 6 on this development). As I show in this chapter, Yannai's conceptualization of the Jewish relationship with the angels contradicts the rabbinic emphasis on imitating God alone. I read Yannai as harnessing popular interest in imitating the angels and responding to Christian preaching that emphasized Christians as angels.

The problems of attribution, challenges of dating transmitted traditions, and anonymous editorial activity do not plague the study of Yannai's liturgical poetry as they do rabbinic literature. Nevertheless, challenging its integration into the field of Jewish studies is the claim that liturgical poetry is obscure and was unintelligible in antiquity. Whereas scholars of Christian hymnography have no doubt that Syriac and Greek liturgical compositions were intended for the laity as well as clergy members, monks, and nuns, Jewish historians have expressed some skepticism about the comprehension of Hebrew piyyutim in Aramaic-speaking Palestine.[16] Such skeptics point out that the language of these poetic compositions is inventive and relied on a fluency in the biblical sources that only the most educated likely possessed. Nonetheless, dismissing comprehension of Hebrew in late antiquity goes too far. The magical handbook *Sefer ha-Razim* was written in fluent expressive Hebrew in Palestine, likely in the fourth century. In his book *Poetry and Society in Jewish Galilee of Late Antiquity*, Joseph Yahalom emphasizes that late antique Roman Palestine experienced a Hebrew renaissance, with literary creations such as the *Tanhuma* midrashim and legal works such as the *Ma'asim L'Bnei Eretz Yisrael*.[17] Yahalom believes that in late antiquity and the early medieval period, "Hebrew speech likely carried connotations of roots, and was spoken still in villages by women and elders dedicated to tradition."[18] Michael D. Swartz, meanwhile, points out that "For all its presumed obscurity and artificiality, piyyut was enormously popular in the ancient synagogue; its ubiquity in the Jewish communities of the medieval Mediterranean is well attested by the vast number of piyyutim found in the Cairo Genizah; and indeed, its very popularity was the source of tension between members of the synagogues and the rabbinic authorities."[19] We may never have decisive proof either way, but I believe that the picture of total linguistic estrangement between congregation and prayer leader is just as speculative and unfounded as its opposite. In any case, the *qedushah*'s Hebrew was lucid and clearly called Jews to prayer with and like the angels.[20]

---

16. See Schwartz's discussion of piyyut, payyetanim, and comprehension in *Imperialism and Jewish Society*, especially under the heading "Judaization," 240–74.

17. Yahalom, *Poetry and Society in Jewish Galilee of Late Antiquity*, 49.

18. My translation of Yahalom, *Poetry and Society*, 49.

19. Swartz, "Translation and the Comprehensibility of Early Piyyut," 43.

20. Elizur, "The Congregation in the Synagogue and the Ancient Qedushta."

It is true that much that we would like to know about sacred song is out of reach. We do not know exactly how or where the popular phenomenon of performing sacred song began in Palestine. We can only assume Yannai performed his works in the synagogues of the Galilee, where the heart of Jewish and rabbinic life existed in his lifetime. Yoseph Yahalom hypothesizes that prayer leaders like Yannai led the morning prayers and then later in the same service, served as the translators for the recitation of the Torah.[21] We are ignorant of what these compositions sounded like, since the entire musical dimension of this poetry is lost. While we know the Syriac church employed female choirs and the Greek church had all male choirs, it is unclear whether there were similar choirs in synagogues.[22] It is evident that Yannai's liturgical poetry contained refrains in the sixth section that invited audience participation.[23] And the possibility of Jewish female participants should not be dismissed out of hand. The prohibition on hearing a woman's voice in the synagogue is a much later medieval development with surprisingly little basis in the Talmudic sources.[24] One of Yannai's poems celebrating the patriarch Jacob calls to the congregation to "Celebrate with fitting songs, with proper melodies, / men *and women* making music upon every melodic instrument."[25] Audience participation was increasingly popular with the generations, but the foundation already existed in each of Yannai's compositions, which drew the congregation into the angelic mode, especially in the ninth poem which led into the *Qedushah*.[26] Liturgical poets like Yannai mediated between the broad Jewish public and the learned rabbinic elite. As Lieber observed, "Yannai was shaped by and

21. Yahalom, *Poetry and Society*, 216.

22. There is evidence that synagogues in the generations after Yannai had professional choirs. See Fleischer, *The Pizmonim of the Anonymus*.

23. Fleischer, *The Pizmonim of the Anonymus*, 20–22. Fleischer discusses a corpus of refrains, recovered from the Cairo Genizah, which an anonymous poet wrote for the *qedushta'ot* of R. Simeon b. R. Megas (he wrote three or four refrains for each *qedushta*); some of these ended up accompanying the *qedushta'ot* of Yannai as well.

24. Saul Berman, "*Kol 'Isha*." One should also keep in mind that women maintained the role of public mourning and keening (see *m. Ketub.* 4:4) from the Second Temple period through the Crusades. See also Yahalom, *Poetry and Society*, 51, who write that according to Karaite testimony, professional mourning women would crowd Jerusalem in the summer, mourning in Hebrew, Persian, and even Arabic.

25. Lieber, trans., *Yannai on Genesis*, Qedushta for Gen 28:10, p. 530. Following Bronznick, *Piyyutei Yannai*, Lieber notes this may be related to 2 Sam 19:36's reference to the sound of male and female singers. Still, if Yannai repeated it, men and women's participation had to have been within the realm of possibility. Lieber discusses this possibility for Jews in Babylonia in her study "Daru in the Winehouse: The Intersection of Status and Dance in the Jewish East."

26. Notably, Lieber highlighted how the seventh poem in each of Yannai's compositions (called the *rahit* and full of repetitions and rhymes), likely drew in the congregation. See *Yannai on Genesis*, 66–73.

was a shaper of the culture of exegesis in which he lived and for which he wrote."[27] With this in mind, we can turn to examining how Yannai shaped conceptions of angels in Jewish life.

JEWS IN THE IMAGE OF THE ANGELS IN YANNAI'S *QEDUSHTA'OT*

Yannai's extant corpus of over one hundred and sixty *qedushta'ot*, almost entirely recovered from the Cairo Genizah, can teach us a great deal about the culture of the synagogue in late Antique Palestine. Just as the ritual evidence showed a spectrum of mediating figures that ancient Jews imagined were available to them, so Yannai's liturgical poetry depicts Jews in the midst of a network of relationships featuring angels alongside biblical heroes from Israel's past. What Yannai adds is an acknowledgment of local community authorities as well, in no way in tension or competition with the winged beings of the invisible realm. If Yannai's entire corpus of piyyutim survived, we would have *qedushta'ot* to 166 lectionary readings composed for the triennial cycle in use in his environs.[28] As it stands, we have fragmentary or whole *qedushta'ot* to 130 ordinary Sabbaths plus about 18 fragmentary and whole piyyutim for festivals and holiday Sabbaths, which brings his piyyutim to a total of 148. Of these, 75 are fragmentary and lack the final one or two poems relevant to the current analysis.

To give a brief overview of my findings: out of the remaining piyyutim with the concluding verses, seven describe *only* the angels reciting the *Qedushah* (only implicitly including the human worshippers).[29] Ten of Yannai's piyyutim have particular biblical patriarchs and heroes reciting the *Qedushah* alongside angels.[30] The rest of the *qedushta'ot* stress the synchronicity and commingling of the voices of Israel and the angels above and below. Of the piyyutim with emphasis on the people of Israel, several uphold specific subgroups within the congregation like priests or Levites, the elders, or women.[31] As I demonstrate through examples

---

27. Lieber, *Yannai on Genesis*, 132.

28. My findings are based on Rabinovitz's critical edition (*The Liturgical Poems of Rabbi Yannai*) and other recent publications of Yannai's poetry.

29. See compositions to Gen 19:1, Gen 28, Gen 43:14, Exod 12:29, Exod 18:1, Num 16, and the composition for Passover.

30. See compositions to Gen 9:18 (sons of Noah), Gen 12:1 (Abraham), Gen 32:4 (Jacob's descendants), Gen 44:18 (Judah, Joseph, and Benjamin), Exod 6:2 (the patriarchs), Exod 18:1 (Jethro), Exod 31:1 (Bezalel), Num 17:16 (Aaron), Num 25:10 (Phineas), Deut 10:1 (on Moses?).

31. I discuss selected examples below and at the end of this chapter. See compositions to Exod 19:6 (on priests, Levites, Israel), Num 18:25 (on Levites), Gen 24 (on elders), Exod 13:1 (on pregnant women), or Lev 15:25 (on pious women). On women in Yannai, see Lieber, "Yannai's Women," 285–95 in *Yannai on Genesis*; Münz-Manor, "All about Sarah: Questions of Gender in Yannai's Poems."

below, these compositions uphold the recitation of "Holy, Holy, Holy" from the congregation of Israel, variously described and celebrated, explicitly or implicitly placing them on the same level as the angels. Judging by this corpus, it seems that synagogue liturgy reflected and reinforced the ideal of assuming angelic status among Jews. Imitating the angels and reciting liturgical praise in fellowship with them went hand in hand.

Yannai's *qedushta* for the first lectionary reading of Genesis sets forth his basic understanding of the angels' relationship to humanity. Although the first five poems of this *qedushta* are no longer extant, the sixth poem picks up with a concise summary of each of God's creative acts. In Yannai's retelling, it is evident that the first humans were made in the image of the angels, not God: "You gathered (your host): 'Let us make man' / According to *their* likeness is the likeness of man." The following verses in the piyyut reference angelic jealousy of humanity's creation (a common topic in the midrashim) and make clear that the angels were the subject of the likeness. Furthermore, three lines later, Yannai writes: "You plucked dust from the earth / With its body being of the earth / . . . like the angels ['*yly mrom*] he was molded."[32] The Hebrew term for angels here, '*yly mrom*, translates as the heavenly beings or literally 'the lofty divine beings," a term found neither in biblical nor in rabbinic literature.[33] Yannai was expressing a belief about angelic resemblance in his own Hebrew vocabulary, but one that would not have been unfamiliar to his audience. Pappias, who asserted that humanity was created in the image of the angels, may have held a minority opinion in the rabbinic movement, but he was not alone in his conceptualization of angelic and human resemblance among ancient Jews.[34]

Yannai's transference of the voicing of the *Qedushah* from the angels to the protagonists of each week's lectionary reading and the congregants was his most significant contribution to late antique Jewish religious life. In Yannai's *qedushta'ot*, what began as a verbal and embodied imitation of the angels in the fixed prayer became a more complex ritual that cultivated new modes of Jewish self-conception, one composition at a time.[35] Each of Yannai's *qedushta'ot* invited the members of the congregation in direct and lucid language to sing the prayer of the angels, now closely associated with ancestral customs, with a biblical figure, or a group before him in the synagogue. The customs that Yannai invokes in a *Qedushah* to Exodus 16:28, for example, would have been practiced by all Jews present in Yannai's

32. Lieber, *Yannai on Genesis*, 304–5.

33. Similarly, in the penultimate poem in this composition (the *silluq*), Yannai reaffirms angelic and human resemblance, this time using the term *bnei elim* (Lieber, *Yannai on Genesis*, 314–15).

34. The only rabbis that support Pappias's line of thought are the anonymous ones that propose that humanity was made in the image of Gabriel (see *Gen. Rab.* 21:5).

35. Here, I am influenced by Krueger's discussion of developments in Christian piety and practice in the sixth century CE; see *Writing and Holiness*, 159–88.

synagogue on the Sabbath. By connecting them with the song of the angels, the customs and the reciters' sense of self would be infused with new meaning:

> Against these three things, which are Shabbat and circumcision and Wisdom, they will thrice say
> *Holy, Holy, Holy, is the Lord of Hosts! The whole earth is filled with His glory!*
> "*Holy*"—from those keeping the Sabbath
> "*Holy*"—from those observing circumcision
> "*Holy*"—from those reciting Torah.[36]

Yannai ties angelic praise to the Jewish practices of keeping the Sabbath, preserving the ritual of circumcision from generation to generation, and reciting verses of the Torah, poetically referred to as Wisdom (*Tushiya*).[37] In this way, Yannai elevates the reciters alongside the rituals and opens a space for the Jews before him to be the reciters of the angelic praise. He makes clear that the congregation itself, by virtue of upholding these fundamental values, is on a par with the angels. It is possible that he chose the verb "recite" (*sh-n-n*) in order to evoke the recitation of the oral Torah, which the rabbinic movement upheld as integral to a full understanding of Jewish Law.

In other compositions, Yannai lingers and makes sure to praise the aspects of observance that were the object of gentile criticism. In his *qedushah* for the *qedushta* to Leviticus 17:1, Yannai addresses Jewish ritual slaughter practices:

> Those being slaughtered in your name and those who offer sacrifices of their
>   slaughter to your name answer and say:
> *Holy, Holy, Holy,* etc.
> "*Holy*"—from those observing [the rules of] slaughter
> "*Holy*"—from those purifying eating
> "*Holy*"—from those abominating the foreign
> *Holy Holy Holy*
> "*Holy*" for the sake of making us pleasing, he commanded us the ritual slaughter
> "*Holy*" for the sake of purifying us, he commanded us purity of eating
> "*Holy*" for the sake of justifying us, he commanded us to keep afar from foreignness
> "*Holy*" from *Chaya*, "*Holy*" from *Ofan*, "*Holy*" from Cherub.[38]

In the first line, there is a play on words that equates Jewish martyrs with those who perform slaughter of animals, no longer as part of temple sacrifices, but as

---

36. Rabinovitz, *The Liturgical Poems of Rabbi Yannai*, 1:314.

37. In emphasizing Sabbath and circumcision for angelic resemblance, Yannai echoes the author of Jubilees. Yannai uses the word *Tushiya* here to stand in for the Torah. Cf. *Pirqe R. El.* 3: "at once the Lord took counsel with the Law, whose name is *Tushiyah*, as to creating the world" (Jastrow, *Dictionary*, 1659).

38. Rabinovitz, *The Liturgical Poems of Rabbi Yannai*, 1:444.

part of Jewish life. Butchery was a profession that even the rabbis derided at times, yet it was a part of ordinary Jewish life.[39] The emphasis on avoiding foreign practices reveals that ways of eating were a particularly fraught aspect of living among others in Byzantine Palestine. Yannai finds a way to respond not just to the biblical laws of Leviticus on slaughter, but to address the people who enact these laws, whether as butchers or as consumers of animals slaughtered according to Jewish law. More than that, Yannai ties norms of Jewish life with angelic praise. Yannai took the most quotidian Jewish practices and connected them with the loftiest angelic creatures.

In the final line, which is found also in fourteen other extant *qedushta'ot*, Yannai evoked the angelic praise from the three divine creatures found in the prophecies of Ezekiel: the *hayyot* (the living creatures), the ophanim (wheels of eyes), and the cherubim.[40] These three divine types appear separately only in chapter 10 of the book of Ezekiel but do not form a series or a triad in biblical texts.[41] Only Yannai makes a triad of the *hayyot*, the ophanim, and the cherubim and makes this triad a refrain in his *qedushta'ot*. Late antique interpreters like Yannai collected terms for angels from the biblical corpus and understood them to be synonymous. Only much later medieval interpreters showed interest in creating a systematic hierarchy of the angels.

We can compare the Jewish customs that Yannai enumerated in these two examples with the way contemporary Christians discussed achieving angelic status. Peter Brown famously brought attention to the phenomenon of celibate Christians aspiring to the angelic life in the Late Antique Mediterranean, writing that "Not to belong to married society was to belong more intensely to others. The Invisible world was magnificently sociable. It was a 'great city' crowded with angelic spirits."[42] He cites the Patriarch the letter of Athanasius of Alexandria, who wrote to Emperor Constantius II that one of the benefits bestowed by Jesus's intercession was that humans "should possess upon earth, in the state of virginity,

---

39. See *m. Qidd.* 4:14, "R. Judah says in his name: Ass-drivers are most of them wicked, camel-drivers are most of them proper folk, sailors are most of them saintly, the best of physicians is destined for Gehenna, and the most seemly among butchers is a partner of Amalek" (trans. Danby, *Mishnah*).

40. The earliest instance of the triad in Jewish texts can be found in the Book of Parables of 1 Enoch 61:10 (Nickelsburg and Vanderkam, *1 Enoch*, 78 lists them as "Cherubin, Seraphin, and Ophannin"). In only one work in his extant corpus, Yannai groups the angels as those of mercy, peace, and the hosts (see *qedushta* to Gen 28:10): "'Holy' from the angels of mercy that accompanied Jacob on his journey/ 'Holy' from the angels of peace that guarded him where he slept / 'Holy' from angels of the hosts who were revealed to him in his dream" (my translation of Rabinovitz, *The Liturgical Poems of Rabbi Yannai*, 1:170–71).

41. In Ezek 10:9–20, the prophet Ezekiel witnesses the departure of God's glory from the temple and realizes that the frightful divine creatures (*hayyot*) he saw in his first vision of God (Ezek 1) are the cherubim, those responsible for carrying God's throne alongside the divine wheels, the ophanim.

42. Brown, *Body and Society*, 171.

a picture of the holiness of the angels. . . . For indeed, this holy and heavenly profession is nowhere established, but only among us Christians, and it is a very strong argument that with us is to be found the genuine and true religion."[43] According to Athanasius, not only did Christian monks and nuns who practiced celibacy achieve angelic status on earth, but their unique status was proof of the truth of Christian claims over and against Judaism and more established Mediterranean religions. Since biblical and rabbinic law did not prize lifetime vows of celibacy, Yannai illustrates how Jews could seek angelic resemblance in other ways that honored their inherited traditions and distinctive practices. Where Christian thinkers emphasized withdrawal from society to achieve the angelic life, Jews like Yannai emphasized remaining with the congregation to achieve angelic resemblance.

The *qedushta* to Numbers 15:1, a chapter on the sacrifices that the Israelites will offer God once they settle in the Land of Israel, becomes in Yannai's work a celebration of the glorious temple of yesteryear and an ode to the merits of prayer in place of sacrifice, again elevated through angelic praise. Yannai's description of Israel's intermingling with the angels becomes a particularly comforting message in the eighth poem:

> Our sacrifices were to you as though you ate and were sated[44] / and our libations were to you as though you drank and were cheered[45] / And our temple was to you like the heavens / and the higher heavens,[46] *zevul, maon, shehakim, arvot,* and the throne of glory, and the *merkavah/*
>
> And each priest [*cohen*] who ministers / ministers like the ministering angels /
> And the Levites composing song / are like the *hayyot* breaking into joy
> And Israel sanctifying and answering amen / is like the seraphim who open with "holy" and close [with *baruch*].[47]

Yannai juxtaposes the past earthly temple in Jerusalem, which was nonetheless heavenly, and the people of the congregation before him, who are like the angels. Incorporating the biblical hierarchy of priests, Levites, and the rest of the people of Israel, Yannai nonetheless equalizes the three categories of priests, Levites, and Israelites, likening them to the ministering angels, the divine creatures, and the

---

43. Athanasius, *Apologia ad Constantium imperatorem* §33; Patrologia Graeca 25: 640B; trans. Atkinson, *Historical Tracts of Saint Athanasius,* 185.

44. Word play on Deut 11:15, the biblical verse said in the traditional blessings over meals (*Birkat Hamazon*).

45. I thank Elie Kaunfer for pointing me to the source Yannai likely alludes to here, Gen 43:34.

46. Novick translates and discusses this middle section in "'Who resembles you? But they resemble you': Israel and the Apophatic in Yannai," 280.

47. Rabinovitz, *The Liturgical Poems of Rabbi Yannai,* 2:56.

seraphim, respectively.[48] In the ninth poem of this composition, he emphasizes the rituals common to all Jews in the aftermath of the temple:

> Pleasing as sacrifices are the words of your desired people who answer and say
> Holy, Holy, Holy, etc.
> "*Holy*"—from the reciters of Shema
> "*Holy*"—from those who prepare prayer [*tefillah*]
> "*Holy*"—from those who answer each blessing [*berakhah*]
> Holy, Holy, Holy, etc.
> "*Holy*"—like a sacrificial offering, the recitation of Shema pleases him
> "*Holy*"—like a whole offering, the offering of prayer pleases him
> "*Holy*"—like the libation of wine, the saying of each blessing pleases him.[49]

Yannai places prayer, whether in the form of the biblically commanded Shema, the fixed prayer referred to simply as *tefillah* (or Amidah), or the blessings said after meals, all on a par with the angelic prayer of the *Qedushah* and with the temple cult of the past. Whereas a rabbinic tradition places the *Qedushah* and the Shema in competition, Yannai brings these prayers together harmoniously. The idea that prayer can substitute for sacrifice, taken for granted today, was still a relatively new development in Judaism at this time. Yannai's works ought to be seen as part of an effort to endow the synagogue liturgy with greater value in Late Antique Jewish culture.

Even the rabbis receive descriptions of angelic resemblance from Yannai. The *qedushta* to Num 11:16, a Torah portion ostensibly on the appointment of elders to lighten Moses's load, provides an opportunity for Yannai to ruminate on the Jewish legal scholars of his day.[50] To understand the following verses fully, one must know of a saying found in the Mishnah: "Warm thyself before the fire of the Sages, but be heedful of their glowing embers lest thou be burned, for their bite is the bite of a jackal and their sting the sting of a scorpion and their hiss the hiss of a serpent, and all their words are like embers of fire."[51] In his composition, Yannai writes of God's relationship with the sages: "Then by sword and by scroll,

48. Yannai describes the congregation in terms taken from biblical traditions (Priests, Levites, and Israel) and incorporated into the Mishnah as legal categories. The Mishnah already takes these categories for granted: see *Pe'ah* 8:6, *Ta'an.* 4:2, *Mid.* 2:6, and *Sanh.* 4:2. Cf. the closing to the *qedushta* to Exod 19:6, discussed below.

49. Rabinovitz, *The Liturgical Poems of Rabbi Yannai*, 2:57.

50. Rabinovitz, *The Liturgical Poems of Rabbi Yannai*, understands the description here to refer to the Palestinian yeshiva in Tiberias. He reads many other subtle references to the yeshiva of Tiberias in Yannai's corpus, but I find these too speculative. I observe three references to the sages (*Ḥakhamim*) as a group in the extant piyyutim. See the *kerova* to Num 11:16 discussed above, the *kerova* to Lev. 15:25, and in the beginning of the Yom Kippur composition, discussed below.

51. See *m. 'Abot* 2:10; trans. Danby, *The Mishnah*, 449.

you grasped them / in a miraculous act you chose them / Like a consuming fire are their embers / in the image of angels you elevated them. . . . From above their appointment is strengthened // "their bite is the bite of a jackal."[52] Yannai interweaves the rabbinic saying with biblical imagery of the fiery angels. He compares the fiery awesomeness of the angels with the fiery brilliance of the rabbis. It is unfortunate that the *qedushah* of this composition does not survive, because we cannot tell how Yannai would have developed this at its culmination.

Where the sages interpret Mal 2:7 conditionally ("For the lips of a priest preserve knowledge and they shall seek Torah from his mouth for he is an angel [*mal'akh*] of the Lord of hosts"), in several of his *qedushta'ot*, Yannai affirms the plain meaning of this text, asserting priestly and angelic identification. Angelic resemblance begins with Aaron and applies to all priests that follow from him: "For permission was not given / except for Aaron to minister / he who looks like the ministering angels."[53] And in composition on the ordination of Aaron and his sons (to Exod 29:1), he writes "Your priests will wear salvation in holiness [They] being like divinities of holiness / In adornment of holiness / Established like angels/ going about in excitement."[54] The *qedushta* to Lev. 21:1 is particularly interesting because Yannai dwells on the destruction of the priesthood and its manifestations in his time. After lamenting their sorry state in Byzantine Palestine, where the gentiles mock the priests and their inability to achieve cultic purity, Yannai describes how priests as a class are destined to resemble the angels in the future. He states, speaking in God's voice: "My priests who (are) above are pure / my priests who (are) below will be pure // above in fire they purify // below in water they will be purified. . . ."[55] Your service will be in holiness // like the ministering angels, the servants of the Holy."[56] Yannai exceeds biblical descriptions of priestly and angelic likeness, offering comfort not only to a dejected class within Israel, but promising all Jews in his audience restoration of their biblically appointed leaders in the future.

More than any other extant *qedushta*, the one on Exodus 19:6 lingers on priestly imagery.[57] The opening crucial line of that week's lectionary reading is "you shall be to Me a Kingdom of priests and a holy nation'" (Exod 19:6). As Martha Himmelfarb discusses in *Kingdom of Priests*, this universalistic statement stands in tension with the exclusive, genealogical framework of the priesthood.[58] Yannai

---

52. Rabinovitz, *The Liturgical Poems of Rabbi Yannai*, 2:47–8.

53. Rabinovitz, *The Liturgical Poems of Rabbi Yannai*, 2:72 (*qedushta* to Num 17:16, line 104–5).

54. Rabinovitz, *The Liturgical Poems of Rabbi Yannai*, 1:346 (the third piyyut in the *qedushta* to Exod 29:1).

55. Rabinovitz, *The Liturgical Poems of Rabbi Yannai*, 1:459 (*qedushta* to Lev 21:1, line 60).

56. Rabinovitz, *The Liturgical Poems of Rabbi Yannai*, 1:460 (*qedushta* to Lev 21:1, line 70).

57. Lieber also examines this composition in "'The Exegesis of Love."

58. Martha Himmelfarb, *Kingdom of Priests*.

shifts between these two models of the priesthood, inclusive of all of Israel, while singling out the priesthood for restoration to its former glory. In the closing poem of this composition, Yannai references the contemporary reality, where the Byzantine Empire deprived Israel of its kingdom and its priests of their cult.

> In the hosts of the camps of angels
> Priests, Levites, Israelites
> Will sanctify you as the King of Kings of Kings
> *Holy, Holy, Holy*, is the Lord of Hosts! The whole earth is filled with His glory!
> "*Holy*" from the standing priests
> "*Holy*" from the watch of the Levites
> "*Holy*" from the course of the Israel
> "*Holy, Holy, Holy*"
> "*Holy*"—He will return the podium to the sons of the priests
> "*Holy*"—He will instill song in the Levites' watch
> "*Holy*"—He will reveal his kingdom to the Kingdom of Israel
> "*Holy*"—from Chaya, Holy from Cherub, Holy from Ophan.[59]

In the end, he emphasizes the unity of distinct worshippers, juxtaposed with the three classes of angels. Overall, his depiction of priests in the piyyut affirms that priests have a distinct sense of identity, but also that they are important symbolically for the nation as a whole.

The comparison of Israel with the angels reaches its climax in the composition for the holiest day of the Jewish liturgical cycle, Yom Kippur. Yannai's composition for Yom Kippur is unusual from a formal perspective and complex in its transmission history.[60] From the standpoint of content, we see Yannai emphasizing the parity of Israel and the angels more explicitly than in any other composition. Interestingly, just as comparison of Israel with the angels reaches new heights, so too is Yannai's profile raised. Yannai speaks out in the first and fourth piyyutim. He prefaces the first poem by stating, "From the council of sages and the learning of colleagues // I will open my mouth and I will praise the Creator," which Rabinovitz interprets as a request for permission from the sages to lead.[61]

59. Rabinovitz, *The Liturgical Poems of Rabbi Yannai*, 1:321 (poem 9, lines 33–42).

60. Yannai's cycle of poems to Yom Kippur can be outlined thus: 1. on Abraham; 2. on Isaac; 3. on Jacob; 4. unique hymn that declares parity of Israel and the angels (trans. below); 5. attribution uncertain: declaration of eternity of covenant; 6. a call to praise God; 7. description of the throne; 8. attribution uncertain, hymn focuses on each body part's experience of the fast; 9. description of the five kingdoms; 10. attribution to Yannai is uncertain: condemnation of Christian empire; 11. attribution uncertain: curses upon Israel's enemies; 12. description of God's love for Israel; 13. prophecy of the end days; 14. short description of God's might in the end days; 15. final summation and comparison of Israel and the angels (full translation offered below).

61. Rabinovitz, *The Liturgical Poems of Rabbi Yannai*, 2:210 and see fn. 1.

This opening might be interpreted differently: Yannai locates himself among the sages, but his works present a distinctive vision of the people of Israel.

In the fourth poem, Yannai makes an extraordinary move. While he usually signs his name in acrostic in the third poem, here he signs his name in the fourth, but the nature of the fourth itself is striking: each verse the hazan sings requires an answering refrain, and in two refrains the respondents alternate. One refrain assumes an angelic voice; the other refrain assumes Israel's voice. Both refrains contain an acrostic of Yannai's name:

> I will declare your wonders God / I will sing until I am exhausted
> Let your eternity glorify you / Let your dear ones praise you "*Holy*" [YNYY]
> Who has understanding? Who can elucidate the limits of your strength?
> May the beauty of the day of homage be upon us to sanctify you "*Holy*" [YNYY]
> The creatures of your host battalions / sparkling embers of flame
> [Angels say]—Let your eternity glorify you / Let your dear ones praise you *Holy!*
> Demand our humble humility / as prayer of confession
> [Israel says]—May the beauty of the day of homage be upon us to sanctify you *Holy!*
> Beauty of the glory of your adornment / the cacophony of harmonizing reciters
> [Angels say]—Let your eternity glorify you . . .
> And today they are alike and equal / the committees above and below.
> [Israel says]—May the beauty of the day of homage . . .
> Each to the other shouting out / a garland of tripled singing.[62]

Yannai trademarks this poem with his name specifically in the lines of the refrains intended for the audience, here envisioned as two groups, Israel and the angels. While ostensibly keeping the earthly and heavenly adorers distinct, Yannai subverts this distinction through a performance that involves members of the congregation, reciting refrains that alternate between the angelic and human personas. Moreover, he states that on Yom Kippur, the differences between angels and the people of Israel have faded. In a dramatic finale, the closing poem makes this unity of the earthly and heavenly explicit:

> Then heavenly with earthly // on this day are equal, perfect, and beautiful
> The joy of the sanctification of the day in a clear language // from above and below
>   the select holy
> Myriads of heavenly holy ones sanctified you // a place where no eating or drinking
> The holy seed below on this day will be sanctified // who desist from food and
>   drink on the tenth day
> Peace is negotiated among the creatures above // together as the Creator desired
>   they are pleasing to each other

---

62. Rabinovitz, *The Liturgical Poems of Rabbi Yannai,* 2:214–15.

Each man will desire his friend on this day // for the sake of making peace among
  themselves
Above they wear white garments // clean from all stains and bleached from sins
Likewise below the cloaks are white today // because from sins they are whitened.
Tis one of the wonders of the heavens that they have no knees//their step is straight
  and barefoot
Our congregation today too in straightness of leg // trembling in barefoot steps
Your name above they will sanctify as one// On the day on which it is One above
  and below.
You will be pleased and comforted as they call one to the other // the sanctification
  of this people / in the sanctification of this day.[63]

In appearance, in character, in their actions, and in status before God, Israel and
the angels have finally achieved identification on Yom Kippur. On this holy day
both the angels and earthly Israel are devoted entirely to prayer; in fasting, the
people of Israel resemble the angels, who never require food or drink; like the
angels, people set aside their differences on Yom Kippur and coexist in complete
harmony; both the angels and the people of Israel dress in white raiment on this
day; the people, standing straight as they pray, imitate the angelic posture. Yannai
brackets the fact that only sinful mortals would require a day of atonement like
Yom Kippur. Instead, he emphasizes the aspects of Yom Kippur that lend themselves to angelic and human parity.

While the heavenly and earthly realms are separated in the abstract, this sep-
aration is subverted by shared recitation on Yom Kippur: in the synagogue at
that time, Israel and the angels are one. Yannai is the authority whose performative utterance creates this reality. To us, his presence is obvious only textually,
in acrostic. To the congregation witnessing his performance, his authority as a
mediating figure, leading the people in prayer, standing front and center, would
have been obvious. On this day above all, he is a pious intermediary, asserting
Israel's—and his own—identification with the angels.

YANNAI'S CONCEPTUALIZATION OF ANGELS

Apart from the question of angelic-human resemblance, Yannai's works offer
us the rare opportunity of understanding how one late antique Jew embedded
in his social context synthesized diverse traditions about the angels themselves.
Close reading of his piyyutim may help us understand more precisely how he,
among other Jews, conceptualized angels. My survey of his corpus suggests that
Yannai used many terms for angels and understood them as synonymous, not

---

63. Rabinovitz, *The Liturgical Poems of Rabbi Yannai*, 2:225–26.

distinguishing a hierarchy among them. In the following poem from the *qedushta* to Num 20:14, he brings together all the known biblical terms for angels.

> And you will rule camps [of angels] / and you will be carried miraculously / and you will ride a storm / and you will be majestic in majesty / and you will be ornamented in wonder / and roar among the hosts / and call out aloud / and ride the winds / and be praised in the name / and lauded powerfully / by countless *shenan* / by those swiftly running ones / by all the sided faces by the seraphim watchers / by the symphony of those saying / by the blazing ranks / by the perceiving *tephsar* / by the glinting [ones of] lightening / by the thanking tumult / by those of height / by flashes of light / by those thrice saying holy.[64]

Storm imagery is prominent in Yannai's description of God's appearance as it is in the theophanies of the Torah (Exod 19:16–20). When Yannai describes angels, he relies on biblical vocabulary, referring to angels as camps, hosts, *shenan*, seraphim, watchers, *tephsar*, as well as other substantive phrases. Yannai was not troubled by discrepancy between the divine creatures with four faces from Ezekiel's vision or the six-winged seraphim of Isaiah's vision. There is no attempt to account for discrepancies or provide hierarchies of angels in Yannai's piyyutim. In the same poetic verse, he brings together Isaiah's seraphim and the late book of Daniel's "watchers." Those saying thrice *kadosh* at the end allude back to the seraphim of Isaiah but also includes the people of Israel in the moment of their recitation of this prayer. Yannai synthesizes biblical sources; he does not present a systematic hierarchy or analysis of them. For Yannai, cataloging the many kinds of angels and their countless number was a way of glorifying God, but it also shows how he understood the multiplicity of angelic types in scripture: they were all divine beings subordinate to God. While the people of Israel rise to the level of the angels in the piyyutim of Yannai, the poet does not invite his congregations to call on angels in the midst of prayer. Prayer with the angels is always directed to the God above them.

Individual names of angels are also rare in Yannai's corpus. Yannai leaves almost all the angels unnamed, except for Michael, Gabriel, and Raphael (who all have some biblical pedigree, the former two from the Book of Daniel and the latter from the book of Tobit). In the extant corpus of his piyyutim, Yannai only names these three angels once, and only in this *qedushta* to Gen 19:1 on the story of the angels arriving in Sodom. Where the biblical source states that two angels came to Lot in Sodom, later interpreters such as Yannai and the sages identified these angels as Gabriel and Raphael.[65] According to Yannai and the sages, Gabriel was sent "to overturn Sodom and her suburbs" and Raphael sent "to spare Lot

---

64. Rabinovitz, *The Liturgical Poems of Rabbi Yannai*, 2:88.
65. See *Gen. Rab.* 50:2 (Theodor and Albeck, 516).

from being swallowed in the enveloping shroud."[66] Michael was the herald who announced the birth of a son to Abraham and Sarah (the topic of the previous lectionary reading and *qedushta*). Ancient interpreters likely assigned each of these angels their particular mission partially because of their name—Raphael, whose name is composed of the root R-P-A, which means "to heal," is sent for saving Lot and his family from death; Gabriel, whose name contains the trilateral root G-B-R, "man," denotes manliness and power and is sent for his great destructive power. Michael, whose name means "who is like God," is the angel associated with the nation of Israel in the book of Daniel, and so he performs the task of telling Abraham of his progeny, who contains within him the destiny of Israel. In his *qedushta* to Gen 19:1, Yannai emphasizes that each of the angels was sent for one task:

> The matter of the mission was singular; it would not be doubled
> and two missions [fall not upon one]
> Does not each his mission do,
> Whether for good or ill, whether of favor or anger?
> Good as done as soon as heard, they rush to their mission.[67]

These verses contain two ideas: a single task per angel and a rhetorical question about the obedience of the angels, regardless of the good or evil outcome of their missions. The attribution of a single mission to each angel is a principle that was shared by ancient learned Jews, the sages, targumists, and Yannai alike.[68] This idea relates less to angelic abilities than to a certain conception of wealth and power in antiquity. The more powerful an individual, the more servants he has at his service, each responsible for a particular duty. The underlying principle in these traditions is that God has so many ministering angels, each need only conduct one mission at a time, and the entire world in all its details functions as he wills it.[69]

In this poem, Yannai also gestures toward the nature of angelic will, which is subordinate to God's will. Yannai writes that a command heard is one executed; even Michael, Gabriel, and Raphael have no room for interiority for emotional reactions in these piyyutim. The subject of angelic will and emotions was not a settled one among Jews, as I will show in the next two chapters. Yannai did not highlight the emotional aspect of angelic-human relations directly because he does not encourage Jews to pray *to* angels, but to pray *with* angels to God. If Jews

66. Lieber, *Yannai on Genesis*, 492 (see the sixth and ninth piyyutim of this *qedushta*).

67. Lieber, *Yannai on Genesis*, 488–89; Rabinovitz 1:158–59.

68. Lieber, *Yannai on Genesis*, 488n9, translating the lacuna filled by Rabinovitz, who himself referenced Targum Neofiti to Gen 18:1 and *Genesis Rabbah* 50:2. On angels in the Targum in general, see Kasher, "Conception of Angels in Jewish Biblical Translations."

69. Indeed, *Sefer ha-Razim* offers no such disclaimer for angelic missions, but does offer six firmaments, each composed of many encampments of myriad angels, each assigned a different sphere of influence.

needed a mediating and compassionate presence, ostensibly Yannai in his role as prayer leader in the synagogue sought to fulfill it for them. And yet Yannai's description of the roles of Michael, Gabriel, and Raphael in the story of Abraham suggests these archangels were too well known to leave out. Jews expected to hear about these leading angels in this foundational story, and some Jews sought the help of these angels in their daily life. As ritual texts attest, the angels' presence would have made sense on a personal level to some Jews in the late antique Mediterranean world.

Although Yannai is clearly interested in inspiring Jews with angels, it seems that Israel and the angels achieve only temporal, not physical commingling. The sixth poem of the *qedushta* to Deut 6:4 states:

> The masses [of angels] do not recite "Holy" above,
> Until the faithful [Israel] recite "Blessed" below;
> When they stand below with words of prayer in their mouth,
> The angels standing above let down their wings.[70]

According to Yannai, Israel and the angels are synchronized in prayer, but the directions "above" and "below" suggest that they are not operating on the same physical plane. The angels remain above—hovering above in the heavens or at the height of the ceiling of the synagogue—but they are attuned to the actions of Israel below.[71] Yannai's verses suggest that angels closely attend to the actions of the praying congregations of Israel, but he does not provide unambiguous evidence that they are physically present alongside Jews the way that the ritual evidence does. Incantation bowls and amulets describe angels present in homes or protecting Jews as they proceed in daily life. In Yannai's mind, it seems that in moments of holiness, in prayer, the congregations of Israel and the angels take part in an imagined community. Yannai writes that both Israel and the angels recite the *Qedushah*, but Israel says it first, and only then, the angels follow.[72] Additionally, when the congregation stands in the synagogues, adopting an upright posture of prayer (itself an imitation of the angelic stance in Ezekiel), the angels in the

---

70. Rabinovitz, *The Liturgical Poems of Rabbi Yannai* 2:144. Translated and analyzed by Wout van Bekkum and Naoya Katsumata in "Piyyut as Poetics: The Example of Yannai's Qedushta for Deut. 6:4," 94.

71. Because they almost never leave traces behind, Synagogue ceilings form a significant gap in the study of ancient Jewish worship. On this, see Stern, "Mapping Devotion in Roman Dura Europos: A Reconsideration of the Synagogue Ceiling."

72. Similarly, in the Targumim, a tradition states that the ministering angels do not say the name of God until Israel has said the *Qedushah* (*Targum Neofiti* and *Fragment Targum* of MS Paris Hebr. 110 and MS Vatican 440 to Deut 32:2). See Shinan, "The Angelology of the 'Palestinian' Targums on the Pentateuch," 187. This may be contrasted with the tradition in *b. Ḥul.* 91b, where the rabbis claim that Israel pronounces God's name in the Shema before the angels do in the *Qedushah*.

heavens relax their wings; perhaps with their wings behind them (not extended) angels look more human too, bringing their appearances closer together.

We can compare this approach to angelic presence with the way Christian congregations in Palestine conceptualized angels in churches, a topic foregrounded by Ellen Muehlberger in her research on angels in ancient Christian catechetical treatises.[73] Likely from the first generations, followers of Jesus brought interest in angelic imitation to the nascent religious movement that became Christianity. After Christianity became an imperial religion in the fourth century CE, the influx of new converts necessitated the composition of books of catechesis that would provide converts with a guide to proper comportment as well as an orientation to the Christian imagination of the invisible realms. As Muehlberger explains, these books of catechesis encouraged Christians "to imagine the angels present, invisibly, at rituals," (178).[74] The earliest treatise, written by Cyril, the bishop of Jerusalem, in 348 CE, invited new Christians to join an "imagined angelic community," encouraging them to bring to their mind's eye the celestial stars, creatures, angels, archangels, cherubim, and finally Isaiah's seraphim saying, "Holy, Holy, Holy."[75] In poetic form, Yannai offers his congregants the same visual framework and ritual recitation, but Cyril's catechesis states the purposes of this directly: "Through this hymning we become fellows in the army above the world."[76] On the topic of imagined community with the angels during prayer, late antique churchgoers and synagogue attendees seem to have been in agreement.

Muehlberger observes that John Chrysostom's writings from fourth-century CE Antioch took angelic-human fellowship a step further, encouraging congregations to imagine angels surrounding holy priests during the ritual of the Eucharist. In his ruminations on the priesthood, the priests' holiness is emphasized by angelic presence "around the priest, and the bema and the place around the altar."[77] At the same time, he offers all catechumens the assurance of angelic attention after baptism, using athletic metaphors: "Not only are humans watching the exercises but the host of angels as well."[78] Chrysostom went further than Yannai in describing angelic presence inside congregational spaces and in relationship with individuals in their daily life. Some Jews may have believed angels were present with them inside and outside of the synagogues too, but Yannai's corpus, perhaps limited by

---

73. Muehlberger, *Angels in Late Ancient Christianity*, 177.

74. Muehlberger, *Angels in Late Ancient Christianity*, 178.

75. Muehlberger, *Angels in Late Ancient Christianity*, 184–87.

76. *Mystagogic Catechesis* 5.6–7. I quote Muehlberger's translation in *Angels in Late Ancient Christianity*, 187 (cf. Yarnold, trans., *Cyril of Jerusalem*, 183).

77. Muehlberger, *Angels in Late Ancient Christianity*, 193, translating *On the Priesthood* 6.4 (cf. *Sur la Sacredoce*, ed. Malingrey, 316).

78. Muehlberger, *Angels in Late Ancient Christianity*, 194, translating *Baptismal Instructions* 3.8.

the genre of liturgical poetry itself, does not directly address this aspect of angelic-human relations.

Angels are gendered masculine in Hebrew's binary language and described as masculine in a number of ancient sources.[79] One tradition, however, found in Yannai's corpus and in *Genesis Rabbah*, suggests Jewish thinkers could conceive of divine feminine messengers.[80] In the *qedushta* on Gen 11:1, the eighth poem begins as a description of God's movement in the heavens and ends in a description of God's creation of divine beings:

> And your mount is a cherub / Your flight is on the wind / Your road is in the storm / Your path is in the gale / Your way is on the water / Your mission is through fire / Thousands upon thousands, myriads upon myriads / Become men / Become women / Become spirits / Become demons / Become every form / And perform every mission / With terror, with dread, with fear, with trembling, with quaking, with shaking, they open their mouths to mention Your holy name.[81]

At the phrase "your mission is through fire," the topic of this poem changes. The keywords are mission and fire. *Shlichut*, translated as mission, derives from the verb to send (*sh-l-ḥ*). At this phrase, what begins as a description of God's powerful presence transitions to a discussion of his fiery messengers, those he sends out. Yannai plays on this double meaning (God in the fire and God creates beings of fire), and the next lines feature those thousands and myriads of God's messengers, which are men (*'anashim*), women (*nashim*), spirits (*ruhot*), demons (*zykym*), and so on. The plain meaning seems to be that God makes myriads of beings, masculine and feminine; incorporeal beings; and demons. The order of beings in this tradition (flaming fire, men, women, spirits) is the same as in *Genesis Rabbah*, and Yannai employs identical Hebrew terminology, except that the rabbis' list ends with angels while Yannai's ends with demons.

This is the only poem by Yannai where feminine divine beings are clearly referenced and it seems that he, in turn, was alluding to the prophetic book of Zechariah 5:9. This book describes Zechariah seeing "two *women* [*nashim*] going forth and the wind was in their wings, for they had wings like a stork."[82] One explanation for this passages is that Yannai and the rabbis who contributed to *Genesis Rabbah*

---

79. In the biblical and Second Temple period, Jews perceived angels as corporeally masculine: the seraphim in Isaiah's vision cover their "legs," a biblical euphemism for genitals (Isa 6:1); according to the author of the book of Jubilees (late second century BCE), the angels were created circumcised (15:27); and in the first century CE, Paul was worried about women seducing angels (1 Cor 11:10).

80. See *Gen. Rab.* 21:9 (Theodor and Albeck, 203). Unfortunately, this passage is part of a larger middle section missing both from MS Vatican 30 and the genizah fragments published by Sokoloff in *The Geniza Fragments of Bereshit Rabba*.

81. Lieber, *Yannai on Genesis*, 384–85.

82. Zech 5:9; cf. *Exod. Rab.* 25:2.

were acknowledging the winged women referenced in the visions of Zechariah. One text in the Hebrew Bible thus provided a point of departure for imagining female beings, even if the rabbis and liturgical poets rarely elaborated on it. I treat this important topic in a separate article, but in this context, it is worth lingering on how the synagogue practice of reciting the *Qedushah* may have opened up space for new possibilities in the Jewish imagination.[83] When Jewish men and women prayed in the synagogue, they recited the angelic praise and assumed the postures of the angels. As women assumed angelic postures in synagogue practice, they made possible the imagining of feminine angels too. Angels, invisible and divine, were also malleable, imitable, and crucial to communal piety in antiquity.

BLURRING THE BOUNDARIES: PRIESTS, RABBIS, AND RITUAL PRACTITIONERS IN THE SYNAGOGUE

Previous chapters have already pointed to the permeability between ritual incantations, rabbinic traditions, and Jewish prayers that appeal to angels. In this section, I wish to dwell on Yannai's perspective, which stands out as unique in its inclusive (even ecumenical) attitude to Jewish society in late antiquity, embracing priests, rabbis, and even ritual practitioners in the angelic congregation before him. Yannai's fragmentary composition to Num 6:22 offers a few tantalizing verses about the role of the priests in the synagogue and, in the process, speaks to the coexistence of different figures of authority in the late antique synagogue. This lectionary reading contains the blessing of the people of Israel, taught by God to Moses, who is instructed to pass it on to the priests (*birkat kohanim*, "the priestly blessing"). Because this *qedushta* is so fragmentary, I paraphrase some of its verses, and explain how this composition evokes the network of relationships that Yannai and ancient Jews inhabited.

In a vivid image that has endured in Jewish interpretation, Yannai wrote that God peeks out between the fingers of the priests during their blessing of the people (1:1–4).[84] Jews, priests and congregants alike, traditionally avert their eyes at this moment of divine intimacy. In this portrayal, the honorific significance of the priest increases dramatically; they stand in as God's angelic mediators, with God directly behind them. In the same piyyut, Yannai wrote that to hear the priests' blessing, many run to the synagogue (4:39).[85] The following fragmentary line begins with the words "sixty letters" and ends with a reference to

83. See Ahuvia, "Gender and the Angels in Late Antique Judaism."

84. Rabinovitz, *The Liturgical Poems of Rabbi Yannai*, 2:29.

85. Rabinovitz, *The Liturgical Poems of Rabbi Yannai*, 2:32. Here the synagogue is referred to as *sh'ar rabim*. Cf. y. B. *Mesi'a* 2:11, which describes people "running" to hear R. Yohanan expounding in R. Benaya's Beit Midrash in Sepphoris.

holding "swords" (4:40).[86] To fill in this fragmentary verse, one must know that the priestly blessing contains sixty letters as well as the content of Song 3:7, which states "Behold, it is the litter of Solomon! Around it are sixty mighty men, of the mighty men of Israel, all equipped with swords / and experts in war, each with his sword at his thigh / guarding against the terrors of the night." To ritual practitioners, the image of King Solomon's bed with sixty warriors guarding against demons of the night was fitting for a sick, bedridden patient, who believed his suffering was caused by demons. Quotations of this verse are found in many ritual texts for anti-demonic purposes.[87] In these contexts, the warriors might have been perceived as angelic warriors. In any case, Yannai was telling his audience that the priestly blessing with its sixty letters was as strong as those sixty swords of the warriors of Solomon invoked by ritual practitioners. Interestingly, the combination of Song 3:7 with the priestly blessing is now part of the nightly Shema as well, alongside the invocation of the angels on four sides, discussed in the previous chapters' closings.[88] Rather than choosing one option, later Jews embraced multiple comforting images: angels on four sides, the sixty armed-warriors around their bed, and the priestly blessing protected them.

In the very next verse of his liturgical composition, Yannai likens the sixty letters of the priestly blessing to the perfectly arranged sixty tractates of the Mishnah: "like the sixty orders which are the *halakhot* / Blessings arranged, ordained, fixed" (4:41).[89] With these descriptions, Yannai brings together the priests' most important ritual function in the synagogue, a biblical motif often quoted by ritual practitioners against demons, and the sages' legal code. We should note that for Yannai, these sources of authority in no way conflict, but the authority inherent in each allusion enlivens the other. Yannai offers us a crucial window into a time in late antique Jewish life when priests, ritual practitioners, and sages coexisted on a spectrum of authority. At the end of this *qedushta*, these leaders and the congregation would have been elevated to angelic status as well.

This composition demonstrates that popular texts and practices were evidently shared among Jewish authorities. This observation, in turn, may help us understand Yannai's rumination on the power of God's name, which can be used to heal, exorcise, and bless (*qedushta* on Exod 6:2).

86. Rabinovitz, *The Liturgical Poems of Rabbi Yannai*, 2:32.

87. For other appearances of this verse, see Naveh and Shaked, *Magic Spells and Formulae*, 24–25. See also Rainbow, "The Song of Songs and the Testament of Solomon."

88. It is possible that this juxtaposition of biblical description and priestly blessing began in the synagogue and impacted ritual texts, but it is also possible that the ritual texts impacted the description of the priestly blessing and that centuries of popular practice later, they entered the fixed liturgy of the Jewish home.

89. Rabinovitz, *The Liturgical Poems of Rabbi Yannai*, 2:32.

And Your name is not to be explicated | (Your Name) is not to be pronounced. . . .
   Your name is not to be profaned Your name is not to be analyzed
Your name is not to be made known And no one knows Your name
You are your name and your name is You.
(Skipping 4 lines)
And those called in Your name will call you in your name /. . . and this is the name
   said over the fire and it goes out / upon water and it dries up / upon the sea and
   it bursts/ upon stone and it explodes / . . . upon the demon and he flees/ upon
   the sick and he heals / upon the dead and he lives / upon the world and it stands
   forever. . . .
(Skipping 3 lines)
For your sake and your legacy those saying your name answer and say
Holy, Holy, Holy, is the Lord of Hosts! The whole earth is filled with His glory!
"Holy"—from the covenant of Abraham,
"Holy"—from the oath of Isaac,
"Holy"—from the promise of Jacob.[90]

Yannai elevates God's name here with references to well-known biblical stories (e.g., Moses's parting of the Red Sea, Moses's drawing of water from stone), but also with references to ritual practices, wherein ritual practitioners invoked God's name (often alongside angels) to exorcise demons, heal the sick, and resurrect the dead. The ritual sources that we have reviewed furnish examples of this use of God's name. Yannai's poetry shows that he understood the use of the divine name for healing as consistent with the covenant of Israel with God. Perhaps Yannai was aware that some ritual practitioners placed amulets invoking God and the angels in synagogues.[91] God's sacred name was sanctioned for the descendants of Abraham, Isaac, and Jacob, whether they were priests reciting their benediction in the synagogue, ritual practitioners in their incantations and amulets, the sages in their legal and exegetical work, or prayer leaders singing God's praise with the angels.

Whereas contemporary readers might want to distinguish between classic rabbinic authorities and "fringe" ritual practitioners, seeing one as acceptable and one as alien to Jewish practice, Yannai and his congregation evidently did not make such distinctions. Yannai does not have a separate categorical name for ritual practitioners. Yannai's views thus undermine our boundaries between "magical" and religious authorities. God's commitment to the Jewish people was expressed in many ways, through many authorities, and Yannai had no problem acknowledging all of them—perhaps because priests, rabbis, prayer and ritual practitioners had much in common as they sought to guide and support the Jews in their communities in their interaction with the invisible realm. Moreover, all of

90. Rabinovitz, *The Liturgical Poems of Rabbi Yannai*, 1:278–79.
91. Stern, "Harnessing the Sacred."

them were present in the synagogue among the congregation of Israel, imitating the angels as they prayed to God.

CONCLUSION: ANGELS IN THE ANCIENT SYNAGOGUE

While some rabbis, following traditions associated with Rabbi Akiva, encouraged Jews to be godly and focus on a singular holiness, Jews in Yannai's synagogues were inspired to emulate angels through Yannai's interweaving of Jewish customs, angelic holiness, and the angelic praise. Although there are parallels in Christian writings on angels in congregational settings from the same period in Palestine, there is nothing Christian per se about Jewish conceptualization of angels. Yannai's works shows us how Jews conceptualized angels on their own terms. Jewish men and women could participate in imitation of the angels in liturgical practice, and it is possible that this practice opened up new possibilities in the Jewish imagination, allowing for women to be angelic too.

In the previous chapter, we saw how the rabbis tried to redirect Jewish attention to God rather than attack Jewish preoccupation with angels. In this, their success was limited. Yannai encouraged fellowship with angels, even as he directed Jewish prayer toward God alone. On the holiest days of the year, Yannai depicted all Jews as equal to the angels. And yet Yannai also illustrates that the worldview of the ritual practitioners was not far from that of the Jew in a synagogue in Galilee, who expected angelic names and God's names to heal. The late antique synagogue was a space not only for the communal liturgy but also for amulets that invoked God and the angels. The popularity of the angels with Jews in the synagogue impacted the rabbinic movement in Palestine and Babylonia. In the next chapter, I will show the shift in rabbinic attitudes toward angels in the latest strata of rabbinic writings, in which the rabbis finally admit the usefulness of conceptualizing the angels all around them.

6

Israel among the Angels

Late Rabbinic Sources

He who enters a bathroom should say: "Be honored, you honorable and holy ones, ministers of the Most High, give honor to the God of Israel. Withdraw from me while I enter and do my business until I come back to you."

Abaye said: a person should not say this lest they abandon the person and go their way. Rather, he says: "Guard me, guard me. Assist me, assist me. Wait for me, wait for me until I have entered and exited, for thus is the way of human beings."

— BABYLONIAN TALMUD

Having examined ritual, liturgical, and early rabbinic traditions, we can now turn to the later rabbinic texts and see the rabbis, at last, coming to terms with the popularity of angels and incorporating conceptualizations of angels into Jewish prayer and practice. The above rabbinic prayers to angels represent a significant shift in rabbinic attitudes toward angels.[1] The fourth generation Babylonian Amora Rabbi Abaye is attributed the development of an existing prayer directed at guardian angels. Evidently, this ritual prayer to angels originated in rabbinic circles.[2] Far more than any previous rabbinic, ritual, or liturgical text, these ritual prayers modeled how to interact with the invisible angels, asking directly for their continued protective presence, their assistance, and their patience in the most human and mundane circumstances.

This and other examples analyzed in this chapter demonstrate that as time passed in late antiquity, rabbinic disciples began to accept the role of angels in other Jews' piety, and gradually rabbinic traditions moved beyond accommodation to exploitation of belief in angels for particularly rabbinic ends. This chapter forms the final part of a survey of angels in rabbinic texts and focuses on traditions

---

1. *b. Ber.* 60b; the first prayer text has a parallel in *y. Ber.* 9:4 (14b).
2. Septimus, "On the Boundaries of Prayer," 24.

that signal a departure from treatment of angels seen in Tannaitic texts. Rather than studying the hundreds, if not thousands, of traditions about angels in later rabbinic midrashim, this focus on departures allows for an exploration of both normative traditions and exceptions to those.[3]

In chapter 3, I argued that the early rabbinic texts tended to discuss angels only indirectly and subtly, displaying a tendency to downplay angels in Israel's foundational narratives. Though the rabbis had to grapple with angels in their commentaries on Exodus, overall, their interpretations discouraged the imagining of angels. At best, a few traditions allowed that the Israelites' time in the wilderness was a time of divine intimacy, when they were close to God and his angels. Based on extant texts, it is difficult to ascertain whether the relative dearth of references to angels in early sources is a product of editing, redaction, and transmission or a self-censoring tendency among the rabbis. Still, comparing earlier and later sources, we can distinguish changes in attitudes toward angels. Especially helpful are traditions that are repeated from early to later generations and reshaped in transmission to reflect developing attitudes. To observe developments in rabbinic attitudes toward angels, I have examined sources diachronically, erring on the side of caution in terms of the accuracy of attributed traditions, and noted especially where the tradition is preserved. At best, we can be certain about the date of the final redaction of sources or trace development of parallel traditions from earlier rabbinic documents to later ones. With this in mind, I treat sources in the Palestinian Talmud as earlier than *Genesis Rabbah* and these two documents as earlier than the texts in the Babylonian Talmud, acknowledging that there may be some overlap in early Babylonian rabbinic traditions and later Palestinian ones. I also acknowledge that what is captured in a certain rabbinic corpus may not reflect all the traditions available to rabbis of that time period or the wider imaginative vocabulary available to contemporaneous Jews.

This chapter begins with a close reading of a story with vivid evocations of angels that is preserved in Tannaitic sources and retold in the Palestinian and Babylonian Talmuds. This story highlights the increasing importance of guardian angels in the Jewish and rabbinic imagination. I then discuss other traditions about such accompanying angels, such as those about the Sabbath that employ guardian angels to encourage right prayer and practice, that can be found in the Babylonian Talmud. To fully elucidate these traditions, I explain the role of good and evil angels as well as angelic freewill and emotions in rabbinic texts. In contrast to Tannaitic rabbinic traditions that begrudgingly admit angels were

3. The recent scholarship of Bill Rebiger has furnished synchronic overviews of angels in later rabbinic literature. His article "Angels in Rabbinic Literature," summarizes rabbinic traditions on the origins of angels, angelic characteristics, numbers and classifications, purposes and functions, angelic proper names, and so on.

a feature of Israel's glorious past, later rabbinic traditions increasingly discuss angels in the people of Israel's present, active in the lives of Jews, and worthy of theological reflection. Studied in the wider context of Jewish sources, we can see that rabbinic attitudes toward angels shifted over time and in dialogue with other Jewish beliefs and practices.

CHANGING CONCEPTIONS OF ANGELS IN THE LATER RABBINIC IMAGINATION

I begin with the story of Rabban Yohanan ben Zakkai and Rabbi Eleazar ben Arach, which captures and reflects the changing attitudes toward angels among the rabbinic storytellers and redactors. This rabbinic story is preserved in the Tosefta, Mekhilta de Rabbi Shimon bar Yohai, the Palestinian Talmud, and the Babylonian Talmud.[4] In the Tosefta this story is presented to illustrate a rabbinic precept limiting discussion of dangerous topics like the heavenly throne (lit. "the works of the chariot," Hebrew *ma'ase merkavah*).[5] In its earliest formulation in Tosefta *Ḥagigah* 2:1, this story had no angels at all: according to the text, two rabbis were on the road when one suggested discussing God's heavenly throne. While the disciple Eleazar b. Arach expounded, the teacher dismounted from his donkey to listen, wrapped himself in his tallit, and sat under an olive tree. According to the story, the elder Rabban Yohanan ben Zakkai listened to the exposition and then, as a mark of his approval, kissed Eleazar's head, and said, "Blessed are you God, the God of Israel, who gave Abraham our father a son such as this who knows to comprehend and to expound the glory of his father in the heavens." The approval of the legendary founder of the rabbinic movement was emphasized in this story, and his praise proved sufficient to convey God's affirmation.[6] As we shall see, this is not the case in the later retellings, where the rabbis inserted angels or took for granted the angels' presence.

---

4. Urbach examined the evolution of this tradition for different reasons in "The Traditions on Merkavah Mysticism in the Tannaitic Period."

5. *Ma'ase merkavah* is the rabbinic term for expositions on the chariot-throne described in Ezek 1 and 10. The biblical book of Ezekiel does not contain the word *merkavah* but describes the divine throne-chariot of God using the Hebrew *kisse* (1 Chron 28:18 is the earliest to refer to the chariot as *merkavah* and Sir 49:8 is the earliest to refer to the visions of the chariot). See chapter 7 for more bibliography on this term.

6. Cf. *Mek. RS, Nezikin* 1 (Nelson, 259–60): in this parallel, no angels descend to bless R. Eleazar ben Arach's exposition, and Rabban Yohanan praises R. Eleazar in similar terms ("Happy is the one who gave birth to you! Happy is Abraham our father, for this one came for your loins!" He used to say, "If all the wise men of Israel were in one side of the scale, with R. Eleazar ben Arach in the second side, he would outweigh them all!"). Yohanan's praise in this source is more pronounced, but still the heavenly realm does not directly intrude into the earthly one.

I begin quoting the story in the Palestinian Talmud's retelling, where new details were added:

> Because Rabbi Eleazar opened his mouth to speak of the works of the chariot, Rabban Yohanan ben Zakkai dismounted from the donkey. He said: it is not fitting that I should hear about the glory of my maker while I am riding a donkey. They went and sat under a tree. And fire descended from the heavens and surrounded them and the ministering angels were skipping about before them like groomsmen rejoicing before the groom. One angel answered from the fire and said, "Just as you say, Eleazar ben Arach, indeed, thus is *ma'ase merkavah.*" Immediately, all the trees joined in song and said praise: "let all the trees of the forest sing for joy" (Ps 96:12).[7]

According to this rendition, rabbinic exposition on an esoteric topic prompted heavenly fire and dancing angels.[8] As we have seen, fire is often associated with the fiery and pure nature of angels.[9] Rather than being frightening, the fiery angels are described as intimately enclosing the rabbis and dancing before them as if they were at a wedding party. From a learned rabbinic perspective, discussing the mysteries of the divine throne is presented as equivalent to the intimacy and joy in the rite of passage associated with nuptial celebrations. This analogy is not surprising in the context of rabbinic comparisons of Torah study with the devotion required of marriage.[10] What should be surprising is that it was deemed necessary to add the angels at all. The presence of angels in this text is not the legacy of biblical interpretation, but the product of the rabbinic imagination, which conceived of legendary first-century CE rabbis interacting with angels and uses angelic presence as a marker of divine approval. That the storytellers who retold and transmitted this story chose to develop it with the presence of the angels is a striking departure from earlier narratives that seem bent on eliminating angels from biblical prooftexts. The rabbis would not have embellished a rabbinic foundation story with angels unless their attitudes toward angels had changed, and now they wanted the affirmation that only angels could bring to a story.

Taking this description of angelic presence one step further, the rabbinic storyteller described one angel as addressing the expounding rabbi and declaring, "Just as you say, Eleazar ben Arach, indeed thus is *ma'ase merkavah.*" Rather than having Rabban Yohanan give Eleazar ben Arach affirmation, here an angel validates his wisdom. (Ostensibly, the ministering angel, having been in the heavens, is validating Eleazar's description with eye-witness experience.) The angel's declaration

---

7. See *y. Ḥag.* 77a (Schäfer and Becker, *Synopse zum Talmud Yerushalmi* II/5–12, 320 [2.1/9–10]).

8. This story is one of the rare sources that describes angels dancing; cf. *b. Ber.* 51a.

9. This goes back to Ps 104:4; *Gen. Rab.* 78:1, *b. Ḥag.* 14a; cf. *b. Pesaḥ.* 118b where the angel Gabriel describes himself as the angelic "prince of the fire."

10. Rubenstein, *Rabbinic Stories*, 139–45.

makes the stationary trees come alive with joy and praise as well; the angel speaks to the rabbis and impacts the natural world. This story may not have encouraged those who heard the story to imagine angels around them explicitly, but it situated legendary founders and disciples with angelic company and associated the exposition of right knowledge with angelic presence. These additions represent an important departure from earlier approaches to angels in rabbinic texts.

Between the redaction of the story into the Tosefta and its redaction into the Palestinian Talmud sometime in the fourth century, the religious landscape had changed in Roman Palestine. In the fourth century CE, the emperor Constantine transformed the notoriously rebellious province into the Holy Land through the construction of countless pilgrimage sites.[11] Constantine's mother-in-law personally intervened with the emperor to ensure a Christian basilica was built on the site of Mamre, where Jews, Christians, polytheists, locals, and Arabs congregated to commemorate the angels' appearance to Abraham (Gen 18–19).[12] As discussed in the previous chapter, contemporary Christian leaders encouraged attention to angels in their teachings of converts, in communal settings, and in the Christian imagination. It is likely no coincidence that a tradition in the Palestinian Talmud explicitly warned Jews not to pray to Gabriel and Michael.[13] Yet this Talmud is also the earliest rabbinic source to include a tradition about the origin of the archangels' names.[14] As time went on, the rabbis could not afford to ignore the presence of angels in biblical traditions or in the popular imagination.

If the sages quoted in the Palestinian Talmud were still ambivalent about the angels, the Babylonian Talmud's redactors were not. In the Babylonian Talmud's rendition of this story, the earlier versions were combined, and some editorial intrusions interrupted the flow, but descriptions of the angels remained and grew. The Stammaim took for granted Jewish traditions associated with the ongoing presence of guardian angels.

> Once upon a time Rabban Yohanan ben Zakkai was riding upon a donkey and was going about the way and Rabbi Eleazar ben Arach was upon a donkey behind him. He said to him, "Rabbi, teach me a chapter of *ma'ase merkavah*. He answered him, "Did I not teach you that this topic could not be expounded on before one, unless he was wise and understood the matter on his own?" [Rabbi Eleazar] said to him, "will you permit me to state before you one matter that I learned?" [Rabban Yohanan]

---

11. Taylor, *Christians and the Holy Places*.

12. Cline offers an excellent analysis of this pilgrimage site and its description in written sources (*Ancient Angels*, 107–18).

13. See *y. Ber.* 9.1, discussed in chapter 3. Raphael is not mentioned in the Palestinian Talmud.

14. See *y. Roš Haš.* 1:2, 6a which has Reish Lakish cite Dan as a prooftext for the names of Michael and Gabriel arising from Babylonia); cf. *Gen. Rab.* 48:9 (Theodor and Albeck, 485); the trio of Michael, Gabriel, and Raphael is also found in the *b. Yoma* 37a and *b. B. Meṣi'a* 86b. The topic of names of angels is discussed in Rebiger, "Angels in Rabbinic Literature," 637–40.

said "speak." Immediately, Rabban Yohanan dismounted from the donkey, covered himself [in his cloak], and sat upon a stone under an olive tree. [Rabbi Eleazar] said to him, "Rabbi, why did you dismount from the donkey?" He answered, "Is it acceptable for you to expound in the *ma'ase merkavah* with the *Shekhinah* with us and the ministering angels accompanying (Hebrew, *melavin*) us and all while I am riding a donkey?"

Immediately, Rabbi Eleazar ben Arach began expounding on the *ma'ase merkavah* and a fire descended from the heavens and encircled all the trees in the field and they all broke out into song.[15]

In this retelling, the guardian angels' presence is referenced before the beginning of the exposition on the *ma'ase merkavah*. Whereas the Palestinian Talmud's version made clear that the angels *descended* as a result of rabbinic engagement with this esoteric topic, Rabban Yohanan's rhetorical question introduces an ambiguity regarding divine presence: he asks whether it is appropriate to discuss *ma'ase merkavah* while he is on a donkey and the "*Shekhinah* with us" and "the ministering angels accompanying (*melavin*)" us. This storyteller took for granted the idea of the accompanying *Shekhinah* and guardian angels. This aspect of the Babylonian rendition recalls the Tosefta source on traveling with the righteous and their angels as well as the invocation of angels on all sides.[16] In the Babylonian Talmud's version of this story, Rabban Yohanan's words seem to allude to such traditions directly, rhetorically asking how Eleazar could be unaware of the *Shekhinah* and the ministering angels "*accompanying*" them, but it is actually only Yohanan's riding on the donkey that renders discussion of the *ma'ase merkavah* inappropriate (as in the Palestinian Talmud's version). In its current form, Eleazar's question and Rabban Yohanan's answer are intrusive to the story, but some editorial need must have prompted these additions. The Babylonian rabbinic storytellers took the belief in accompanying angels and the *Shekhinah* for granted and, unlike previous generations, seem to have anticipated such questions about divine presence from fellow rabbinic disciples. In the Babylonian Talmud's version of this story, the angels are just as important for signifying divine sanction, but more than that, we can discern that conceptions of angels are part of a larger constellation of beliefs that the redactors could draw on at will.[17]

15. b. *Hag.* 14b. In the Babylonian Talmud, this story continues incorporating details found in the Tosefta, the Mekhilta, and the Palestinian Talmud, plus a few other minor editorial interventions.

16. See t. '*Abod. Zar.* 1:17 (chapter 3), which advised journeying within three days of a righteous person in order to benefit from the angels of peace "accompanying" him (*melavin* is the verb there as well).

17. According to the next story in b. *Hag.* 14b, when Rabbi Yehoshua and Rabbi Yose ha-Kohen discussed *ma'ase merkavah* on a clear summer day, clouds and a rainbow suddenly appeared, and the ministering angels gathered around them to listen like people gathering to hear music at a wedding. In the Palestinian Talmud, the same story follows, but a *bat kol* is the divine voice who signals approval for those rabbis.

We can see how such traditions about angelic guardianship continued to develop among the rabbis with the next tradition from the medieval Midrash on Psalms, which clearly has some relationship to the Toseftan tradition of traveling with the righteous and their angels as well as the rabbinic principle of imitation of God. The tradition is attributed to a sage named Rabbi Joshua ben Levi, who lived at the beginning of the third century CE and around whom circulated many angelic traditions.[18] The following tradition synthesized a number of other rabbinic attitudes toward the invisible realm. Rather than seeing the imitation of God and imitation of angels as competing, here they are in harmony and combined with beliefs in angelic guardianship: "Rabbi Joshua ben Levi: At the time that a person sets out on a journey, a procession of angels walks before him, declaring and saying: "Give way before the icon[19] of the Holy One, blessed be He!"[20] Unlike the Tosefta tradition that offered travel advice and conceptualized angels of peace for the righteous and adversarial angels for the wrongdoer, this tradition celebrates the dignity of each human being as an icon of God, a message that is amplified by a procession of angels that precedes a person. The procession, a fixture of religious life in the Greco-Roman world, usually bore the icons of a Greco-Roman divinity, but here the angels carry an icon for every person, who himself is an icon of God (going back to Gen 1:24 "in the image of God"). This tradition, far more than the earlier Toseftan one, encouraged Jews to imagine themselves preceded and celebrated by angels. It also transcended the theme of rivalry between angels and humans, understanding the angels as celebrating humans' relationship to God. Angels accompanied people as they celebrated a relationship with the divine. This tendency toward synthesis and harmonization of previous sources is characteristic of later medieval rabbinic traditions.

ANGELS IN PRAYER AND PRAXIS
IN TALMUDIC SOURCES

Once the rabbis accepted the concept of angelic company or guardianship, they had to attend to a number of repercussions: How do you acknowledge the angels'

18. According to a story in *b. Ketub.* 77b, R. Joshua b. Levi tricked the Angel of Death into allowing him to see Paradise. This story grew into a medieval legend called *Ma'aseh R. Joshua b. Levi*, which was adapted by Muslim sources into a story of Enoch's encounter with the Angel of Death. See Reeves and Reed, *Enoch from Antiquity to the Middle Ages*, 1:200–209.

19. A play on words is more readily seen in the Hebrew, where the Greek loan word *eikonya* (plural of Greek εἰκόνιον) appears twice in the Hebrew, once signifying the kind of icon-laden procession of angels that sets out and once referring to the individual, who is the icon of God. Jastrow suggests the singular possessive makes more sense here and that the doubling of the form *ikonya* is likely a copyist error (*Dictionary*, 60).

20. *Midrash Tehillim, Mizmor* 17:8 (Buber, p. 131).

presence (with or without God)? Do guardian angels follow you into the bathroom? How do you request the leave of your guardian angels without risking abandonment? The rabbinic prayers to angels with which this chapter begins addressed these questions. The earlier prayer was careful to outline the angels' subordinate role ("ministers of the Most High, give honor to the God of Israel"), while the prayer attributed to Abaye addressed the angels without titles and without bringing God into the recitation itself. Both of these prayers evince a concern with maintaining angelic presence and addressing angels respectfully, not taking their presence for granted nor ignoring them. Surviving rabbinic traditions suggest that other questions emerged regarding human behavior around the angels and, conversely, imagining how the angels might respond to the conduct of Jews in their ordinary lives. In the following examples, I examine rabbinic traditions that focus on angels in Jewish prayer and practice.

The belief that angels are transmitters of prayer is the underlying assumption in a tradition attributed to Rabbi Yohanan (third century CE Roman Palestine). This tradition about the language of the angels is found only in the Babylonian Talmud: "Prayer: It is supplication and may be said however one wishes. And may prayer (be said) in every language? Rav Yehuda said: a person ought never ask for his needs in Aramaic as Rabbi Yohanan said, 'whoever asks for his needs in Aramaic, the angels do not attend to him, as the angels do not understand the Aramaic tongue!'"[21] This tradition grappled with a practical problem, engaging with the questions of prayer language, efficacy, and the angels. Notably, the prayer to guardian angels attributed to Abaye was in Hebrew even as the comments about maintaining the angelic presence were in Aramaic—Aramaic, of course, was the colloquial language of Jews in late antiquity.[22] Though readers are often struck by the idea that angels are monolingual, what is even more striking is that this influential rabbi is said to take for granted that Jews were in fact praying to the angels and the angels do play a role in conveying Jewish prayers to God. According to this tradition, Palestinian and Babylonian rabbis were encouraging Jews to pray in Hebrew if they wanted the angels to attend to their prayers. Only the belief that angels attended to the prayers of Hebrew-speaking Jews makes sense of the converse opinion: that they do not attend to the prayers of Aramaic-speaking Jews. This rabbinic assertion about the proper language of prayer should not be taken at face value for many reasons, as Joseph Yahalom thoroughly explained: it must be understood in the context of rabbinic assertion of authority over the

---

21. See *b. Šabb.* 12b and *b. Soṭah* 33a.

22. To clarify, acc. to *b. Ber.* 60b, "Abaye said [in Aramaic]: a person should not say this lest they abandon the person and go their way. Rather, he says [in Hebrew]: "Guard me, guard me. Assist me, assist me. Wait for me, wait for me until I have entered and exited, for thus is the way of human beings."

informal prayer of other Jews.[23] This tradition evinced a concern about personal and informal Jewish prayer in Aramaic and cited Rabbi Yohanan's opinion as encouragement to other rabbinic Jews to pray in Hebrew instead. What matters for our purpose is that, in the process of arguing over prayer language, this rabbinic tradition assumed that angels have a role in attending to people's prayers. The later rabbis indirectly acknowledged that Jews prayed through angels and expected angels to convey their prayers to God. Meanwhile, the evidence of the ritual texts suggests that Jews prayed to angels in Aramaic, both in Palestine and Babylonia and that Rabbi Yohanan's opinion on angelic language was not widely shared by Jews.

The fullest description of the role of angels in the mechanics of prayer may be discerned in a story found in the Palestinian Talmud. According to the story, when the idolatrous biblical king Manasseh was captured by the Babylonians, he called on all the other gods to rescue him. When none came to his aid, he finally remembered his own father's prayers, and the God of his fathers, and figuring he had nothing to lose, he prayed to God. The angels intervened:

> The ministering angels sealed the windows [of the heavenly palace] so that his prayer would not reach God. And the ministering angels said before the Holy One, blessed be He, "Master of the universe, a man that took part in idolatry and erected a statue in the Holy of Holies—are you going to accept his repentance? He responded, "If I were to reject Manasseh's repentance, I would have to lock the doors before all those who seek repentance." What did he do for him? The Holy One, blessed be He, created an opening for him beneath his glorious throne and heard his pleas from there. Hence it is written "He prayed to him, and he granted his prayer, heard his plea, and returned him" [2 Chron 33:13].[24]

The image of God sitting on his glorious throne and needing to create another opening for prayer requires conjuring up the image of a heavenly throne room. Although set in the era of the biblical monarchy, this story assumes a worldview wherein God receives prayers in a heavenly throne room attended by ministering angels. The angels have a role in conveying prayers to God, and they can even stop one's prayers from reaching the heavenly throne room. In this story, the angels apparently did not relent after hearing God's explanation for receiving Manasseh's repentance, and thus God had to open a channel just for

23. See Yahalom, "Angels Do Not Understand Aramaic." As Yahalom points out, already ca. 1000 CE Rav Sherira and Hai Gaon were writing that they had never "seen or heard that the sages refrained from praying in the Aramaic tongue" (33). In addition to the Hebrew liturgical poetry of Yannai and other early medieval poets, see Sokoloff and Yahalom, *Jewish Palestinian Aramaic Poetry from Late Antiquity.*

24. See *y. Sanh.* 10:2 (28c). My translation.

the prayers of Manasseh to reach him. The unspoken assumption is that other prayers reach God with the aid of the angels, who act as messengers or gatekeepers for the transmission of prayers. That angels were such mediating figures was also assumed in an amulet from Turkey, directed to Michael, Raphael, and other angels who stand before the throne and that asks for the words of the incantation to "rise up to heaven at the side of the throne of the great, powerful, awful, sacred, magnified and praised, and exalted God."[25] Prayer from people in the earthly realm had to reach the heavenly throne room and many ancient people believed that angels had to carry their prayers to God. By the time of the redaction of the Babylonian Talmud, the belief that angels conveyed prayers was taken for granted by the rabbis too.

Other Babylonian rabbinic traditions exposed the invisible realm of the angels, as it were, revealing what people's guardian angels were doing in response to proper or improper Jewish behavior. In a passage about conduct in times of famine, the rabbis used the imagining of angelic guardians to encourage Jewish solidarity: "Our rabbis taught: in times when the people of Israel are suffering in sorrow and one of them separates himself from them, the two ministering angels that accompany a person come to him and place their hands upon his head and say: 'may this one who separated from the community never see the consolation of the community.'"[26] This is the first of three traditions in the Babylonian Talmud that assumes that Jews are each accompanied by a pair of angels. Rather than acting as guardian angels, however, in this rabbinic conceptualization, the ministering angels police behavior in the invisible realm. The ministering angels offer their charge (the perceived deserter) a malediction, not protection or a blessing. The rabbis wished to emphasize that the ministering angels sided with the community of Israel; they placed Jewish communal interests above the individual's. Like the rabbinic emphasis on the angels speaking Hebrew only, this tradition probably reflects not popular belief about angels but rabbinic preoccupation with boundary drawing and upholding communal cohesion. While it is linguistically similar to other traditions found in the Babylonian Talmud, conceptually it is unique.

The next tradition in the Babylonian Talmud about the accompanying angels clearly bears some relationship to the one just discussed but is attributed to a first-generation Babylonian Amora named Mar Ukba. It appears in a section of the Talmud urging Jews to enjoy the Sabbath and its attendant obligations, where the Stammaim brought together a number of traditions to encourage recitation of prayers and the preparation of the home for the weekly holy day (Šabb. 119b). These traditions again used guardian angels as a way of encouraging right practice:

25. See chapter 2; Naveh and Shaked, *Amulets and Magic* Bowls, 68–77, amulet no. 7.
26. *b. Ta'an.* 11a.

Rav Hisda said in the name of Mar Ukba: "One who prays on the eve of the Sabbath and recites 'Thus the heavens and earth were completed,' etc. [Gen 2:1], the two ministering angels that accompany that person place their hands on his head and say to him, "your iniquity is taken away and your sin is forgiven" [Isa 6:7].

With this tradition, the rabbis encouraged fellow Jews to integrate a biblical verse into their prayer on the eve of the Sabbath. In the Amoraic period, the Sabbath liturgy had not yet been standardized among Jews, so in order to make their case for the inclusion of the recitation of these verses from Genesis, the rabbis employed the belief in the presence of angels. Rather than encouraging Jews to address the angels directly, as the tradition attributed to Abaye does, this tradition let Jews know what the angels were doing in response to their recitation. It taught them how to visualize the angels' reactions. In this case, the angels responded with a benediction offering forgiveness of sins.

To understand how angels could be assigned this role in forgiveness of sins, we must revisit two biblical sources on angels, one from Isaiah's vision and one from Jacob's deathbed blessing. In Isaiah's vision of the seraphim in the temple, the modest prophet protests his unworthiness to stand before God: "I am a man of unclean lips," he says, and so a seraph takes a coal from the temple's altar, touches it to his lips, and tells him that his sins are now forgiven and he can stand before God without fear (Isa 6:5–7). According to the Talmudic passage above, some rabbis imagined the angels similarly blessing and exonerating any ordinary Jew who prayed on the eve of the Sabbath. The idea that angels have the authority to redeem Jews also has biblical precedent in Jacob's deathbed blessing of his son Joseph and his grandsons Ephraim and Manasseh in Gen 48:15–16, verses that still form a part of the nighttime Shema:

> The God before whom my fathers Abraham and Isaac walked,
> the God who has been my shepherd all my life long to this day,
> the angel who redeems me from all evil,
> bless the boys and in them let my name be carried on,
> and the name of my fathers Abraham and Isaac;
> and let them grow into a multitude in the midst of the earth.

This blessing invokes both God's protection and angelic redemption, having Jacob recall the God and angel who protected him in his lifetime and calling on them to protect Jacob's grandchildren. Evidently, some rabbinic disciples found the idea of angelic redemption inspiring and useful in encouraging right practice. The idea that angels can redeem people was used here to encourage participation in Shabbat rituals. This tradition is a reminder that some Jews, even rabbinic Jews, saw angels as playing a significant role in their lives, not just accompanying them, but even forgiving them their misdeeds and rewarding them for their pious deeds.[27]

The next tradition in this section of the Babylonian Talmud (Šabb. 119b) further elaborated on the identity of the two angels who accompany every Jew home from the synagogue and employed angels to encourage Jews to prepare their homes for the Sabbath. As mentioned in the introduction to this book, this tradition about angelic visitation is attributed to Yose ben Judah, a contemporary of Judah the Patriarch, the figure most closely associated with the redaction of the Mishnah. Whether this attribution is historical or not, this story locates angelic presence and blessings with the founding generation of rabbinic Judaism:

> Rabbi Yosi bar Yehuda said: two ministering angels accompany a man on the eve of the Sabbath from the synagogue to his home, one good (*tov*) and one evil (rā'). And when he arrives at his house, if a lamp is lit and a table is prepared and his bed covered, the good angel says, "may it be like this on another Sabbath too" and the evil angel answers "amen" against his will. And if it is not, the evil angel says, "May it be like this on another Sabbath too" and the good angel answers "amen" against his will.

This tradition takes more interest in domestic arrangements and encourages good Sabbath routine from the synagogue to the home: tidiness, a lit lamp, and a set table prompt the blessing of the angels. Negligence also prompts an angelic response: an undesirable malediction. This source also requires grappling with the topic of evil angels as well as the free will of the angels, each of which I treat in turn. These discursions serve to show that angels were integral to ancient Judaism and rabbinic theology, rooted in the biblical texts and in dialogue with later religious developments in late antiquity.

ANGELS OF EVIL AND DESTRUCTION

Angels are described neither as good nor evil in the Hebrew Bible. Instead, angelic messengers execute God's will for ends that readers might regard as positive (e.g., heralding the birth of a child, protecting God's chosen people) or as destructive (e.g., bringing plague as punishment upon the Israelites, bringing accusations

---

27. One midrash attributed to R. Yohanan makes light of angelic redemption as compared with the sustenance that God provides but does not deny that angels fulfill this role in Jewish life. His response to Gen 48:15–16 appears in only two manuscripts of *Genesis Rabbah* (see 97:3, Theodor and Albeck, 1245). Cf. *b. Pesaḥ.* 118a: "R. Yohanan said [providing] the sustenance of a person is harder than [bringing about his] redemption, as about redemption it is written 'the angel who has redeemed me from all evil' (Gen 48:16), merely an angel, and about sustenance it is written, 'the God who shepherds me . . .' (Gen 48:15)." This quotation follows the Vilna MS (paralleled by Venice Print 1520); Other MSS cite R. Levi as the speaker of this statement (see JTS 1623, Vatican 109, Munich 6; New York Columbia X 893). MS Oxford Opp Add. Fol. 23 has R. Eliezer.

against pious men like Job). Ancient Jews like the rabbis and ritual practitioners spoke of angels of good and angels of evil, but they understood all of these angels to be under God's control.[28] So-called evil angels were not in the same category as demons. Neither in the Hebrew Bible nor in later Jewish sources does God enlist demons (*mazzikin*) to execute his will nor send demons to torment people. Only "angels of satan" or "angels of destruction," angels whose job it is to monitor wrongdoing, are imagined policing Jews from the invisible realm. In the above tradition attributed to Rabbi Yosi bar Yehuda, the so-called evil angel (*mal'akh rā'*) is evil only insofar as it is his duty to attend to the evil actions of his charges.

Modern readers sometimes struggle with the idea that both good and evil come from God, a belief stated most clearly by Second Isaiah: "I form light and create darkness, make peace and create woe" (Isa 45:7; woe in Hebrew is *rā'*, the same word used above to describe the "evil" angel). Second Isaiah emphasized that the Babylonian destruction and Persian ascendance were part of God's plan to make known His might "from east to west;" the traumatic defeat of Judah and (seventy years later) the spectacular triumph of Cyrus ensured the fame of God among new peoples and foretold the ultimate redemption of God's chosen people from any empire that would oppress them. What was devastating in the early sixth century CE became a story of hope for Jews for centuries to come. The rabbis inherited this belief, internalizing that what seemed like defeat could be part of God's plan in the long term. This is affirmed in the Mishnah and Talmudic commentaries: "A person is obligated to bless upon the bad just as he blesses upon the good as it says, 'And you shall love the Lord your God with all your heart and all your soul and with all your might' (Deut 6:5)."[29] Blessing whatever happens, for good or not, is a sign of accepting God's will and judgment. The Toseftan tradition of angels of satan that accompany the impious man on his journey hint that this conceptualization of angels was within the frame of reference of the early rabbis, but only the Babylonian rabbis elaborated more traditions about angels of evil or destruction and harnessed fear of the angels of destruction to encourage proper behavior in the present.[30]

Like traffic police, these angels of destruction were conceptualized as necessary to upholding a functioning society, but they were not popular, and the rabbis relate a few traditions about how to avoid these angels' scrutiny. One Talmudic tradition states that, based on a person's deeds in life, they would either be greeted by three bands of ministering angels or by three bands of angels of destruction

---

28. A recently published bowl seeking to expel entities from the shop of the clients lists, among others, Samiel and Qaspiel, the angels of destruction (*ḥblh*): see Bhayro et al., *Aramaic Magic Bowls*, VA. 2182, pp. 11–15.

29. See *m. Ber.* 9:5. See rabbinic discussion of this mishnah in *b. Ber.* 60b.

30. For more on angels of destruction, see *b. Šabb.* 55a and 88a.

upon their death.[31] This tradition stands in tension with Jewish belief in bodily resurrection, but it speaks to the popularity of angels in the imagination, especially in association with the experience of the soul after death.

According to another Babylonian tradition, Rabbi Yishmael ben Elisha recounted that Suriel, the angelic prince of the Presence, related to him that the angels of destruction lie in wait to attack the man who relies on human intermediaries too much: for example, relying on a servant to fetch his cloak in the morning (rather than fetching it himself), ritually washing his hands in the water brought by a servant (who had not ritually washed his hands), and passing off a cup of medicinal brew to another person (rather than back to the person who gave it to him).[32] In other words, Suriel the angelic mediator reveals to a sage how to avoid the angels of destruction when interacting with human servants or slaves. This cleverly constructed story comments on intermediaries on three levels: heavenly angels as a source of proper protocol, earthly angels as monitors of human behavior, and improper reliance on human intermediaries. This story reinforces that angels of destruction are part of the heavenly hierarchy that even some rabbis envisioned in their daily life.

Another late tradition about destructive angels stands out from the others, naming a feminine angel as their leader, and it deserves more attention. It begins with a prohibition attributed to Rabbi Yose and spoken to Rabbi Judah the Patriarch: "Do not go out alone at night."[33] In explanation, the Stammaim cite a Baraita, which explains that, on the evening before Wednesday and the evening of the Sabbath, a figure named Agrat the daughter Maḥlat alongside "180,000 angels of destruction" goes out, and "each one of them has permission to cause destruction on his own." The Stammaim add that once upon a time, these angels of destruction would go out every night to do their work until Rabbi Hanina ben Dosa encountered Agrat and they had a conversation that limited the scope of her and her retinue of destructive angels. According to the story, Agrat said to the rabbi: "'If it were not for the fact that there is a proclamation in heaven (saying): Beware of Hanina and his (knowledge of the) Torah, I would put you in danger.' He said to her: 'If I have a considerable position in heaven, I decree against you that you should never go through an inhabited place.' She said to him: 'Please give me a

---

31. See *b. Ketub.* 104a. The belief in angelic escorts after death was common in late antiquity (see Cline, *Ancient Angels*, 94–97). Roman-era Jewish sarcophagi depict winged beings, attesting to popular belief in the presence of angels at death as well. For the archaeological evidence, see Burrus, "Remembering the Righteous." One example appears on the cover of this book.

32. See *b. Ber.* 51a. My thanks to Drew Kaplan of the Rabbinic Drinking podcast for pointing out that *asparagus* refers to a medicinal elixir well known in the ancient Mediterranean world.

33. See *b. Pesaḥ.* 112b. Ronis's dissertation "Do Not Go Out Alone at Night" invokes the beginning of this tradition as its title. Ronis reads the Talmudic story through the lens of the ritual texts, identifying Agrat as a demon at the heads of demonic minions, a characterization I disagree with.

little respite', and he allowed her (to roam about) on the eves of the Sabbath and Wednesday." It is evident that the story of Hanina ben Dosa as it appears in the Talmud serves to uphold the value of Torah study as effective against Agrat and her fellow angels of destruction. Readers may recall that Hanina ben Dosa figures in ritual incantations where he encounters an unnamed evil spirit and recites a verse of psalm against her; no other conversation is reported between them (see chapter 1). Though Agrat does appear in other incantation bowls among other demons, she never appears with a retinue of angels of destruction nor opposite Hanina ben Dosa in extant ritual texts.[34] Because of these and other divergences, the publishers of *Aramaic Bowl Spells* hypothesize that the Talmudic tradition and the historiola found in the ritual incantations are independent traditions with distinct trajectories of development; neither is an adaptation of the other.[35] I agree with their observation; each tradition is best evaluated on its own terms as it hints at the different outlooks on the heavenly hierarchies, which operated concurrently among Jews. In the incantation bowls, practitioners invoked Hanina ben Dosa as a folk-hero sage with the power to displace evil spirits with his quotation of a psalm; other angelic figures assist him. In the Talmud, Hanina ben Dosa is confronted with Agrat and her retinue of destructive angels; his Torah is effective.

For the purpose of this study on angels, it seems worth lingering on the fact that these angels of destruction are led by a female angelic being named Agrat.[36] The Baraita is explicit that these angels of destruction operate with permission, and their number (a multiple of 18, a number signifying "life" in gematria) suggests their alignment with divine will. Agrat herself also seems knowledgeable of the heavens and obligated to negotiate with this miracle-working sage. In the context of this *sugya*, it is noteworthy that Agrat is never explicitly identified as a demon or as an evil spirit.[37] Reading the story separately from the incantation texts, we may entertain the possibility that in this story she is an angelic figure, albeit an angel of destruction, perhaps the logical counterpart to named angels like Michael, Gabriel or Suriel: a named angelic leader designated female to emphasize her lower status in the divine realm. The fact that Hanina ben Dosa "decrees upon

34. See Shaked, "'Peace Be Upon You, Exalted Angels': On Hekhalot, Liturgy, and Incantation Bowls," 216 (commenting on Moussaieff bowl no. 6). In this incantation Agrat bat Mahlat is accompanied by her chariot (*merkavta*). As Shaked points out, Agrat is also mentioned in *Exod. Rab.* 12:3 with her chariot. Notably there, Ps 91:5 is interpreted to mean that one need not fear Agrat and her chariot, nor the demons (*mazzikin*) who have dominion in the night. Agrat's retinue and the demons of the night are separate entities.

35. Shaked, Ford, Bhayro, *Aramaic Bowl Spells*, 53.

36. Cf. discussion of feminine angels in the previous chapter and Ahuvia, "Gender and the Angels in Late Antique Judaism."

37. Elsewhere in this *sugya*, Agrat is mentioned among names spoken by witches, presumably Jewish women outside rabbinic circles (*b. Pesaḥ.* 111a).

her" is in keeping with his characterization as a powerful sage in the Babylonian Talmud.[38] It also reflects the beliefs of some Jewish practitioners and mystics who believed they could command God's angels to do their bidding.[39]

In summary, angels of good and angels of evil that acted in alignment with God's will can be found throughout all the layers of rabbinic literature. Whereas only one tradition in Tannaitic literature references the conception of these two classes of accompanying angels, several later traditions assume belief in such angels and elaborate on these conceptions. While earlier rabbinic traditions seem to avoid referencing angels, the later rabbis found them more useful and creatively elaborated traditions about them. When rabbinic stories invoked the ministering angels or angels of peace, they did so to encourage right behavior; at the same time, they invoked the specter of angels of evil to deter Jews from impiety.

DO ANGELS HAVE A WILL OF THEIR OWN?

Returning to the Talmudic traditions on the angels who accompany a person home on the Sabbath (b. Šabb. 119b), we find that the good and evil angels were obligated to bless for good or ill in accordance with divine will. And yet, that tradition also states that each angel was obligated to bless "against his will."[40] This suggests that angels have a will of their own in the rabbinic storyteller's imagination, a remarkable detail. Many readers will be familiar with the angelic characteristics summarized by Bill Rebiger: "Angels are the most perfect creation of God. . . . They could not sin. . . . They are not allowed to take a step without the command of God."[41] Others might be more familiar with the Talmudic maxim comparing Jews and angels which states, "The Torah was not given to the ministering angels," recently illuminated by Christine Hayes in her studies of divine law in ancient Judaism.[42] Such descriptions are precisely the reason many readers find angels boring: obedient automatons do not make for exciting companions. My survey of the rabbinic sources on angels suggests that, while angels could *not* act out of divine alignment, they could have emotional responses nonetheless, because they cared about their charges. Describing angels as perfect emotionless beings diminishes the complexity of the portrayal of angels in rabbinic storytelling and makes the ancient Jewish interest in angels less intelligible.[43] Because the rabbinic traditions on angels as incapable of sin is well-traversed ground, in this section I

38. Bokser, "Wonder-Working and the Rabbinic Tradition."

39. See next chapter and discussion of ritual magic in Cairo Genizah at end of chapter 2.

40. Cf. *m. 'Abot* 4:22, where Rabbi Eleazar Ha-Kappar discusses humanity's lack of freewill.

41. Rebiger, "Angels in Rabbinic Literature," 631–32.

42. See *b. Qidd.* 54a, *b. Ber.* 25b, *b. Me'il* 14b, and *b. Yoma* 30a, and *b. Sanh.* 94a; analyzed and contextualized by Hayes in "'The Torah Was Not Given to Ministering Angels': Rabbinic Aspirationalism."

43. In the conclusion, I discuss the Jewish thinkers that promoted such views of the angels.

only briefly review the most important developments in Jewish theology about angels and then foreground lesser-known traditions that portray the emotional investment of angels in their Jewish charges.

The most famous story of angelic disobedience, the myth of the fallen Watchers, was categorically rejected by the rabbis. Incompatible with their understanding of the nature of good and evil in the world, human responsibility and free will as described above, this story was not part of their imaginative library or vocabulary. Rabbinic midrashim read Gen 6:4 not as sons of God (*bnei ha-elohim*), but as judges.[44] Ignoring alternative interpretations of these verses, the rabbis never directly reckon with the idea of fallen or disobedient angels.

Only one early midrash explicitly describes the angels as indiscriminately obedient. In Exod 12:22, where Moses warned the Israelites to stay in their homes while the final plague is executed, the rabbis stated: "'*And None of You Shall Go Out*,' etc. This tells that the angel, once permission to harm is given him, does not discriminate between the righteous and the wicked."[45] That Moses orders the Israelites to mark their doorposts with blood suggested to the sages the work of an indiscriminate angel, one who could not differentiate between Israelite and Egyptian households, but is on a mission of execution. Although later sources undermine such a portrayal, this and other traditions suggest a general belief in angels as God's obedient subordinates with no will or motivations of their own.[46]

A well-known motif in later rabbinic literature differentiates between humans, who are susceptible to evil inclination, and angels who are immune to it. It is instructive to look at an example of this tradition and scholarship on it because it clarifies a misconception about emotions and impulses in antiquity. In *Genesis Rabbah* 48:11, commenting on Abraham's invitation to the angels to refresh themselves (Gen 18:5, literally "feast your heart"), the rabbis note "it does not say 'And feast your hearts,' but 'feast your heart.' Hence it is said that the Evil Inclination (*yetzer ha-rā'*), does not control the angels." The singular heart of the verse in Genesis is read as evidence that the angels have one unified heart, not divided hearts like humans do. It is humanity's divided heart that makes them susceptible to the demonic. As Ishay Rosen-Zvi explained in *Demonic Desires: Yetzer Hara and the Problem of Evil in Late Antiquity*, the rabbis attributed the source of sin to the *yetzer ha-rā'*, "a demon-like figure limited to the heart," which can and "should be resisted."[47] The *yetzer* was neither an independent demonic entity nor merely a physical impulse. Rosen-Zvi compellingly argues

---

44. *Gen. Rab.* 26:5 states "R. Simeon b. Yohai cursed all who called them "sons of God" (Theodor and Albeck, 247). Discussed in Reed, *Fallen Angels*, 137.

45. *Mek. RI, Bo* §11 (Horowitz and Rabin 38; Lauterbach, 60).

46. Cf. *Gen. Rab.* 48:11, *Lev. Rab.* 24:8, b. *Šabb.* 88b–89a.

47. Rosen-Zvi, *Demonic Desires*, 127.

that scholars have misread rabbinic rhetoric on the *yetzer* through Hellenistic models of psychology, attributing to the rabbis a belief in body/soul dualism or a Hellenistic frame of mind that seeks to subdue lower irrational and appetitive parts of the soul.

What can seem surprising to modern readers is that in the rabbinic imagination, absence of an evil *yetzer* does not mean an absence of emotions or passions. Just as scholars have attributed to the rabbis Hellenistic psychological frameworks (as Rosen-Zvi notes), so too experts on Judaism have tended to attribute to ancient Jews Hellenistic attitudes on divine figures as unmoved, passionless, higher beings. In this, modern readers seem more committed to Hellenistic models than the rabbis themselves do. The late antique rabbinic traditions show that the rabbis did attribute emotions to God and angels, whether spontaneous joy and sadness or compassion and rage, as several examples below will illustrate. It is important to place such stories within the wider context of debates by Jews and Christians in late antiquity on the topic of divine beings and emotions. The rabbis, again, never address this issue systematically, but the writings of Augustine do, and it is helpful to compare Augustine's systematic approach with the rabbis' midrashim.

In *City of God* 9:5, Augustine wrote, "We follow the conventions of human language in applying to the angels the words denoting these passions [anger, compassion, fear, love], but this is perhaps because of the analogy between their actions and those of men, not because they are subject to the infirmity of our passions."[48] Christians steeped in Hellenistic culture imagine God and his angels as undisturbed, omniscient, omnipotent perfect beings. If humans write about them in emotional terms, it is only because of the limits of human perception and language, not because God or the angels actually suffer a tempest of emotions. As Muehlberger explains, "Like God, angels can seem to be angry, but remain philosophically undisturbed."[49] I posit that it would be unwise to attribute to late antique rabbinic Jews such Hellenistic attitudes. The rabbis did not abide by Hellenistic philosophical standards applied to divinities. Stories of God's laughter, anger, and sadness abound in rabbinic storytelling. So too do examples of angels reacting to human successes and losses. Angels may not have had demonic impulses, but they still had emotions and compassion for Israel according to the late antique and early medieval texts of the rabbis.

Above, we encountered the story about the angels celebrating the rabbinic discussion of *ma'ase merkavah* in the Palestinian Talmud. The angels skipped about the two rabbis as if they were at a wedding party. Similarly, a story in the Mekhilta tells of the angels rejoicing before Jochebed, Moses's mother: "And there were [even] ministering angels rejoicing before her like grooms and brides, upholding

48. Quoted in Muehlberger, *Angels in Late Ancient Christianity*, 55.
49. Muehlberger, *Angels in Late Ancient Christianity*, 55.

what is said in Scripture, '[He sets the childless woman among her household] as a happy mother of children.'"[50] The contributors to *Genesis Rabbah* emphasize that it was an angel (not God) who came to the matriarchs in their time of need. An angel defended Sarah when she was taken by Pharaoh and at risk of being raped, consulting with her about when to strike and when to stop afflicting Pharaoh (*Gen. Rab.* 52:13). It is because angels were imagined to care about their charges that Jews, in turn, cared about their guardian angels.

A poignant story can be found in *Genesis Rabbah* 56:5, the story of the Binding of Isaac (Gen 22:1–19), which provoked three comments on the angels' reactions: first, when it seems that Abraham will slaughter Isaac, the angels weep and lament the unnatural act of a father slaying his son with his own hands and that such a pious and hospitable host would merit this command. The rabbis stress the angelic presence in Gen 22:9 ("And they came to that place which God commanded and Abraham built an altar there and arranged the wood and he bound Isaac his son and laid him on the altar *above* the wood"), stating "and whoever tells you that these verses do not refer to the ministering angels, note that it says here "*above*" (Hebrew "*mi-ma'al*") and it is said there "above" as in "The Seraphim stood *above* him" (Isa 6:2). The weeping angels witnessing the binding of Isaac are linked to the attendant seraphim of Isaiah's vision through the rabbinic principle of *gzerah shavah*, linking two verses in the Hebrew Bible that employ the same words. Second, when the angel of the Lord calls out to the patriarch from the heavens, saying "Abraham, Abraham," Rabbi Hiyya explains that this repetition was "an expression of affection and encouragement." The response attributed to Rabbi Hiyya implies that angels have affection for humans, a belief that is not explicitly stated in earlier sources, where angels protect humans under God's orders. The final comment on the reaction of the angels can be found when the rabbis explain what happened to the knife that Abraham was holding out to slaughter his son: "Three tears fell from the ministering angels and the knife disintegrated."[51] The weeping of the angels described earlier is re-invoked, now explaining what happened to this weapon that almost destroyed Isaac and implicitly the people of Israel. Taken together, these traditions in *Genesis Rabbah* portray angels who can only act in alignment with God (they have no evil/adversarial impulse), and yet they have emotional interiority and attachment to humans.

Most early rabbinic sources describe the angels assisting Jews under God's direct orders.[52] Later Talmudic sources portray the archangels actively assisting

---

50. *Mek. RS* (Nelson, 8); Textual Source: JTS Rab. 2404, folios 1–2 and Notes of Rav Abraham Ha-Laḥmi.

51. My translation of *Gen. Rab.* 56:7 (Theodor and Albeck, 2:603).

52. See traditions associated with the Exodus narrative: God causing Israel to see the squadrons of angels supporting them (*Mek. RI, Beshallah* §2 [Horowitz and Rabin, 94; Lauterbach, 141]); God

the heroes of Israel's past without mention of God's orders, suggesting a more fully developed conceptualization of angels acting of their own accord. In *b. Yoma* 77a the rabbis dwell at length on verses from the books of Daniel and Ezekiel on the Babylonian destruction of the temple in order to assign unnamed cherubim and the nameless "man clothed in linen" the identities of the archangels Michael, Gabriel, and other ministering angels, following the rabbinic tendency to provide anonymous figures with names.[53]. Michael is credited with asking God to leave a remnant among Israel (implying there must be a minority of good people worth saving). God responds that since the good did not rebuke the wicked, no remnant is worthy of rescue. God then orders Gabriel to burn the city. Gabriel does not fully comply and is credited with carrying out God's orders in such a way that a remnant of the Jewish people does survive. It is striking that both of these archangels are attributed more compassion than God toward Israel, signaling a departure from previous attitudes toward angels, which diminished the angels' care for Israel compared with God's. Interestingly, when Gabriel reports to God that he fulfilled his mission, Rabbi Yohanan reports that the other angels cast Gabriel out, ostensibly because he should have kept quiet about completing a destructive mission, as is the usual protocol. This odd moment in the text is as close as the rabbinic storytellers come to implying angelic disobedience.

Gabriel's compassion continues to be on display in the continuation of the story in the Talmud. The angelic prince of the Persians, Dubbiel, takes over Gabriel's place in the heavenly palace.[54] When Dubbiel decides that the Jews and the sages ought to pay taxes (taxes being an issue of cosmic importance, then and now), Gabriel protests this decree, but he is overridden by the other angels. Gabriel then calls out to God, reminding him of his service to Daniel, and God welcomes him back to His inner sanctum. Gabriel confronts Dubbiel, but only manages to mitigate the tax load that falls upon the Jews, thus supposedly explaining why some Jews pay taxes and others do not in the rabbis' contemporary Persia. Closing the story, Dubbiel says, "When I depart from him, the prince of Greece comes" (quoting Dan 10:20), meaning that Greek armies are about to conquer the Kingdom of Judea, foreshadowing more suffering for the ancient Jews. The story closes with Gabriel's reaction to the Persian angel's statement: "He wept and wept and

---

orders angels to help "their brothers" when they are terrified of the theophany on Sinai and flee (*Mek. RI, Bahodesh* §9 [Horowitz and Rabin, 236; Lauterbach, 340]); God sent the heavenly stars against Sisera and the angel of the Lord against Sennacherib (*Sifre Num* 84); God sends two angels in disguise to prevent gentiles from looting the home of two Jews on pilgrimage (*y. Peah* 17b).

53. *Gen. Rab.* 78:1 (rabbis argue over whether Michael or Gabriel wrestled with Jacob); *Gen. Rab.* 63 (Michael and Gabriel together helped Jacob); *Gen. Rab.* 44 (Michael rescued the three—Hananiah, Mishael, and Azaria—from the fiery furnace described in Dan 3); *Gen. Rab.* 50:2 (Raphael rescued Lot from the destruction of Sodom).

54. Dubbiel literally means "Bear of God" (Jastrow, *Dictionary*, 2:282).

none listened to him."[55] What is striking about this story is that it portrays both Michael and Gabriel as more compassionate and merciful than God. Gabriel is not described as transgressing God's orders, but there is an implication that he has gone his own way in carrying out his mission. Like the angels of *Genesis Rabbah*, Gabriel weeps when thinking about what Israel is about to endure. In the Babylonian rabbinic perspective, the archangels Michael and Gabriel have become the fitting intermediaries that earlier rabbinic sources rejected.[56]

Taking all of these stories into account, we may now return to the question of what it means to relate that the angels accompanying a Jew home from the synagogue on the Sabbath inspect her home and bless her, with the respective angel responding "'amen' against his will." The angels in rabbinic perspective seem to be as governed by their emotions, as God is in rabbinic perspective. In many rabbinic stories God is surprised, delighted, anguished, angered, and moved by his faithful flock. Just so, the Babylonian rabbis could imagine the angels to be moved to compassion or righteous anger as well, defiantly compassionate to the people of Israel. In these stories, we can see the emotional intimacy of Jews and the angels. Only by acknowledging the emotional appeal of angels can we understand why they became significant to ancient Jews and were invoked in prayer and ritual practice as well.

BLURRING THE BOUNDARIES: RABBINIC INTERMEDIARIES IN LATE ANTIQUITY

The rabbis never produced angelology, but their texts do preserve some nonsystematic speculation about the angelic realms. A high number of traditions cluster together in Babylonian Talmud *Ḥagigah* 12b–16a. The basic teaching that frames this section of the tractate is Mishnah *Ḥagigah* 2:1, which states "The subject of forbidden relations may not be expounded in the presence of three, nor the work of creation (*maʿaseh bereshit*) in the presence of two, nor *maʿaseh merkavah* in the presence of one, unless he is a sage and understands of his own knowledge."[57] We have already examined the story of the journeying rabbis discussing the heavenly throne and the angels therein. The topics of creation and *maʿaseh merkavah* provided opportunities for more vivid discussions of the angelic realm. They reveal that later rabbis were engaged in theological speculation about the heavenly realm

---

55. Of nine manuscripts in the Lieberman database, only the Vilna MS does not have the last line about Gabriel's protest.

56. See earlier discussion of *y. Ber.* 9.1, 13a: "If a person faces trouble, he should cry out neither to Michael nor to Gabriel, but should cry out to Me, and I will answer him immediately."

57. This statement, unusual in rabbinic literature, has provoked a great deal of scholarship. See Furstenberg, "The Rabbinic Ban on Maʿaseh Bereshit;" Halperin, *Faces of the Chariot*, 23–31; Swartz, "Jewish Visionary Tradition in Rabbinic Literature."

usually not associated with rabbis, or with Jews more generally. Analyzing these traditions shows how the rabbinic ideas about angels developed over time and in dialogue with other Jewish beliefs and practices.

In *b. Ḥagigah* 12b, the rabbis put forth another version of the idea of the seven heavens, a motif we already encountered in the treatise of *Sefer ha-Razim* and one that can also be found in the liturgical poetry of Yannai.[58] Although locating the divine beings was a shared interest among ancient Jews, the names of the seven heavens varied among these different learned authorities. According to the rabbis, the seven heavens are called Vilon, Rakia, Sheḥakim, Zebul, Maon, Makon, and Araboth. The rabbis placed the planets and constellations, elsewhere evoked as the celestial beings, in the second heaven of Rakia. In the fourth heaven, Zebul, they imagined the heavenly Jerusalem where "Michael the great prince" was high priest. In the fifth heaven, Maon, they imagined the companies of ministering angels dwelling, singing by night and silent by day so that Israel's prayer may be heard from below (cf. Yannai's conception of Israel's and the angels' synchronized singing). Finally, in the seventh heaven of Araboth dwell the souls of the righteous, the spirits and souls yet to be born, as well as the ophanim, the seraphim, the holy living creatures, more ministering angels, and the throne of God. There was not a shared cosmology in antiquity among Jews, but such variation reminds us that the rabbis, liturgical poets, and ritual practitioners were engaged in similar conversations.

In this section of the *sugya* (13b), the rabbis depart from other traditions in trying to distinguish various angelic creatures. They analyze and define the divine creatures from Ezekiel's vision.[59] The rabbis engage in an interesting comparison of Isaiah's and Ezekiel's winged creatures, recognizing that the descriptions of angelic creatures vary significantly between the two prophets: Isaiah sees seraphim with six wings while Ezekiel sees four-winged creatures. Anonymous teachings correlate the destruction of the first temple with the loss of a pair of angelic wings and perhaps the diminution of the number of angels in the heavenly family. This is one of the few rabbinic traditions that dwells on the nature of the angels directly and shows the rabbis harmonizing divergent traditions about angels by asserting that angels changed through history (as, indeed, conceptions of them did change in the Hellenistic period).

---

58. On the topic of the seven heavens in ancient Judaism, see Schäfer, "In Heaven as It Is in Hell," 252–66. For Yannai's list of the seven heavens, see the eighth poem to the *qedushtah* for Gen. 11:1 (Lieber, *Yannai on Genesis*, 384–85). Yannai's list does not match the one in *b. Ḥag* 12b. For seven heavenly palaces in Palestinian piyyut, see Swartz, "Hekhalot and Piyyut," in *Mechanics of Providence*, 262–69, esp. 264.

59. For example, they suggest that *ḥashmal* (Ezek 1:4) is a tripartite portmanteau of the words "creatures of fire who speak" (*ḥayyot 'sh memallelot*); Rabbi Eliezer suggests that *ophan* refers to the angel Sandalfon, who stands on Earth and whose head reaches the divine creatures of the Chariot), and that *cherubim* refers to angels with the faces of babies.

While the rabbis of *Genesis Rabbah* were concerned with the *original* creation of the angels as befitting that midrash, the rabbis of the Babylonian Talmud speculated about the *ongoing* creation of the angels. In part, these traditions reflect Babylonian rabbis' eagerness to display their acuity as they scoured the Bible to speculate about God's power and the angelic nature (*b. Ḥag.* 14a). With flourish, Shmuel tells Hiyya Bar Rav about one of the great things his father Rav used to say: "Every day ministering angels are created anew from the River of fire [cf. Dan 7:10's *nehar dinur*] and they cease to exist after singings God's praise as it is said 'They are new every morning; great is Your faithfulness'" (Lam 3:23). This opinion both connects the fiery nature of the angels with the book of Daniel's river of fire and proposes a new idea about how angels are created and pass away on a daily basis. The idea that angels pass away each day is unique to Rav. It will be contradicted in another rabbinic tradition, shortly, but nonetheless this tradition shows us the rabbis playing with biblical sources to speculate about the angels in new ways. Immediately after quoting Rav's tradition, the redactors cited another opinion attributed to Rabbi Yonatan, claiming that "an angel is created from each and every utterance that comes out of the mouth of the Holy, blessed be He," as it is said "By the word of the Lord the heavens were made, and by the breath of His mouth all their hosts" (Ps 33:6). Just as God spoke the world into being in Genesis, the rabbis use Psalms to imagine God creating angels through speech. Rabbi Yonatan's opinion on angels being created with every word would prove particularly popular among later Jewish mystics, who enjoyed dwelling on the idea of God's endless numbers of angels. These two opinions offer new origin stories for the angels (either from the river of fire or with every utterance of God) and show a willingness to engage in angelic speculation not seen in earlier rabbinic sources.

One final tradition from this textual unit seeks to elucidate the nature of humans and demons through comparison with the angels, summarizing some motifs we have encountered before and introducing a few new ones (*b. Ḥag.* 16a). The first comparison focuses on demons and the second on humans:

> The rabbis taught: six things are said about demons; in three respects [they are] like ministering angels and in three respects like humans.
>
> In three respects they are like ministering angels: they have wings like the ministering angels and they fly from one end of the earth to the other like the ministering angels and they know the future like the ministering angels. They know? They hear from behind the curtain of heaven like the ministering angels.
>
> And in three ways they are like mortals: they eat and drink like mortals, multiply like mortals, and die like mortals.
>
> Six things were said about humans, in three respects [they are] like the ministering angels and in three respects like beasts.

> In three respects they are like the ministering angels: they have wisdom like the ministering angels, they walk about upright like the ministering angels, and they speak the holy tongue like the ministering angels.
>
> In three respects like beasts: they eat and drink like beasts and multiply like beasts and they defecate like beasts.

Overall, these two lists rank angels, demons, humans, and beasts from most divine to most animalistic. This rabbinic tradition is unusual in thinking about angels and demons together. Though people often think of angels and demons as intertwined, my research shows that angels appear in Jewish sources quite independently of demons. In this case the rabbis note that, like the angels, the demons too are winged, flying, knowledgeable creatures, but they eat, drink, and copulate like humans. Demons, created on twilight of the sixth day according to the Mishnah (see chapter 3), reproduced thereafter on their own according to the Babylonian rabbis. From the Babylonian incantation bowls, we can see that some Jews believed that demons copulated not just with each other but with humans as well (hence the performative ritual *divorcing* of demons in incantation bowls, which is attributed to Rabbi Joshua ben Perahia). The rabbis do not mention the ritual technique of divorcing demons or the incantation bowls, but they do show themselves able to take on demons through their own ritual techniques.[60]

Although angels are not the rabbis' direct subject of inquiry here, we learn quite a lot about angels from this tradition: (1) the angels have wings; (2) they can fly to any corner of the earth; (3) they have access to divine knowledge and know the future; (4) they have wisdom; (5) they walk about upright like humans; and (6) they speak the holy language Hebrew. To take each idea in turn: when the rabbis imagined angels, they visualized winged upright beings, powerful and able to reach any destination, and they associated them with biblical and holy Hebrew. This emphasis on the angels speaking Hebrew is unique to the Babylonian Talmud (see discussion on pp. 150–51) and was not widely shared by other Jews, but it may be that this emphasis on Hebrew was more about associating God's servants with his holy people in particular. The idea that the angels are wise and have access to heavenly knowledge ("behind the curtain of heaven" implies secret divine knowledge) was to prove particularly inspiring to Jewish mystics, who imagined gaining access to heavenly secrets through the angels. The Babylonian rabbis, by contrast, seem to emphasize that humans can attain the same wisdom as the angels, likely through their study of Torah.

According to this rabbinic comparison of demons and humans, demons die like mortals and therefore, presumably, demons are not immortal like angels. This idea

---

60. See the story of the rabbi who wrote a client an amulet to get rid of demons in *b. Pesaḥ.* 111b, discussed in Bohak, *Ancient Jewish Magic*, 375–76.

stands in contrast with the tradition associated with Rav about the angels ceasing to exist after singing God's praise. Within the same *sugya*, we can see that there was variation in how the rabbis thought about the angels and that the rabbis felt no need to systematize and harmonize their speculations about angels. These short lists are as close as the rabbis get to engaging in angelology or demonology.[61] Angels and demons were discussed separately for the most part, suggesting they were not as linked in the rabbinic imagination as they are in the imagination of people today.

Keeping in mind that the rabbis were not a monolithic group and were affected by the same trends as other Jews, we should expect a variety of intermediaries from them as well. Indeed, the angels alongside other mediating figures were important to the rabbis; alongside the archangels Gabriel and Michael, the Angel of Death, and Elijah the prophet received much attention in rabbinic literature.[62] One Babylonian rabbinic tradition ranks Michael, Gabriel, Elijah, and the Angel of Death by their comparative strength in flight to reach their destination (cf. how many connections one needs to make in transit): "It was taught Michael in one [flight], Gabriel in two [flights], Elijah in four [flights] and the Angel of Death in eight [flights], except in times of plague when it is one."[63] This underlines my theory that intermediaries existed on a spectrum in the Jewish imagination, available for Jews to choose from.

In stories in the Babylonian Talmud, Elijah is described as an intimate interlocuter of the rabbis and a supernatural figure who can navigate the heavenly and earthly realms.[64] Medieval Kabbalists and later rabbinic authorities extrapolated that Elijah was an angel all along, or that he later became an angel.[65] In light of my studies of intermediaries, I am not sure this interpretive leap is necessary: not every Jewish intercessory figure needed to be an angel. In ritual texts, angels were useful protectors, messengers, and empowering figures, but they did not figure in every incantation text; sometimes other figures like biblical heroes or folk heroes took their place. I see Elijah as just such a human figure. Elijah's biblical biography was marked with miraculous occurrences that made him suitable for later

---

61. Cf. *Gen. Rab.* 8:11 which compares humans to upper beings (angels) on the one hand and lower beings (animals) on the other (Theodor and Albeck, 65).

62. Cf. *b. Yoma* 37a that ranks Michael as best, Gabriel as second best, and Raphael as third best.

63. *b. Ber.* 4b.

64. See Lindbeck, *Elijah and the Rabbis*.

65. See Cordovero, *Pardes Rimmonim*, 24:14 on the opinions of Moses ben Shem Tov de Leon (d. 1305) and Moses ben Jacob Cordovero (d. 1570): the former believed Elijah was always an angel, while the later that he transformed into an angel. These are discussed in Horodezky, "Elijah: In Mysticism." Also relevant is *Terumat HaDeshen* 2:102 by Israel Isserlin (d. 1460), which uses the idea of Elijah transforming into an angel as *halakhic* precedent for dissolving marital case. Most recently, this stance was adopted by Rabbi Eliezer Waldenberg (d. 2006) in his opinion on transgender Jews, comparing them to those who transformed into angels, and therefore did not need a *get* (discussed in Rabinowitz, "Status of Transsexuals").

retellings in which he could intervene once more.[66] And the book of Malachi's prediction that Elijah would return to herald the Day of the Lord (3:34) made him an exceptional hero, who could be imagined lingering through the ages. Based on surviving sources, it seems that Elijah's previous human life and his promised return made him an ideal intermediary figure.

The Angel of Death is fourth in the above list, after Elijah, and this rank is a measure of how much the Angel of Death was domesticated by the rabbis and by other Jews in late antiquity. The Angel of Death is individuated in every stratum of rabbinic literature from the Mekhilta and *Sifrei Netzavim* through to the Babylonian Talmud; although nameless he resembles Michael and Gabriel in this respect.[67] Strikingly, in all rabbinic sources, he is not a source of chaos or fear but is like the "evil angels" who play a role in managing order on earth from the invisible realm.[68] Part of imagining the invisible realm with positive and negative figures is that it brought the chaos of life into order. The statement attributed to Reish Lakish that "Satan is the *yetzer ha-rā* is the Angel of Death" (*b. B. Bat.* 16a) needs to be understood in the context of the "analogical thinking" that was a feature of the ancient world, where categories are understood in relationship to each other, not through deductive logic.[69] The Angel of Death was like *yetzer ha-rā* and like Satan in that these three beings, while they had evil connotations, were an integral part of God's order and could be warded off with devotion to Torah. Comfortable with the invisible realm, the later rabbis modeled how to engage with all of the invisible figures in it.

CONCLUSION: BABYLONIAN RABBIS AMONG THE ANGELS

In this chapter, I surveyed late fourth- to sixth-century CE rabbinic texts, which I argue demonstrate that later rabbis came to accept the popularity of angels among

---

66. See Bohak's discussion of Elijah's relevance to the study of Jewish magic in *Ancient Jewish Magic*, 20–39.

67. See *Sifre Devarim Nitzavim* 3; *Mek. RI, Bahodesh* 9 (Horowitz and Rabin, 237; Lauterbach, 2:341), *y. Šabb.* 19b, *b. Šabb.* 30b, *b. Šabb.* 89a, *b. Yoma* 77b, *b. Sukkah* 53a, etc. The Angel of Death appears in about seventeen traditions in the Babylonian Talmud, a significant number on par with Michael and Gabriel, but far fewer than Elijah's.

68. In *b. Ber.* 51 the Angel of Death is described as a grim reaper–like figure, dancing with a sword in front of women returning from the cemetery, but it also tells the rabbis how to avoid his fatal attention: reciting the verse from Zechariah 3:2 ("the Lord said to satan, 'The Lord rebuke you, satan, may the LORD who has chosen Jerusalem rebuke you! For this is a brand plucked from the fire'") warded off the Angel of Death. Interestingly, in this rhetorical strategy, the rabbis and ritual practitioners of Babylonia were in agreement: this was the most commonly quoted biblical verse in incantation bowls. See Angel, "Use of the Hebrew Bible in Early Jewish Magic," 788–93.

69. Douglas, *Leviticus as Literature*, 18.

Jews, allowed angels to take a more active role in their worldview, and even harnessed beliefs in angels to encourage rabbinic norms of prayer and practice. Each retelling of the story about Rabban Yohanan ben Zakkai and Rabbi Eleazar ben Arach enlarged the role of the angels: whereas they were absent in the Toseftan version, by the time of the Babylonian Talmud the presence of the angels is taken for granted. Angelic approval became important to the rabbis. Discussions of how to pray through angels and even to angels can be found in these later rabbinic texts.

We also find more speculation about the angels although, again, little that could be termed an angelology. Later rabbis took for granted that the angels were God's creation (even if they could not agree on the exact timing of their origin), that the archangels and angels had an abode in the multilayered heavens, that angels carried the prayers of Jews from the earth to the heavens, and that they accompanied Jews wherever they went—even to the bathroom, where their patience might be politely requested. Several rabbinic traditions about angelic presence cluster around preparation for the Sabbath, which have endured in Jewish prayer and practice to this day. According to rabbinic stories, the angels were immune to acting out of divine alignment, but they still had emotional responses to their charges, the people of Israel. The Torah may not have been given to angels, but angels of good and angels of evil monitored the behavior of ancient Jews for obedience to the Torah, enforcing justice in the invisible realm.

The picture of angelic and human relations found in later rabbinic sources is very different from the one foregrounded by Tannaitic and Amoraic traditions, which emphasized that a direct and loving relationship with God was enough; no angelic mediators were necessary. By the time of the redaction of the Babylonian Talmud, many rabbis had come to accept that angels could play a significant role in Jewish life. Even as the rabbis themselves sought to become intermediaries for the Jewish people, they also accepted mediation of angels in the invisible realm.

And yet, these many ways of engaging with the invisible realm offered by Jewish thinkers in late antiquity proved insufficient for the circles of mystics who desired more control over their own destiny. The Jewish mystics examined in the next chapter did not merely want to pray with the angels on the Sabbath in the synagogue; they wanted to sing the angelic praise all the time. Moreover, they did not merely want to communicate with the angels; they wanted to command angels to do their bidding. Rejecting the doctrine that the Torah was *not* given to angels, they asserted that power of mastery over Torah was given to the angels, to the Angel of the Torah in particular, and to achieve mastery over Torah and Talmud, secret knowledge was necessary.

7

Jewish Mystics and the Angelic Realms

Early Mystical Sources

Said Rabbi Ishmael: Which are the hymns recited by one who wishes to behold the vision of the Merkavah (the divine throne-chariot), to descend in peace and to ascend in peace?

The greatest thing of all is that they [the angels] are bound to him, lead him, and bring him into the palace chambers of the seventh heaven, and place him to the right of the throne of his glory, and sometimes he stands opposite TʿTzS, the Lord, the God of Israel, in order to see everything that they do before the throne of his glory and to know everything that will occur in the world in the future.

—OPENING OF HEKHALOT RABBATI

To fully understand ancient Jewish attitudes toward angels and other intermediaries, we must turn our attention to Jewish mystics, who in the fifth to sixth century CE began gathering traditions related to God's heavenly places. Half a millennium before the first Kabbalistic treatises were written and one thousand years before Kabbalah erupted into the public sphere, circles of Jewish men were engaged in a different mode of mysticism. The passage above gestures at their mysterious and esoteric ideals: reciting hymns to attain a vision of God's throne, to *descend* and *ascend* in peace (more on this language below), and to bind angels to oneself so that one can go where previously only angels could go and know what the angels know.[1] These mystics represent the radical extreme of what was possible for Jews to imagine about angels in late antiquity.

---

1. Hekhalot Rabbati, §81, trans. Schäfer, *Origins of Jewish Mysticism*. Cf. Morton Smith's translation, which is widely available online.

Far more explicitly than Yannai, the men who recited the hymns of Hekhalot Rabbati aspired to sing with the angels and recite liturgical praise with them at any time and all the time. Whereas the Babylonian rabbis asserted that the Torah was *not* given to the ministering angels, one famous Hekhalot narrative stated the opposite: the Torah *was* given to the angels and esoteric knowledge was necessary to gain access to it. Far more confident than most other ritual practitioners, some of the mystics even dared to command the angels to do their bidding. In the early mystical texts examined in this chapter, we encounter Jews who believed they had access to the angels, displaced the angels, or could become as powerful as angels to possess the Torah themselves.

Studying Hekhalot Rabbati requires its own unique set of tools and approaches, which I describe in the first section of this chapter, after which I offer a close reading of attitudes toward angels in three distinctive subunits of Hekhalot Rabbati: the liturgical sections, where we can see the mystics aspired to sing with the angels all the time; the *Sar ha-Torah* narrative, where we find looking to the angels for Torah-mastery; and the Gedullah hymns, where we find Jews who command the angels to do their bidding. After these close-readings, I shift to broader observations of angels in the ascent accounts of Hekhalot Rabbati, demonstrating how the Jews that redacted these texts were in conversation with rabbis, synagogue poets, and ritual practitioners but charted their own course as well. To provide a full account of the significance of angels in ancient Jewish society, we must look even at Jews like these, who were probably cliquish and exclusive, because they nonetheless expanded the boundaries of what was possible to imagine about angels in late antiquity, and they left their imprint on Jewish society through the medieval period and into modernity.

METHODS, HISTORY OF SCHOLARSHIP, DEFINITION OF TERMS

Of all Jews, the mystics were most preoccupied with the heavenly realms and composed what has come to be known as Hekhalot literature. *Hykl* in Hebrew refers to the temple, especially its holiest inner sanctum; in the Hekhalot texts (plural of *hykl*), the Hekhalot refers to the heavenly chambers and palace of God. Hekhalot literature designates an early medieval group of texts preoccupied with the heavenly realms, its angels, and God's throne room. Angels, angelic names, and angelic hymns fill the pages of Hekhalot literature, which is generally agreed to be comprised of Hekhalot Rabbati, Hekhalot Zutarti, *ma'aseh merkavah*, *Merkavah Rabbah*, and 3 Enoch.[2] The longest and likely also the earliest of these texts, Hekhalot

2. Schäfer surveyed the role of angels in each of these macroforms in *The Hidden and Manifest God*.

Rabbati, includes descriptions of the ascent of several famous sages through the seven heavens, acquiring power over gate-keeping angels, and finally joining the highest ranks of the angels in liturgical worship of God.[3]

While the stories of ascent to the heavens feature famous rabbinic sages, the content of the corpus does not resemble the style or content of the writings of the rabbis. Hekhalot Rabbati is anthological, containing short narratives, apocalypses, instructions, and poetic-liturgical sections. Hekhalot literature defies precise textual delimitation as well as geographical and chronological location and thus requires a different set of approaches than most ancient Jewish texts. As Peter Schäfer has compellingly argued, in this corpus there is no original *ur*-text to be reconstructed.[4] There was never a fixed original text that one author or school composed: there is much variation among the manuscripts of this text, and it is often unclear where one "work" ends and another begins. Schäfer's publication of a synoptic edition of several ancient manuscripts of this work in *Synopse zur Hekhalot-Literatur* enables researchers to see that variation and tread more carefully in making claims about the characteristics of the texts.[5] Following his lead, some specialists use such terms as macroforms and microforms to refer to the different subsets of the literature, terms that serve to highlight the flexible boundaries of these compositions. *Macroform* refers to the larger "imaginary single text" (e.g., Hekhalot Rabbati), while *microform* refers to smaller redactional units within it, as short as a few sentences or as long as a subunit of several pages.[6] Following Schäfer's framework, the published macroform of Hekhalot Rabbati spans the units §§81–306.[7] Within the macroform of Hekhalot Rabbati, we may discern the microforms that scholars refer to as the *Gedullah* hymns, the *Qedushah* hymns, the Ten Martyrs Narratives, the Apocalypses, the Hymns of Praise, the ascent accounts, and the *Sar ha-Torah* Traditions.[8] Each of these microforms reflects its own conceptions of angels and the relationship of the mystics to angels and the heavenly realm. In this chapter, I focus on the portrayal of angels in the

---

3. On the topic of the seven heavens in ancient Judaism, see Schäfer, "In Heaven as It Is in Hell," 252–66. The rabbis offer a list in *b. Ḥag.* 12b. For Yannai's list of the seven heavens, see the eighth poem to the *qedushtah* for Gen 11:1 (Lieber, *Yannai on Genesis*, 384–85).

4. Schäfer, *Origins of Jewish Mysticism*, 244.

5. See Schäfer, Schlüter, and von Mutius, *Synopse zur Hekhalot-Literatur*. The importance of the synoptic edition is explained by Halperin, "A New Edition of the Hekhalot Literature." *Hekhalot Literature in Context*, a conference volume edited by Boustan, Himmelfarb, and Schäfer, celebrated the thirty years to this landmark publication, convening an array of scholars from different disciplines and highlighting both the advances and lingering questions surrounding the corpus. See also Swartz, "Three-Dimensional Philology" in *Mechanics of Providence.*

6. Schäfer, *Hekhalot-Studien*, 199ff.; *Hidden and Manifest God*, 6n14.

7. I follow his numbering and identify which manuscripts I follow where relevant.

8. Schäfer, *Origins of Jewish Mysticism*, esp. chapter 8.

Qedushah hymns, the *Sar ha-Torah* narratives, the *Gedullah* hymns, and the ascent accounts, placing each of these portrayals in the context of broader Jewish attitudes to angels.

In the previous chapter, we encountered Babylonian rabbinic traditions on *ma'aseh merkavah*, the works of the divine chariot, which some have associated with the Jewish mysticism of Hekhalot literature. Traditions in rabbinic literature are frustratingly opaque about the content of these *merkavah* speculations, and scholars have tried to fill in the gap for generations. In his foundational work *Major Trends in Jewish Mysticism*, Gershom Scholem asserted that Hekhalot texts were representative of "*Merkavah* mysticism," Jewish mysticism centered on the divine throne-chariot first described in the book Ezekiel, which continued to develop through the Second Temple period. Scholem posited that Hekhalot literature reflected a later phase of Jewish mysticism, contemporary with rabbinic Judaism and preceding the medieval development of Kabbalah in the thirteenth century CE. Much of Scholem's initial work has been challenged, and Hekhalot texts are now generally dated to the post-Talmudic period.[9] The consensus is that circles of men composed these texts over the course of the fifth to ninth centuries CE in Palestine and Babylonia but attributed them to famous second-century CE sages like Rabbi Ishmael in the passage above.[10] Pseudonymously attributing traditions to rabbis like Ishmael and Akiva, they sought to endow these works with legitimacy and authority.[11] I limit my focus to Hekhalot Rabbati, as it is more or less contemporaneous with the liturgical poetry of the synagogue in Palestine, the redaction of the Babylonian Talmud, and the commissioning of incantation bowls and amulets in the late antique Mediterranean.

David Halperin cogently argued that the rabbinic term *ma'aseh merkavah* referred not to Hekhalot literature, but only to exegesis of Ezekiel 1, sections of the Torah that needed to be interpreted with caution, especially in public.[12] Whether the term *mysticism* correctly expresses and reflects the interests of the composers of this corpus has also been challenged by later scholars. As Joseph Dan observed, historically the term *mysticism* belongs to the Christian tradition and only began being applied by scholars to Jewish and Islamic traditions in the nineteenth century.[13] In its Christian context, mysticism refers to an experience of union with the Godhead. As Schäfer pointed out in a succession of studies, this is not the goal

---

9. Summarized most accessibly in Boustan, "The Study of Heikhalot Literature." See also his introduction in Boustan, et al., *Hekhalot Literature in Context*.

10. Another accessible overview to these texts can be found in Swartz, "Mystical Texts." For a brief introduction to these texts including excerpts from each in translation, see Ahuvia, "Ancient Mystical Texts."

11. Boustan, "The Study of Heikhalot Literature," 132.

12. Halperin, *Faces of the Chariot*.

13. Dan, *Kabbalah*, 8.

of the Hekhalot texts: their goal is not self-annihilation or union with God but seems to be what he termed *unio liturgica*, liturgical union with the angels.[14] In this chapter, I place the significance of this angelic ideal in the context of Jewish preoccupation with praying with angels in late antiquity more broadly.

As the opening passage of this chapter shows, Hekhalot Rabbati makes idiosyncratic use of the language of ascent and descent to the heavenly throne, probably reflecting the insider language of exclusive circles (some scholars refer to the users of this corpus as *yordei merkavah*, lit. "the descenders to the chariot").[15] The only sociological variable regarding this exclusive group upon which all scholars agree is that only men engaged with the composition of these texts, banishing the feminine—and women themselves—from their texts and practices.[16] As Rebecca Lesses puts it: "It was a male-only world, and women were mentioned only as possible threats to the sexual or ritual purity of the male practitioners."[17] Whereas in liturgical, ritual, and rabbinic texts we can point to some evidence for Jewish conceptualization of feminine angels, no such hint can be found in extant manuscripts of Hekhalot Rabbati. Extant evidence for women engaged in mysticism dates only to sixteenth-century Kabbalistic mysticism.[18] Generations of men between Babylonia and Palestine composed what came to be known as Hekhalot literature, and these texts were transmitted through medieval copyists to the present (the manuscripts in *Synopse zur Hekhalot-Literatur* date to 1300–1550).[19]

It is difficult to say much more about the identity of these exclusive male Jewish mystics. Boustan cautions that "the range of ideological perspectives articulated in various Hekhalot compositions undermines unitary or homogenizing accounts of the religious phenomena or social groups thought to stand behind the surface of the Hekhalot texts."[20] It would be more prudent to discuss the worldview that each text projects. And yet, behind all of these compositions were Jews who were part of Jewish society, albeit with competing visions of the divine realm. They were just as diverse in their outlook as the ritual practitioners we encountered in chapter 1 and just as diverse in their perspectives as the rabbis were over time.

---

14. Most recently summarized in *The Origins of Jewish Mysticism*, 243–330.

15. Schäfer, Scholem, and Halperin have proposed various explanation for this language. See summary of approaches in Schäfer, *Origins of Jewish Mysticism*, 247. See also Wolfson, "*Yeridah la-Merkavah*: Typology of Ecstasy and Enthronement in Ancient Jewish Mysticism."

16. Lesses, "Women and Gender in Hekhalot Literature."

17. Lesses, "Women and Gender in Hekhalot Literature," 279–80. Lesses does analyze one exception in the manuscript tradition, which she describes as "an idiosyncrasy of the medieval redactor of the text" (282).

18. For example, Rachel Aberlin and Sarah Francesa of Safed, on whom see Taitz, Henry, and Tallan, eds., *The JPS Guide to Jewish Women*, 170–71.

19. Boustan, "The Study of Heikhalot Literature," 137.

20. Boustan, *Hekhalot Literature in Context*, xiv.

Schäfer states that the authors share the values of the rabbinic movement but that their compositions are post-rabbinic, and he finds a redactional context in Babylonia more likely than Palestine.[21] Himmelfarb posits that the diversity of surviving texts "suggests small circles of mystics operating independently of other such circles, shaping common traditions in different ways."[22] Like them, I use the term *mystics* for the sake of convenience.

Other scholars have ventured to name more specific groups behind these compositions, and each perspective illuminates a facet of these texts' themes. James Davila, Rebecca Lesses, and Michael Swartz each highlight the commonalities of the ritual texts and Hekhalot texts according to their area of expertise. Davila begins his study from the anthropological standpoint that the "descenders to the Chariot" may be understood as shamans and sees the ritual texts as the practical counterpart to the Hekhalot texts. He writes that the "evidence of the other texts of ritual power fills out this picture and shows that the tradents of the Hekhalot literature used their powers to heal, protect, and exorcise demons from clients."[23] Lesses also takes a wider cross-cultural perspective, arguing that "revelatory adjurations of Hekhalot literature, *Sefer ha-Razim*, the Greco-Egyptian ritual texts, and the Aramaic amulets all belong to a larger complex of practices of adjuration that was widespread in the Greco-Roman world in the late antiquity."[24] Michael D. Swartz, who specializes in liturgical poetry and medieval ritual texts, has long noted the relationship of the mystics with the synagogue poets of late antique Palestine.[25] In more recent scholarship, Swartz argues for a Palestinian provenance for these texts, observing that "it is now possible to show that the basic elements of the ascent narratives of Hekhalot literature—travel through the seven Hekhalot, admission through the gates of the palaces by angelic guards, and vision of the divine throne—were known to Palestinian Jews in Late antiquity."[26] Building on recent publications of piyyut, Swartz makes a persuasive case that the content of Hekhalot literature was shared knowledge among Jews in the early period of classical piyyut, the fifth to the early seventh centuries CE in Palestine.[27] Behind these anonymously transmitted texts, we can reconstruct small circles of Jewish

---

21. Schäfer, *Origins of Jewish Mysticism*, 245.

22. Himmelfarb, "Heavenly Ascent and the Relationship of the Apocalypses and the Hekhalot Literature," 88.

23. In *Descenders to the Chariot*, Davila writes that the "religious functionaries portrayed in the Hekhalot texts, the 'descenders to the chariot' as they are sometimes called, were real people, practitioners of the rituals described in the Hekhalot literature and the writers of that literature." (254–55).

24. Lesses, *Ritual Practices to Gain Power*, 284; Lesses, "Speaking with Angels," 45.

25. Swartz, *Scholastic Magic*, esp. 220.

26. Swartz, "Hekhalot and Piyyut," in *Mechanics of Providence*, 259.

27. In "Hekhalot and Piyyut," Swartz cites the work of Michael Rand, "More on the *Seder Beriyot*," in particular.

men who were experimenting with Jewish identity, ritual practices, and relating to the invisible realms. We will return to the question of the authors' social location at the end of this chapter, but for now, equipped with an understanding of these texts and their origins, we can delve into a close reading of some microforms and better evaluate the mystics' envisioning of human interaction with angels.

THE *QEDUSHAH* HYMNS OF HEKHALOT RABBATI: ANGELS ALL THE TIME

In chapter 5, I foregrounded how Yannai depicted Israel singing in synchronicity with the angels every sabbath during the prayer service. The *Qedushah*, the angelic praise of God from Isaiah, which became the third benediction in the fixed liturgy of the Jews, was Yannai's point of departure. The *Qedushah* would receive special attention from the Jewish mystics as well. Much of Hekhalot Rabbati consists of heavenly hymns that the authors pictured the angels reciting. My readings of these liturgical sections have led me to conclude that the mystics took the practice of reciting the *Qedushah* to a radical extreme, originating the idea of praying with the angels *all the time*. Although the rabbis upheld God's preference for the Shema prayer as the prayer of Israel par excellence, in Hekhalot literature, the *Qedushah* takes the place of honor, especially in microforms §§94–106, aptly referred to as the *Qedushah* hymns, and the related microforms §§152–97, also called the *Qedushah* hymns and hymns of praise.[28] These are the most stable "poetic-liturgical" sections within the manuscript tradition of Hekhalot Rabbati.[29] Focusing on them, we can discern the mystics' conception of time and how these texts might have served as their liturgy, one that remained flexible and varied between circles of mystics. Much has been written about the character and purpose of the hymns in Hekhalot Rabbati, especially as they relate to the ascent material.[30] Scholars have asked how the hymns could put the mystic into a trance or assisted or protected him as he ascended to heaven; they have also mined the hymns for descriptions of the heavenly goals of the *yordei merkavah*. Indeed, limiting the scope of my discussion to these microforms highlights their shared stylistic traits, content, and assumptions about time. As I explain the features of this liturgical collection, I will highlight how the mystics imagine themselves in sync with angelic time to an unprecedented extent.

28. Schäfer, "The Merkavah Mystics," in *Origins of Jewish Mysticism*.

29. Schäfer, *Origins of Jewish Mysticism*, 246.

30. Altmann, "Kedushah Hymns in the Earliest Hechaloth Literature; Scholem, *Major Trends in Jewish Mysticism*, 57–63; Maier, "'Attah hu' Adon"; Wewers, "Die Überlegenheit des Mystikers"; Gruenwald, "Angelic Songs, the Qedushah and the Problem of the Origin of the Hekhalot Literature"; Swartz, *Mystical Prayer in Ancient Judaism*.

In contrast to the rabbinic emphasis on calendrical time (e.g., development of halakhah around Shabbat and holidays), the hymns of Hekhalot Rabbati emphasize a present and continuous sense of sacred time.[31] Indeed, there is no mention of Shabbat or any other holidays in Hekhalot literature. The liturgical collection of Hekhalot Rabbati is undergirded by a unique conception of time that focuses on the heavenly realm. On the one hand, it is easy to miss the few references to time in the prayers of Hekhalot Rabbati. Here and there we encounter a reference to the time of creation (§166) and to dawn (§173 "at sunrise"). For the singing divine creatures, there "is no night and no day" (§270). On the other hand, references to the "day" and especially "every day" or "each and every day" are commonplace, but they carry no mundane connotation. Rather the opposite is the case: the "everyday" generally refers to the perennial, uninterrupted, and most holy heavenly activity of God and the angelic creatures.[32] For example, a *Qedushah* hymn states:

> From the praise and song of each and every day
> From the joy and exultation of each and every twenty-four hours
> And from the recitation which comes from the mouth of the Holy ones
> And from the melody which wells up from the mouth of the servants
> Behold fire and hills of flame are piled up and hidden and poured out each day.
> As it is said, "Holy, holy, holy, is the Lord of Hosts.[33]

Similarly, note the references to "day and night" alongside echoes of thrice-daily prayer in the following hymn:

> For how many of the mighty are they
> Who bear up the throne of the glory of this mighty King,
> Standing laden, day and night,
> Evening and morning and noon, in trembling and in terror,
> In fright, in shivering, in shaking and in fear!
> And how great strength is there in you, you servants of our God,
> That you recall to Him and cause Him to hear
> The reminder of His name, in the height of the world!
> There is no searching out and no telling the sound and the strength.
> As it is said, "Holy, Holy, Holy."[34]

The joyous angelic activity happens every day and continually so that the "every-day" takes on a sacred quality. The assumption of present, simultaneous, and

---

31. Cf. discussion of sacred time in Stökl Ben Ezra, *The Impact of Yom Kippur on Early Christianity*.

32. §§92, 95, 99, 100, 153, 159, 163, 165, 168, 169, 173, 189, 269.

33. §95 based on MS Oxford 1531(henceforth O1531); trans. Smith, *Hekhalot Rabbati* with minor corrections.

34. §168 O1531; trans. Smith, *Hekhalot Rabbati* with minor corrections.

ongoing holy time permeates the prayers collected in these sections of Hekhalot Rabbati. "Each and every day, at the rising of the dawn," God asks his heavenly creatures to be silent while he listens to the prayers of his sons on earth (§173). The adherents of this liturgy began each morning imagining God in tune with their prayers, which inherently demanded the highest level of devotion.

Within the framework of the day, the authors of the Hekhalot Rabbati foreground another way of ordering time, which is shared by the inhabitants of the heavenly and earthly realms alike: the punctuation of the day with three liturgical moments. The division of the day into three parts is emphasized in several contexts in the hymns: the divine throne bows before God three times a day (§99); the Prince of the Presence comes and goes upon the firmament three times daily (§100); God hears Israel's prayers during morning, afternoon, and evening prayers (§163); God embraces and kisses the icon of Jacob engraved on his throne thrice daily (§164); the exaltation of the faces of the angels on high occurs three times each day (§169); the Prince of the Presence "kneels and falls and prostrates" himself before the holy creatures (§171);[35] all creation declares His sanctification with triple Sanctus (§273 and §274).

The thrice-daily occasion for intimacy between God and those praying with their eyes cast on heaven is most striking in the following hymn.[36] It is the only explicit depiction of coordinated earthly and heavenly activity in the liturgical collection (aside from God listening to the morning prayers in §173):

> Blessed are you to the heavens and to the earth who descend to the chariot
> If you declare and say to my sons
> What I do during the morning, afternoon, and evening prayer
> On each day and at every hour that Israel say before me "Holy"
> Teach them and tell them: lift your eyes to the horizon opposite your houses of
>   prayer at the time that you say "Holy"
> [Teach them] that there is no greater joy before me in all the world that I created as
>   in that time when your eyes are lifted to my eyes
> And my eyes are reflected in your eyes at the time that you say before me "Holy"
> Because the voice that comes from your mouth at that hour carries and ascends
>   before me like a pleasant aroma.[37]

35. Three times a day according to the Oxford MS, but three thousand times according to the rest of the MSS.

36. This text is a much-discussed unit (§163): see Schäfer, *The Origins of Jewish Mysticism*, 260; Münz-Manor, "A Prolegomenon to the Study of Hekhalot Traditions in European Piyyut," 239.

37. §163 (my translation based on O1531). There is some inconsistency in the manuscript tradition, probably because the scribes tried to resolve a mystifying aspect of the text: God addresses the *Yordei Merkavah* and tells them what He does during the *shacharit*, *minchah* and *arvit* prayer whenever Israel recites the "Holy," seemingly alluding to the *Qedushah*. The problem is that the *Qedushah* was not said thrice daily according to normative rabbinic liturgical practice. This will be addressed below.

This is a beautiful and moving text about a very intimate moment in prayer. Here the angelic *Qedushah* stands at the center and serves as the moment when the select group of mystics can encounter the eyes of God, an activity in which even the angels are not described as partaking. In late antiquity, the *Qedushah* was recited communally only weekly, on the Sabbath, in Palestine. Today, following Babylonian custom, the *Qedushah* is recited in the morning and afternoon prayer as part of the fixed liturgy on a daily basis, but it is not clear when this custom was established.[38] The mystics, perhaps before other Babylonian Jews, seem to have adopted an idiosyncratic practice, reciting the angelic praise three times a day, at every prayer time, in imitation of their sense of the divine time of the heavens, which was eternally holy, punctuated only three times a day by praise.

Perhaps the adoption of the recitation of the *Qedushah* on a daily basis began in early medieval Babylonia as another rabbinic concession to popular practice and engagement with the angelic praise. What is certain is that while the rabbis worked at consolidating a Jewish calendar with Sabbath and festivals, this circle of mystics focused on angelic time, eternally holy, always in the company of God. As Sarit Kattan Gribetz has suggested, repetitive activity is a way of expressing continuity and eternity in the only ways humans feasibly could.[39] The mystics seem to have adopted the language of repetition to express their sense of eternal heavenly time.

I speculate that the *Qedushah* hymns circulated as a collection of prayers— prayers so sacred in themselves that they would turn every moment into the most sacred moment (later, they were incorporated into Hekhalot Rabbati alongside apocalypses and ascent accounts). Reciting them, the individual could shift into holy time and participate in the heavenly liturgy. In the same way Jews today might associate hearing the ancient hymn U-Netanne Tokef with the Jewish high holidays or Christians associate Christmas music with the holidays, ancient mystics associated hymns with their own communal sense of time.[40] But they attributed much more importance to this liturgy than their fellow Jews did. For them, when one excelled in his devotion to prayer, he was, in effect, praying before the throne and making eye contact with God.[41]

38. See discussion of this topic in Langer, "Individual Recitation of the Kedushah," in *To Worship God Properly*.

39. Gribetz, *Time and Difference in Rabbinic Judaism*.

40. In his book *The Mysteries of Jewish Prayer and Hekhalot*, 51–53, Bar Ilan points out one of U-Netanne Tokef's stanza's similarities to §82. A Cairo Genizah manuscript of Yannai's poetry includes U-Netanne Tokef, which has led to speculation that it was composed by Yannai. Elizur has laid out a compelling case for this view in "New Discoveries on the Origin of the Thrilling Piyyut 'U-Netanneh Tokef.'" If she is right, perhaps Yannai's corpus did reach Babylonia where mystics were developing these *Qedushah* hymns.

41. The equation of reciting the liturgy and viewing the *merkavah* lends weight to Scholem's suggestion that the terminology of *yeridah la-merkavah* (descent to the chariot) is related to the idea of

Certainly, the authors of this corpus valued the liturgy far more than the rabbis did. In "Some Liturgical Issues in the Talmudic Sources," Reif draws attention to the controversial theological status of prayer in late antique rabbinic circles. Reviewing the Talmudic discussions of this topic, he writes that "The authentic successor to the temple liturgy and, thus, the ideal form of worship is being portrayed as Torah-study, and Prayer is accorded no more than a junior place in comparison."[42] Where the rabbis devalued prayer, never acknowledging the poets of the synagogue, Yannai placed the priests, the rabbis, and himself on equal footing (see conclusion to chapter 5). The mystics went a step further, making their angelic liturgical practices the heart of their identity formation.

The hymns of the mystics do precisely that which the rabbis criticize: they multiply the epithets of God. Interestingly, the sages, in Reif's words, were "anxious to limit the praise of God to statutory proportions."[43] We have already encountered one example of this tendency with the unusual reference to synagogue practice in the Mishnah, examined in chapter 3, where Akiva is attributed a criticism of the prayer "Let us bless the Lord our God, the God of Israel, the God of Hosts, Who sits upon the cherubim, for the food that we have eaten" and suggests limiting it to the shorter version "Let us bless the Lord, our God." Echoes of this attitude are found in the later traditions of the Babylonian Talmud. Rabbi Yohanan is quoted as saying that "the one who recounts the praises of Holy One, blessed be He, excessively will be uprooted from the world" (*b. Meg.* 18a). Likewise, the sage Hamnuna seems to have extended his prayers, perhaps in just such a manner, and in reaction, Rava complained that "some set aside the matters of the world to come and instead occupy themselves with transient matters" (*b. Šabb.* 10a). In the same section, the redactors brought a story about Rabbi Zeira and Rabbi Yirmeya: when the latter was hurrying to finish study and pray, Rabbi Zeira applied a proverb to him, "He who turns his ear from hearing Torah, his prayer is an abomination" (Prov 28:9). Such traditions may point to a reality wherein there was tension between the rabbis who upheld Torah study and mystics who valued liturgical praise imitating the angels. These learned Jews likely inhabited the same communities, but tension animated their relationship, of which only traces remain in the written record.

Piyyut made its way to Babylonia and flourished there, even as Babylonian rabbis opposed piyyut and Palestinian liturgical innovations.[44] Still, the liturgical

---

yeridah lifnei ha-teiva (descent to the ark in the synagogue, where the prayer leader would stand)—not because "the ark containing the scrolls of the Torah is like the throne," however, but because descending into prayer mode was tantamount to attaining intimacy with God. See Scholem, *Jewish Gnosticism, Merkabah Mysticism, and Talmudic Tradition*, 20n1.

42. Reif, "Some Liturgical Issues in the Talmudic Sources," 193 (his capitalization).

43. Reif, "Some Liturgical Issues in the Talmudic Sources," 201.

44. Rosen and Yassif, "Hebrew Literature in the Middle Ages," 268.

prayers adopted in the end by the Babylonian rabbis look very different from the corpus of Hekhalot. Comparing the liturgy of the *yordei merkavah* and the siddur, Philip Alexander comes to the conclusion that "We are dealing, in effect with two independent liturgical styles, two independent liturgical traditions;" he calls this "a startling fact, the socio-religious implications of which have yet to be properly assessed."[45] While the respective liturgies are both in rabbinic Hebrew and in Aramaic, the Hekhalot prayers' style, especially their propensity to stack synonyms, distinguishes them from the prayers of the siddur. Hekhalot prayers present an approach not taken (liturgically) by most medieval Jews.

I would further argue that the hymns of Hekhalot Rabbati also reveal a conception of realized eschatology, by which I mean a sense of time where every day is celebrated in the presence of God and calls for the highest standards of conduct, on the same level as the most sacred day in the Jewish calendar, the day of judgment, Yom Kippur.[46] The mystics stand apart from their rabbinic (and Christian) counterparts in their conception of the judgment day. For the mystics, at least when they used this book of hymns, every day was as holy as the judgment day.

Two conceptions of the judgment day seem to have existed among Jews in the first century CE. Some ancient Jews as well as the nascent Jesus movement conceptualized the judgment day as a single and final eschatological event.[47] The first-century CE Jewish thinker Paul writes about a final judgment day in 1 Thess 5:2, telling his followers to be prepared for the day of the Lord that will come like a "a thief in the night," and reassuring his followers that those who died in the meantime will be resurrected and precede those who are already alive, who will also be granted eternal life.[48] For Christians through the centuries, the day of judgment has remained a future (and ever-looming) event. In contrast, in the first century CE, Philo writes about the annual Day of Atonement, stating that even Jews who are usually not observant show piety during this period.[49] In late antiquity, the sages further de-emphasized the future judgment day and elaborated its meaning as an annual event, whereby humanity is judged on Rosh Hashana and its fate sealed on Yom Kippur.[50] A third position was offered by the composers of the *Qedushah* hymns, who in their liturgical texts convey an ever-present sense of sacred time.

---

45. Alexander, "Prayer in the Heikhalot Literature," 61.

46. Schäfer, Wewers, and Boustan have written about the heroes of Hekhalot literature as eschatological judges; my argument here builds on their research, and their work will be discussed more in the next sections. See Schäfer, *Hidden and Manifest God*, 42–43; Wewers, "Die Überlegenheit des Mystikers," 21; Boustan, *From Martyr to Mystic*, 200.

47. See *b. Roš Haš.* 16b. My thanks to Israel Yuval for bringing this to my attention.

48. See also the book of Revelation's lengthy depiction of the final judgment.

49. Philo, *De Specialibus Legibus* 1:186; LCL, Philo 7:205–6.

50. See *y. Roš. Haš.* 57a and *b. Roš. Haš.* 16b.

THE *SAR HA-TORAH* MYTH: THE TORAH
WAS ~~NOT~~ GIVEN TO ANGELS

The most famous section of Hekhalot Rabbati is probably the *Sar ha-Torah* myth, the myth of the angelic Prince of the Torah (§§281–298).[51] This myth describes the Jews returning to Palestine to rebuild the temple after the Babylonian destruction in the sixth century BCE and their frustrations with completing their physical labor alongside Torah study. In answer to their complaints, God agrees to reveal to them the means of calling up the Angel of the Torah (Hebrew, *Sar ha-Torah*), who can grant them perfect memorization of the Oral and Written Torah. If the rabbis of the Babylonian Talmud argued that the Torah was given to Israel (whether at Sinai through Moses or later through Ezra), these mystics argued the opposite: the Torah was given to the angels and it was still with the angels.[52] In this imagined scenario (as elsewhere) the angels object to sharing the mystery of Torah with the earthly people of Israel. According to the text, God recounts:

> My servants waged a great battle with me,
> An accuser, the greatest of the ministering angels, [appeared and] this was his plea:
> "Let not this secret go forth from your storehouse,
> and mystery of wisdom from your treasuries;
> Let not flesh and blood be as our equals, suppose not the children of men our substitute.[53]

The "secret" and "mystery" of Torah was in the heavenly storehouses and treasuries; the angels argue against sharing it, but according to the myth's inner chronology, the Torah was already revealed at this time and yet still out of reach of the laboring Jew. God continues his speech, saying "this secret will go forth from my storehouse, this mystery of wisdom from my treasuries" (§293). The emphasis is on the Torah, secrecy, and access only through the mystics' secret practices.

After this section, near the end of the macroform of Hekhalot Rabbati, the adjuration of angels is affirmed as the means of the ascent with the goal of Torah mastery as its end (§§302–4). The authority of Rabbis Ishmael, Akiva, and Eliezer the elder are evoked to approve of this method.

> Let him conjure up those twelve [angels]
> by the name Yofiel:

51. For full text, translation, and analysis, see Vidas, "Hekhalot Literature, the Babylonian Academies, and the Tanna'im," 141–76, esp. 146ff.

52. Contrast also with the tradition found in *t. Šabb.* 6:1 and elsewhere that at the end of days the angels would "learn the mysteries of heaven from the righteous" (Rebiger, "Angels in Rabbinic Literature," 630).

53. §§291–92 of O1531 (cf. Smith, *Hekhalot Rabbati*). See also *b. Šabb.* 88b.

he is the splendor of [heaven on] high because of the permission of his King;
by the name Sarakhiel:
he belongs to the princes of the Chariot;
by the name Sahadariel:
he is a beloved prince;
by the name Hasdiel: six hours every day he is called to the divine power.
Let him again conjure up the last [named] four princes
by the great seal and the great oath,
by the name AZBWGH:
he is the great seal;
and by the name SWRTQ:
the holy name and the awesome crown.

After the course of twelve days
he will reach all the types of the Torah he desires,
whether that is Bible,
whether that is Mishnah,
whether that is Talmud,
whether it is even the vision of the Chariot.

. . .

Rabbi Ishmael said:
So spoke Rabbi Akiva in the name of Rabbi Eliezer the Elder:
Blessed is he to whom the merit of his fathers comes as aid
and whom the righteousness of his parents assists:
he will avail himself of this crown and this seal,
[the angels] will be bound up with him,
and he will rise up proudly in the sublimity of the Torah.[54]

In this microform, mastery of the angels and of the Torah are inextricably tied together. Moreover, the vision of the heavenly throne is placed on the same level of importance as knowledge of the rabbinic curriculum.

Hekhalot Zutarti and *ma'aseh merkavah*, which postdate Hekhalot Rabbati, largely repeat its traditions on the means of adjuration (see §§417–19 and §§560–69) with microform §562 framing this practice more explicitly: "You are YY the living God in the heavens who gave permission to the ranks of your glory to be bound to human beings." Like the ritual practitioners who see themselves as operating within a hierarchy that God created, those who composed these traditions see their adjuration of angels as acting out a world order that God put in place for them. But unlike most of the ritual practitioners, the mystics are stationed above the angels.

For many scholars, the identification of the social group behind this corpus rests on the interpretation of the *Sar ha-Torah* myth, even though this narrative

---

54. Based on Vatican 228; trans. Schäfer, "Aim and Purpose," in *Hekhalot-Studien*, 282.

circulated independently from the rest of the Hekhalot texts.[55] What kind of Jews would think up such a myth? Many theories have been suggested by scholars, and each hypothesis raises important considerations. David Halperin believes the *am ha'aretz*, the non-rabbinic ordinary Jews of late antique Palestine, who were derided in rabbinic literature, could have been responsible for conceiving this foundation myth and the Hekhalot corpus as a whole.[56] His argument identifies a few microforms' emphasis on leveling the playing field, as it were, for the brilliant and the less gifted.[57] Moulie Vidas proposes identifying certain members of the rabbinic movement as possible authors and carriers of this text. He suggests locating the authors of the Hekhalot texts squarely within the rabbinic movement, among the tanna'im, the Jewish men responsible for memorizing and reciting oral traditions (not to be confused with the early rabbis who are referred to as Tannaim).[58] In a scholastic environment before print books, their role in the study house and academy as "living books" was crucial, albeit taken for granted among the scholars. Polemical accounts in the Babylonian Talmud indicate that these reciters were of inferior status in the study house, aspired to the status of the legal scholars, and engaged in some of the same activities as the scholars (like juxtaposition and emendations of traditions), but that other scholars ridiculed them.[59] If the ideals contained in Hekhalot literature emerged from this subset of the rabbinic movement, their texts would likely share many values with the rabbis but also reformulate some rabbinic traditions about angels for their own personal ends. In light of the above theories, it is worth revisiting the closing of the myth of *Sar Ha-Torah*:

> Sit before my throne as you sit in the yeshiva and seize the crown and accept the seal and study this order of the Prince of Torah, how you shall perform it, how you shall expound it, how you shall use it, how you shall raise the paths of your hearts, how your hearts shall gaze into Torah!"
>
> At once Zerubbabel the son of Shaltiel stood up before him like a translator and explained the names of the Prince of the Torah, one by one, with his name, the name of his crown and the name of his seal."[60]

According to the myth, the ancient Davidic king Zerubbabel received the names of the Prince of Torah, and now this knowledge is available to the hearers of this

---

55. Schäfer, "Handschriften zur Hekhalot Literatur," in *Hekhalot-Studien*, 212–13.

56. *Am ha'aretz* is literally "people of the land" (cf. the original meaning of *pagan*, "people of the hills").

57. Halperin, *The Faces of the Chariot*, esp. 437.

58. Vidas, "Hekhalot Literature, the Babylonian Academies, and the Tanna'im."

59. See *b. Soṭah* 22a and *b. B. Meṣi'a* 33a–b.

60. §298 of O1531; I reproduce Vidas's translation from *Tradition and Formation*, 193 with minor changes.

esoteric tradition. This passage references the rabbinic context of the yeshiva, the *meturgeman* or translator of the synagogue context, and teaches the ritual process of invoking seals and names of the Prince of Torah to grasp secrets of Torah. These references suggest that, rather than being confined to one movement or place, the mystics behind the myth of the Angelic Prince of the Torah were Jews who could be found in rabbinic study circles, in synagogue prayer circles, and engaging in ritual practices. It may be that Hekhalot Rabbati as a whole reflects the variety of mystical practices in which late antique Jews engaged: some were more liturgical in their approach; some were more preoccupied with rabbinic values of Torah mastery. Through a focus on traditions about angels, we can see that the different registers of Jewish culture were interacting in late antiquity. Ideas about angels flowed among rabbis, ritual practitioners, synagogue poets, and mystics.

COMMANDING THE ANGELS IN THE *GEDULLAH* HYMNS

The beginnings and endings of manuscripts are notoriously flexible and difficult to date. It is with this observation in mind that I now evaluate conceptions of angels in the *Gedullah* hymns (§81–93), which at some point in time were adjoined to the beginning of Hekhalot Rabbati. This microform begins with the enigmatic words "The greatest thing of all is that they [the angels] are bound to him, to admit him and to bring him in to the chambers of the palace of the seventh heaven" (§81). To restate it more clearly, the mystics behind this microform celebrated authority over the angels as the greatest feat.[61] Far more than any other genre of Jewish texts and more explicitly than any other microform in Hekhalot Rabbati, the composers of this section promote the view that the mystics were entitled to command the angels to obey their will. Jews engaged with Hekhalot mysticism composed ritual texts in which they commanded the angels to do their bidding.[62] The idea that one can command angels implies a very different attitude to the self, the heavenly realm, and authority. It implies a different placement of oneself in the hierarchy

61. Schäfer, "Aim and Purpose," in *Hekhalot-Studien*, 277–95; idem, "Engel und Menschen in der Hekhalot-Literatur." Already in his 1988 collection of studies on Hekhalot Literature, Schäfer collected the literary evidence for adjuration in the corpus and noted that adjuration of angels was no minor theme in the Hekhalot literature, but central to all the works in this corpus, as central as the ascent itself

62. As previously mentioned, several scholars have highlighted the commonalities between the Hekhalot literature and ritual-magical texts: Schäfer, "Jewish Magic Literature in Late Antiquity and the Early Middle Ages"; Shaked, "'Peace Be Upon You, Exalted Angels': On Hekhalot, Liturgy, and Incantation Bowls"; Davila, *Descenders to the Chariot*, esp. chap. 8; Swartz, *Scholastic Magic*; Dan, *The Ancient Jewish Mysticism*; Naveh and Shaked, *Amulets and Magic Bowls*; Levene, *A Corpus of Magic Bowls*, esp. 44–50 (Bowl M102).

stretching between the mortal and divine realm. How did these Jewish mystics come to situate themselves so highly in the hierarchy stretching from the lowest (children, women, and slaves) to the highest, the angelic princes and God?

As Schäfer and Boustan have argued, these mystics upheld a world of realized eschatology wherein they conceived of themselves as messianic godlike figures, superior to their fellow men, on the same level or superior to the angels.[63] To observe the mystics' inflated self-conception, one need only look at more of the *Gedullah* hymns that follow on the introductory promises of this macroform (§83): "Greatest of all is that he sees all the deeds of human beings which they do even in the most hidden chambers, whether they are good deeds or corrupt deeds; if a person steals he knows and recognizes it (in him); if a person commits adultery, he knows and recognizes it (in him)," and the list goes on, naming other fundamental transgressions enumerated in the Ten Commandments.[64] As Schäfer observes, the mystics equated the ability to see into the innermost chambers of God with the ability to see into their fellows' souls, where they found only corrupt deeds.[65] This positioned the self-proclaimed descender to the chariot as superior to his fellows and in a position to look down on them. In the previous chapter, we also encountered the angels of good and evil that monitored behavior from the invisible realm, but the rabbinic traditions were not explicit about what the angels of evil would do in response to misdeeds. In the *Gedullah* hymns the angels are depicted as the avengers of the pious and righteous mystics when they are wronged:

> Greatest of all is the fact that all who raise their hand against him and strike him [the mystic], they [the angels] clothe him in plagues, and they cover him in leprosy and adorn him in blisters.
> Greatest of all is the fact that all who speak of him in gossip, they take up and throw upon him punishing blisters, terrible bruises and wounds, out of which moist boils seep.[66]

63. Schäfer, *Hidden and Manifest God*, 43 and *Origins of Jewish Mysticism*, 245–53; for Boustan, the mystics' sense of realized eschatology is confirmed by a different section of the text; he analyzed the way the "Story of the Ten Martyrs" was emended and inserted into Hekhalot Rabbati (§§107–21). This story describes a decree coming from Rome that sentenced four great sages to death and how in response, Rabbi Nehunia ben Hakanah descended to the *Merkavah* and sought the intervention of the angelic princes to avert this tragedy. The angelic princes duly intervene and promise vengeance in graphic detail upon Rome and its emperor; the sages rejoice. Boustan explains that "this fantasy of revenge is recounted in the present tense. This temporal shift transforms what in the conventional martyrology is the *future* punishment of Rome into a tale of *immediate* revenge. . . . Like other parts of *Heikhalot Rabbati*, the 'inverted' martyrology emphasizes the immediate power of the mystical fellowship to intervene in worldly events" (*From Martyr to Mystic*, 200).

64. Schäfer, *Origins of Jewish Mysticism*, 250–51.

65. Schäfer, *Origins of Jewish Mysticism*, 250–51.

66. My translation of §84 following O1531; cf. Schäfer, *Origins of Jewish Mysticism*, 250.

This vivid portrayal of angels promises the present intervention of the angels, punishing people who have wronged the mystics, and represents a departure from previous texts. In *Genesis Rabbah*, we saw that some traditions portray the angels as executors of God's wrath and defenders of the matriarch's honor but nothing quite so graphic or grotesque as this microform. Even the ritual texts do not depict angels engaging in such vengeful labor. We see both extremes in Hekhalot Rabbati's traditions: extreme violence between angels and people and at times heightened intimacy between angels and worthy mystics.

The next unit combines praise and a warning to others as well (§85): "Greatest of all is the fact that he is distinguished from all humans and awe-full by all measures and honored by heavenly ones and earthly ones (or lofty ones and lowly ones)."[67] And it warns that anyone who struck him would be struck down by the heavenly law court. But it is the following microform that uses the most evocative biblical imagery, recalling descriptions of the messenger who prepares the people for the day of judgment in the biblical book of Malachi 3–4, namely Elijah. In §86 the mystic depicts himself as a judge-like or Elijah-like figure:[68]

> The greatest thing of all is the fact
> that all the creatures will be before him
> like silver before the silversmith, who perceives
> which silver has been refined,
> which silver is impure,
> and which silver is pure
> He even sees (*tzofeh*) into the families,
> how many bastards there are in the family,
> how many sons sired during menstruation,
> how many with crushed testicles,
> how many with mutilated penis,
> how many slaves,
> and how many sons from uncircumcised (fathers).[69]

Here the mystics claimed to achieve the power and perception to determine who was halachically Jewish in their community, a power usually reserved for God, the angels, Elijah the prophet, or God's chosen one—the messiah. As we saw in the previous chapter, the rabbis treated Elijah as an intermediary, on a par with the angels, who revealed hidden things to them. The mystics claimed they could do what Elijah was destined to do even in their own time. As Schäfer notes, the mystic, in assuming an Elijah-like role, "has rendered the Messiah

---

67. My translation of §85 O1531.
68. Schäfer, *Origins of Jewish Mysticism*, 252.
69. §86, trans. Schäfer, *Origins of Jewish Mysticism*, 251.

superfluous."[70] The future arrival of Elijah, the messiah, and even the intervention of the angels was irrelevant to the mystics, who saw themselves in a framework of realized eschatology.

The *Gedullah* Hymns, too, convey the idea of an ever-present or everyday judgment in a more punitive light than the *Qedushah* Hymns with their continuous sacred tempo.[71] Such a conception of time explains the features of the following text, which seem to describe a scenario wherein judgment and excommunication take place in the heavenly court three times every day:

> Greatest of all [is] that the courthouse of the heavens
> Sounds the long blast, and the short blast, and the long blast [on the trumpet][72]
> and then excommunicates [*menadin*] and returns and excommunicates [*menadin*]
>   and excommunicates [*machrimin*] three times on each day
> . . . the one who stands before him contemplating the *merkavah* and leaves it.[73]

Again, the emphasis is on daily recurring action, simultaneously celebratory and punitive. The penalty for neglecting or leaving the activity of contemplation of the chariot is great indeed. Excommunication from God and the heavenly court seems to resemble being written into the book of life and death. This seems to fit Jewish norms in the Geonic period: according to Simcha Assaf, at this time the "banished (*menudeh*) and the ex-communicated (*muchram*) were thought of as dead, taken from life and distanced a great distance from the public."[74] To further the parallel, in the Geonic period part of the ritual of excommunication was to blow the shofar in the synagogue; this heavenly court scene may have been familiar to earlier generations of Jews too.[75] For these Jewish mystics, intense devotional liturgical prayer became the way of relating to God and his angels.[76]

Taken together, the *Qedushah* and *Gedullah* hymns' conception of time allows for the judgment and punishment of Israel's antagonists to be celebrated alongside

70. Schäfer, *The Hidden and Manifest God*, 43.

71. While scholars have studied the *Gedullah* hymns (§§81–93) and *Qedushah* hymns productively as separate units, looking at these together proves compelling and productive; Alexander suggested as much in "Prayer in the Heikhalot Literature," 48.

72. The terms *tekiah* and *truah* refer to the two types of trumpet (or shofar) sounds to be made on holy occasions (see Lewis, "Shofar" in *Encyclopedia Judaica* 18:506–8). Jastrow translates *tekiah* as the "plain note" and *truah* as "to blow tremolo" (see Jastrow, "Rua'," *Dictionary*, 1462).

73. My translation of part of §92 O1531. NB: *nidui* is a lesser degree of excommunication than *cherem* (Jastrow, *Dictionary*, 903).

74. Assaf, *Ha-Onashin Acharei Chatimat HaTalmud*, 31 (my translation).

75. Assaf, *Ha-Onashin*, 32. It is also worth noting that during the Geonic period and the tenth century especially, the excommunications became more common and severe in their application. Abrahams, *Jewish Life in the Middle Ages*, 53; Assaf, *Ha-Onashin*, 32.

76. Swartz maps out this process for the prayers of *Ma'aseh Merkavah* in *Mechanics of Providence*, 220–30, summarizing his earlier work in *Mystical Prayer in Ancient Judaism*.

other hymns that praise the daily activity of the king, the throne, and the angelic creatures. Each day is a day of judgment and victory, and an occasion for partaking in prayers in tune with the angels. It seems that for the mystics who engaged with these hymns, time above and below operated at the same sacred tempo. The *Gedullah* and *Qedushah* hymns of Hekhalot Rabbati demonstrate how some of the mystics, using liturgical language, tapped into heavenly time—the angelic rhythm—and achieved angelic status for themselves. These mystics already saw themselves as perfect as the angels and some of them dared to command the angels as well.

ANGELS IN THE ASCENT ACCOUNTS
OF HEKHALOT RABBATI

Having analyzed conceptions of angels and Jewish identity in three of the most famous microforms, I now turn to a synchronic overview of angels in the ascent accounts of Hekhalot Rabbati in light of my research on angels in late antique Jewish society. This approach shifts us from late antique microforms to the early medieval macroform; what we lose in methodological precision, we gain in being able to form an overall impression of how the redactors' conceptions of angels relate to broader late antique views about angels.

As Swartz's work highlights, all late antique Jews were discussing the seven-layered heavens: we find the cosmology of seven heavens, each with its respective ranks of angels in the ascent accounts of Hekhalot Rabbati (§§198–268) as well as in *Sefer ha-Razim*, in traditions in later rabbinic literature and in liturgical poetry—although each of these texts differs on the precise names associated with each level.[77] Hekhalot Rabbati §206–15 purports to transmit the names of gatekeeping angels associated with each of the seven heavenly palaces. According to this microform, at the threshold of each palace stand eight guardians, four to the right of the threshold and four to the left of the threshold. One may recall Gen 3:24, where God stations fierce cherubim with flaming swords to guard the entrance to the Garden of Eden from the recently exiled humans.[78] In this macroform of Hekhalot Rabbati, the guardian angels replace the cherubim and are imagined in the heavens, not at the boundary of the earthly garden.[79] Like the cherubim, these angels are fierce, threat-

---

77. See Hekhalot Rabbati §232. In rabbinic literature see *b. Ḥag.* 12b; in Yannai's liturgical poetry see the *silluq* to the *qedushtah* on Gen 11:1, and the recent work of Swartz on *Seder Beriyot* (Swartz, "Hekhalot and Piyyut," in *The Mechanics of Providence*, esp. 261–69). For a survey of ancient Jewish cosmologies see Schäfer, "In Heaven as It Is in Hell," 233–74. Schäfer points out precedents for these cosmologies in the *t. Levi* 2–5 and *Mart. Ascen. Isa.* 6–11.

78. These descriptions relate to ancient Near Eastern conceptions of guardian divinities, in turn. See Hartenstein, "Cherubim and Seraphim in the Bible."

79. On the shift of the Garden of Eden from earth to the heavens in ancient Jewish literature, see Ratzon, "Placing Eden in Second Temple Judaism."

ening, and dangerous to the would-be ascender. The mystics who ascend to the heavens are doing so by their own will, not at God's invitation, and therefore they warrant the skepticism and hostility of the gatekeeping angels. Himmelfarb explains that this hostility needs to be understood in light of the idea that the heavens mirror the sacred space of the Jerusalem temple, whose cult "is fraught with danger for those who are not fit or who err in its performance."[80] The heavens are imagined, then, as a place of strict purity and order and the arrival of a mortal (especially an unqualified one) is potentially destabilizing. The angels are described in most vivid terms at the entrance to the highest and most sacred palace:

> And at the entrance to the seventh palace, wrathfully stand all the mighty ones,
>   warlike, vehement, harsh, awful, fearful, taller than mountains and more honed
>   than hills. Their bows are strung and stand before them; their swords are honed
>   in their hands. And lightning strikes and issues forth from the balls of their eyes,
> And lashes of fire from their nostrils and torches of fiery coals from their mouths.
> And they are equipped with helmets and with coats of mail, and javelins and spears
>   are hung upon their arms.[81]
> Their horses are horses of gloom
> Horses of the shadow of death
> Horses of darkness,
> Horses of fire,
> Horses of blood,
> Horses of hail,
> Horses of iron,
> Horses of fog,
> The horses upon which they ride, which stand before feeding troughs of fire,
> filled with glowing juniper coals.[82]

Although we have encountered descriptions of fiery angels before, this description is far more detailed, adding military armor and weapons to the angels as well as supernatural horses. This recalls imagery of the Second Temple period like the book of Maccabees' descriptions of people seeing visions of angelic equestrians battling in the skies, wearing gold armor, armed with spears and with the horses' bridles flashing in the sunlight (2 Macc. 5). Likewise, the book of Revelation, written by a late first-century CE Jew, famously describes the fire-breathing horses of the angelic beings, now remembered as the horsemen of the apocalypse (9:17).[83] From this description in Hekhalot Rabbati, we can see that

---

80. Himmelfarb, "Heavenly Ascent," 85.

81. §213 (based on Smith trans. *Hekhalot Rabbati*, with my corrections).

82. §214 (trans. Schäfer, "Aim and Purpose," *Hekhalot-Studien*, 281).

83. For example, Rev 9:17–18. Cf. Thackeray, trans., Josephus, *The Jewish War* 6.299, discussed in chapter 4.

Jews and Christians shared the imagery of terrifying divine warriors on horses. The earlier conceptions of angels were composed in times of imperial clashes between the kingdom of Judea and the Seleucid and Roman Empires respectively, and, naturally, those visions of angels had national and cosmic dimensions. We can speculate that the battling equestrian angels of Hekhalot Rabbati reflect the Byzantine imperial context.[84] In this case, however, the horsemen remain in the heavens and their targets are potential individuals who ascend to them.

In traditions describing mystical ascension, the gatekeeping angels are not merely hostile, but capricious and unreliable. In the following unit, it seems that the angels are testing the would-be mystic:

> If he is worthy to descend to the Merkavah—
> If they [the angels] say to him: Enter! [but] he does not enter [immediately], and
>   they once again say to him: Enter! and he [then] immediately enters, [then] they
>   praise him and say: Surely this one is [one] of the *yordei merkavah*.
> If he, however, is not worthy to descend to the Merkavah, [and] if they say to him:
>   Enter! and he [then immediately] enters, [then] they immediately throw pieces of
>   iron at him.[85]

The angels' invitation is not what it seems. Violating angelic etiquette results in an attack on the human visitor with bars of iron (or molten coals in a parallel in Hekhalot Zutarti).[86] Looking at the variation in this microform among the manuscripts, one has the impression that even the early copyists themselves struggled with the apparent meaning of this passage, that angels would be so capricious, and therefore they changed the text in §258 so that the unworthy mystic would be at fault for transgressing the angel's instructions. The point of this story seems to be to heighten the sense of danger, secrecy and privilege surrounding the experience of ascent.[87] In the process of describing the heavens as dangerous, the composers of this tradition introduced behavioral traits previously not associated with angels.

84. Boustan, *From Martyr to Mystic*, has especially drawn attention to the Byzantine Palestinian context of some sections of Hekhalot Rabbati. See also Hermann, "Jewish Mysticism in Byzantium."

85. §258 (Schäfer, *Hidden and Manifest God*, 37).

86. See Hekhalot Zutarti §407: "Whomever was worthy of seeing the king in his beauty, they would set it into his heart. If they [the angels] said to him "enter," he did not enter immediately, and they repeated and said 'enter' and he immediately entered, then they would praise him and say certainly he is worthy of seeing the King in his beauty. And whomever was not worthy of seeing the king in his beauty, they would set it into his heart and since they said 'enter,' he would enter; immediately they seized him and threw him into molten coals." Schäfer notes this parallel in *Hidden and Manifest God*, 38.

87. Similarly, the mystic is imagined confronting hostile angels in Hekhalot Zutarti as well: reaching the sixth heavenly palace, he sees what appear to be hundreds of thousands of waves of water (in actuality the beautiful, polished marble floor). According to the microform, if he asks, "These waters, what is their nature?" the angels immediately pursue him to stone him and denounce him as a descendant of the sinful Israelites who kissed the golden calf in the wilderness (§408). These are no merciful

The names of these angels differ among the manuscript traditions, but most would *not* be familiar to readers, except in that they all end with the suffix "el" like Michael and Gabriel. The angelic title "prince" (Hebrew "*sar*") is often used with prominent angels in this text, both on its own and with a modifier (e.g., *Sar ha-Panim*, the Prince of the Presence or Countenance, or *Sar ha-Torah*, the Prince of the Torah).[88] Yannai only records the names of three archangels, and the rabbis record a few more angelic names in their vast commentaries (e.g., Dubbiel, Lyla, and Metatron).[89] But the Hekhalot Rabbati introduces a plethora of angelic names, such as Anafiel, Dumiel, T'tzs, and many more that are unpronounceable and that vary among the manuscripts. The many unfamiliar names of angels in this macroform recall those names we have encountered in ritual texts. As elsewhere, angelic names do not connote angels having a fixed identity or reputation. Only Metatron and Anafiel receive phrases beyond a name and a title in Hekhalot Rabbati.[90] It is noteworthy that despite the wide variety of angelic names in these macroforms, no one doubts the Jewish identity of these mystical texts. Like the ritual texts, the early mystical texts challenge us to expand our view of the religious vocabulary of ancient Jews and ancient Judaism more broadly.

As in the Babylonian Talmud, only a few microforms in Hekhalot literature discuss the continuous creation and destruction of the angels. Where the rabbinic tradition stated that the angels ceased to exist after they sang God's praise, Hekhalot offers a more violent twist, stating that some angels are destroyed in rivers of fire whenever they accidentally depart from harmony when they sing in the heavenly choirs (§185).[91] According to another microform, exposure to the radiance of God's countenance causes the angels to waste away (§184, §189). While also glorifying them more than other texts do, this corpus also portrays the angels at their most disposable.

We have seen that rabbinic traditions diverged on the need for angelic intercession, with some traditions asserting mediators were unnecessary and other traditions taking angelic mediation for granted. By contrast, microforms in Hekhalot

---

angels tolerant of human musings. The next two microforms emphasize that this story ought to be a lesson to "future generations, that a person not misspeak at the entrance to the sixth heavenly palace" (§§409–10).

88. Cf. Dan 10:20–21 and *t. Ḥul.* 2:18. "*Sar ha-Torah*" is found in Hekhalot Rabbati §§281–99 in O1531, in §299 in Munich 40; "*Sarah shel Torah*" is found in Vatican 228 §297.

89. See Bar-Ilan, "The Names of Angels;" Olyan, *Thousand Thousands Served Him*.

90. See §420 where Anafiel is described in a few lines and relatedly, Idel, "Holding an Orb in His Hand." On Metatron, see §277, §310 in V228, §148 of N8128 = §316 of V228; also see Paz, "Metatron Is Not Enoch."

91. Cf. *b. Ḥag.* 14a; Schäfer, *Hidden and Manifest God*, 17, 26–27.

Rabbati describe angels whose precise function is to intercede for Israel before God. The angels are praised as:

> Those who annul decrees, those who unbind oaths, those who make [His] wrath
> pass, those who turn back [His] jealousy, those who mention love, the love of
> Abraham our father before the King
> When they see him angry at his sons, what do they do?
> They throw down their crowns, loosen their loins, and strike their heads, and fall
> on their faces and say:
> Release, Release, Creator of all creation
> Forgive, forgive, Noble one of Jacob
> Pardon, Pardon Holy one of Israel
> Because you are the most glorious King.[92]

These angels are presented in far more active terms than the ones encountered in ritual or rabbinic texts. These angels annul decrees, unbind oaths, and assuage God's anger. They also amplify the needs of the people of Israel below and can sway God toward forgiveness. While some rabbis took for granted that the angels conveyed the (Hebrew) prayers of Israel to God, here these circles of mystics imagined that the angels played a far greater role, interceding on behalf of Israel whenever necessary.

When a *worthy* mystic ascends to the heavens, he could receive beneficent angelic guardianship. According to one microform, a man who has internalized all of the biblical, rabbinic teachings, as well as kept all the laws going back to Sinai may be received in favor by Dumiel, the angelic prince in the sixth heaven (§§230–36). Recognizing the positive attributes of one such mystic, Dumiel calls on Gabriel to write the descender a seal that declares his right to enter before the divine throne. Then these two angels along with Qatzpiel lead the mystic, now in a traveling coach of his own, to the seventh heaven. When the guardians of the entrance to the seventh heaven see the three angels proceeding before the worthy mystic's wagon, they cover their scowling faces and retract their weapons. The mystic shows proof of worthiness (the seal and a crown) and is then led into the throne room, where the angels take out musical instruments, sing, "and raise him and seat him among the cherubim, among ophanim, and among holy creatures" (§236). The rabbinic tradition that imagined angels processing before righteous Jews on their journeys on earth is transposed here to the heavenly realms. Threatening angels become beneficent, their bows and swords are exchanged for musical instruments, and the mystic is imagined seated among the angels in the very throne room of God.

92. §158 and §190 (my translation; cf. Schäfer, *Origins of Jewish Mysticism*, 267).

In the following tradition, we see a vivid depiction of intimacy between an angel and a rabbinic hero. In a microform of Hekhalot Rabbati known as the David Apocalypse (§122–26), the famous sage Rabbi Ishmael is imagined receiving revelation while sitting in the embrace of the angelic prince Senuniel:

> Rabbi Ishmael said: Senuniel, the Prince of the Presence said to me
> "My friend, sit in my lap." And he was looking at me and was crying and the tears
>   fell from his eyes upon my face and I said to him, "Splendid one of lofty radiance,
>   why do you weep?"
> He said to me, "My friend come and I will take you in and show you what they have
>   in store for Israel, the holy people."[93]

Dwelling in the company of the angels, sitting with them, is a significant theme in Jewish texts of late antiquity, but this microform takes it further, poignantly noting that the angel's tears fell on the face of the sage in his embrace (*hyq* can be translated as "bosom"). Such intimacy between humans and angels may be compared with a Jewish incantation text from sixth-century Nippur, where angels were described embracing a lovelorn wife, clothing her with divine grace, and sitting with her.[94] Schäfer believes this theme of revelation is a later addition to the text, noting it is "not the most characteristic of all Hekhalot texts."[95] But in terms of its depiction of angels, I see this conceptualization of angelic emotion and intimacy as parallel to the vivid depictions of angelic malevolence and benevolence in this corpus, as well as Jewish imaginings elsewhere. With the full range of representations of angelic and human relations in mind, we can see that this tradition was within the realm of possibility in the late antique Jewish imagination.

For some, the idea of the sage in the lap of an archangel may also bring to mind the image of Jesus in the lap of his enthroned mother Mary, an icon popularized in the fifth century in the Eastern Empire after Mary's role as God-bearer (*theotokos*) was formally adopted.[96] Late antique Jews were not immune to the visual and religious vocabulary of their day; sometimes they incorporated this vocabulary and reproduced it in Jewish terms.[97] This particular microform is an evocative example of that practice. Angels could embrace sages and weep with them for the

---

93. My translation of the microform from B238. Boustan cataloged the circulation of this text within and independently of Hekhalot Rabbati in *From Martyr to Mystic*, 44.

94. Montgomery, *Aramaic Incantation Texts*, no. 13, discussed in chapter 1.

95. Schäfer, *Origins of Jewish Mysticism*, 343. Boustan, *From Martyr to Mystic*, 43–45, also cautions against treating this larger series of microforms on David as part of Hekhalot Rabbati, but this particular unit is not his target.

96. See Vassilaki, *Images of the Mother of God*.

97. For a fascinating example of Jews adapting Marian imagery, see Himmelfarb, *Jewish Messiahs in a Christian Empire*, 35–59.

sorrows of the Jewish people. That conceptions of angels were shared with others did not make them any less significant to late ancient Jews.

CONCLUSION: ANGELS IN JEWISH MYSTICISM AND IN JEWISH SOCIETY

Hekhalot Rabbati is chronologically the latest source examined in this book. Angelic pervasiveness reaches its climax in this corpus of texts. The Jews who composed these texts imagined the heavenly realms and the angels more vividly than any of their counterparts. While we find commonalities with rabbinic, liturgical, and ritual texts, we also find very distinctive views in Hekhalot Rabbati. For these Jews, daily life meant something completely different than for other Jews. They strove to live not on rabbinic annual calendrical time but according to the rhythms of the heavenly realms. I have suggested that they accessed this time through their prayer books, both within and outside the synagogue. What most Jews experienced in weekly prayer services in Palestine or annually on Yom Kippur in the synagogue, these Jews sought to experience all the time. Some of them imagined the angels as territorial, wrathful, and hostile yet also emotional, compassionate, and loyal to the people of Israel. In a way, the circles of mystics humanized the angels, giving them the full range of a person's emotional spectrum. And yet, they depicted the angels as all powerful: they may embrace mortals and show them the future but also cast them out from the heavens; they stand at the entrance of every level of heaven yet also exist close enough to earth to punish any transgressions against the mystics. Some mystics imagined that angels could also be commanded to do their bidding. It is difficult to decide whether these adjurations of angels are an expression of the mystics' confidence in themselves or whether they betray a deep insecurity in their own potential: perhaps they evince both sentiments.

The attitudes described in this chapter can be read as taking Jewish conceptions about angels to their logical conclusion. No "blurring the boundaries" section is necessary. Hekhalot texts are undoubtedly Jewish texts upheld by exclusive circles of Jewish men, but they reflect broader cultural trends. From the perspective of late antique Jewish texts, some of Hekhalot Rabbati's attitudes toward angels seem strikingly radical, but, judging them from the perspective of medieval Jewish ritual texts, we see that some of their beliefs about angels became normative. These mystics' approach to the angels, becoming angelic or commanding them to do their bidding, would come to dominate the ritual practices found in the Cairo Genizah.[98] Medieval copyists combined Palestinian ritual formulas with Hekhalot

---

98. See Bohak, "Magic."

texts, which suggests that the copyists understood the texts to be homologous.[99] Rabbis and their disciples, mystics, and ritual practitioners expressed their Jewish identity in strikingly different ways in late antique communities, but not so differently that they were no longer in dialogue with one another. In their texts we can see that the nature of authority, God, and the angels was still a matter for debate in late antique Jewish society. Circles of men continued to engage with Hekhalot texts through the medieval period. The conceptions of angels innovated by Hekhalot mystics would be maintained by Jews engaged in Kabbalah, the form of mysticism that would take the European Jewish world by storm in the sixteenth century.

---

99. See the Genizah fragment housed in the Jewish Theological Seminary (JTSL ENA 3635.17) and the fragment in the Cambridge University Library (K 1.56) published by Schäfer and Shaked in *Magische Texte* 1:17–45. Discussed by Schäfer, "Jewish Liturgy and Magic."

Conclusion

Angels in Judaism and the Religions
of Late Antiquity

Angels were an integral part of late antique culture for Jews and the other inhabitants of the late antique Mediterranean. Focusing on angels brings to the foreground the local idiosyncrasies of Jewish belief as well as the shared religious outlook of ancient Jews, whether they were rabbis, ritual practitioners, synagogue leaders, mystics, or ordinary men and women. Just as no one approach (whether rabbinic, ritual, liturgical) to Judaism prevailed in antiquity, no systematic angelology prevailed among Jews. This lack of angelology never prevented an individual Jew from praying for angelic assistance, imagining the angels around them in their home or accompanying them out and about in their daily life. Belief in angels was not limited to any one stratum of society or one group but was shared by all Jews. To form a more accurate and full account of the role of angels in Jewish society, we must bring into consideration the ritual-magical incantations, the mystical hymns, and the liturgical poetry that existed alongside, in conversation with, and in tension with rabbinic sources. Only with this array of sources can we see how Jews and rabbis developed their ideas about angels over time.

To restate my definition of angels in late antique Judaism, angels were powerful intermediary beings who were subordinate to God and acted in alignment with divine will. Angels were ever present with the people of Israel, carrying their prayers to the heavens and available for the faithful in times of need; angels of destruction were also imagined to be present on earth to enforce order and proper norms. Although people today may think of angels and demons as inseparable, the ancients conceptualized angels independently of the demonic realm. Angels were beings with abodes in the heavens and obligations on earth. A combination of biblical descriptions, the Hellenistic visual vocabulary, and local traditions likely shaped how late antique Jews imagined angels in the invisible realm, but what angels looked like was much less important to ancient Jews than what angels could do for them on a daily basis. In what follows, I highlight themes that cut across all the corpora and then summarize the contributions of my research according to the chronology of the evidence, beginning with the Tannaitic texts and ending with Jewish mystical writings.

Ancient biblical psalms promised their hearers that God commanded angels to guard them wherever they journeyed (Pss 34:8 and 91:11). This belief in guardian angels proves to be the most widely attested belief among ancient Jews. The variety of texts examined in this book all provide evidence of belief in angelic guardianship, whether applied to the individual Jew, to the Jewish household, or to the Jewish people as a whole. Traditions in the Tosefta show that some sages took for granted that angels accompanied people on their journeys.[1] Later Talmudic traditions affirm that the sages harnessed this belief to promote rabbinic Sabbath observance and general piety. Guardian angels monitored good deeds and transgressions, giving rise to descriptions of good angels and evil angels.[2] Rabbinic midrashim may have seeded imagery for the divine presence surrounding the community, which, reframed as angels on all sides of the person, became so popular in later ritual and liturgical texts.[3] Incantation bowls from Babylonia and amulets from Palestine demonstrate that angels were believed to protect familial households as well as individual men and women. Whereas Christian ascetic trends encouraged monks to find the angels by withdrawing from society, later rabbinic traditions encouraged Jews to stay within the community for angelic guardianship.[4]

Although relatively few references to angels can be found in the earliest strata of rabbinic literature, there is no question that the early sages had to grapple with the presence of angels in the popular imagination, among disciples within their movement as well as among non-rabbinic Jews. In the decades after the destruction of the second temple, the rabbis were most concerned with assuring fellow Jews that God was still in covenant with them. How to relate to God and the rest of the beings of the divine realm was a crucial question in the first centuries of the common era. Close reading of the Tannaitic midrashim show a concerted effort to downplay the role of the angels in foundational Jewish narratives and uphold a direct relationship with God, but a few isolated traditions reveal underlying rabbinic assumptions about the presence of guardian angels. While people tend to emphasize rabbinic Judaism as a religion of laws or Torah-study, this relational aspect of classical Jewish belief should not be overlooked.

1. See discussions of *t. 'Abod. Zar.* 1:17 and *t. Šabb.* 17:2 in chapter 3.
2. See discussions of *b. Šabb.* 119b in chapter 6.
3. See "Blurring the Boundaries" at the end of chapter 1 and chapter 3.
4. See chapters 5 and 6.

The rabbis were not a monolithic group, and close study of their texts reveals that some rabbis took the role of angels in the rhythms of Jewish life for granted while others opposed what they perceived as over-preoccupation with the angels. That angels were subordinates of God was obvious: the question was how much this mediating role of the angels ought to matter to Jews. Traditions attributed to Rabbi Akiva and others in successive generations made an effort to stress God's direct and loving relationship with the people of Israel, emphasizing humanity's creation in the image of God, and God's disclosure of love for Israel through the Torah. This approach encouraged relating to God without intermediaries and emphasized study of Torah as a way of anchoring oneself between the earthly and heavenly realms.

The attraction to imitation of the angels can be traced back to Hellenistic-era Jewish myths, expansions of biblical texts, and sectarian liturgical practices. Once imagined, it never ceased to inspire later generations of Jews who adapted angels as role models to suit their needs. I argue that we can only fully understand rabbinic pronouncements against comparison with the angels in the context of a wider conversation about relating to angelic beings in late antiquity. When we compare the rabbinic and liturgical evidence, we can see how the rabbinic principle of imitation of God competed with a regional trend of imitating the angels. The payyetan Yannai celebrated the creation of humanity in the image of the angels.[5] His poetry described how, by following ancestral customs or praying in the synagogue, the community of Israel was on a par with the lofty angels and in synchronicity with the angels in the heavens. This conception, richly elaborated across many poetic compositions, must be understood in the context of the popularity of sacred song in late antiquity and the practices in churches in the Roman Near East, where Christians were encouraged to imagine themselves surrounded by angels as they prayed. If Christian thinkers upheld nuns as images of angels, in Yannai's qedushta'ot, women, priests, and the sages were likened to angels too. If Christian monks and nuns achieved angelic bodies through celibacy, Jews achieved angelic status through pure circumcised bodies and reproduction. If Christians believed they were surrounded by angels in church ceremonies, rabbis came to say that angels followed Jews home from the synagogue as well, blessing them or cursing them, depending on their merits.

Only with the evidence of ritual and liturgical texts can we see that the rabbis found themselves on the losing side of the argument against angelic preoccupations. Ritual practitioners and synagogue leaders offered avenues to relating to the divine through angels that the rabbis themselves ended up accepting. And so, we find in later rabbinic midrashim and traditions of the Babylonian Talmud that the rabbis harnessed interest in the angels to encourage Jews to follow their halakhah.

5. See chapter 5.

Comparing earlier and later rabbinic texts, we can see how attitudes toward angels shifted in the rabbinic movement: traditions about accompanying and guardian angels became linked with stories about rabbinic authority and expertise, the rabbis offered multiple origin stories for the angels and their own account of the names of the seven heavens to compete with the cosmologies offered by synagogue poets and ritual practitioners, and finally, the sages used angels to encourage prayer and practice.

Although a great deal of speculation about angels can be found in the Babylonian Talmud, those seeking a precise definition to compare with Christian theological pronouncements will be disappointed. The rabbis did not engage in systematic angelology, and only limited coherence among their traditions may be discerned: God has subordinate angels and his ministering angels acted in alignment with divine will, but, like the Jews themselves, the angels did not always agree with God's interventions in history. The rabbis, like the ritual practitioners and synagogue poets, came to teach fellow Jews how to visualize the angels' reactions to their behavior and to God's orders. According to Talmudic tradition, the Babylonian sage Abaye offered a prayer directed at his guardian angels for fellow Jews to recite; several traditions related what angels did on the Sabbath evening for the pious Jews.[6] A number of midrashim ruminate on the angels' compassionate response to Jewish suffering as well their ruthless response to wickedness. Later rabbinic traditions about angels demonstrate that angelic intimacy became important to the sages as well and that the sages came to recognize the need for intermediary relationships between God and Israel. The sages positioned themselves as intermediaries, of course, but they also relied on their own mediators: archangels, the Angel of Death, or Elijah the prophet. The rabbis, like other Jews, could envision themselves in relationship with a variety of figures in the invisible realm.

The incantation bowls and amulets allow us to see most vividly how Jews envisioned angels as operatives on earth alongside other equally important mediators of God: prophets, priests, meritorious ancestors, miracle workers, ritual practitioners, and even sages turned folk heroes. The Jews of Babylonia and Palestine had many options and many ways of interacting with the invisible realm in their earthly communities. These relationships with human practitioners and beings in the invisible realm were foundational to Jewish practice. While some Jews appealed to God alone in their time of need, others preferred to appeal to God, the angels, or a heroic figure from the past. According to my analysis of the incantation bowls, appealing to God alongside the angels was the most popular approach of ancient Jews. From the variety of approaches found in incantation bowls, we can learn to be wary of overgeneralization about the religious outlook of people

6. See discussion of *b. Ber.* 60b and *b. Šabb.* 119b in chapter 6.

in the ancient world. People in antiquity were as complex as they are today and related to the divine realm in inconsistent ways.

The angels might be invoked to help negotiate the anxiety of in-laws in a large household or called to a room where a woman was giving birth. From a gendered stance, it is important to note that men and women commissioned ritual objects that appealed to angels in almost equal numbers; similarly, angels could surround and support men, women, and children. Men and women commissioned and wore necklace amulets that invoked the angels to accompany them and protect them wherever they went. Jewish evidence indicates that angels could be imagined as fiery bodiless beings or as gendered beings.[7] Gendered notions of impurity did not pose challenges to angelic intimacy. Angels were invoked for a variety of reasons, not only to repel demons but also to heal or stave off illness or restore love to a marriage.

The exclusive circles of men who engaged with the traditions of Hekhalot Rabbati themselves had differences in relating to angels, reflecting the diversity of late antique Jewish society. Some took liturgical norms of reciting prayer with the angels to an extreme, striving to live in angelic synchronicity all the time. If the rabbis asserted that the Torah was given to Israel, some circles of Jewish mystics asserted the Torah was still with the angels and accessible through their ritual techniques alone. And some mystics considered authority over the angels to be their greatest distinguishing achievement. They saw themselves as messiah-like figures, superior even to the heavenly angels, whom they could command. Jewish ritual formulas commanding the angels can be found in incantation bowls and in the texts of the Cairo Genizah, showing that these views of angels as biddable became normative in medieval Jewish society.

Overall, my book contributes to telling the story of how the Jewish culture came to be rabbinic.[8] As many scholars have noted, the rabbis were not hegemonic authorities in late antiquity. My project centers other authorities: ritual practitioners and synagogue leaders. For the rabbinization of Jewish culture to take place, the rabbis themselves had to accommodate and appropriate popular Jewish beliefs about angels, even as synagogue poets and ritual practitioners in turn adapted rabbinic midrashim and accepted rabbinic authority on other matters. The authority of the rabbis rested in their ability to persuade people to seek them out, and to convince them that the rabbinic approach to the divine world was most compelling. The rabbis preserved multiple views on engaging God and the angels in their literature, but close reading shows that their earlier approach,

---

7. Discussed at greater length in Ahuvia, "Gender and the Angels in Late Antique Judaism."

8. Schwartz, *Imperialism and Jewish Society*, 250–74; Boustan, "Rabbinization and the Making of Early Jewish Mysticism."

downplaying the angels and angelic imitation, lost out to an approach that welcomed guardian angels into Jewish religiosity.

While studies of authority in antiquity tend to emphasize competition between different groups, the study of angels brings into view the relationship networks that transcended these differences and knit communities together. Yannai's communally focused *qedushta'ot* celebrate priests and sages in the synagogue and even allude to techniques of the ritual practitioners, using angelic models as an aspiration to equality. This provides an important corrective perspective to our understanding of Jewish society in late antiquity. The ritual technology of the incantation bowl was limited to Babylonia, but incantation formulas found in the bowls are also found in amulets in Palestine and echoed in rabbinic midrashim, and some popular formulas entered the fixed liturgy of the Jews, reminding us that the boundaries between magic and prayer may be more artificial and academic than rigid in practice. Extant evidence shows that ancient Jews argued with each other about the invisible realm of the angels and God, but also that they agreed with each other at times. In their discourses about angels, Jews were very much at home in the wider culture of the Mediterranean.

ANGELS IN THE RELIGIONS OF LATE ANTIQUITY

Divine messenger figures who were accessible to ordinary worshippers became a feature of all of late antique religions, whether Hellenic, Jewish, Christian, Mandaic, Manichean, Sasanian Zoroastrian, or Islamic.[9] In every religious movement that arose in late antiquity, the role and function of mediating figures was negotiated and developed gradually over time even as different groups consolidated their authority, foundational texts were codified, and new ritual practices were established. Each of the above-mentioned religious communities had mediating divine beings in keeping with their respective cosmologies and adapted to the needs of religious authorities as well as ordinary worshippers: Neoplatonists upheld a hierarchy of divinities within which archangels and angels played a role, distinct from but not totally estranged from Jewish precedents.[10] Angels, as I have defined them in the Jewish context, may be compared with the *yazatas* of Zoroastrianism, the *'utras* in Mandaean religion, and the heavenly twins of Mandean and Manichean belief, each of which is discussed below. Just as a focus on Jewish ritual and liturgical practice brought ordinary Jews and their relationship with angels into view, so too does a focus on liturgical and ritual practice of these other

9. Scholars generally agree that divine messengers antedate ancient Israelite religion, but become more popular over time. See Reiterer et al., *Angels: The Concept of Celestial Beings*.

10. Brisson et al., eds., *Neoplatonic Demons and Angels*, 4.

religious communities bring their mediators into view. Situating Jewish beliefs on angels in a wider context serves to highlight how Jews participated in late antique trends, at times influencing the practice of adjacent communities, while maintaining their own distinctive beliefs and customs.

In *Angels in Late Ancient Christianity*, Ellen Muehlberger shows persuasively that belief in guardian angels, the pursuit of the angelic life, and celebration of the angelic liturgy on earth were central to Christian piety in late antiquity. Much the same can be said about late antique Judaism. Whereas extant Christian texts allowed Muehlberger to trace the development of these tropes among Christian thinkers, surviving Jewish writings are not susceptible to such analysis. Ancient Jews like the rabbis did not produce systematic theology or strive to explain themselves to others. The rabbis do not explain *why* Jews need guardian angels or *how* they might attract them; traditions simply state that pious Jews are accompanied by angels or have angelic guardians when they observe the commandments of the Torah. Jewish and Christian traditions about angels developed concurrently, might serve some of the same functions, and in some cases overlapped or were in dialogue with each other. But it is important to stress that, while Jews and Christians shared a wide range of angelological traditions from the Second Temple period, Jewish and Christian conceptions took distinct forms.

Like Cyril the bishop of Jerusalem, Yannai the payyetan in Galilee encouraged imagining the angels' recitation of the *Qedushah* during the liturgical service. Having said that, whereas John Chrysostom insisted that the angels were present around the bema and the altar during worship, Yannai only conceded that the heavenly angels prayed in synchronicity with the people of Israel. Whether ordinary Jews grasped this nuance cannot be ascertained: it is possible some Jews closed their eyes in the synagogue and did imagine the angels praying alongside them just as they imagined the angels accompanying them home (as rabbinic traditions and ritual evidence suggests). The strategies involving angels that drew Christians to churches in Byzantine Palestine may have been adopted to draw Jews to the synagogue. Alternatively, the belief in angelic presence in liturgical services may have become commonplace by late antiquity, no longer the province of temple priests and Jewish sectarians alone.

In terms of practice, the nature of imitating angels differed for Jews and Christians. For Christians, thanks to Paul's apocalyptic perspective, celibacy became associated with Christian gendered norms and angelic behavior in the writings of later Church leaders. Nuns and monks thus achieved the angelic life on earth. By abstaining from sexual reproduction, Christian women could claim to be sexless like the angels. Similarly, the early Jewish mystics eschewed contact with women and women's impurity when they imagined accessing the heavens through their liturgical recitations. Still, imitation of angels was a malleable ideal and available to men and women. As Yannai emphasized in his liturgical poetry, continuing to follow God's prescription to be fruitful and multiply could be conceived of as angelic as well.

Like the incantation bowls written for Jews, incantation bowls written for Christians in Syriac scripts also invoke an array of intermediaries, among them familiar rabbinic folk heroes and angels. Apparently, Rabbi Joshua ben Peraḥia's reputation transcended communal boundaries and inspired confidence in Christians living in proximity to Jews. Only a few Syriac incantation bowls invoke distinctive Christian terms like the Trinitarian formula ("In the name of the Father, in the name of the Son and the Living and Holy Spirit") or invoke "Jesus the healer."[11] It is noteworthy how much Syriac and Jewish incantations have in common. At times, Syriac incantation formulas are only distinguished from Jewish incantations by dialect. In this context, we must heed Boustan and Sanzo's observation that "concerns of ritual efficacy and boundary demarcation could be mutually reinforcing, and, on occasion, could overlap in ways that eclipsed the distinctions between Jews and Christians that ecclesiastical elites frequently promoted and that contemporary historians of religion have so often assumed."[12] The characteristics of angelic invocation in ancient Syriac incantation bowls and the proportion of appeal to angels as opposed to other mediators deserves more study and remains an area for future research.

Mandaeans are often described as an Iranian gnostic sect, but the category of gnostic here only points to the fact they were considered heretical by other Christians. According to their own mythology, the Mandaeans originated from a Jewish community in the Jordan Valley, upheld John the Baptist as prophet, and sought refuge in the tolerant atmosphere of the Persian Empire, where they eventually codified their sacred text the Ginza (the treasure).[13] More recent scholarship suggests the Mandaeans as a community date to the late fifth-century Sasanian Empire.[14] In their cosmology, people are in a fallen state and seek to return to the heavenly world of light above with the help of angelic guardians called 'utras (lightbeings).[15] Scholars have observed that in their sacred texts, Mandaeans were careful to distinguish their benevolent divine messengers from Jewish angels, incorporating the famous archangel Gabriel, for example, merely as a "messenger" (shlyha, not mal'akha).[16] Nevertheless, some of the same angels invoked in Jewish Aramaic incantation bowl texts are invoked as sources of support in Mandaic incantation

---

11. For the Trinitarian formula see Moriggi, *Corpus of Syriac Incantation Bowls*, Bowl 2, p. 28. and for "Jesus the healer," bowl 6, p. 48.

12. Sanzo and Boustan, "The Shared Magical Culture of Late Antiquity," 220.

13. Foltz, *Religions of Iran*, 127.

14. van Bladel, *From Sasanian Mandaeans to Ṣābians of the Marshes*, 79.

15. Yamauchi, *Mandaic Incantation Texts*, 36.

16. Yamauchi, *Mandaic Incantation Texts*, 37.

bowls as well.[17] This is a particularly good example of how attractive angels were to ancient peoples and how they could be used to draw communal boundaries at the same time. Mandaic texts are distinguished only by their Aramaic dialect and the divine names distinctive to Mandaean worldview, reminding us of the shared ritual practices and beliefs of the late antique Mesopotamian world.

Mani, the founder of Manichaeism, lived between 216 and 276 CE and over the course of sixty years set the stage for a world religion that would thrive for one thousand years.[18] He grew up among the Elchasaites, a Jewish-Christian sect on the Tigris River, and constructed a synthesizing religious system that drew on Jewish, Christian, Mandaean, and Buddhist elements, as well as Zoroastrian. Within a strictly dualist framework that contrasted the powers of darkness (associated with matter, pollution, and femininity) with the powers of light (ruled over by the spirit, purity, masculinity, salvation) there were angelic and demonic emanations with which humans interacted. In their daily prayers, Manichean catechumens would pray toward the sun or moon, depending on the time of day (four times a day if they were lay members; seven times a day if they were members of the elect). The preamble to prayers would bless Mani as "Our guide, the paraclete, the apostle of light; Blessed are his angels, the guardians; Praiseworthy are his luminous armies!"[19] Each of the following ten sections of prayer (or prostrations) addressed and glorified the angelic armies of the Father of the Lights. This liturgy was likely composed by Mani himself in Aramaic.[20] It praised the angels more explicitly than any Jewish or Christian prayers from antiquity: "I worship and glorify the great powers, the shining angels: Having come forth with their own wisdom, and having subjected the darkness and its arrogant powers that were desiring to make war with the one who is first of all; these are they who put heaven and earth in order, and bound in them the whole foundation of contempt."[21] Perhaps because the Father of Lights was portrayed as more distant, the angels in the Manichean worldview were more active and significant. Mani himself claimed to have received his first revelation at the age of twelve from an angelic twin.[22] The belief in angelic doubles can be found in Mandean religion as well as other Mediterranean religions and may have been echoed in the tradition in the Tosefta, where a tradition records that Rabban Gamaliel asked after the angel of Akiva's heart in what sounds like idiomatic speech.

17. Yamauchi, *Mandaic Incantation Texts*, 37, notes that "Gabriel (27:3), and Raphael (9:5), but not Michael," are found in Mandaic incantations.

18. Foltz, *Religions of Iran*.

19. Gardner, "Manichaean Ritual Practice at Ancient Kellis," 249.

20. Gardner, "Manichaean Ritual Practice at Ancient Kellis," 259.

21. Gardner, "Manichaean Ritual Practice at Ancient Kellis," 252 (prayer 3).

22. Mani Codex 22.8, discussed in its Christian context in Peter Brown, *Body and Society*, 197. See also Michel Tardieu, *Manichaeism*, 10.

Near Eastern conceptions of divine beings impacted Greco-Roman beliefs over the course of centuries, beginning in the seventh and sixth centuries BCE, and continuing through to late antiquity.[23] Angelic hierarchies played an important role in the last revival of Hellenic religions in late antiquity in the theurgical traditions associated with Syrian Platonist Iamblichus (ca. 240–325 CE) and Neoplatonists after him.[24] Since Philo in the first century CE, Platonist philosophers had identified the intermediary beings Plato called daemons as angels.[25] Iamblichus conceived of a hierarchy of divinities stretching from the supreme god (the World Soul) to the celestial gods, archangels, angels, daemons, heroes, archons, and human souls (De Mysteriis II.3): the gods were associated with transcendent perfection, uniform power, and stable governance and these qualities decreased with the archangels, angels, and so on down until the human soul, which was described as imperfect, powerless, and given to inclinations.[26] In Neoplatonic theology, angels were believed to assist the soul in reaching higher realms of light and divinity, drawing it away from the material disorder of the earthly realm (n.b., no negativity or evil is associated with earthly realm per se).[27] The successfully ascended soul, according to Iamblichus, could transform into an angel (De Mysteriis II.2).[28] More precisely, theurgy ("god-work") or theurgical rituals enabled the human to receive higher levels of divinity, become both "man and god" or "an icon" of god.[29] No treatise by Iamblichus on theurgical rituals survives, so we do not have a sense of the mechanics of this aspect of his philosophy. The surviving Jewish incantations and Hekhalot texts do demonstrate that Jewish ritual practitioners and Jewish mystics were engaged in practices that connected them to their own Jewish heroes and gave them a sense of their own elevation to the angelic ranks, but specifically within the framework of Jewish monotheism.

Neoplatonic conceptualization of angels may explain a remarkable cemetery in the Aegean islands of Thera (Santorini) where approximately sixty stelae commemorate the deceased by invoking their angels.[30] The belief that one could become

23. Speyer, "The Divine Messenger," 43–44.

24. Shaw, Theurgy and the Soul.

25. See Casas, "Ontology, Henadology, Angelology." Philo also identified daemons as heroes.

26. Iamblichus: De Mysteriis, trans. and eds. Clarke, Dillon, and Hershbell, 89. See Shaw, Theurgy and the Soul, esp. 39–42 and 78–79.

27. According to the Chaldean Oracles, the so-called "pagan Bible" (Brisson, O'Neill, and Timotin, "Introduction" to Neoplatonic Demons and Angels, 3); Seng, "Demons and Angels in the Chaldean Oracles," 70.

28. Discussed in Seng, "Demons and Angels in the Chaldean Oracles," 71.

29. Shaw, Theurgy and the Soul, 50–51. Conversely, according to Proclus, "the soul of an angel can descend from its place and live and operate through a human body as a theurgist." Seng, "Demons and Angels in the Chaldean Oracles," 74–76. See also Brisson, "The Angels in Proclus: Messengers of the Gods."

30. Discussed in Cline, "Angels of the Grave" in Ancient Angels, 77–104.

an angel after death was shared by many people in late antiquity, Jewish and non-Jewish alike.[31] The religious identity of the men and women who died in Thera in the third century CE cannot be definitively ascertained; they only identified themselves on their tombstones as angels, for example, "the angel of Tryphon," "the angel of Herakleon," or "the angel of Epikto the Eldress."[32] Only stylized rosettes decorate the tombs, similar to ones that appear on other late Roman tombs as well. I agree with Rangar Cline's assessment that these tombs cannot be identified as Christian or Jewish by iconography, prosopography, or by their belief in angelic self-identification.[33] As he observes, the "Theran epitaphs demonstrate how democratic the belief in guardian angels could be, as the large number and variety in quality of Theran *angelos* epitaphs suggest that the possession of a guardian *angelos* was not restricted to a few holy men, or even the wealthy of the community."[34] His study of angels in Roman religions serves as an important reminder of the significance of angels in the local religions of the Roman Mediterranean world.

Angels were such a fixture of religious life in late antiquity outside Jewish and Christian communities that later Byzantine Christian theologians had to vociferously deny any continuity between pagan divinities and Christian devotion to angels. Apparently, some polytheists did understand angels as equivalents to their own local gods, and such nominal Christians could bring the specter of idolatry into churches. As Glenn Peers's book *Subtle Bodies: Representing Angels in Byzantium* chronicled, the visual representation of angels as images in worship was a very fraught issue for Christians in the centuries leading up to the iconoclasm of the eighth and ninth centuries. He observed that the "rejection of images of angels was directly related to that fear of idolatry, but it also involved other issues of primary concern in the early church, namely the worship of angels as gods and pagan attempts to equate Christian angels with their own Gods."[35] Medieval Jewish and rabbinic sources had no need to engage in such debates, mainly because they were aimed at an internal Jewish audience, but still, Jews were not immune from the ideological battles of the Byzantine era. The iconoclastic era left its mark on the archaeological record of the synagogues of Byzantine Palestine where Jews themselves likely carried out the disfiguring of images in synagogue architectural

31. See Daube, "On Acts 23: Sadducees and Angels," where he notes that the Sadducees believed in angels but differentiated themselves from the Pharisees by refuting the idea that people became angels after death and before their resurrection. See the descriptions of the resting places of the righteous with the angels in *Epistle of Enoch* 104:2–6 and the *Book of Parables* 39:4–5. Discussed in Collins, *The Apocalyptic Imagination*, 184.

32. See Kiourtzian, "Stèles funéraires de Théra portant le mot 'ange,'" in *Recueil des inscriptions grecques chretiennes des Cyclades*, 249, 254, and 263.

33. Cline, "Angels of the Grave," in *Ancient Angels*, esp. 88–92.

34. Cline, "Angels of the Grave," 104.

35. Peers, *Subtle Bodies*, 15.

features.[36] Of particular interest for this study is the fact that winged figures on synagogue lintels were targeted.[37] While winged figures were once acceptable in synagogue art, after the iconoclastic era, the depiction of angels would be limited to illuminated manuscripts.[38]

Turning to the religions of Iraq and Iran, we must remember that by the time of the redaction of the Babylonian Talmud, Jews had been living in Babylonia for over one thousand years. Over the course of the same period, Jewish and Iranian religions developed and changed a great deal, and no monolithic Judaism can be compared with monolithic Zoroastrianism of the Sasanian Empire.[39] Many recent studies are focused on situating Judaism in its Persian and Iranian context, and a few mention Zoroastrian demonology, but none center on their conceptualization of angels and subordinate divinities.[40] Though this topic deserves a monograph in its own right, some preliminary remarks on their shared negotiations with subordinate divine beings may be ventured here. The Zoroastrian sacred text, the Avesta, has a long and complex history (to put it lightly), with some archaic passages contemporary with the earliest oral traditions of the Torah and most of it only codified in the late Sasanian period, roughly contemporary with the redaction of the Babylonian Talmud.[41] To give a general sense of the contents, the Avesta consists of the Yasna (the earliest liturgy of the Zoroastrian community, possibly composed by Zoroaster himself), the Yašts or Yashts (later priestly hymns of praise devoted to various divinities), and the Videvdat (a priestly manual for keeping away demons).[42] It is the Yashts that are of particular significance to this study. In the process of promoting Ahura Mazda to a supreme position, other Iranian gods and goddesses came to occupy a lower status as divine beings termed *yazatas*, "literally 'beings worthy of sacrifice.'"[43] Medieval observers of Zoroastrianism understood yazatas as angels, but scholars of Zoroastrianism lack consensus on whether these terms

36. Hachlili observed that the "damage to the lintels and the gable reliefs was carefully carried out, indicating that it was probably done by Jews" (*Ancient Synagogues*, 276).

37. Hachlili, *Ancient Synagogues*, 276. At Bar'am, for example, Hachlili noted that the lintels had either "eagles or Nikae," which were disfigured.

38. See the angels in Epstein, *Skies of Parchment, Seas of Ink: Jewish Illuminated Manuscripts*, 133 and 146: The Munich Mahzor (fifteenth century; Munich, Bayerische Staatsbibliothek, MS Cod. Heb 3/1–II, fol. II, 95v; The Golden Haggadah (1320; Spain; British Museum Library MS Add. 27210, fol. 2vd.).

39. Elman, "Middle Persian Culture and the Babylonian Sages," 190; Shaked, *Dualism in Transformation*.

40. For a recent overview of this field of research, see Gross, "Rethinking Babylonian Rabbinic Acculturation in the Sasanian Empire" and Secunda, *The Iranian Talmud*.

41. I owe this overview to Foltz's *Religions of Iran*. Another excellent introduction is provided by Boyce, *Textual Sources for the Study of Zoroastrianism*.

42. West, *The Hymns of Zoroaster*.

43. Foltz, *Religions of Iran*, 37.

are interchangeable.[44] The hymns codified in the Yashts of the Avesta petition a range of divine beings from the goddess of water Anahita to Mithra, the god of light, to Sraosha, "The Best protector of the poor."[45] All of them begin with a preamble that stresses the primacy of Ahura Mazda before celebrating the divinity that forms the subject of the Yasht. Since they are petitioned as divinities, subordinates to Ahura Mazda, who nonetheless offer benefits to humankind, they may be compared to angelic beings.[46] The hymn to Anahita begins by stating, "On my account, worship her, O Zarathustra Spitama . . . the one "who purifies the semen of all males, who purifies for conception the wombs of all females, who gives easy delivery to all females, who gives milk to all females regularly and at the proper time."[47] While acknowledging the supreme deity Mazda, the hymn still celebrates the role of the female divinity Anahita in the conception of children, particularly the purification of men's seed and women's wombs. This recalls the Babylonian Talmud's description of the role of the angel Lyla (Hebrew, "Night"), who protects women during pregnancy: "the angel that is appointed over pregnancy, Lyla is his name, he carries the drop and presents it before the Holy One, blessed be He."[48] In both sources, mediating beings oversee women's pregnancy and are particularly concerned with the men's furnishing of pure semen for the conception of children.

Meanwhile, the hymns to Mithra describe him in terms that recall the same functions that angels fulfilled for Jews in incantation bowls and in prayers, supporting, healing, and helping them in everyday life: "May he come hither to us in order to help (us). May he come hither to us for spaciousness. May he come hither to us to support (us). May he come hither to us to (grant us) mercy. May he come hither to us to cure (us of disease). May he come hither to us so that we are able to defeat our enemies. May he come hither to us to (grant us) a good life."[49] In the Zoroastrian pantheon, Mithra was second in importance only to Mazda himself, associated variously with covenants, friendship, protection, and even with the sun as a solar deity.[50] The words of this ancient hymn, which evoke Mithra's protection, also recall the requests and prayers of ancient Jews to angels. In these cases, powerful beings closely associated with God are asked to intervene

44. See sources collected in Boyce, *Textual Sources for the Study of Zoroastrianism*, 68–69 and 143–45.

45. Darmesteter, ed., *The Zend-Avesta*, 160.

46. See Hutter, "Demons and Benevolent Spirits in the Ancient Near East," which focuses on the ancient Iranian context.

47. See Malandra, trans. and ed., *An Introduction to Ancient Iranian Religion: Readings from the Avesta*, 120 (Yasht 5).

48. See *b. Nidd.* 16b, briefly discussed in Rebiger, "Engel und Dämonen," 16.

49. See Malandra, trans. and ed., *Readings from the Avesta*, 59 (Yasht 10).

50. Malandra, *Readings from the Avesta*, 55–58.

personally to support and protect their charges. Richard Foltz understands these hymns devoted to divine beings as religious rites created by popular demand, "an accommodation to the desires of the patrons and not necessarily those of the priests."[51] These Yashts devoted to ancient Iranian male and female gods and goddesses stand in tension with Zoroaster's focus on worship of Ahura Mazda alone. It seems that, like the rabbis, Sasanian Zoroastrian authorities struggled with and accommodated people's preoccupation with divine beings subordinate to the supreme deity.[52]

Tracking traditions about angels into the Qur'an and Islamic interpretation shows that early Muslims participated in the same conversations about angels as the other communities investigated in this book, incorporating famous beliefs about angels into foundational stories and everyday piety, resolving some theological difficulties related to angels, and developing influential angelologies that would dominate philosophical discourse throughout the medieval period.[53] More than any prior sacred text, the Qur'an is explicit about the place of angels in the religious imagination, averring that righteous Muslims believe in "Allah, the Last Day, the angels, the scriptures, and the prophets" (Q. 2:177 and cf. Q. 2:285). Belief in angels forms one of the pillars of Islam, upheld at the same level as believing in God and God's prophets, who brought scriptures to every community in every age.[54] The angels were understood as the carriers of "news" (naba) as well as the implementers of "command" (amr).

Gabriel's reputation as the revelatory angel that visited the prophet Daniel and Mary the mother of Jesus likely explains why he is identified with the spirit that reveals the Quran to the prophet Muhammad (Q. 16:102).[55] The angels Gabriel and Michael (Arabized into Jibrā'īl / Jibrīl and Mīkā'īl) were upheld alongside Isrāfīl and the Angel of Death as the four leading archangels, and their role in the present and future was elaborated upon in Hadith.[56] The Jewish and Christian belief in a good and bad angel that hovers over each human and records their deeds can also be found in the Qur'an, combined with the idea of angelic guardianship

---

51. Foltz, *Religions of Iran*, 43. Foltz's approach echoes modern perception of angels found elsewhere as well as perhaps the perspective of some ancient authorities, who frowned on interest in angels.

52. Foltz, *Religions of Iran*, 60.

53. For this topic, see Burge, *Angels in Islam*; a concise overview of angels in Islamic sources including all references to angels in the Qur'an can be found in Kassim, "Nothing Can Be Known or Done without the Involvement of Angels." My thanks to Hamza Zafer for these insights about Islamic practice and interpretation.

54. Alavi, "Pillars of Religion and Faith," offers an excellent description of angels in contemporary Islamic piety.

55. See Burge, "Gabriel."

56. Kassim, "Nothing Can Be Known," 647, citing Ibn Kathir, Tuhfat al-Nabala' 8; see also Burge, "The Angels' Roles in Death and Judgement." The Angel of Death is identified as 'Izrā'īl in later sources.

(Q. 50:17, Q. 82:10–12, and Q. 86:4). Muslim interpreters would have agreed with the rabbis that God values humans over and above the angels—the guarded is more valued than the guardian.[57] Similarly, sages of the respective communities would have agreed that humans, when they prove pious, are more commendable than the angels, who were created perfectly obedient (Q. 21:27; see chapter 6). Where the rabbis have to provide historical explanations to resolve the diversity of descriptions of winged beings in biblical texts, the Qur'an simply asserts that Allah created the angels as "messengers having wings, two or three or four" (35:1).[58] Interestingly, ʿAisha, the second wife of Muhammad, is credited with the tradition that angels were created from the light of fire, which is comparable to biblical and Jewish associations of angelic bodies with fire.[59]

As with Jewish and Christian communities, Muslim worshippers believed that they imitated the angels in their liturgical practices (when they circumambulated the Kaaba, for example).[60] While some Jews welcome the angels into their home each Sabbath evening, some Muslims welcome the descending angels to their homes with lights and candles on the Night of Power, one of the last nights of Ramadan, which commemorates Muhammad's first revelation. Ritual practices invoking angels and other mediating beings flourished among Muslims as much as among medieval Jews and Christians.[61] The early Islamic myth of "fallen angels" reframes the story with angelic obedience in mind, explicating that Allah *sent* the two angels to Babylon to experience the travails of humanity and that these two angels transmitted magical knowledge to humans, which was abused by some people in time (Q. 2:102).[62] The Cairo Genizah provides intriguing examples of Jewish and Islamic sharing of ritual-magical formulas and angelic motifs, a topic that deserves more research.[63] Finally, Muslim philosophers, informed by Neoplatonic traditions, developed new branches of knowledge that combined angelology,

57. See *Gen. Rab.* 78:1 (discussed in Schäfer, *Rivalität zwischen Engeln und Menschen*, 192–93). The superiority of humans over the angels is made explicit in Q. 2:31 with Adam proving more knowledgeable than the angels, which also recalls the story in *Gen. Rab.* 8:4 (Schäfer, *Rivalität zwischen Engeln und Menschen*, 92). More comparative work on angels in Jewish midrash and early Islamic interpretation is a desideratum.

58. See the discussion on the six-winged seraphim vs. four-winged cherubim in *b. Hag.* 13b (chapter 6); on the Qur'anic text, see Burge, "Angels in *Sūrat al-Malāʾika*: Exegeses of Q 35:1."

59. Kassim, "Nothing Can Be Known," 647 and 653. According to later Islamic texts, angels were made of the light of fire, Jinns of the flames of fire, and satans from the smoke of fire.

60. See Burge, *Angels in Islam*, §489, and Burge, "Angels, Ritual, and Sacred Space in Islam."

61. Zadeh, "Magic, Marvel, and Miracle in Early Islamic Thought." See also Bohak, "Magic."

62. Kassim, "Nothing Can Be Known," 652; Zadeh, "Magic, Marvel, and Miracle in Early Islamic Thought," 240.

63. Naveh and Shaked said as much in *Magic Spells and Formulae*. See also Shaked, "Medieval Jewish Magic in Relation to Islam." More recently, see Cohen, "Goitein, Magic, and the Genizah."

cosmology, and epistemology, shaping Christian and Jewish philosophical and mystical trajectories in turn.[64]

This brief survey highlights that intermediary beings were a feature of all religions of late antiquity even as authorities dealt with them in different ways. Against this backdrop, we can see that the early rabbinic tendency to avoid angels was quite countercultural. Angels drew people to synagogues and churches when prayer leaders deployed them. Alternatively, to access angels or other intermediary beings, ancient people turned to ritual practitioners, priests, and theurgists. The integrity of angels in the religious outlook was deeply grounded in the ancient Near Eastern worldview and yet the significance of angels in people's lives varied based on their respective cosmologies, personal and familial preference, regional customs, and communal practice.

ANGELS AFTER ANTIQUITY

Certainly, the written record captures Jewish ambivalence toward angels alongside Jewish preoccupation with them, but in surveying the corpus of late antique Jewish writings, one cannot deny that angels were a rich part of Jewish culture in the formative period of late antiquity as well as long after. Medieval Jewish texts indicate that belief in angels continued unabated among Jews until modernity. Rabbinic midrashim like *Exodus Rabbah* or *Lamentations Rabbah* multiplied the roles of angels in the biblical past and in the people of Israel's present.[65] In surviving ritual texts and amulets from the Cairo Genizah, we can see that the techniques of ritual practitioners from Palestine and Babylonia continued to be used and commissioned by Jews.[66] In ritual amulets and books of magic, angels continued to play essential roles. Liturgical poetry produced after Yannai continued to evoke angelic imagery and the integration of this evidence into the study of religion is an important area for future research.[67]

Eleazar of Worms (1165–1240 CE), one of the last great thinkers among *hasidei Ashkenaz*, the group that transmitted the Hekhalot literature to Europe, wrote *The Book of Raziel the Angel*, which purports to contain the secrets the angels told the first man.[68] Such works demonstrate that new productions about angelic

---

64. See Davidson, *Alfarabi, Avicenna, and Averroes, on Intellect."* Briefly discussed in Kassim, "Nothing Can Be Known," 654.

65. For these later sources, see Rebiger, "Angels in Rabbinic Literature" or Urbach's chapter on angels in *The Sages*.

66. See Swartz, *Hebrew and Aramaic Incantation Texts from the Cairo Genizah*; Saar, *Jewish Love Magic*; Bohak, "The Magical Rotuli from the Cairo Genizah."

67. Elizur's *Sod Meshalshei Qodesh* publishes much new material deserving of more attention.

68. See *Sefer Raziel haMalach* (ed. ben Shabtai).

knowledge continued through the medieval period among Jews. Engagement with Hekhalot texts also continued through the medieval period, but the works' liturgical and ritual modes were no match for the eventual popularity of a different approach to the divine, the one embodied in Kabbalah, which innovated an exegetical approach to biblical and Jewish texts. The religiosity of Kabbalah leaped from elite circles into the public sphere with the aid of the printing press at the same time that the Catholic Church banned the printing of the Talmud in Italy (1553).[69] Both Hekhalot mysticism and Kabbalistic mysticism empowered and centered the individual in the universe, and angels acted as important supporting cast members in people's imaginings of the world.[70] Angels were a feature of Jewish religiosity long before Kabbalah, but this form of mysticism's spread may have enlarged their role in some Jews' imagination.

Alongside mystical speculations about angels, a separate trajectory can be found in the works of the Jewish philosopher Maimonides (1138–1204 CE), who devoted sections of his treatises to angels but rationalized and depersonalized them, turning them into natural forces and intelligences.[71] He shared the view with Christian theologians and Islamic philosophers that angels were immaterial or bodiless.[72] He was radical among Jews in his time, rejecting the depiction of and ruminations on angels found in rabbinic midrashim, liturgical poetry, and mystical texts and building instead on Hellenistic philosophical trends, particularly Aristotelianism, through Islamic and Arabic transmission.[73] Maimonides "agreed with Muslim theological hardliners in upholding the absolute simplicity, immateriality, and transcendence of God."[74] There was no room for emotional, individuated angels in his philosophical approach. In the twelfth and thirteen centuries, in part in response to Maimonides's writings, some Jews demoted angels

69. Dweck, *The Scandal of Kabbalah*, 7.

70. Kabbalists hold that there are ten ranks, but their contents vary (see *Zohar* Exod 43 or *Maseket Azilut*). See also the 1820 text attributed to Hayim Vital, *Sefer Segulut Bedukot u-muvhakot meod*, including *ktav malachim ve-chotmei hamalachim hashonim*.

71. Maimonides, *Yesodei ha-Torah*, 2:3–8; see also Maimonides, *A Guide to the Perplexed*, 1:39 and 2:6–7. Kellner cites and analyzes the relevant passages in full in his "Angels," in *Maimonides' Confrontation with Mysticism*, 265–85.

72. This conception of angels builds on Ps 104:4 (for reception history, see Kaduri, "Windy and Fiery Angels"); for medieval angelology, see Tobias Hoffmann, ed., *A Companion to Angels in Medieval Philosophy*.

73. Kellner, "Angels."

74. Adamson, *Philosophy in the Islamic World*, 239. Adamson credits Abraham Ibn Daud with showing Maimonides "how Judaism and Aristotelianism could be harmonized" (225). He also notes that it was Ibn Daud who identified "angels with the heavenly intellects of the Aristotelian system" in his book the *Exalted Faith*.

in favor of more abstract divine emanations (*sefirot*).[75] Ironically, Maimonides's philosophical approach is much more influential today than it was in his own day or throughout the medieval period.

Maimonides's rationalistic approach to angels did not stop Kabbalists from co-opting his legal works and reinterpreting them through their own mystical lens. In Safed, the combination of Kabbalah and Jewish law lay at the heart of an influential cultural renaissance led by Isaac Luria (1534–1572).[76] For Kabbalistic mystics, there was no contradiction between a deep engagement with legal texts and a relationship with the angelic realm. Many Jewish legends celebrate the holiness of Isaac Luria and his relationship to angels, who revealed secrets to him and whom he could bid to help him in his endeavors.[77] Luria's leading disciple, Hayyim ben Joseph Vital (1543–1620), wrote: "Every word that is uttered creates an angel. . . . Consequently, when a man leads a righteous and pious life, studies the Law, and prays with devotion, then angels and holy spirits are created from the sounds which he utters . . . and these angels are the mystery of *maggidim*, and everything depends on the measure of one's good works."[78] Extrapolating from the rabbinic tradition that "every utterance of God creates an angel" (*b. Ḥag.* 14a, discussed in chapter 6), Vital drew the conclusion that every pious individual can create angels with his utterances. Vital upheld devotion to the halakhah, prayer, and the angels in his influential synthesis of Jewish mysticism. Alongside Luria and Vital in Safed lived the influential legal thinker and mystic Joseph Karo (1488–1575 CE), who composed the *Shulhan Arukh*, still the authoritative summary of Talmudic law for Orthodox Jews. Karo was known to have communicated with a personification of the Mishnah, a maggid, understood by some witnesses as an angelic being.[79] This angelic being revealed to him how to interpret texts. For Karo there was no tension between a rationalist approach to halakhah and a belief in angels.

Until the twentieth century, most Jews lived in a world full of angels. A turning point can be seen in a 1908 *Jewish Encyclopedia* entry on angels, where Ludwig Blau duly cataloged the angels in Jewish texts through the ages and, in closing, lamented, "After the victorious advance of the Cabala, opposition to the highly fanciful belief in angels was no longer made; and mystical Angelology lured the Occident as well as the Orient into its charmed circle, from which a portion of

---

75. See Weiss, "Prayers to Angels and the Early Sefirotic Literature," who examines the emergence of sefirotic literature as "a conservative rabbinic reaction to Jewish medieval mythical and magical beliefs that were suspected of being contradictory to monotheism" (22).

76. Dweck, *Scandal of Kabbalah*, 8.

77. Howard Schwartz, ed. *Gabriel's palace*.

78. Vital, *Sefer ha-Gilgulim* (Frankfurt, 1684), 32b; trans. and quoted in Werblowsky, *Joseph Karo*, 78.

79. See Werblowsky, *Joseph Karo*, 22–23.

Judaism has not yet liberated itself."[80] Blau evidently believed that Jews *ought* to liberate themselves from "the highly fanciful belief in angels." For Blau, angels were just a "fanciful belief," apparently not integral to Jewish life. Blau credited the Kabbalistic writings with the spread of belief in angels, but my research shows that long before the Kabbalists and even apart from mystical preoccupations, angels were a significant part of Jewish religion and culture.

Blau may be seen as representative of German Jewish scholars engaged in the *Wissenschaft des Judentums* (the "science of Judaism"), a movement of learned men in Europe and America, which sought to present Judaism as a philosophically "mature" and utterly monotheistic religion. These *Wissenschaft* scholars were responding to anti-Semitic bias in academic circles and sought to provide ordinary Jews with a history and religious heritage of which to be proud.[81] The *Jewish Encyclopedia* has been a lasting achievement and legacy of the nineteenth-century *Wissenschaft des Judentums* and aimed to subject all biblical and Jewish traditions to rigorous criticism and research.[82] This authoritative source evinced discomfort with angels in the context of modernity.

If most American Jews today believe angels are irrelevant to Judaism, credit must also go to Yehezkel Kaufmann's influential *The Religion of Israel*, which popularized the view that exclusive monotheism was the invention and contribution of ancient Israel, the popular expression of the Israelite people, who recognized an utterly transcendent God, devoid of both myth and idolatry.[83] For Kaufmann, only polytheists saw personalized mediators around them. Jews needed no mediators to fill the gap between God and themselves. While acknowledging that angels appeared in biblical texts, Kaufmann deprived them of any function or personalized aspect and relegated them to the distant heavens. According to his book, the angels of the Hebrew Bible "are the featureless 'host of god' or his manifestation. They lack even the elementary mythological distinction of the sexes."[84] While Kaufmann's work has been challenged in academic scholarship, his view of angels as non-Jewish still persisted in many

80. Blau, "Angelology."

81. Dinur, "*Wissenschaft des Judentums*," 112.

82. The *Jewish Encyclopedia* continues to inform many people about Jewish beliefs today as it is freely available online and reproduced in most Wikipedia entries on Judaism.

83. Kaufmann, *The Religion of Israel*, 63. In "Monotheism—A Misused Word in Jewish Studies?" Hayman credits a different book called *The Religion of Ancient Israel*, by Theodorus Vriezen, which was translated in 1967, with the same misconception of Jewish monotheism. Kaufmann's *Religion of Israel* (1960) was an abridgment and translation of the eight-volume work *Toldot Ha-Emuna Ha-Israelit* (1937–57). While Kaufmann acknowledged that God had a celestial entourage, his reconstruction of the religion of Israel relegated angels to the margins.

84. Kaufmann, *The Religion of Israel*, 63. In this section Greenberg translated Kaufmann almost word for word (see *Toldot Ha-Emuna Ha-Israelit* [Jerusalem: Bialik, 1937], 2:264).

circles and has been passed on into the popular imagination through seminaries training rabbis.[85]

Kaufmann's contribution was in keeping with other trends in the academic study of religion in the twentieth century.[86] As Robert Orsi has elucidated, the academic study of religion has privileged a "true religion" that is "rational, respectful of persons, noncoercive, mature, nonanthropomorphic in its higher forms, mystical (as opposed to ritualistic), unmediated and agreeable to democracy (no hierarchy in gilded robes and fancy hats), monotheistic (no angels, saints, demons, ancestors), emotionally controlled, a reality of mind and spirit, not body and matter."[87] For much of US history, this unmediated form of religion was seen as suitable for the modern nation state, where citizens were expected to engage with their elected representatives and in turn their representatives were to avoid discussing religion publicly. (Until the Carter presidency, doing so was "bad manners.")[88] Scholars and institutional leaders who followed in the footsteps of the *Wissenschaft* participated in the project of re-presenting Judaism as a "modern" religion. In doing so, they disavowed a great deal of traditional Jewish beliefs and practices. They omitted angels from their teaching of Judaism and contributed to the contemporary belief that Judaism lacks emphasis on personal and intimate relationships with the invisible realm.

Returning angels to the history of Jewish religion offers both a more accurate view of the past and important insights into Jewish beliefs and practices today. As the task of the historian is to make the foreign familiar, my book has sought to recover a neglected dimension of late antique Jewish experience, one often conceived as foreign to Judaism as well as to modern secular citizenship. While belief in angels was shared among Christian and polytheists in late antiquity, some conceptions of angels were quintessentially Jewish. Angels pervaded the world of ancient Jews, especially during the formative period of late antiquity when Jewish men and women mediated biblical traditions into practices that would be continued for generations and into the present.

---

85. In *Angels in the Bible*, Rofé writes that the composers of Deuteronomy and the priestly sources subordinated foreign gods to angelic status in an attempt to reconcile popular polytheism with Israelite monotheism. In other words, they were monotheistic, but angels were their concession to polytheism. On seminary training, see Uffenheimer, "Some Reflections on Modern Jewish Biblical Research."

86. At about the same time, the Christian theologian Karl Barth articulated a similar view of angels, asserting they were "essentially marginal figures," not worthy of examination (*Church Dogmatics*, 371); discussed in Muehlberger, *Angels in Late Ancient Christianity*, 7.)

87. Orsi, *Between Heaven and Earth*, 188.

88. Prothero, *Religious Literacy*, 41.

Table of Incantation Bowls

This table of incantation bowls represents a best effort to categorize the diverse ways Jews imagined themselves in relation to the crowded invisible realm. While this dataset accounts for a large proportion of the few hundred published bowls to date, it represents only 5 percent of the two thousand incantation bowls estimated to exist in various museums and private collections around the world.[1] As more incantation bowls come to light and are published, these proportions may change. My results are reproducible, but others might categorize these incantations differently.[2]

---

1. On the number of incantation bowls estimated to exist, see Brodie, "The Market Background to the April 2003 plunder of the Iraq National Museum," 44–54.

2. For example, in most incantations, the names of angels are obvious, but in *AIT* 11, my guess is that the names listed are not only variations on God's name but refer to angels as well (based in part, on partial parallels to these names found elsewhere). Others might disagree with my analysis, reading angelic names where I see a reference only to God (as in SD12, discussed in chapter 2). Nine out of the 100 incantation bowls I analyzed stood out as anomalous: AIT 19 invokes "60 male gods and 80 female goddesses," some Greek and some Persian; BM 047A calls on planetary deities like the Sun, Dalibat, Bel, etc.; BM 049A closes in the name of "*tyqws yhwh* of Hosts"—*Yhwh* of Hosts is common; *tyqws* is difficult; Gordon E & F call on angels and known archangels, *Yhwh* God of Israel as well as "Yokabarziwa the son of Rabbe" (identity unknown), "the signet ring of Aspanadas-Dwia, the jinnee of King Solomon;" Isbell 4 invokes God, angels, Hermes, "Yahu-is-Yahu and Abbahu the great and Abraxas the great," and "Parnagin the son of Parnagin" (alternative reading Farangin); BOR invokes "your God, Sariah, *Yhwh*, Jesus," possibly the Holy Ghost, "and the Ishtars." See the list of abbreviations in this appendix.

Table of Incantation Bowl Study

Incantation bowl texts with provenance (58 total)

God 24%	Angels 4%	God and Angels 40%	God, Angels, Hero 13%	God, Hero 5%	No Beings 5%	Other 9%
AIT 1		*AIT* 3	*AIT* 8	*AIT* 17	*AIT* 6	*AIT* 19
AIT 11 / 18 / etc.	BM 021A	*AIT* 5	*AIT* 9	Gordon A	*AIT* 21, 22, 23	BM 047A
AIT 16	Gordon-Teheran	*AIT* 7	*AIT* 10			
AIT 24		*AIT* 12	*AIT* 14			BM 049A/M-K "Unique"
AIT 26	*AIT* 4	*AIT* 13	BM 034A			
AIT 2★		*AIT* 15	Gordon B			Gordon E & F
AIT 27★	BM 003A –	*AIT* 20	Faraj-Moriggi 62265			
AIT 29	Refrain A (x12)	*AIT* 25	Oriental Institute A17877			Isbell 4
BM 015A /016A		*AIT* 28	Gordon 1932.620			
BM 026A		BM 010A				BOR
		BM 013A				
Kaufman-Nippur★		BM 014A				
Gordon K		BM 017A				
		BM 028A				
Gordon 9		BM 065A				
		Gordon C				
		Gordon L				
		Gordon 8				
		Gordon I (x2)				
		Isbell-De Menil				
		Isbell N-IV				
		Faraj-Moriggi 71180				

Incantation Bowl text without provenance (42 total)					
BM 038A	Gordon D	MS 1927/2	MS 1927/9	036A	MS 1929/6 and MS 2053/170
Oberman1	Gordon H	MS 1927/8 x10	Isbell 66	AMB-B7	
Gordon 2	Gordon 1	M117	VA 3854x2	AMB-B8	Oberman 2
Gordon 4	Gordon 5	M123			
Gordon 11	Gordon 6	AMB-B5			M102
Gordon G	Gordon 7				
MS 2053/183	Gordon IM-9736				
M108	M101				
M121	M103 (x4)				
Isbell 68	M107				
Mor 2	M112*Names				
	Isbell 64-65				
	Isbell 67				
	Isbell 69				
	Isbell 70				
	SD12				
	Mor1				
	AMB-B6				

ABBREVIATIONS USED IN THE TABLE

AIT: Montgomery, *Aramaic Incantation Texts*.

AMB–B5 and *AMB*–B6: Naveh and Shaked, *Amulets and Magic Bowls* (1985).

BM: British Museum, follows Segal and Hunter's *Catalogue of the Aramaic and Mandaic Incantation Bowls in the British Museum* (*CAMIB*).

BOR: Harviainen, "An Aramaic Incantation Bowl from Borsippa," 1981.

Faraj-Moriggi: Faraj and Moriggi, "Two Incantation Bowls from the Iraq Museum"; 71180 is from Nippur while 62265 was found a few kilometers south of Baghdad.

Gordon followed by a numeral: Gordon, "Aramaic Incantation Bowls" (1941, pp. 116–41). Of these, only Gordon 8 and 9 have firm provenance from Kish.

Gordon 1932.620: Gordon, "Aramaic Incantation Bowls" (1941, pp. 279–80).

Gordon followed by letters A–E: Gordon, "Aramaic Magical Bowls in the Istanbul and Baghdad Museums." As Gordon explains, bowls A–C in the Istanbul Museum originated from the Pennsylvania expedition in Nippur (like those published by Montgomery); he does not offer provenance for Bowl D, now in the Baghdad Museum, but Bowl E and its duplicate originated in Kish.

Gordon followed by letters H–L: Gordon, "Aramaic and Mandaic Magical Bowls." Gordon asserted bowls I through K originated in Nippur (p. 85), and with some names overlapping with names of clients from Nippur, his assertion seems trustworthy.

Gordon IM: Iraq Museum, Gordon, "Aramaic Incantation Bowls" (1941, pp. 339–60). I counted only one, the most complete bowl that Gordon discusses. As for provenance, he says that Iraqi *fellahin* bring these bowls to the Iraq Museum.

Gordon-Teheran: Gordon, "Two Magic Bowls in Teheran"; the Aramaic bowl invoking only Metatron was excavated at Khuzistan.

Isbell: Isbell, *Corpus of the Aramaic Incantation Bowls* (1975); I cite five incantations first translated by Isak Jeruzalmi in 1964 in an unpublished dissertation and reproduced by Isbell in his book. Isbell 4 is a reprint of Myhrman's publication of a bowl from Nippur.

Isbell De-Menil and Isbell N-IV: Isbell, "Two New Aramaic Incantation Bowls," (1976): 15–23.

Kaufman: Kaufman, "A Unique Magic Bowl from Nippur."

M followed by a number: Levene, *A Corpus of Magic Bowls*.

M-K: Müller-Kessler and Kwasman, "A Unique Talmudic Aramaic Incantation Bowl;" they offer a better translation of 049A from *CAMIB*.

Mor1 and Mor2: Gordon, "Magic Bowls in the Moriah Collection" (1984).

MS: bowls in the Schoyen collection first published by Shaked, "Form and Purpose in Aramaic Spells," and collated in Shaked, Ford, and Bhayro, *Aramaic Bowl Spells*.

Oberman: Oberman, "Two Magic Bowls" (1940).

Oriental Institute No. A17877: Cook, "An Aramaic Incantation Bowl from Khafaje."

Refrain A–003A (a.k.a. BM 117883): was found in Abu Habbah; see Hunter, "Manipulating Incantation Texts: Excursions in Refrain A."

SD12: Levene, Marx, and Bhayro, "'Gabriel Is on Their Right': Angelic Protection in Jewish Magic and Babylonian Lore."

VA 3853 and VA 3854: Levene, "Heal O' Israel."

BIBLIOGRAPHY

Abelson, Joshua. *The Immanence of God in Rabbinical Literature*. London: Macmillan and Co., 1912.

Abrahams, Israel. *Jewish Life in the Middle Ages*. Philadelphia: Jewish Publication Society, 1993.

Adamson, Peter. *Philosophy in the Islamic World: A History of Philosophy without Any Gaps*. Vol. 3. Oxford: Oxford University Press, 2016.

Ahuvia, Mika. "Ancient Mystical Texts." *The Posen Library of Jewish Culture and Civilization, volume 2: Emerging Judaism, 332 BCE–600 CE*. Edited by Carol Bakhos. New Haven, CT: Yale University Press, forthcoming.

———. "Darkness upon the Abyss: Depicting Cosmogony in Late Antiquity." In *In the Beginning: Jewish and Christian Cosmogony in Late Antiquity*, edited by Lance Jenott and Sarit Kattan Gribetz, 255–70. Tübingen: Mohr Siebeck, 2013.

———. "Gender and the Angels in Late Antique Judaism." *Jewish Studies Quarterly*, 28 (2021): 1–21.

———. "Jewish Towns and Neighborhoods." In *The Blackwell Companion to Late Ancient Jews and Judaism*, edited by Naomi Koltun-Fromm and Gwynn Kessler, 33–52. Malden, MA: Blackwell Publishing, 2020.

———. "Memra." *Encyclopedia of the Bible and Its Reception*. Edited by Barry Walfish. Berlin: De Gruyter, 2020.

———. "Metatron." In *Encyclopedia of the Bible and Its Reception*. Edited by Barry Walfish. Berlin: De Gruyter, 2020.

———. "Popular Religion and Magic." In *The Oxford Encyclopedia of the Bible and Gender Studies*. Edited by Julia O'Brien. Oxford: Oxford University Press, 2014.

———. "The Spatial and Social Dynamics of Jewish Babylonian Incantations." In *Placing Ancient Texts: The Rhetorical and Ritual Use of Space*, edited by Mika Ahuvia and

Alexander Koçar, 243–69. Texts and Studies in Ancient Judaism 174. Tübingen: Mohr Siebeck, 2018.

Ahuvia, Mika, and Sarit Kattan Gribetz. "The Daughters of Israel: An Analysis of the Term in Late Ancient Jewish Sources." *Jewish Quarterly Review* 108, no. 1 (2018): 1–27.

Alavi, Karima Diane. "Pillars of Religion and Faith." In *Voices of Islam, Volume 1: Voices of Tradition*, edited by Vincent J. Cornell, 5–42. London: Praeger, 2007.

Alexander, Philip. "From Son of Adam to Second God: Transformations of the Biblical Enoch." In *Biblical Figures Outside the Bible*, edited by Michael E. Stone and Theodore A. Bergren, 87–122. Harrisburg, PA: Trinity Press International, 1998.

———. *The Mystical Texts: Songs of the Sabbath Sacrifice and Related Manuscripts*. London: T & T Clark, 2006.

———. "Prayer in the Heikhalot Literature." In *Prière, Mystique et Judaïsme*: Colloque de Strasbourg (10–12 September 1984, edited by Roland Goetschel, 43–64. Paris: Presses Universitaires de France, 1987.

Altmann, Alexander. "The Gnostic Background of the Rabbinic Adam Legends." *Jewish Quarterly Review* 35 (1944/45): 371–91.

———. "Kedushah Hymns in the Earliest Hechaloth Literature (From an Oxford Manuscript)." *Melilah* 2 (1946): 1–24 (Hebrew).

Angel, Joseph. "The Use of the Hebrew Bible in Early Jewish Magic." *Religion Compass* 3, no. 5 (2009): 785–98.

Assaf, Simcha. *Ha-Onashin Acharei Chatimat HaTalmud*. Jerusalem: HaPoel HaZair, 1922.

Atkinson, Miles, trans. and ed. *Historical Tracts of Saint Athanasius*. Oxford: Parker, 1843.

Bagnall, Roger. "Writing on Ostraka." In *Everyday Writing in the Greco-Roman East*, 117–38. Berkeley: University of California Press, 2011.

Bar-Ilan, Meir. *The Mysteries of Jewish Prayer and Hekhalot*. Ramat-Gan: Hotsa'at Universitat Bar-Ilan, 1987 (Hebrew).

———. "The Names of Angels." In *These Are the Names: Studies in Jewish Onomastics*, edited by Aaron Demsky, Joseph Reif, and Joseph Tabory, 33–48. Ramat Gan: Bar-Ilan University Press, 1997 (Hebrew).

———. "Prayers of Jews to Angels and other Mediators in the First Centuries CE." In *Saints and Role Models in Judaism and Christianity*, edited by Marcel Poorthuis and Joshua Schwartz, 79–95. Leiden: Brill, 2004.

Barth, Karl. *Church Dogmatics III.3: The Doctrine of Creation*. 1960. Reprint, London: T & T Clark, 2004.

Beard, Mary, John North, and Simon Price. *Religions of Rome*. New York: Cambridge University Press, 1998.

Ben Shabtai, Israel. *Sefer Raziel haMalach*. Bnei Brak: dfus Cohanim, 1882 (Hebrew).

Berman, Saul. "Kol 'Isha." In *The Rabbi Joseph H. Lookstein Memorial Volume*, edited by Joseph Hyman Lookstein and Leo Landman, 45–66. New York: Ktav Publishing, 1980.

Berner, Christoph. "The Four (or Seven) Archangels in the First Book of Enoch and Early Jewish Writings of the Second Temple Period." In *Angels: The Concept of Celestial Beings—Origins, Development and Reception*, edited by Friedrich Reiterer, et al., 395–412. New York: de Gruyter, 2007.

Betz, Hans Dieter. *Greek Magical Papyri in Translation, Including the Demotic Spells*. Chicago: University of Chicago Press, 1986.

Bhayro, Siam, James Nathan Ford, Dan Levene and Ortal-Paz Saar. *Aramaic Magic Bowls in the Vorderasiatisches Museum in Berlin: Descriptive List and Edition of Selected Texts*. Magical and Religious Literature of Late Antiquity 7. Boston: Brill, 2018.

Blau, Ludwig, and Kaufmann Kohler. "Angelology." In *Jewish Encyclopedia*. 1901–6. Reprint, Brooklyn, NY: KTAV, 1960.

Bohak, Gideon. *Ancient Jewish Magic: A History*. Cambridge: Cambridge University Press, 2008.

——. "Babylonian Jewish Magic in Late Antiquity: Beyond the Incantation Bowls." In *Studies in Honor of Shaul Shaked*, edited by Yohanan Friedman, 70–122. Jerusalem: The Israel Academy of Sciences and Humanities, 2019.

——. "Conceptualizing Demons in Late Antique Judaism." In *Demons and Illness from Antiquity to the Early-Modern Period*, edited by Siam Bhayro and Catherine Rider, 111–33. Magical and Religious Literature of Late Antiquity 5. Leiden: Brill, 2017.

——. "Jewish Amulets, Magic Bowls, and Manuals in Aramaic and Hebrew." In *Guide to the Study of Ancient Magic*, edited by David Frankfurter, 388–415. Religions in the Graeco-Roman World 189. Leiden: Brill, 2019.

——. "Magic." In *The Cambridge History of Judaism V. Jews in the Medieval Islamic World*. Edited by Phillip Lieberman. Cambridge: Cambridge University Press, 2021.

——. "The Magica Rotuli from the Cairo Genizah." In *Continuity and Innovation in the Magical Tradition*, edited by Gideon Bohak, Yuval Harari, and Shaul Shaked, 321–40. Leiden: Brill, 2011.

Bokser, Baruch M. "Wonder-Working and the Rabbinic Tradition: The Case of Ḥanina Ben Dosa." *Journal for the Study of Judaism in the Persian, Hellenistic, and Roman Period* 16, no. 1 (1985): 42–92.

Boustan, Raʿanan. *From Martyr to Mystic: Rabbinic Martyrology and the Making of Merkavah Mysticism*. Texts and Studies in Ancient Judaism 112. Tübingen: Mohr Siebeck, 2005.

——. "Rabbinization and the Making of Early Jewish Mysticism." *Jewish Quarterly Review* 101, no. 4 (2011): 482–501.

——. "The Spoils of the Jerusalem Temple at Rome and Constantinople: Jewish Counter-Geography in a Christianizing Empire," In *Antiquity in Antiquity: Jewish and Christian Pasts in the Greco-Roman World*, edited by Gregg Gardner and Kevin Osterloh, 327–72. Texts and Studies in Ancient Judaism 123. Tübingen: Mohr Siebeck, 2008.

——. "The Study of Heikhalot Literature: Between Mystical Experience and Textual Artifact." *Currents in Biblical Research* 6 (2007): 130–60.

Boustan, Raʿanan, and Michael Beshay. "Sealing the Demons, Once and for All: The Ring of Solomon, the Cross of Christ, and the Power of Biblical Kingship." *Archiv für Religionsgeschichte* 16, no. 1 (2015): 99–130.

Boustan, Raʿanan, Martha Himmelfarb, and Peter Schäfer, eds. *Hekhalot Literature in Context: From Byzantium to Babylonia*. Texts and Studies in Ancient Judaism 153. Tübingen: Mohr Siebeck, 2013.

Boyarin, Daniel. "Beyond Judaisms: Metatron and the Divine Polymorphy of Ancient Judaism." *Journal for the Study of Judaism* 41 (2010): 323–65.

Boyce, Mary, ed. and trans. *Textual Sources for the Study of Zoroastrianism.* Chicago: University of Chicago Press, 1984.

Breed, Brennan. "Reception of the Psalms: The Example of Psalm 91." In *The Oxford Handbook of the Psalms,* edited by William P. Brown, 297–310. Oxford: Oxford University Press, 2014.

Brettler, Marc. "Shalom Aleikhem: Bible." In *My People's Prayer Book: Traditional Prayers, Modern Commentaries.* Volume 7: *Shabbat at Home.* Edited by Lawrence A. Hoffman. Jewish Lights Publishing, 2004.

Brisson, Luc. "The Angels in Proclus: Messengers of the Gods." In *Neoplatonic Demons and Angels,* edited by Luc Brisson, Seamus O'Neill, and Andrei Timotin, 209–30. Studies in Platonism, Neoplatonism, and the Platonic Tradition 20. Leiden: Brill, 2018.

Brisson, Luc, Seamus O'Neill, and Andrei Timotin, eds. *Neoplatonic Demons and Angels.* Studies in Platonism, Neoplatonism, and the Platonic Tradition 20. Leiden: Brill, 2018.

Brock, Sebastian. "Syriac and Greek Hymnography: Problems of Origin." *Studia Patristica* 16 (1985): 77–81.

Brodie, Neil. "The Market Background to the April 2003 Plunder of the Iraq National Museum." In *The Destruction of Cultural Heritage in Iraq,* edited by Peter G. Stone and Joanne Farchakh Bajjaly, 41–54. London: Boydell Press, 2008.

Brooten, Bernadette. "Female Leadership in the Ancient Synagogue." In *From Dura to Sepphoris: Studies in Jewish Art and Society in Late Antiquity,* edited by Lee I. Levine and Ze'ev Weiss, 215–23. Portsmouth, RI: Journal of Roman Archaeology, 2000.

Bronznick, Nachum M. *Piyyutei Yannai: Be'urim ve-Perushim* 2 Vols. Jerusalem: Re'uven Mas, 2000 (Hebrew).

Brown, Peter. *The Body and Society: Men, Women, and Sexual Renunciation in Early Christianity.* 1988. Reprint, New York: Columbia University Press, 2008.

———. *The Making of Late Antiquity.* Cambridge, Mass.: Harvard University Press, 1976.

Buber, Salomon. *Midrash Tehillim.* Vilna: Vagshal, 1891.

Bülow-Jacobsen, Adam. "Writing Material in the Ancient World." In *The Oxford Handbook of Papyrology,* 3–29. Oxford: Oxford University Press, 2009.

Burge, Stephen. *Angels in Islam: Jalal al-Din al-Suyuti's al-Haba'ik fi akhbar al-mala'ik.* New York: Routledge, 2015.

———. "The Angels in *Surat al-Mala'ika*: Exegeses of Q. 35:1." *Journal of Qur'anic Studies* 10 (2008): 50–70.

———. "Angels, Ritual, and Sacred Space in Islam." *Comparative Islamic Studies* 5, no. 2 (2009): 221–45.

———. "The Angels' Roles in Death and Judgement: Al-Suyūṭī's Approach to Hadith." In *The Meeting Place of British Middle Eastern Studies: Emerging Scholars, Emergent Research and Approaches,* edited by Amanda Phillips and Refqa Abu Remailleh, 40–59. Newcastle, UK: Cambridge Scholars Press, 2009.

———. "Gabriel." In *Encyclopedia of the Bible and Its Reception.* Vol. 9. Boston: De Gruyter, 2014.

Burrus, Sean. "Remembering the Righteous: Sarcophagus Sculpture and Jewish Patrons in the Roman World." PhD Diss., Duke University, 2017.

Casas, Ghislain. "Ontology, Henadology, Angelology: The Neoplatonic Roots of Angelic Hierarchy." In *Neoplatonic Demons and Angels*, edited by Luc Brisson, Seamus O'Neill, and Andrei Timotin, 231–68. Studies in Platonism, Neoplatonism, and the Platonic Tradition 20. Leiden: Brill, 2018.

Clarke, Emma, John Dillon, and Jackson Hershbell, trans. and eds. *Iamblichus: De Mysteriis*. Writings from the Greco-Roman World 4. Atlanta, GA: Society of Biblical Literature, 2003.

Cline, Rangar. *Ancient Angels: Conceptualizing Angeloi in the Roman Empire*. Religions in the Graeco-Roman World 172. Leiden: Brill, 2011.

Cohen, Mark. "Goitein, Magic, and the Geniza." *Jewish Studies Quarterly* 13 no, .4 (2006): 294–304.

Cohen, Naomi G. "Jewish Names as Cultural Indicators in Antiquity." *Journal for the Study of Judaism in the Persian, Hellenistic, and Roman Period* 7, no. 2 (1976): 97–128.

Cohen, Shaye. *The Beginnings of Jewishness: Boundaries, Varieties, Uncertainties*. Hellenistic Culture and Society 31. Berkeley: University of California Press, 1999.

Cohn, Yehudah. *Tangled Up in Text: Tefillin and the Ancient World*. Brown Judaic Studies 351. Providence, R.I.: Brown University Press, 2008.

Collins, John Joseph. *The Apocalyptic Imagination: An Introduction to Jewish apocalyptic Literature*. Grand Rapids, Mich.: Eerdmans Publishing 2016.

———. "From Prophecy to Apocalypticism: The Expectation of the End." In *The Encyclopedia of Apocalypticism*, edited by John Joseph Collins, Bernard McGinn, and Stephen J. Stein, 1:129–61. New York: Continuum, 1998.

Cook, E. M. "An Aramaic Incantation Bowl from Khafaje." *Bulletin of the American Schools of Oriental Research* 285 (1992): 79–81.

Dan, Joseph. *The Ancient Jewish Mysticism*. Tel Aviv: Ministry of Defense, 1989 (Hebrew).

———. *Kabbalah: A Very Short Introduction*. Oxford: Oxford University Press, 2006.

Danan, Julie H. "The Divine Voice in Scripture: *Ruah Ha-Kodesh* in Rabbinic Literature." PhD diss., The University of Texas at Austin, 2009.

Danby, Herbert. *The Mishnah: Translated from the Hebrew with Introduction and Brief Explanatory Notes*. Oxford: Oxford University Press, 1933.

Darmesteter, James, trans. and ed. *The Zend-Avesta*, Part II: *The Sirozahs, Yashts and Nyayesh*. Sacred Books of the East 23. 1883. Reprint, Delhi: Motilal Banarsidass, 1965.

Daube, David. "On Acts 23: Sadducees and Angels," *Journal of Biblical Literature* 109, no. 3 (1990): 493–97.

Davidson, Herbert A. *Alfarabi, Avicenna, and Averroes, on Intellect: Their Cosmologies, Theories of the Active Intellect, and Theories of Human Intellect*. Oxford: Oxford University Press, 1992.

Davidson, Israel. *Thesaurus of Mediaeval Hebrew Poetry*. 4 vols. Edited by Gerson D. Cohen. 1930. Reprint, Brooklyn, NY: KTAV, 1970 (Hebrew).

Davila, James. *Descenders to the Chariot: The People Behind the Hekhalot Literature*. Supplements to the *Journal for the Study of Judaism* 70. Boston: Brill, 2001.

Dimant, Devorah. "Men as Angels: The Self Image of the Qumran Community." In *Religion and Politics in the Ancient Near East*, edited by Adele Berlin, 93–103. Bethesda: University Press of Maryland, 1996.

Dinur, Benzion. "*Wissenschaft des Judentums.*" In *Encyclopaedia Judaica*, edited by Michael Berenbaum and Fred Skolnik, 21:105–14. 2nd ed. Detroit: Macmillan Reference USA, 2007.

Douglas, Mary. *Leviticus as Literature*. Oxford: Oxford University Press, 2000.

Dweck, Yaacob. *The Scandal of Kabbalah: Leon Modena, Jewish Mysticism, Early Modern Venice*. Jews, Christians, and Muslims from the Ancient to the Modern World 43. Princeton, NJ: Princeton University Press, 2011.

Edmonds, Radcliffe. *Drawing Down the Moon: Magic in the Ancient Greco-Roman World*. Princeton, NJ: Princeton University Press, 2019.

Elizur, Shulamit. "The Congregation in the Synagogue and the Ancient Qedushta." In *Knesset Ezra: Literature and Life in the Synagogue*, edited by Shulamit Elizur, 171–90. Jerusalem: Yad Ben Zvi, 1994.

———. "New Discoveries on the Origin of the Thrilling Piyyut 'U-Netanneh Tokef.'" The National Library of Israel. September 17, 2017. https://blog.nli.org.il/unetanneh_tokef/ (Hebrew).

———. *Sod Meshalshei Qodesh: The Qedushta from Its Origins until the Time of Rabbi El'azar Berabbi Qillir*. Sources for the Study of Jewish Culture 22. Jerusalem: World Union of Jewish Studies: 2019 (Hebrew).

Ellis, T. "Jewish Relics." In *Discoveries in the Ruins of Nineveh and Babylon*. Edited by A. H. Layard. London: John Murray, 1853.

Elman, Yaakov. "Middle Persian Culture and the Babylonian Sages: Accommodation and Resistance in the Shaping of Rabbinic Legal Tradition." In *The Cambridge Companion to the Talmud and Rabbinic Literature*, edited by Charlotte Elisheva Fonrobert and Martin S. Jaffee, 165–97. Cambridge: Cambridge University Press, 2007.

Epstein, Jacob N. "Commentary on Babylonian-Aramaic Words." *Mehkarim beSifrut haTalmud ve-beLeshonot Shemiot* 1 (1921–22): 329–374 (Hebrew).

Epstein, Jacob N., and Ezra Z. Melamed. *Mekhilta de-Rabi Shim'on ben Yohai*. Jerusalem: Mekitse Nirdamim, 1955 (Hebrew).

Epstein, Marc Michael. *Skies of Parchment, Seas of Ink: Jewish Illuminated Manuscripts*. Princeton, NJ: Princeton University Press, 2015.

Eshel, Hanan, and Rivka Leiman. "Jewish Amulets Written on Metal Scrolls." *Journal of Ancient Judaism* 1, no. 2 (2010): 189–99.

Faraj, Ali H., and Marco Moriggi. "Two Incantation Bowls from the Iraq Museum." *Orientalia* 74, no. 1 (2005): 71–82.

Fine, Steven. *Art and Judaism in the Greco-Roman World: Toward a New Jewish Archaeology*. Cambridge: Cambridge University Press, 2005.

Finkelstein, Louis. *Sifre Devarim*. 1939. Reprint, New York: Jewish Theological Seminar, 1969.

Fischer, Alexander A. "Moses and the Exodus-Angel." In *Angels: The Concept of Celestial Beings—Origins, Development and Reception*, edited by Friedrich Reiterer et al., 79–94. New York: de Gruyter, 2007.

Fishbane, Michael. *Biblical Myth and Rabbinic Mythmaking.* Oxford: Oxford University Press, 2003.

Fisher, Clarence Stanley. *Excavations at Nippur.* Stechert, 1905.

Fleischer, Ezra, ed. *The Pizmonim of the Anonymus.* Jerusalem: Israel Academy of Sciences and Humanities, 1974 (Hebrew).

———. "The *Qedusha* of the *Amida* (and other *Qedushot*): Historical, Liturgical, and Ideological Aspects." *Tarbiz* 67, no. 3 (1998): 301–50 (Hebrew).

Flusser, David. *Judaism of the Second Temple Period.* Trans. Azzan Yadin. Grand Rapids, Mich.: Eerdmans, 2007.

———. "There Are Two Ways." In *Jewish Sources in Early Christianity,* 232–52. Tel Aviv: Poalim, 1979 (Hebrew).

Foerster, Gideon. "The Zodiac in Ancient Synagogues and Its Place in Jewish Thought and Literature." *Eretz Israel* 19 (1988): 225–54 (Hebrew).

Foltz, Richard. *Religions of Iran: From Prehistory to the Present.* London: Oneworld Publications, 2013.

Fraade, Steven. "Rabbinic Views on the Practice of Targum, and Multilingualism in the Jewish Galilee of the Third–Sixth Centuries." In *The Galilee in Late Antiquity,* edited by Lee I. Levine, 253–87. New York: Jewish Theological Seminary of America, 1992.

Frankfurter, David. *Evil Incarnate: Rumors of Demonic Conspiracy and Ritual Abuse in History.* Princeton, NJ: Princeton University Press, 2006.

———. "Scorpion/Demon: On the Origin of the Mesopotamian Apotropaic Bowl." *Journal of Near Eastern Studies* 74, no. 1 (2015): 9–18.

Frühauf, Tina. *Experiencing Jewish Music in America: A Listener's Companion.* New York: Rowman & Littlefield, 2018.

Furstenberg, Yair. "The Rabbinic Ban on Ma'aseh Bereshit: Sources, Contexts and Concerns." In *Jewish and Christian Cosmogony in Late Antiquity,* edited by Lance Jenott and Sarit Kattan Gribetz, 39–63. Texts and Studies in Ancient Judaism 155. Tübingen: Mohr Siebeck, 2013.

Gafni, Isaiah. "Babylonian Rabbinic Culture." In *Cultures of the Jews,* edited by David Biale, 223–66. New York: Schocken Books, 2002.

———. "The Political, Social, and Economic History of Babylonian Jewry, 224–638 CE." In *The Cambridge History of Judaism IV: The Late Roman-Rabbinic Period,* edited by Steven T. Katz, 792–820. Cambridge: Cambridge University Press, 2006.

———. "Yeshiva and Metivta." *Zion* 43, nos. 1–2 (1978): 12–37 (Hebrew).

Gardner, Iain. "Manichaean Ritual Practice at Ancient Kellis: A New Understanding of the Meaning and Function of the So-Called Prayer of the Emanations." In *In Search of Truth: Augustine, Manichaeism and Other Gnosticism, Studies for Johannes Van Oort at Sixty,* edited by Jacob Albert van den Berg, Annemaré Kotzé, Tobias Nicklas, and Madeleine Scopello, 245–62. Nag Hammadi and Manichaean Studies 74. Leiden: Brill, 2011.

Geertz, Clifford. *The Interpretation of Cultures.* New York: Basic Books, 1973.

Geller, Markham J. *Joshua b. Perahia and Jesus of Nazareth: Two Rabbinic Magicians.* University Microfilms, 1999.

Gerhards, Albert. "Crossing Borders—the Kedushah and the Sanctus: A Case Study of the Convergence of Jewish and Chrisitan Liturgy." In *Jewish and Christian Liturgy and Worship: New Insights into Its History and Interaction*, edited by Albert Gerhards and Clemens Leonhard, 27–40. Jewish and Christian Perspectives 15. Leiden: Brill, 2007.

Gibson, McGuire. *Excavations at Nippur: Eleventh Season*. Oriental Institute Communications 22. Chicago: University of Chicago Press, 1976.

Goldin, Judah. "Not by Means of an Angel and Not by Means of a Messenger." In *Religions in Antiquity: Essays in Memory of Erwin Ramsdell Goodenough*, edited by Jacob Neusner, 412–24. Leiden: Brill, 1968.

Goldschmidt, Daniel. *Haggadah Shel Pesach Ve-Toledoteha*. Jerusalem: Bialik, 1960 (Hebrew).

Goodblatt, David. *Rabbinic Instruction in Sasanian Babylonia*. Leiden: Brill, 1975.

Gordon, C. H. "Aramaic and Mandaic Magic Bowls." *Archiv Orientální* 9 (1937): 84–106.

———. "Aramaic Incantation Bowls." *Orientalia N.S.* 10 (1941): 116–41, 272–84, 339–60.

———. "Aramaic Magical Bowls in the Istanbul and Baghdad Museums." *Archiv Orientální* 6 (1934): 319–34.

———. "Magic Bowls in the Moriah Collection." *Orientalia N.S.* 53, no. 2 (1984): 220–41.

———. "Two Magic Bowls in Teheran." *Orientalia N.S.* 20 (1951): 306–15.

Gordon, Richard, and Francisco Marco Simón, eds. *Magical Practice in the Latin West: Papers from the International Conference held at the University of Zaragoza, 30 Sept.–1 Oct. 2005*. Religions in the Graeco-Roman World 168. Leiden: Brill, 2010.

Gottstein, Alon Goshen. "The Body as Image of God in Rabbinic Literature." *Harvard Theological Review* 87, no. 2 (1994): 171–95.

Green, Deborah A. *The Aroma of Righteousness: Scent and Seduction in Rabbinic Life and Literature*. University Park: Penn State University Press, 2011.

Gribetz, Sarit Kattan. *Time and Difference in Rabbinic Judaism*. Princeton, NJ: Princeton University Press, 2020.

———. "*Zekhut Imahot*: Mothers, Fathers, and Ancestral Merit in Rabbinic Sources," *Journal for the Study of Judaism* 49, no. 2 (2018): 263–96.

Gross, Simcha. "Rethinking Babylonian Rabbinic Acculturation in the Sasanian Empire." *Journal of Ancient Judaism* 9 (2019): 280–310.

Gruenwald, Ithamar. "Angelic Songs, the Qedushah and the Problem of the Origin of the Hekhalot Literature." In *From Apocalypticism to Gnosticism: Studies in Apocalypticism, Merkavah Mysticism and Gnosticism*, 145–73. Beiträge zur Erforschung des Alten Testaments und des Antiken Judentums 14. New York: Peter Lang, 1988.

Häberl, Charles. "Production and Reception of a Mandaic Incantation." In *Afroasiatic Studies in Memory of Robert Hetzron: Proceedings of the 35th Annual Meeting of the North American Conference on Afroasiatic Linguistics*, edited by Charles Häberl, 130–48. Newcastle upon Tyne: Cambridge Scholars Publishing, 2009.

Hachlili, Rachel. *Ancient Mosaic Pavements: Themes, Issues, and Trends*. Boston: Brill, 2009.

———. *Ancient Synagogues—Archaeology and Art: New Discoveries and Current Research*. Leiden: Brill, 2013.

Halperin, David. *Faces of the Chariot: Early Jewish Responses to Ezekiel's Vision*. Tübingen: J.C.B. Mohr, 1988.

———. "A New Edition of the Hekhalot Literature." *Journal of the American Oriental Society* 104, no. 3 (1984): 543–52.

Hamilton, Gordon. "A New Hebrew-Aramaic Incantation Text from Galilee: 'Rebuking the Sea,'" *Journal of Semitic Studies* 41, no. 2 (Autumn 1996): 215–49.

Hammond, Dorothy. "Magic: A Problem in Semantics." *American Anthropologists* 72, no. 6 (1970): 1349–56.

Hannah, Darrell D. "Guardian Angels and Angelic National Patrons in Second Temple Judaism and Early Christianity." In *Angels: The Concept of Celestial Beings—Origins, Development and Reception*, edited by Friedrich Reiterer et al., 413–35. New York: de Gruyter, 2007.

Harari, Yuval. *Jewish Magic before the Rise of Kabbalah*. Detroit: Wayne State University Press, 2017.

———. "The Sages and the Occult." In *Literature of the Sages II*, edited by Shmuel Safrai, Zeev Safrai, Peter J. Tomson, and Joshua Schwartz, 521–64. *The Literature of the Jewish People in the Period of the Second Temple and the Talmud* 3. Philadelphia: Fortress Press, 2006.

———. "Shaul Shaked on Jewish Magic." In *Studies in Honor of Shaul Shaked*, edited by Yohanan Friedmann and Etan Kohlberg, 19–28. Jerusalem: Academy of Sciences and Humanities, 2019.

Hartenstein, Friedhelm. "Cherubim and Seraphim in the Bible and in the Light of Ancient Near Eastern Sources." In *Angels: The Concept of Celestial Beings—Origins, Development and Reception*, edited by Friedrich Reiterer et al., 155–88. New York: de Gruyter, 2007.

Harviainen, Tapani. "An Aramaic Incantation Bowl from Borsippa: Another Specimen of Eastern Aramaic 'koiné.'" *Studia Orientalia* 51, no. 14 (1981): 3–25.

Hayes, Christine. "'The Torah Was Not Given to Ministering Angels': Rabbinic Aspirationalism." In *Talmudic Transgressions: Engaging the Work of Daniel Boyarin*, edited by Charlotte Elisheva Fonrobert, Ishay Rosen-Zvi, Aharon Shemesh, Moulie Vidas, in collaboration with James Adam Redfield, 123–60. Boston: Brill, 2017.

Hayman, Peter. "Monotheism—A Misused Word in Jewish Studies?" *Journal of Jewish Studies* 42 no. 1 (1991): 1–15.

Herman, Geoffrey. "Babylonia of Pure Lineage: Notes on Babylonian Jewish Toponymy." In *Sources and Interpretation in Ancient Judaism: Studies for Tal Ilan at Sixty*, edited by Meron Piotrkowski, Geoffrey Herman, and Saskia Doenitz, 191–228. Ancient Judaism and Early Christianity 104. Leiden: Brill, 2018.

Hermann, Klaus. "Jewish Mysticism in Byzantium: The Transformation of Merkavah Mysticism in 3 Enoch." In *Hekhalot Literature in Context: From Byzantium to Babylonia*, edited by Ra'anan Boustan, Martha Himmelfarb, and Peter Schäfer, 85–116. Texts and Studies in Ancient Judaism 153. Tübingen: Mohr Siebeck, 2013.

Hezser, Catherine. *Jewish Travel in Antiquity*. Texts and Studies in Ancient Judaism 144. Tübingen: Mohr Siebeck, 2011.

———, ed. *The Oxford Handbook of Jewish Daily Life in Roman Palestine*. Oxford University Press, 2010.

Hilprecht, Hermann Vollrat, Fritz Hommel, Immanuel Benzinger, Peter Jensen, and Georg Steindorff. *Explorations in Bible Lands during the 19th century*. AJ Holman, 1903.

Himmelfarb, Martha. *Ascent to Heaven in Jewish and Christian Apocalypses*. Oxford: Oxford University Press, 1993.

———. "Heavenly Ascent and the Relationship of the Apocalypse and the Hekhalot Literature." *Hebrew Union College Annual* 59 (1988): 73–100.

———. *Jewish Messiahs in a Christian Empire: A History of the Book of Zerubbabel.* Cambridge, Mass.: Harvard University Press, 2017.

———. *A Kingdom of Priests: Ancestry and Merit in Ancient Judaism.* Philadelphia: University of Pennsylvania Press, 2006.

Hoffmann, Tobias, ed. *A Companion to Angels in Medieval Philosophy.* Leiden: Brill, 2012.

Hopkins, Keith. *A World Full of Gods: The Strange Triumph of Christianity.* London: Free Press, 2000.

Horbury, William. "Jewish and Christian Monotheism in the Herodian Age," In *Early Jewish and Christian Monotheism,* edited by Loren Stuckenbruck and Wendy North, 16–44. New York: T & T Clark International, 2004.

Horodezky, Samuel Abba. "Elijah: In Mysticism." In *Encyclopedia Judaica,* edited by Michael Berenbaum and Fred Skolnik, 6:331–37. 2nd ed. Detroit: Macmillan Reference USA, 2007.

Horowitz, Hayim Saul. *Sifre de-bei Rav: Sifrei al sefer Bemidbar ve-Sifrei Zuta: Im hilufei girsa'ot ve-he'arot.* 1966. Reprint, Jerusalem: Shalem Books, 1992 (Hebrew).

Horowitz, Hayim Saul, and Israel Abraham Rabin. *Mekhilta de-Rabi Yishma'el.* 1930. Reprint, Jerusalem: Sifre Vahrman, 1970.

Houtman, Cornelis. *Der Himmel im Alten Testament: Israels Weltbild und Weltanschauung.* Leiden: Brill, 1993.

Hunter, Erica. "Incantation Bowls: A Mesopotamian Phenomenon?" *Orientalia N.S.* 65, no. 3 (1996): 220–33.

———. "Manipulating Incantation Texts: Excursions in Refrain A." *Iraq* 64 (2002): 259–73.

———. "Two Incantation Bowls from Babylon." *Iraq* 62 (2000): 139–47.

———. "Who Are the Demons? The Iconography of Incantation Bowls." *Studi epigrafici e linguistici sul Vicino Oriente antico* 15 (1998): 95–115.

Hutter, Manfred. "Demons and Benevolent Spirits in the Ancient Near East: A Phenomenological Overview." In *Angels: The Concept of Celestial Beings—Origins, Development and Reception,* edited by Friedrich Reiterer et al., 21–34. New York: de Gruyter, 2007.

Idel, Moshe. "Holding an Orb in His Hand: The Angel 'Anafiel and a Late Antiquity Helios Mosaic." *Ars Judaica* 9 (2013): 19–44.

Ilan, Tal. *Lexicon of Jewish Names in Late Antiquity II: Palestine 200–650.* Texts and Studies in Ancient Judaism 148. Tübingen: Mohr Siebeck, 2012.

———. *Silencing the Queen: The Literary Histories of Shelamzion and Other Jewish Women.* Texts and Studies in Ancient Judaism 115. Tübingen: Mohr Siebeck, 2006.

Isbell, Charles. *Corpus of the Aramaic Incantation Bowls.* Missoula, Mont.: Scholars Press, 1975.

———. "The Story of the Aramaic Incantation Bowls." *The Biblical Archaeologist* 41, no. 1 (1978): 5–16.

———. "Two New Aramaic Bowls." *Bulletin of the American Schools of Oriental Research* 223 (1976): 15–23.

Jaffee, Martin, trans. *Sifre Devarim.* Seattle, WA: Stroum Center for Jewish Studies, 2016. *https://jewishstudies.washington.edu/book/sifre-devarim/.*

Jastrow, Marcus. *A Dictionary of the Targumim, the Talmud Babli, and Yerushalmi, and the Midrashic Literature*. Luzac, 1903. Reprint, Peabody, MA: Hendrickson, 1943.

Jones, David Albert. *Angels: A History*. Oxford: Oxford University Press, 2010.

Juusola, Hannu. "Who Wrote the Syriac Incantation Bowls?" *Studia Orientalia Electronica* 85 (1999): 75–92.

Kaduri, Yaakov. "Windy and Fiery Angels: Prerabbinic and Rabbinic Interpretations of Psalm 104:4." In *Tradition, Transmission, and Transformation from Second Temple Literature through Judaism and Christianity in Late Antiquity*, edited by Menahem Kister, Hillel Newman, Michael Segal, and Ruth Clements, 134–49. Studies on the Texts of the Desert of Judah 113. Leiden: Brill, 2015.

Kalmin, Richard. "The Evil Eye in Rabbinic Literature of Late Antiquity." In *Judaea-Palaestina, Babylon and Rome: Jews in Antiquity*, edited by Benjamin Isaac and Yuval Shahar, 11–28. Texts and Studies in Ancient Judaism 147. Tübingen: Mohr Siebeck, 2012.

Kasher, Rimon. "The Conception of Angels in Jewish Biblical Translations." In *Angels: The Concept of Celestial Beings—Origins, Development and Reception*, edited by Friedrich Reiterer et al., 555–84. New York: de Gruyter, 2007.

Kassim, Husain. "Nothing Can Be Known or Done without the Involvement of Angels: Angels and Angelology in Islam and Islamic Literature." In *Angels: The Concept of Celestial Beings—Origins, Development and Reception*, edited by Friedrich Reiterer et al., 645–62. New York: de Gruyter, 2007.

Kaufman, Stephen A. "A Unique Magic Bowl from Nippur." *Journal of Near Eastern Studies* 32, nos. 1–2 (1973): 170–74.

Kaufmann, Yehezkel. *The Religion of Israel*. Translated and abridged by Moshe Greenberg. Chicago: Chicago University Press, 1960.

Kedar, Dorit. "Who Wrote the Incantation Bowls." PhD Diss., Freie Universität Berlin, 2018.

Kellner, Menachem. *Maimonides' Confrontation with Mysticism*. Littman Library of Jewish Civilization. Liverpool University Press, 2006.

Kiourtzian, Georges. *Recueil des inscriptions grecques chretiennes des Cyclades: De la fin du IIIe au VIIe siècle après J.-C.* Paris: de Boccard, 2000.

Kister, Menahem. "Metatron, God, and the Problem of the Two Powers: Investigating the Dynamics of a Tradition, Interpretation, and Polemics." *Tarbiz* 82, no. 1 (2013): 43–88 (Hebrew).

Knibb, Michael A. *The Qumran Community*. Vol. 2. Cambridge: Cambridge University Press, 1987.

Knohl, "Sacred Architecture: The Numerical Dimensions of Biblical Poems." *Vetus Testamentum* 62, no. 2 (2012): 189–97.

Köckert, Matthias. "Divine Messengers and Mysterious Men in the Patriarchal Narratives of the Book of Genesis." In *Angels: The Concept of Celestial Beings—Origins, Development and Reception*, edited by Friedrich Reiterer et al., 51–78. New York: de Gruyter, 2007.

Koltun-Fromm, Naomi. "Aphrahat and the Rabbis on Noah's Righteousness in Light of the Jewish and Christian Polemic." In *The Book of Genesis in Jewish and Oriental Christian Interpretation: A Collection of Essays*, edited by Judith Frishman and Lucas Van Rompay, 57–71. Traditio Exegetica Graeca 5. Louvain: Peeters, 1997.

Kosior, Wojciech. "A Tale of Two Sisters: The Image of Eve in Early Rabbinic Literature and Its Influence on the Portrayal of Lilith in the Alphabet of Ben Sira." *Nashim: A Journal of Jewish Women's Studies & Gender Issues* 32 (2018): 112–30.

Kotansky, Roy. "A Jewish Liturgical Fever-Amulet." In *Greek Magical Amulets: The Inscribed Gold, Silver, Copper, and Bronze Lamellae—Part I Published Texts of Known Provenance*, edited by Roy Kotansky, 312–25. *Papyrologica Coloniensia* 22, no. 1. Opladen: Westdeutscher Verlag, 1994.

———. "Two Inscribed Jewish Aramaic Amuelts from Syria." *Israel Exploration Journal* 41, no. 4 (1991): 267–81.

Kraemer, Joel L. "Women Speak for Themselves." In *The Cambridge Genizah Collections: Their Contents and Significance*, edited by Stefan C Reif and Shulamit Reif, 178–216. Cambridge: Cambridge University Press, 2002.

Krueger, Derek. *Writing and Holiness: The Practice of Authorship in the Early Christian East*. Divinations: Rereading Late Ancient Religion. Philadelphia: University of Pennsylvania Press, 2011.

Labuschagne, Casper. "Significant Compositional Techniques in the Psalms: Evidence for the Use of Number as an Organizing Principle." *Vetus Testamentum* 59 (2009): 583–605.

Langer, Ruth. "Revisiting Early Rabbinic Liturgy: The Recent Contributions of Ezra Fleischer." *Prooftexts* 19, no. 2 (2000): 179–94.

———. *To Worship God Properly*. Cincinnati: Hebrew Union College Press, 1998.

Lapin, Hayim. "Epigraphical Rabbis: A Reconsideration." *Jewish Quarterly Review* 101, no. 3 (2011): 311–46.

Lauterbach, Jacob Z. *Mekhilta De-Rabbi Ishmael*. 2 vols. 1933. Reprint, Philadelphia: Jewish Publication Society, 2004.

Layard, A. H., ed. *Discoveries in the Ruins of Nineveh and Babylon*. London: John Murray, 1853.

Lesses, Rebecca. "Exe(o)rcising Power: Women as Sorceresses, Exorcists, and Demonesses in Babylonian Jewish Society of Late Antiquity." *Journal of the American Academy of Religion* 69, no. 2 (2001): 343–75.

———. *Ritual Practices to Gain Power: Angels, Incantations, and Revelation in Early Jewish Mysticism*. Harvard Theological Studies 44. Cambridge, MA: Harvard University Press, 1998.

———. "Speaking with Angels: Jewish and Greco-Egyptian Revelatory Adjurations." *The Harvard Theological Review* 89, no. 1 (1996): 41–60.

———. "Women and Gender in Hekhalot Literature." In *Hekhalot Literature in Context: From Byzantium to Babylonia*, edited by Ra'anan Boustan, Martha Himmelfarb, and Peter Schäfer, 279–312. Texts and Studies in Ancient Judaism 153. Tübingen: Mohr Siebeck, 2013.

Levene, Dan. *A Corpus of Magic Bowls: Incantation Texts in Jewish Aramaic from Late Antiquity*. London: Kegan Paul, 2003.

———. "Curse or Blessing: What's in the Magic Bowl?" Pamphlet. Southampton, UK: Parkes Institute, 2002.

———. "Heal O' Israel: A Pair of Duplicate Magic Bowls from the Pergamon Museum in Berlin." *Journal of Jewish studies* 54, no. 1 (2003): 104–21.

———. *Jewish Aramaic Curse Texts from Late-Antique Mesopotamia.* Magical and Religious Literature of Late Antiquity 2. Leiden: Brill, 2013.

Levene, Dan, and Siam Bhayro. "'Bring to the Gates . . . Upon a Good Smell and Upon Good Fragrances': An Aramaic Incantation Bowl for Success in Business." *Archiv für Orientforschung* 51 (2005/2006): 242–46.

Levene, Dan, Dalia Marx, and Siam Bhayro. "'Gabriel Is on Their Right': Angelic Protection in Jewish Magic and Babylonian Lore." *Studia Mesopotamica: Jahrbuch für altorientalische Geschichte und Kultur* 1 (2014): 185–98.

Levine, Lee I. *The Ancient Synagogue: The First Thousand Years.* New Haven, Conn.: Yale University Press, 2005.

Lewis, Albert L. "Shofar." In *Encyclopaedia Judaica,* edited by Michael Berenbaum and Fred Skolnik, 18:506–8. Detroit: Macmillan Reference USA, 2007.

Lieber, Laura. "Daru in the Winehouse: The Intersection of Status and Dance in the Jewish East." *The Journal of Religion* 98, no. 1 (2018): 90–113.

———. "The Exegesis of Love: Text and Context in the Poetry of the Early Synagogue." *Review of Rabbinic Judaism* 11, no. 1 (2008): 73–99.

———. "Portraits of Righteousness: Noah in Early Christian and Jewish Hymnography" *Zeitschrift für Religions und Geistesgeschichte* 61, no. 4 (2009): 332–55.

———. *Yannai on Genesis: An Invitation to Piyyut.* Cincinnati: Hebrew Union College Press, 2010.

Lieberman, Saul, ed. *Tosefta Ki-Feshutah.* 10 vols. New York: Jewish Theological Seminary, 1955–88 (Hebrew).

Lightstone, Jack. *Commerce of the Sacred: Mediation of the Divine Among Jews in the Graeco-Roman Diaspora.* 1984. Reprint, New York: Columbia University Press, 2006.

Lindbeck, Kristen H. *Elijah and the Rabbis: Story and Theology.* New York: Columbia University Press, 2010.

Lorberbaum, Yair. *In God's image: Myth, Theology, and Law in Classical Judaism.* New York: Cambridge University Press, 2015.

Mach, Michael. *Entwicklungsstadien des jüdischen Engelglaubens in vorrabbinischer Zeit.* Texte und Studien zum Antiken Judentum 34. Tübingen: Mohr Siebeck, 1992.

Magness, Jodi. "Heaven on Earth: Helios and the Zodiac Cycle in Ancient Palestinian Synagogues." *Dumbarton Oaks Papers* 59 (2005): 1–52.

Maier, John. "'Attah hu' Adon (Hekhalot Rabbati XXVI 5)." *Judaica* 21 (1965): 129–33.

Malandra, William. *An Introduction to Ancient Iranian Religion: Readings from the Avesta and the Achaemenid Inscriptions.* Minneapolis: University of Minnesota Press, 1983.

Malingrey, Anne-Marie, ed. *Sur la Sacredoce.* Sources Chrétiennes 272. Paris: Éditions du Cerf, 1980.

Manekin-Bamberger, Avigail. "Jewish Legal Formulae in the Aramaic Incantation Bowls." *Aramaic Studies* 13 (2015): 69–81.

———. "The Vow-Curse in Ancient Jewish Texts." *Harvard Theological Review* 112, no. 3 (2019): 340–57.

———. "Who Were the Jewish 'Magicians' behind the Aramaic Incantation Bowls?" *Journal of Jewish Studies* 71, no. 2 (2020): 235–54.

Margalioth, Mordecai. *Midrash va-yikra rabah* (*Leviticus Rabbah*). 5 vols. 1953–1960. Reprint, Jerusalem: Keren Yehuda, 1972 (Hebrew).

———. *Sefer Ha-Razim: A Book of Magic from the Talmudic Period.* Tel Aviv: Yediot Ahronot, 1966 (Hebrew).

Marmorstein, Arthur. *The Old Rabbinic Doctrine of God.* 2 vols. Oxford University Press, 1937 and 1969.

Martin, Dale. "When Did Angels Become Demons?" *Journal of Biblical Literature* 129, no. 4 (2010): 657–77.

Martinez, Florentino Garcia. *The Dead Sea Scrolls Translated: The Qumran Texts in English.* Leiden: Brill, 1994.

McCollough, Thomas, and Beth Glazier-McDonald. "Magic and Medicine in Byzantine Galilee: A Bronze Amulet from Sepphoris." In *Archaeology and the Galilee: Texts and Contexts in the Graeco-Roman and Byzantine Period*, edited by D. R. Edwards and C. T. McCollough, 43–49. Atlanta, GA: Scholars Press, 1997.

McGuckin, John Anthony. "Poetry and Hymnography." In *The Oxford Handbook of Early Christian Studies*, edited by Susan Ashbrook Harvey, 641–56. Oxford: Oxford University Press, 2008.

McNamara, Martin, trans. and ed. *The Aramaic Bible: Targum Neofiti 1: Genesis.* Collegeville, Minn.: Liturgical Press, 1992.

Melammed, Renée Levine, and Uri Melammed. "Epistolary Exchanges with Women." *Jewish History* 32 (2019): 411–18.

Meyer, Marvin. "The Prayer of Mary in the Magical Book of Mary and the Angels." In *Prayer, Magic, and the Stars in the Ancient and Late Antique World*, edited by Scott Noegel, Joel Walker, and Brannon Wheeler, 57–68. University Park: Pennsylvania State University Press, 2003.

Meyer, Marvin and Richard Smith. *Ancient Christian Magic: Coptic Texts of Ritual Power.* Princeton, NJ: Princeton University Press, 1999.

Meyers, Carol L., and Eric M. Meyers *Haggai, Zechariah 1–8: A New Translation with Introduction and Commentary.* Garden City, NY: Doubleday, 1987.

Miller, Michael. "Folk-Etymology, and Its Influence on Metatron Traditions." *Journal for the Study of Judaism* 44, no. 3 (2013): 339–55.

Miller, Stuart S. "'Epigraphical' Rabbis, Helios, and Psalm 19." *Jewish Quarterly Review* 94, no. 1 (2004): 27–76.

Montgomery, James. *Aramaic Incantation Texts from Nippur.* Philadelphia, 1913.

———. "Some Early Amulets from Palestine." *Journal of the American Oriental Society* 31, no. 3 (1911): 273–79.

Morgan, Michael, trans. *Sepher Ha-Razim: The Book of the Mysteries.* Chico, CA: Scholars Press, 1983.

Moriggi, Marco. *A Corpus of Syriac Incantation Bowls: Syriac Magical Texts from Late-Antique Mesopotamia. Magical and Religious Literature of Late Antiquity 3.* Leiden: Brill, 2013.

Morony, Michael. "Magic and Society in Late Sasanian Iraq." In *Prayer, Magic, and the Stars in the Ancient and Late Antique World*, edited by Scott Noegel and Joel Walker, 83–107. University Park: Pennsylvania State University Press, 2003.

———. "Religion and the Aramaic Incantation Bowls." *Religion Compass* (2007): 414–29.

Muehlberger, Ellen. *Angels in Late Ancient Christianity.* Oxford: Oxford University Press, 2013.

Müller-Kessler, Christa. "Die Zauberschalensammlung des British Museum." *Archiv fur Orientforschung* 48–49 (2001–2002): 115–45.

Müller-Kessler, Christa, and Theodore Kwasman. "A Unique Talmudic Aramaic Incantation Bowl." *Journal of the American Oriental Society* 120, no. 2 (2000): 159–65.

Münz-Manor, Ophir. "All About Sarah: Questions of Gender in Yannai's Poems on Sarah's (and Abraham's) Barrenness." *Prooftexts* 26, no. 3 (2006): 344–74.

———. "*In Situ*: Liturgical Poetry and Sacred Space in Late Antiquity." In *Placing Ancient Texts: The Rhetorical and Ritual Use of Space,* edited by Mika Ahuvia and Alexander Koçar, 87–100. Texts and Studies in Ancient Judaism 174. Tübingen: Mohr Siebeck, 2018.

———. "Liturgical Poetry in the Late Antique Near East: A Comparative Approach." *Journal of Ancient Judaism* 1, no. 3 (2010): 336–61.

———. "A Prolegomenon to the Study of Hekhalot Traditions in European Piyyut." In *Hekhalot Literature in Context: From Byzantium to Babylonia,* edited by Ra'anan Boustan, Martha Himmelfarb, and Peter Schäfer, 231–42. Texts and Studies in Ancient Judaism 153. Tübingen: Mohr Siebeck, 2013.

Naveh, Joseph, and Shaul Shaked. *Amulets and Magic Bowls: Aramaic Incantations of Late Antiquity.* Jerusalem: Magnes Press, 1985.

———. *Magic Spells and Formulae: Aramaic Incantations of Late Antiquity.* Jerusalem: Magness Press, 1993.

Neis, Rachel. *The Sense of Sight in Rabbinic Culture.* Cambridge: Cambridge University Press, 2013.

Nelson, David, ed. and trans. *Mekhilta De-Rabbi Shimon Bar Yohai.* New York: Jewish Publication Society, 2006.

Neusner, Jacob. *A History of the Jews in Babylonia.* 5 vols. Leiden: Brill, 1966.

Neusner, Jacob, and Richard Sarason, trans. and ed. *The Tosefta.* 6 vols. New York: Ktav, 1977–86.

Newsom, Carol. "Angels: Old Testament." In *Anchor Bible Dictionary.* New York: Doubleday, 1992.

———. "'He Has Established for Himself Priests': Human and Angelic Priesthood in the Qumran Sabbath *Shirot*." In *Archaeology and History in the Dead Sea Scrolls.* Edited by Lawrence H. Schiffman, 101–20. Sheffield: Sheffield Academic Press, 1990.

———. *Songs of the Sabbath Sacrifice: A Critical Edition.* Atlanta: Scholars Press, 1985.

Nickelsburg, George W. E., and James C. Vanderkam, *1 Enoch: The Hermeneia Translation.* Minneapolis: Fortress Press, 2012.

Noegel, Scott. "On the Wings of the Winds: Towards an Understanding of Winged Mischwesen in the ancient Near East." *Kaskal* 14 (2017): 15–54.

Novick, Michael Tzvi. "'Who resembles you? But they resemble you': Israel and the Apophatic in Yannai." *Journal of Jewish Studies* 63, no. 2 (2012): 263–84.

Noy, David, Alexander Panayotov, and Hanswulf Bloedhorn, eds. *Inscriptiones Judaicae Orientis: Eastern Europe.* Texts and Studies in Ancient Judaism 101. Tübingen: Mohr Siebeck, 2004.

Obermann, Julian. "Two Magic Bowls: New Incantation Texts from Mesopotamia." *American Journal of Semitic Languages and Literatures* 57, no. 1 (1940): 1–31.

Olyan, Saul. *A Thousand Thousands Served Him: Exegesis and the Naming of Angels in Ancient Judaism*. Texts and Studies in Ancient Judaism 36. Tübingen: Mohr Siebeck, 1993.

Oppenheimer, Aharon. *Babylonia Judaica in the Talmudic Period*. Wiesbaden: L. Reichert Verlag, 1983.

———. *Between Rome and Babylon: Studies in Jewish Leadership and Society*. Edited by Nili Oppenheimer. Texts and Studies in Ancient Judaism 108. Tubingen: Mohr Siebeck, 2005.

Orlov, Andrei. *The Enoch-Metatron Tradition*. Texts and Studies in Ancient Judaism 107. Tubingen: Mohr Siebeck, 2005.

———. *Yahoel and Metatron: Aural Apocalypticism and the Origins of Early Jewish Mysticism*. Texts and Studies in Ancient Judaism 169. Tübingen: Mohr Siebeck, 2017.

Orsi, Robert A. *Between Heaven and Earth: The Religious Worlds People Make and the Scholars Who Study Them*. Princeton, NJ: Princeton University Press, 2005.

———. *History and Presence*. Cambridge, MA: Harvard University Press, 2016.

Paz, Yakir. "'Meishan Is Dead': On the Historical Contexts of the Bavli's Representations of the Jews in Southern Babylonia." In *The Aggada of the Bavli and Its Cultural World*, edited by Geoffrey Herman and Jeffrey Rubenstein, 47–99. Providence, RI: Brown University Press, 2018.

———. "Metatron Is Not Enoch: Reevaluating the Evolution of an Archangel. *Journal for the Study of Judaism* 50 (2019): 1–49.

Peers, Glenn. *Subtle Bodies: Representing Angels in Byzantium*. Los Angeles: University of California Press, 2001.

Peeters, John. *Nippur; or, Explorations and Adventures on the Euphrates*. Philadelphia: University of Pennsylvania, 1904.

Prothero, Stephen. *Religious Literacy: What Every American Needs to Know and Doesn't*. New York: Harper, 2007.

Quine, Cat. "The Host of Heaven and the Divine Army: A Reassessment." *Journal of Biblical Literature* 138, no. 4 (2019): 741–55.

Rabinowitz, Mayer. "Status of Transsexuals," *Committee on Jewish Law and Standards of the Rabbinical Assembly* (YD 336.2003).

Rabinovitz, Zvi Meir. *The Liturgical Poems of Rabbi Yannai*. 2 volumes. Jerusalem: Bialik, 1985 (Hebrew).

Rainbow, Jesse. "The Song of Songs and the Testament of Solomon: Solomon's Love Poetry and Christian Magic." *Harvard Theological Review* 100, no. 3 (2007): 249–74.

Rand, Michael. "More on the Seder Beriyot." *Jewish Studies Quarterly* 16, no. 2 (2009): 183–209.

Ratzon, Eshbal "Placing Eden in Second Temple Judaism." In *Placing Ancient Texts: The Rhetorical and Ritual Use of Space*, edited by Mika Ahuvia and Alexander Koçar, 15–52. Texts and Studies in Ancient Judaism 174. Tübingen: Mohr Siebeck, 2018.

Rebiger, Bill. "Angels in Rabbinic Literature." In *Angels: The Concept of Celestial Beings— Origins, Development and Reception*, edited by Friedrich Reiterer et al., 629–44. New York: de Gruyter, 2007.

———. "Engel und Dämonen im rabbinischen Denken und in der jüdischen Magie." *Chilufim* 25 (2019): 3–38.

Reed, Annette Yoshiko. *Fallen Angels and the History of Judaism and Christianity*. Cambridge: Cambridge University Press, 2005.

Reeves, John, and Annette Yoshiko Reed, eds. *Enoch from Antiquity to the Middle Ages: Sources from Judaism, Christianity, and Islam*. 2 vols. Oxford: Oxford University Press, 2018.

Reif, Stefan C. "Some Liturgical Issues in the Talmudic Sources." *Studia Liturgica* 15 (1982): 188–206.

Reiterer, Friedrich, Tobias Nicklas, and Karin Schöpflin, eds. *Angels: The Concept of Celestial Beings—Origins, Development and Reception*. New York: de Gruyter, 2007.

Rofé, Alexander. *Angels in the Bible: Israelite Belief in Angels as Evidenced by Biblical Traditions*. Jerusalem: Carmel, 2012.

———. *The Belief in Angels in the Bible and in Early Israel*. 2 vols. Jerusalem: Hotsa'at Makor, 1979 (Hebrew).

Rollston, Christopher A. "The Crisis of Modern Epigraphic Forgeries and the Antiquities Market: A Palaeographer Reflects on the Problem and Proposes Protocols for the Field." *SBL Forum* (2005): 1–8.

Ronis, Sara. "Do Not Go Out Alone at Night: Law and Demonic Discourse in the Babylonian Talmud." PhD Diss., Yale University, 2015.

Rosen, Tova, and Eli Yassif. "Hebrew Literature in the Middle Ages." In *The Oxford Handbook of Jewish Studies*, edited by Martin Goodman and Jeremy Cohen, 241–94. Oxford: Oxford University Press, 2002.

Rosen-Zvi, Ishay. *Demonic Desires: "Yetzer Hara" and the Problem of Evil in Late Antiquity*. Divinations: Rereading Late Ancient Religion. Philadelphia: University of Pennsylvania Press, 2011.

Rubenstein, Jeffrey. *Rabbinic Stories*. New York: Paulist Press, 2002.

Saar, Ortal-Paz. *Jewish Love Magic: From Late Antiquity to the Middle Ages*. Magical and Religious Literature of Late Antiquity 6. Boston: Brill, 2017.

Sanzo, Joseph, and Ra'anan Boustan. "Christian Magicians, Jewish Magical Idioms, and the Shared Magical Culture of Late Antiquity." *Harvard Theological Review* 110, no. 2 (2017): 217–40.

Schäfer, Peter. "Engel und Menschen in der Hekhalot-Literatur." *Karios* 22 (1980): 201–25.

———. *Hekhalot-Studien*. Tübingen: J.C.B. Mohr, 1988.

———. *The Hidden and Manifest God: Some Major Themes in Early Jewish Mysticism*. Translated by Aubrey Pomerance. SUNY Series in Judaica. Albany: State University of New York Press, 1992.

———. "In Heaven as It Is in Hell: The Cosmology of *Seder Rabbah Di-Bereshit*." In *Heavenly Realms and Earthly Realities in Late Antique Religions*, edited by Ra'anan Boustan and Annette Yoshiko Reed, 233–74. Cambridge: Cambridge University Press, 2004.

———. *Jesus in the Talmud*. Princeton, NJ: Princeton University Press, 2007.

———. *The Jewish Jesus: How Judaism and Christianity Shaped Each Other*. Princeton, NJ: Princeton University Press, 2012.

———. "Jewish Liturgy and Magic." In *Geschichte-Tradition-Reflexion: Festschrift Fur Martin Hengel Zum 70*, edited by Hubert Cancik, Hermann Lichtenberger, and Peter Schäfer, 541–55. Tubingen: JCB Mohr, 1996.

———. "Jewish Magic Literature in Late Antiquity and the Early Middle Ages." *Journal of Jewish Studies* 41 (1990): 75–91.

———. "Magic and Religion in Ancient Judaism." In *Envisioning Magic: A Princeton Seminar and Symposium*, edited by Peter Schäfer and Hans Kippenberg, 19–43. Boston: Brill, 1997.

———. *The Origins of Jewish Mysticism*. Princeton, NJ: Princeton University Press, 2009.

———. *Rivalität zwischen Engeln und Menschen: Untersuchungen zur Rabbinischen Engelvorstellung*. Berlin: de Gruyter, 1975.

Schäfer, Peter, and Hans-Jürgen Becker. *Synopse zum Talmud Yerushalmi*. Texte und Studien zum Antiken Judentum. Tübingen: Mohr-Siebeck, 1991–2000.

Schäfer, Peter, and Bill Rebiger. *Sefer ha-Razim*. Texts and Studies in Ancient Judaism 125 and 132. 2 Vols. Tübingen: Mohr Siebeck 2009.

Schäfer, Peter, Margarete Schlüter, and Hans-Georg von Mutius. *Synopse Zur Hekhalot-Literatur*. Texte Und Studien Zum Antiken Judentum 2. Tübingen: J.C.B. Mohr, 1981.

Schäfer, Peter, and Shaul Shaked. *Magische Texte Aus Der Kairoer Geniza*. Texts and Studies in Ancient Judaism 42. Tübingen: JCB Mohr, 1994.

Schiffman, Lawrence H., and Michael D. Swartz. *Hebrew and Aramaic Incantation Texts from the Cairo Genizah: Selected Texts from Taylor-Schechter Box K1*. Semitic Texts and Studies 1. Sheffield, England: JSOT Press, 1992.

Schipper, Bernd. "Angels or Demons? Divine Messengers in Ancient Egypt." In *Angels: The Concept of Celestial Beings—Origins, Development and Reception*, edited by Friedrich Reiterer et al., 1–20. New York: de Gruyter, 2007.

Scholem, Gershom. *Jewish Gnosticism, Merkabah Mysticism, and Talmudic Tradition*. New York: The Jewish Theological Seminary of America, 1960.

———. "Magen David." In the *Encyclopaedia Judaica*, edited by Michael Berenbaum and Fred Skolnik, 13:336–39. 2nd ed. Detroit: Macmillan Reference USA, 2007.

———. *Major Trends in Jewish Mysticism*. New York: Schocken, 1946.

Schultz, Joseph. "Angelic Opposition to the Ascension of Moses and the Revelation of the Law." *Jewish Quarterly Review* 61 (1970/71): 282–307.

Schwartz, Howard. "The Book of Raziel." In *Tree of Souls: The Mythology of Judaism*, 253–55. Oxford: Oxford University Press, 2004.

———. *Gabriel's Palace: Jewish Mystical Tales*. Oxford: Oxford University Press, 1994.

Schwartz, Seth. *Imperialism and Jewish Society: 200 B.C.E. to 640 C.E.* Princeton, NJ: Princeton University Press, 2001.

———. "The Political Geography of Rabbinic Texts." In *The Cambridge Companion to the Talmud and Rabbinic Literature*, edited by Charlotte Elisheva Fonrobert and Martin S. Jaffee, 75–96. Cambridge: Cambridge University Press, 2007.

Scurlock, "Popular Religion and Magic: Ancient Near East." In *The Oxford Encyclopedia of the Bible and Gender Studies*. Edited by Julia O'Brien. Oxford: Oxford University Press, 2014.

Secunda, Shai. *The Iranian Talmud: Reading the Bavli in Its Sasanian Context*. Divinations: Rereading Late Ancient Religion. Philadelphia: University of Pennsylvania Press, 2013.

Segal, J. B., and Erica Hunter. *Catalogue of the Aramaic and Mandaic Incantation Bowls in the British Museum*. London: British Museum, 2000.

Seng, Helmut. "Demons and Angels in the Chaldean Oracles." In *Neoplatonic Demons and Angels*, edited by Luc Brisson, Seamus O'Neill, and Andrei Timotin, 46–85. Studies in Platonism, Neoplatonism, and the Platonic Tradition 20. Leiden: Brill, 2018.

Septimus, Gerald. "On the Boundaries of Prayer: Talmudic Ritual Texts with Addressees Other Than God." PhD diss., Yale University, 2008.

Shaked, Shaul. *Dualism in Transformation: Varieties of Religion in Sasanian Iran*. Jordan Lectures in Comparative Religion 16. London: School of Oriental and African Studies, 1994.

———. "Form and Purpose in Aramaic Spells: Some Jewish Themes." In *Officina Magica: Essays on the Practice of Magic in Antiquity*, edited by Shaul Shaked, 1–30. Leiden: Brill, 2005.

———. "Medieval Jewish Magic in Relation to Islam: Theoretical Attitudes and Genres." In *Judaism and Islam: Boundaries, Communications and Interaction: Essays in Honor of William M. Brinner*, edited by Benjamin H. Hary, John L. Hayes, and Fred Astren, 97–109. Leiden: Brill, 2000.

———. "'Peace Be Upon You, Exalted Angels': On Hekhalot, Liturgy, and Incantation Bowls." *Jewish Studies Quarterly* 2 (1995): 197–219.

———. "The Poetics of Spells. Language and Structure in Aramaic Incantations of Late Antiquity." In *Mesopotamian Magic: Textual, Historical, and Interpretative Perspectives*, edited by Tzvi Abusch and Karel van der Toorn, 173–95. Groningen: Styx Publications, 1999.

———. "Rabbis in Incantation Bowls." In *The Archaeology and Material Culture of the Babylonian Talmud*, edited by Markham Geller, 97–120. Boston: Brill, 2015.

Shaked, Shaul, James Nathan Ford, and Siam Bhayro, eds. *Aramaic Bowl Spells: Jewish Babylonian Aramaic Bowls*. Magical and Religious Literature of Late Antiquity 1. Leiden: Brill, 2013.

Shaw, Gregory. *Theurgy and the Soul: The Neoplatonism of Iamblichus*. University Park: Penn State University Press, 1995.

Shinan, Avigdor. "The Angelology of the 'Palestinian' Targums on the Pentateuch." *Sefarad* 43, no. 2 (1983): 181–98.

Smith, Morton, ed. and trans. *Hekhalot Rabbati: The Greater Treatise Concerning the Palaces of Heaven*. Corrected by Gershom Scholem and transcribed by Don Karr. Public domain, 2009.

———. "Helios in Palestine." *Eretz-Israel* 16 (1982): 199–214.

Sokoloff, Michael. *A Dictionary of Jewish Babylonian Aramaic of the Talmudic and Geonic Periods*. Baltimore: The Johns Hopkins University Press, 2002.

———, ed. *The Geniza Fragments of Bereshit Rabba*. Jerusalem: Israel Academy of Sciences and Humanities, 1982.

Sokoloff, Michael, and Joseph Yahalom. *Jewish Palestinian Aramaic Poetry from Late Antiquity*. Jerusalem: Publications of the Israel Academy of Sciences and Humanities, 1999 (Hebrew).

Speyer, Wolfgang. "The Divine Messenger in Ancient Greece, Etruria and Rome." In *Angels: The Concept of Celestial Beings—Origins, Development and Reception*, edited by Friedrich Reiterer et al., 35–47. New York: de Gruyter, 2007.

Steinberg, Jonah. "Angelic Israel: Self-Identification with Angels in Rabbinic Agadah and Its Jewish Antecedents." PhD diss., Columbia University, 2003.

Stern, David, and Mark Jay Mirsky, eds. *Rabbinic Fantasies: Imaginative Narratives from Classical Hebrew Literature*. New Haven, CT: Yale University Press, 1998.

Stern, Karen. "Harnessing the Sacred: Hidden Writing and 'Private' Spaces in Levantine Synagogues." In *Inscriptions in the Private Sphere in the Greco-Roman World*, edited by Rebecca Benefiel and Peter Keegan, 213–47. Brill, 2016

———. "Mapping Devotion in Roman Dura Europos: A Reconsideration of the Synagogue Ceiling." *American Journal of Archaeology* (2010): 473–504.

Stökl Ben Ezra, Daniel. *The Impact of Yom Kippur on Early Christianity*. Wissenschaftliche Untersuchungen zum Neuen Testament 163. Tübingen: JCB Mohr, 2003.

Stone, Michael E., Aryeh Amihay, and Vered Hillel, eds. *Noah and His Book(s)*. Atlanta, GA: SBL, 2010.

Stuckenbruck, Loren. *The Myth of Rebellious Angels: Studies in Second Temple Judaism and New Testament Texts*. Grand Rapids: Eerdmans Publishing Co., 2017.

Swartz, Michael D. *Hebrew and Aramaic Incantation Texts from the Cairo Genizah*. Vol. 1. London: A & C Black, 1992.

———. "Jewish Magic in Late Antiquity." In *The Cambridge History of Judaism IV: The Late Roman Period*, edited by Steven T. Katz, 699–720. Cambridge: Cambridge University Press, 2006.

———. "Jewish Visionary Tradition in Rabbinic Literature." In *The Cambridge Companion to the Talmud and Rabbinic Literature*, edited by Charlotte Elisheva Fonrobert and Martin S. Jaffee, 198–221. Cambridge: Cambridge University Press, 2007.

———. "'Like the Ministering Angels': Ritual and Purity in Early Jewish Mysticism." *AJS Review* 19 (1994): 135–67. Reprinted in *The Mechanics of Providence: The Workings of Ancient Jewish Magic and Mysticism*. Texts and Studies in Ancient Judaism 172. Tübingen: Mohr Siebeck, 2018.

———. *The Mechanics of Providence: The Workings of Ancient Jewish Magic and Mysticism*. Texts and Studies in Ancient Judaism 172. Tübingen: Mohr Siebeck, 2018.

———. *Mystical Prayer in Ancient Judaism: An Analysis of Maaseh Merkavah*. Texts and Studies in Ancient Judaism 28. Tübingen: Mohr Siebeck, 1992.

———. "Mystical Texts." In *The Literature of the Sages*, edited by Shmuel Safrai, 2:393–420. Philadelphia: Fortress Press, 1987.

———. *Scholastic Magic: Ritual and Revelation in Early Jewish Mysticism*. Princeton, NJ: Princeton University Press, 1996.

———. "Three-Dimensional Philology: Some Implications of the *Synopse zur Hekhalot-Literatur*." In *Envisioning Judaism: Studies in Honor of Peter Schäfer on the Occasion of his Seventieth Birthday*, edited by Ra'anan Boustan, Klaus Herrmann, Reimund Leicht, Annette Yoshiko Reed, and Giuseppe Veltri, 1:529–50. Tübingen: Mohr Siebeck, 2013.

———. "Translation and the Comprehensibility of Early Piyyut." In *Giving a Diamond: Essays in Honor of Joseph Yahalom on the Occasion of his Seventieth Birthday*, edited by Wout van Bekkum and Naoya Katsumata, 39–50. Leiden: Brill, 2011.

Tabory, Joseph. "The Prayer Book (Siddur) as an Anthology of Judaism." *Prooftexts* (1997): 115–32.

Taitz, Emily, Sondra Henry, and Cheryl Tallan, eds. *The JPS Guide to Jewish Women: 600 B.C.E. to 1900 C.E.* Philadelphia: JPS, 2003.

Talgam, Rina. *Mosaics of Faith: Floors of Pagans, Jews, Samaritans, Christians, and Muslims in the Holy Land.* University Park: Penn State University Press, 2014.

Tardieu, Michel. *Manichaeism.* Translated by M. B. DeBevoise. Urbana: University of Illinois Press, 2008.

Taylor, Joan. *Christians and the Holy Places: The Myth of Jewish-Christian Origins.* Oxford: Clarendon Press, 1993.

Thackeray, Henry St. J. *Josephus, The Jewish War.* Vol. 3: Books 5–7. Loeb Classical Library 210. Cambridge, MA: Harvard University Press, 1928.

Theodor, Julius, and Chanoch Albeck, eds. *Berischit Rabba mit Kritischem Apparat und Kommentar.* 3 vols. Jerusalem: Wahrmann Books, 1965.

Uffenheimer, Benjamin. "Some Reflections on Modern Jewish Biblical Research." In *Creative Biblical Exegesis: Christian and Jewish Hermeneutics through the Centuries*, edited by Henning Graf Reventlow and Benjamin Uffenheimer, 161–74. Sheffield, UK: Sheffield Academic Press, 1988.

Urbach, Ephraim E. *Hazal: Pirkei Emunot ve-Deot.* Translated by Israel Abrahams as *The Sages: Their Concepts and Beliefs.* Jerusalem: Magnes, 1975.

———. "The Traditions on Merkavah Mysticism in the Tannaitic Period." In *Studies in Mysticism and Religion Presented to Gershom Scholem on his 70th birthday*, edited by Efraim Elimelech Urbach, Raphael Jehudah Zwi Werblowsky, and Chaim Wirszubski, 1–28. Jerusalem: Magnes Press, the Hebrew University, 1967 (Hebrew).

van Bekkum, Wout, and Naoya Katsumata. "Piyyut as Poetics: The Example of Yannai's Qedushta for Deut. 6:4." In *Giving a Diamond: Essays in Honor of Joseph Yahalom on the Occasion of His Seventieth Birthday*, edited by Wout van Bekkum and Naoya Katsumata, 83–107. Leiden: Brill, 2011.

van Bladel, Kevin T. *From Sasanian Mandaeans to Ṣābians of the Marshes.* Leiden: Brill, 2017.

VanderKam, James. *The Book of Jubilees.* Sheffield: Sheffield Academic Press, 2001.

van der Toorn, Karel. "The Theology of Demons in Mesopotamia and Israel: Popular Belief and Scholarly Speculation." In *Die Dämonen: die Dämonologie der israelitisch-jüdischen und frühchristlichen Literatur im Kontext ihrer Umwelt*, edited by Armin Lange, Hermann Lichtenberger, and K. F. Diethard Römheld, 61–83. Tübingen: J.C.B. Mohr, 2003.

van der Toorn, Karel, Bob Becking, and Pieter Willem van der Horst, eds. *Dictionary of Deities and Demons in the Bible.* Grand Rapids, Mich.: Wm. B. Eerdmans Publishing, 1999.

Vassilaki, Maria, ed. *Images of the Mother of God: Perceptions of the Theotokos in Byzantium.* New York: Routledge, 2017.

Vidas, Moulie. "Hekhalot Literature, the Babylonian Academies, and the Tanna'im." In *Hekhalot Literature in Context: From Byzantium to Babylonia*, edited by Ra'anan Boustan, Martha Himmelfarb, and Peter Schäfer, 141–76. Texts and Studies in Ancient Judaism 153. Tübingen: Mohr Siebeck, 2013.

——. *Tradition and the Formation of the Talmud.* Princeton University Press, 2014.

Vilozny, Naama. *Lilith's Hair and Ashmedai's Horns: Figure and Image in Magic and Popular Art between Babylonia and Palestine in Late Antiquity.* Jerusalem: Yad Izhak Ben-Zvi, 2017 (Hebrew).

Vriezen, Theodorus Christiaan. *The Religion of Ancient Israel.* Translated by Hubert Hoskins. London: Lutterworth, 1967.

Weiss, Dov. *Pious Irreverence: Confronting God in Rabbinic Judaism.* Philadelphia: University of Pennsylvania Press, 2017.

Weiss, Tzahi. "Prayers to Angels and the Early Sefirotic Literature." *Jewish Studies Quarterly* 27, no. 1 (2020): 22–35.

Weiss, Zeev. "The Sepphoris Synagogue Mosaic and the Role of Talmudic Literature in Its Iconographical Study." In *From Dura to Sepphoris: Studies in Jewish Art and Society in Late Antiquity,* 15–30. Portsmouth, RI: JRA, 2001.

Werblowsky, R. J. Zwi. *Joseph Karo: Lawyer and Mystic.* Philadelphia: the Jewish Publication Society of America, 1977.

West, M. L. *The Hymns of Zoroaster: A New Translation of the Most Ancient Sacred Texts of Iran.* New York: I.B. Tauris, 2010.

Wewers, Gerd A. "Die Überlegenheit des Mystikers: Zur Aussage der Gedulla-Hymnen in Hekhalot-Rabbati 1.2–2.3." *Journal for the Study of Judaism in the Persian, Hellenistic and Roman Period* 17 (1986): 3–22.

Wolfson, Elliot R. "*Yeridah la-Merkavah*: Typology of Ecstasy and Enthronement in Ancient Jewish Mysticism." In *Mystics of the Book: Themes, Topics, and Typologies,* edited by Robert Herrera, 13–44. New York: Peter Lang, 1993.

Yahalom, Joseph. "Angels Do Not Understand Aramaic: On the Literary Use of Jewish Palestinian Aramaic in Late Antiquity." *Journal of Jewish studies* 47, no. 1 (1996): 33–44.

——. *Poetry and Society in Jewish Galilee of Late Antiquity.* Tel Aviv: HaKibbutz Hameuchad, 1999 (Hebrew).

Yamauchi, Edwin. "Aramaic Magic Bowls." *Journal of the American Oriental Society* 85 (1965): 511–23.

——. *Mandaic Incantation Texts.* New Haven, CT: American Oriental Society, 1967.

Yarnold, Edward, trans. *Cyril of Jerusalem.* New York: Routledge, 2000.

Yassif, Eli. *The Tales of Ben Sira in the Middle Ages: A Critical Text and Literary Studies.* Jerusalem: Magnes Press, 1984 (Hebrew).

Young, Gary. *Rome's Eastern Trade: International Commerce and Imperial Policy 31 BC–AD 305.* London: Routledge, 2001.

Youngblood, Ronald. "Divine Names in the Book of Psalms: Literary Structures and Number Patterns." *Journal of the Ancient Near Eastern Society* 19, no. 1 (1989): 171–81.

Yuval, Israel. *Two Nations in Your Womb: Perceptions of Jews and Christians in Late Antiquity and the Middle Ages.* Berkeley: University of California Press, 2006.

Zadeh, Travis. "Magic, Marvel, and Miracle in Early Islamic Thought." In *The Cambridge History of Magic and Witchcraft in the West: From Antiquity to the Present,* edited by David J. Collins, 235–67. Cambridge University Press, 2015.

Zuckermandel, Moses, ed. *Tosefta.* 1937. Reprint, Jerusalem: Wahrmann, 1970.

Founded in 1893,
UNIVERSITY OF CALIFORNIA PRESS
publishes bold, progressive books and journals
on topics in the arts, humanities, social sciences,
and natural sciences—with a focus on social
justice issues—that inspire thought and action
among readers worldwide.

The UC PRESS FOUNDATION
raises funds to uphold the press's vital role
as an independent, nonprofit publisher, and
receives philanthropic support from a wide
range of individuals and institutions—and from
committed readers like you. To learn more, visit
ucpress.edu/supportus.

Made in the USA
Monee, IL
09 June 2026

6490b8ed-2ecd-47cf-a142-0fd6a45c8de2R01